PRENTICE HALL MATHEMATICS

GRADE 6, 7, and 8

Middle School Math Skills Review and Practice

PEARSON

Prentice Hall

Boston, Massachusetts
Upper Saddle River, New Jersey

Pearson Prentice Hall™ is a trademark of Pearson Education, Inc.
Pearson® is a registered trademark of Pearson plc.
Prentice Hall® is a registered trademark of Pearson Education, Inc.

ISBN: 0-13-201391-6
5 6 7 8 9 10   09 08 07

Table of Contents

Table of Contents (continued)

Table of Contents (continued)

Table of Contents *(continued)*

Table of Contents *(continued)*

Grade 8 Topics (Course 3)

Table of Contents *(continued)*

Table of Contents (continued)

Review 1

Understanding Whole Numbers

Millions Period			Thousands Period			Ones Period		
Hundreds	Tens	Ones	Hundreds	Tens	Ones	Hundreds	Tens	Ones
		4	2	0	1	5	7	8

4 million   201 thousand   578

- *Standard form:* 4,201,578
- To find the value of a digit, multiply the digit by its place value.

  4 stands for $4 \times 1{,}000{,}000$, or 4,000,000
- *Expanded form:*
  $4{,}201{,}578 = 4{,}000{,}000 + 200{,}000 + 1{,}000 + 500 + 70 + 8$

Write each number in standard form.

1. six thousand one hundred four

   _____

2. fifteen million twenty-one thousand

   _____

3. sixty thousand one hundred twelve

   _____

4. 2 billion, 9 million, 6 thousand, 1

   _____

5. seventeen thousandths

   _____

6. twenty-nine hundredths

   _____

7. eight thousand two hundred ninety

   _____

8. one billion thirty thousand fifty

   _____

Use < or > to complete each statement.

9. 523 ☐ 567

10. 1,292 ☐ 1,192

11. 47 ☐ 45

12. 9,120 ☐ 912

13. 53,010 ☐ 53,100

14. 4,293 ☐ 4,239

15. 783 ☐ 738

16. 4,121 ☐ 4,212

17. 35,423 ☐ 34,587

18. 241,796 ☐ 242,976

19. 182 ☐ 1,820

20. 8,751 ☐ 8,715

Write in order from least to greatest.

21. 782, 785, 783, 790

   _____

22. 1,240; 1,420; 1,346; 1,364

   _____

23. 6,214; 6,124; 6,421; 6,241

   _____

24. 92,385; 92,835; 93,582; 93,258

   _____

25. 45,923; 54,923; 45,932; 54,932

   _____

26. 1,111; 1,011; 1,101; 1,110

   _____

Review 2

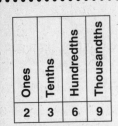

2 and 369 thousandths

- *Standard form:* 2.369
- To find the value of a digit, multiply the digit by its place value.

  9 stands for 9×0.001 or 0.009
- *Expanded form:*

  $2.369 = 2 + 0.3 + 0.06 + 0.009$

Write each decimal in expanded form.

1. 3.6

   _____

2. 4.72

   _____

3. 1.283

   _____

4. 21.5

   _____

5. 7.03

   _____

6. 15.308

   _____

7. 32.27

   _____

8. 6.475

   _____

Write each decimal in words.

9. 0.2

   _____

10. 0.15

    _____

11. 0.29

    _____

12. 0.11

    _____

13. 0.60

    _____

14. 0.9

    _____

15. 0.50

    _____

16. 0.4

    _____

17. 0.37

    _____

Write each decimal in standard form.

18. seven tenths

    _____

19. one tenth

    _____

20. four hundredths

    _____

21. seven hundredths

    _____

22. twenty-two hundredths

    _____

23. forty-six hundredths

    _____

24. eighty hundredths

    _____

25. thirty hundredths

    _____

26. three hundredths

    _____

Review 3

Use >, < , or = to show how 4.092 and 4.089 compare.

① Write the numbers on grid paper with the decimal points lined up.

② Compare digits in the greatest place. Move to the right until you find digits that are not the same.

4 ones = 4 ones
0 tenths = 0 tenths
9 hundreths > 8 hundreths

So, 4.092 > 4.089.

4	.	0	9	2
4	.	0	8	9

To order numbers from least to greatest:

① Write the numbers on grid paper (decimal points lined up) and compare.

② Then arrange the numbers from least to greatest.

4.089, 4.09, 4.092

4	.	0	9	2
4	.	0	8	9
4	.	0	9	

Use <, =, or > to complete each statement.

1. 0.01 ☐ 0.15
2. 0.25 ☐ 0.21
3. 0.30 ☐ 0.26
4. 0.10 ☐ 0.12
5. 0.35 ☐ 0.34
6. 0.1 ☐ 0.4
7. 34.4 ☐ 34.40
8. 0.207 ☐ 0.27
9. 0.08 ☐ 0.40
10. 0.32 ☐ 0.309
11. 6.12 ☐ 6.099
12. 0.990 ☐ 0.99
13. 2.36 ☐ 2.036
14. 0.05 ☐ 0.15
15. 1.19 ☐ 1.91

Use place value to order the decimals from least to greatest.

16. 3.46, 3.64, 3.59
17. 22.97, 21.79, 22.86
18. 43, 43.22, 43.022

19. 10.02, 10.2, 1.02
20. 1.09, 1.9, 1.1
21. 7.54, 75.4, 7.4

Order each set of numbers on a number line.

22. 0.67, 0.7, 0.6
23. 0.03, 0.29, 0.019
24. 8.36, 8.01, 8.1

Course 1 Topics

Review 4

To *round* $76.38 to the nearest dollar:

① Find the rounding place. $7<u>6</u>.38

② Look at the digit to the right. $76.<u>3</u>8

③ If that digit is less than 5, leave the digit in the rounding place as is. If the digit is 5 or greater, round up.

$76.38 rounds to $76.

You can use rounding to estimate a sum.

$$3.76 + 0.85 + 4.09$$

Round each number to the ones place.

$$3.76 \longrightarrow 4$$
$$0.85 \longrightarrow 1$$
$$4.09 \longrightarrow \underline{4}$$

Then add.　　9

The sum is about 9.

You can estimate decimal products, quotients, sums, and differences by using *compatible numbers*.

Example 1 Estimate the product 9.47×3.81

$$9.47 \longrightarrow 10$$
$$\underline{\times 3.81} \longrightarrow \underline{\times\ 4}$$
$$40$$

Change to compatible numbers—numbers that are easy to multiply.

The product is about 40.

Example 2 Estimate the quotient $23.96 \div 4.78$.

$$23.96 \div 4.78$$
$$\downarrow \qquad \downarrow$$
$$24 \div 4 = 6$$

Change to compatible numbers—numbers that are easy to divide.

The quotient is about 6.

Round each decimal to the nearest hundredth.

1. 1.679 _____

2. 4.981 _____

3. 12.602 _____

4. 32.9744 _____

5. 0.159 _____

6. 2.008 _____

Round each decimal to the nearest tenth.

7. 6.457 _____

8. 15.0886 _____

9. 0.1235 _____

10. 1.036 _____

11. 25.671 _____

12. 6.390 _____

Estimate each sum or difference.

13. $2.98
+ 7.22

14. $5.33
+ 2.91

15. $10.02
− 6.89

16. $15.84
+ 37.12

Use compatible numbers to estimate.

17. $7.21 \div 3$

18. $31.74 \div 5$

19. $522 + 81$

_____

_____

_____

20. $908 - 445$

21. $477 + 78$

22. $73 + 229$

_____

_____

_____

Review 5

Add 3.25 + 12.6 + 18.93.

First estimate.

3.25	→	3
12.6	→	13
+ 18.93	→	19
		35

Then follow these steps.

① Line up the decimal points. Write in any needed zeros.

$$
\begin{array}{r}
3.25 \\
12.6\mathbf{0} \\
+ 18.93 \\
\end{array}
$$

② Add as you would add whole numbers. Regroup when needed.

$$
\begin{array}{r}
\overset{11}{3.25} \\
12.60 \\
+ 18.93 \\
\hline
34\,78 \\
\end{array}
$$

③ Place the decimal point.

$$
\begin{array}{r}
3.25 \\
12.60 \\
+ 18.93 \\
\hline
34.78 \\
\end{array}
$$
← Compare to your estimate.

To subtract decimals, follow similar steps. Work from right to left and regroup when needed. Place the decimal point to complete the subtraction.

First estimate and then find each sum.

1. 0.9 + 6.7

Estimate _____

Sum _____

2. 3.1 + 9.4

Estimate _____

Sum _____

3. 4.88 + 8.19

Estimate _____

Sum _____

Use mental math to find each sum.

4. 14.05 + 9.75

_____

5. 6 + 0.22 + 0.78

_____

6. 9.104 + 5.01 + 7.99

_____

First estimate and then find each difference.

7. 8.5 − 4.2

Estimate _____

Difference _____

8. 7.2 − 3.05

Estimate _____

Difference _____

9. 5.07 − 2.8

Estimate _____

Difference _____

10. 6.347 − 2.986

_____

11. 14.2 − 9.86

_____

12. 13.45 − 5.001

_____

13. 22.7 − 12.06

_____

14. 16.1 − 10.88

_____

15. 1.79 − 0.879

_____

Review 6

Lincoln Middle School needs new smoke alarms. The school has $415 to spend. Alarms with escape lights cost $18, and alarms with a false-alarm silencer cost $11. The school wants 4 times as many escape-light alarms as silencer alarms. How many of each kind can the school purchase?

Read and Understand

What facts are needed to solve the problem? *You need the costs of the alarms, $18 and $11; the amount to be spent, $415; and the fact that 4 times as many escape-light alarms as silencer alarms will be bought.*

Plan and Solve

You can try values and check them to solve this problem.
Try: Buy 12 escape-light alarms and 3 silencer alarms.

$$Check: 12 \times \$18 = \$216$$
$$3 \times \$11 = \underline{\$\ 33}$$
$$Add: \quad \$249$$

$249 is a lot less than the $415 that the school has to spend. Continue with different values until you solve the problem.

Buy 20 escape-light alarms and 5 silencer alarms.

$$20 \times \$18 = \$360$$
$$5 \times \$11 = \underline{\$\ 55}$$
$$Add: \quad \$415$$

Look Back and Check

Check to see whether your answer agrees with the information in the problem. *Is the total amount spent $415, or slightly less? Are there 4 times as many escape-light alarms as silencer alarms?*

Choose a strategy to solve each problem.

1. Tina needs batteries. AA batteries cost $3 per pack. D batteries cost $4 per pack. If she has $26 to spend and buys 3 times as many packs of AA batteries as D batteries, how many packs of each does she buy?

2. Ian needs cassette tapes for his recorder. One package of 3 tapes sells for $5. Another pack of 2 costs $4. If Ian has $19 and buys 11 cassettes, how many packs of each kind does he buy?

3. Hyugen has $50 to spend on CDs. New ones cost $9 and used cost $7. He wants to buy more new CDs than used. How many of each can he buy?

4. Frank has $41 to spend on computer disks. A pack of 10 ES brand costs $13 and a pack of 11 CW brand costs $14. How many packs of each can he buy if he spends all his money?

Review 7

Multiplying Decimals

Multiply 0.3 × 1.4. This drawing can help you find 0.3 × 1.4.

**Each small square is 1 hundredth or 0.01.
Each column or row is 10 hundredths
or 1 tenth or 0.1.**

① Shade 3 rows across to represent 0.3.

② Shade 14 columns down to
represent 1.4.

③ The area where the shading overlaps
is 42 hundredths or 0.42.

0.3 × 1.4 = 0.42

Compare the result from the model to the
result of multiplying the factors.

```
    0.3   ←  1 decimal place
  × 1.4   ← +1 decimal place
    1 2
 + 0 3 0
   0.42   ←  2 decimal places
```

When multiplying decimals, first multiply the
factors as though they are whole numbers.
Then add the number of decimal places in each
factor to find the number of decimal places in the
product.

Write a multiplication statement to describe each model.

1.

_____

2.

_____

For each product place the decimal point in the correct place.

3.   0.9
        ×2.8
        252

_____

4.   3.1
        ×77
        2387

_____

5.   6.22
        × 8
        4976

_____

6.   19.6
        ×2.03
        39788

_____

Find each product.

7.   1.6
        ×3.7

8.   8.12
        ×59

9.   12.3
        ×6.1

10.   5.9
         ×1.2

11.   23.4
         ×5.2

_____

12.   4.8
         ×42

_____

13.   9.2
         ×12.4

_____

14.   120
         ×7.6

_____

15.   3.15
         ×2.3

_____

Review 8

Multiplying and Dividing Decimals by 10, 100, and 1,000

Example 1: Multiply 10×0.65.

There is one zero in 10 so move the decimal point one place to the right.

$10 \times 0.65 = 6.5$

Check your answer using a paper and pencil.

$$0.65 \quad \leftarrow \quad \text{2 decimal places}$$
$$\underline{\times 10} \quad \leftarrow \quad \text{0 decimal places}$$
$$6.50 \quad \leftarrow \quad \text{2 decimal places}$$

$6.50 = 6.5$

Example 2: Divide $15.5 \div 100$.

There are two zeros in 100 so move the decimal point two places to the left.

$15.5 \div 100 = 0.155$

Check your answer using a paper and pencil.

$$
\begin{array}{r}
0.155 \\
100\overline{)15.5} \\
-100 \\
\hline
550 \\
-500 \\
\hline
500 \\
-500 \\
\hline
0
\end{array}
$$

Use mental math to find each product.

1. 2.7×10

2. $2.5(10)$

3. $100(0.21)$

_____

_____

_____

4. 0.77×100

5. $10 \times 0.2 \times 1$

6. $5 \times 0.2 \times 100$

_____

_____

_____

7. 2.64×100

8. $7.5 \cdot 1{,}000$

9. $0.5 \times 2 \times 20$

_____

_____

_____

Use mental math to find each quotient.

10. $0.4 \div 10$

11. $2.3 \div 100$

12. $7 \div 100$

_____

_____

_____

13. $52.3 \div 10$

14. $3 \div 1{,}000$

15. $41 \div 100$

_____

_____

_____

Use <, =, or > to complete each statement.

16. $2.2 \times 10 \ \Box \ 2.2(10)(0.1)$

17. $1.1 \div 10 \ \Box \ 110 \div 100$

18. $60 \div 100 \ \Box \ 600 \div 10$

19. $5 \times 0.3 \times 2 \ \Box \ 10 \times 0.3$

20. $0.22 \div 10 \ \Box \ 0.22 \div 0.1$

21. $0.004 \times 100 \ \Box \ 10 \times 10 \times 0.004$

22. $5.5 \times 2 \times 10 \ \Box \ 5.5 \times 100$

23. $(2 \times 5) \, 0.14 \ \Box \ 0.14 \, (10)$

Name _____ Class _____ Date _____

Review 9

Find the quotient 1.52 ÷ 0.4.

You can use a model to estimate the quotient.

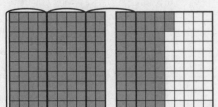

← Draw a model for 1.52.

← Since each square is 0.01, 40 squares represent 0.4. Circle groups of 0.4.

There are close to four groups of 0.4. The quotient is about 4.

① Multiply the dividend and divisor by 10 so that the divisor is a whole number.

$$0.4\overline{)1.52}$$

② Divide as with whole numbers.

$$\begin{array}{r} 38 \\ 4\overline{)15.2} \\ -12 \\ \hline 32 \\ -32 \\ \hline 0 \end{array}$$

③ Place the decimal point in the quotient above its place in the dividend. Insert zeroes as placeholders if necessary.

$$\begin{array}{r} 3.8 \\ 4\overline{)15.2} \\ -12 \\ \hline 32 \\ -32 \\ \hline 0 \end{array}$$

3.8 is close to 4.

Estimate, then find each quotient.

1. $3\overline{)1.35}$ _____

2. $4\overline{)2.68}$ _____

3. $8.4 \div 6$ _____

4. $8\overline{)27}$ _____

5. $12.96 \div 5$ _____

6. $5\overline{)\$11.30}$ _____

7. $0.4 \div 16$ _____

8. $9\overline{)13.86}$ _____

9. $20\overline{)47.6}$ _____

Use the model to find each quotient.

10.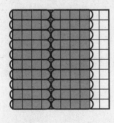

$0.8 \div$ _____ $= 20$

11.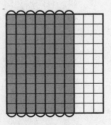

$0.70 \div 0.1 =$ _____

12.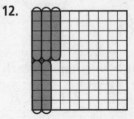

_____ $\div 0.05 =$ _____

Find each quotient.

13. $3 \div 0.12$ _____

14. $1.5\overline{)84}$ _____

15. $78 \div 15.6$ _____

16. $6.4\overline{)23.68}$ _____

17. $7.28 \div 9.1$ _____

18. $3\overline{)4.11}$ _____

19. $0.9\overline{)1.35}$ _____

20. $0.5\overline{)0.935}$ _____

21. $1.9\overline{)19.95}$ _____

Review 10

To find the value of an expression follow the *order of operations*.

First, do all operations inside parentheses.
Next, multiply and divide from left to right.
Then, add and subtract from left to right.

Example 1 Find the value of $6 + (3 + 4) \times 2$.

① Work inside parentheses. $\longrightarrow$ **(3 + 4) = 7**

$$6 + \mathbf{7} \times 2$$

② Multiply next. $\longrightarrow$ **7 × 2 = 14**

$$6 + \mathbf{14}$$

③ Then, add.

$$6 + 14 = 20$$

Example 2 Compare $10 - (6 \div 2) + 1$ and $(10 - 6) \div 2 + 1$.

First, find the value of each expression.

$10 - (6 \div 2) + 1$	$(10 - 6) \div 2 + 1$
$10 - \quad 3 \quad + 1$	$4 \quad \div 2 + 1$
$7 \qquad + 1$	$2 \quad + 1$
8	3

Then, use $<, =,$ or $>$ to compare.

$$8 > 3$$

So,

$$10 - (6 \div 2) + 1 > 10 - 6) \div 2 + 10.$$

Find the value of each expression.

1. $3 + (4 + 1) \times 2$

　　a. $4 + 1 =$ _____

　　b. _____ $\times 2 =$ _____

　　c. $3 +$ _____ $=$ _____

2. $24 \div (5 + 3) - 2$

　　a. $5 + 3 =$ _____

　　b. $24 \div$ _____ $=$ _____

　　c. _____ $- 2 =$ _____

3. $2 + 6 \times 3 \div 3 =$ _____

4. $(6 + 2) \times 3 \div 4 =$ _____

5. $7 + 5 \times 2 - 6 =$ _____

6. $12 \div 3 \times 5 - 6 =$ _____

Use $<, =,$ or $>$ to complete each statement.

7. $9 + 3 \times 4 \ \square \ 9 + (3 \times 4)$

8. $(12 - 4) \times 3 \ \square \ 12 - (4 \times 3)$

9. $6 \div 3 + 4 \times 2 \ \square \ (6 \div 3) + 4 \times 2$

10. $3 \times (12 - 5) + 2 \ \square \ 3 \times 12 - (5 + 2)$

11. $15 - (12 \div 3) \ \square \ (15 - 12) + 3$

12. $8 + 2 \times (9 - 7) \ \square \ 8 + (2 \times 9) - 7$

13. $10 + (10 \div 5) \ \square \ 10 + 10 \div 5$

14. $20 - (2 \times 6) \ \square \ (20 - 2) \times 6$

Review 11

Find the next three numbers in the pattern.

3, 9, 15, 21, ?, ?, ?

Look at how the second number can be found from the first.

3, 9, 15, 21   or   3, 9, 15, 21

× 3   {3 × 3 = 9}   + 6   {3 + 6 = 9}

Look at how the third number can be found from the second.

3, 9, 15, 21   or   3, 9, 15, 21

× 3   {3 × 3 is not 15.}   + 6 + 6   {9 + 6 = 15}

Try adding 6 to the third number.

3, 9, 15, 21

+ 6 + 6 + 6   {15 + 6 = 21}

Now you can write a rule to describe the pattern. The rule is *Start with the number 3 and add 6 repeatedly.*

3, 9, 15, 21, 27, 33, 39

The next three numbers in the pattern are 27, 33, and 39.

Find the next three numbers and write a rule for each number pattern.

1. 2, 5, 8, 11, _____, _____, _____

_____

_____

2. 3, 6, 12, 24, _____, _____, _____

_____

_____

3. 9, 18, 27, 36, _____, _____, _____

_____

_____

4. 64, 56, 48, 40, _____, _____, _____

_____

_____

5. 1, 4, 16, 64, _____, _____, _____

_____

_____

6. 75, 70, 65, 60, _____, _____, _____

_____

_____

7. 90, 81, 72, 63, _____, _____, _____

_____

_____

8. 4, 8, 16, 32, _____, _____, _____

_____

_____

Name _____ Class _____ Date _____

Numerical expressions are made up of numbers and operation symbols.

Example 1:

$6 + 3$ $\qquad$ $9 \times 2 + 1$

Algebraic expressions contain one or more variables. A *variable* is a letter that stands for an unknown number.

Example 2:

$x + 4 \times 2$ $\qquad$ $a - b$

You can model algebraic expressions using objects.

> The 3 paper clips represent 3 of the same variable.

$$3p + 4$$

You can evaluate the algebraic expression $3p + 4$ if you know a value for p.

① Think of each paper clip as having a value of 6.

$3p + 4$ for $p = \mathbf{6}$ means $3 \times \mathbf{6} + 4$

② Then use the order of operations to evaluate.

$3p + 4 = 3 \times 6 + 4$
$\qquad\quad = 18 + 4$
$\qquad\quad = 22$

Write an algebraic expression for each model.

1.

_____

2.

_____

3.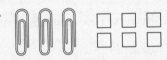

_____

Evaluate each expression.

4. $3t - 4$ for $t = 8$

$3 \times$ ____ $- 4 =$ ____

5. $7c$ for $c = 6$

$7 \times$ ____ $=$ ____

6. $k \div 2$ for $k = 20$

____ $\div 2 =$ ____

7. $15 + m$ for $m = 6$

_____

8. $2x + 1$ for $x = 3$

_____

9. $5y - 10$ for $y = 6$

_____

10. $4m + 8$ for $m = 5$

_____

11. $3(4h)$ for $h = 2$

_____

12. $9 - 3r$ for $r = 2$

_____

13. $a - b$ for $a = 5$ and $b = 4$

_____

14. $3ab$ for $a = 3$ and $b = 4$

_____

15. $x + 2y$ for $x = 3$ and $y = 2$

_____

Review 13

These terms are used to describe mathematical operations.

Addition	Subtraction	Multiplication	Division
sum more than increased by total added to	difference less than fewer than decreased by	product times multiplied by	quotient of divided by

You can use the terms above to write algebraic expressions for word phrases.

Word Phrase		**Algebraic Expression**
the sum of m and 17	$\longrightarrow$	$m + 17$
the difference of x and 12	$\longrightarrow$	$x - 12$
3 times w	$\longrightarrow$	$3w$
the quotient of q and 6	$\longrightarrow$	$q \div 6$

Write an expression to describe the relationship of the data in each table.

1.

n	■
2	10
4	12
6	14

_____

2.

n	■
1	3
2	6
3	9

_____

3.

n	■
8	6
10	8
12	10

_____

Write an expression for each word phrase.

4. 6 increased by y

_____

5. the quotient of 8 and e

_____

6. the difference of h and 3

_____

7. 4 times w

_____

8. the difference of s and 8

_____

9. r divided by 2

_____

10. 5 more than n

_____

11. the product of 6 and m

_____

Review 14

Problem Solving: Make a Table and Look for a Pattern

Stony Hollow School District has a softball playoff each spring for its 8 schools. Each school plays 1 game against every other school. The winner is the school with the greatest number of victories. How many playoff games are played in all?

Read and Understand

What does the problem ask you to find? *You need to find the total number of playoff games.*

How many times will one school play any other school? *1 time*

Plan and Solve

How can you simplify the problem? *Draw a diagram for a few schools. Look for a pattern.*

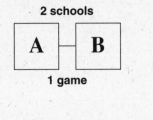

2 schools

1 game

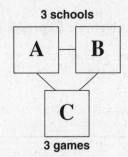

3 schools

3 games

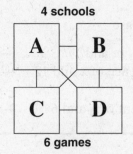

4 schools

6 games

Make a table. Use the pattern you discovered to extend the table to 8 schools.

28 games must be played.

Number of Schools	Number of Games	
2	1	+2
3	3	+3
4	6	+4
5	10	+5
6	15	+6
7	21	+7
8	28	

Look Back and Check

Does the pattern make sense? *Yes. Each school added to the table plays each of the other schools once. So the number of games added is 1 less than the total number of schools.*

Solve each problem by making a table and looking for a pattern.

1. School C won the Stony Hollow School District softball tournament. How many games did School C play in all?

   _____

2. If the Stony Hollow School District had 10 schools, how many playoff games would there be in all?

   _____

3. Each umpire is paid $25 per game. There are 2 umpires for each game. What is the total amount paid to umpires for an 8-team playoff?

   _____

4. Suppose one team wins all of its games. Why is it impossible for there to be a tie for the championship?

   _____

Review 15

Using Number Sense to Solve One-Step Equations

One way to solve some equations is to use mental math.

Example 1: Find the solution to the equation.
$a + 5 = 10$

What you think:
If I add 5 to 5, the sum is 10.
$5 + 5 = 10$
So, $a = 5$.

Example 2: Find the solution to the equation.
$y - 9 = 15$

What you think:
If I subtract 9 from 24, the difference is 15,
$24 - 9 = 15$
So, $y = 24$.

Example 3: Find the solution to the equation.
$w \div 5 = 100$

What you think:
$w \div 5$ means w divided by 5.
I know that $500 \div 5 = 100$.
$500 \div 5 = 100$

So, $w = 500$.

Example 4: Find the solution to the equation.
$4w = 24$

What you think:
$4w$ means 4 times w.
I know that $4 \cdot 6 = 24$.

So, $w = 6$.

Use mental math to solve each equation.

1. $4q = 12$

2. $3w = 15$

_____

_____

3. $h + 7 = 16$

4. $h + 2 = 8$

_____

_____

5. $h \div 3 = 12$

6. $m \div 2 = 10$

_____

_____

7. $y - 8 = 12$

8. $w - 5 = 8$

_____

_____

Tell whether each equation is true or false.

9. $100 \div 8 = 25$

10. $18 + 25 = 43$

11. $1{,}100 - 200 = 900$

_____

_____

_____

12. $16 \times 4 = 32$

13. $18 = 9 \div 2$

14. $32 = 16 + 16$

_____

_____

_____

15. $77 + 12 = 99$

16. $2 \times 9 = 81$

_____

_____

Course 1 Topics

Review 16

Addition Equations	**Subtraction Equations**
There are 4 more than needed to fill the *x* box.	$r - 3 = 9$

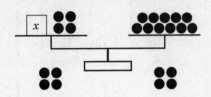

$$x + 4 = 11$$

To *solve* this equation, find the value of *x* that makes the scales balance.

Since 4 is added to *x*, subtract 4 from both sides.

$$x + 4 = 11$$
$$x + 4 - 4 = 11 - 4$$
$$x = 7$$

The *solution* to the equation is $x = 7$.

To *solve* this equation, find the value of *r*.

Since 3 is subtracted from *r*, add 3 to both sides.

$$r - 3 = 9$$
$$r - 3 + 3 = 9 + 3$$
$$r = 12$$

The *solution* to the equation is $r = 12$.

Solve each equation.

1. $a + 15 = 31$

   $a + 15 - \underline{\quad} = 31 - \underline{\quad}$

   $a = \underline{\quad}$

2. $5 = x - 20$

   $5 + \underline{\quad} = x - 20 + \underline{\quad}$

   $\underline{\quad} = x$

3. $19 + t = 51$

_____

4. $p - 11 = 12$

_____

5. $60 = n + 30$

_____

6. $71 = b - 29$

_____

7. $86 + m = 107$

_____

8. $w + 349 = 761$

_____

9. $50 - y = 30$

_____

10. $d - 125 = 75$

_____

11. A car dealer purchased a car for $2,000 and then sold it for $3,200. Write and solve an equation to find the profit.

_____

Review 17

What value of w makes the scales balance?

$4w = 12$ ⟶

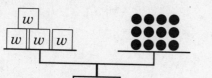

To solve the multiplication sentence, use division.

$$4w = 12$$

$$4w \div 4 = 12 \div 4 \longleftarrow \text{Divide both sides by 4.}$$

$$w = 3$$

The solution is $w = 3$.

To solve a division sentence, use multiplication.

$$y \div 3 = 7$$

$$y \div 3 \times 3 = 7 \times 3 \longleftarrow \text{Multiply both sides by 3.}$$

$$y = 21$$

The solution is $y = 21$.

State whether the number given is a solution to the equation.

1. $3g = 36; g = 12$

   _____

2. $t \div 8 = 2; t = 4$

   _____

3. $h \div 7 = 21; h = 3$

   _____

4. $18 = 3m; m = 6$

   _____

5. $6a = 18; a = 3$

   _____

6. $36 = r \div 9; r = 4$

   _____

Solve each equation.

7. $12 = 4y$

   $12 \div \underline{\quad} = 4y \div \underline{\quad}$

   $\underline{\quad} = y$

8. $n \div 9 = 4$

   $n \div 9 \times \underline{\quad} = 4 \times \underline{\quad}$

   $n = \underline{\quad}$

9. $23n = 115$

   _____

10. $z \div 9 = 9$

    _____

11. $48 = 12h$

    _____

12. $10w = 150$

    _____

13. $34 = t \div 14$

    _____

14. $105 = 21t$

    _____

15. $64 = e \div 9$

    _____

16. $8v = 32$

    _____

17. $22 = t \div 4$

    _____

18. $3s = 66$

    _____

19. $21 = b \div 2$

    _____

20. $15n = 45$

    _____

Review 18

An *exponent* tells how many times a number is used as a factor.

$3 \times 3 \times 3 \times 3$ shows the number 3 is used as a factor 4 times.

$3 \times 3 \times 3 \times 3$ can be written 3^4.

In 3^4, 3 is the *base* and 4 is the exponent.

Read 3^4 as "three to the fourth power."

• To *simplify* a power, first write it as a product.

$2^5 = 2 \times 2 \times 2 \times 2 \times 2 = 32$

• When you simplify expressions with exponents, do all operations inside parentheses first. Then simplify the powers.

Example: $30 - (2 + 3)^2 = 30 - 5^2$
$= 30 - 25$
$= 5$

Name the base and the exponent.

1. 3^6

base _____

exponent _____

2. 6^2

base _____

exponent _____

3. 8^4

base _____

exponent _____

Write each expression using an exponent. Name the base and the exponent.

4. $9 \times 9 \times 9$

_____

5. $6 \times 6 \times 6 \times 6$

_____

6. $1 \times 1 \times 1 \times 1 \times 1$

_____

Simplify each expression.

7. 6^2

_____

8. 3^5

_____

9. 10^4

_____

10. $4^2 + 5^2$

_____

11. $2 \times 6 - 2^3$

_____

12. $6^2 + 4^2$

_____

13. $5 + 5^2 - 2$

_____

14. $24 \div 4 + 2^4$

_____

15. $9 + (40 \div 2^3)$

_____

16. $(4^2 + 4) \div 5$

_____

17. $10 \times (30 - 5^2)$

_____

18. $12 + 18 \div 3^2$

_____

Name _____ Class _____ Date _____

Review 19

The Distributive Property

The *Distributive Property* allows you to break numbers apart to make mental math easier.

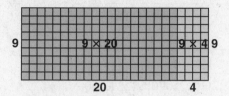

Multiply 9×24 mentally.
Think: $9 \times 24 = 9 \times (20 + 4)$
$= (9 \times 20) + (9 \times 4)$
$= 180 + 36$
$= 216$

The Distributive Property may also help you to simplify an expression.

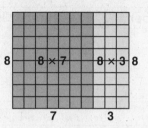

$(8 \times 7) + (8 \times 3) = 8 \times (7 + 3)$
$= 8 \times 10$
$= 80$

Use the Distributive Property to find the missing numbers in the equation.

1. $(\boxed{} \times 4) + (3 \times \boxed{}) = 3 \times (4 + 8)$

2. $(6 \times \boxed{}) - (\boxed{} \times 3) = 6 \times (5 - 3)$

3. $4 \times (\boxed{} - 3) = (\boxed{} \times 9) - (4 \times \boxed{})$

4. $(\boxed{} \times 7) - (6 \times \boxed{}) = 6 \times (7 - 5)$

5. $(4 \times 5) + (\boxed{} \times 7) = 4 \times (\boxed{} + 7)$

6. $\boxed{} \times (12 + 8) = (6 \times \boxed{}) + (\boxed{} \times 8)$

Use the Distributive Property to rewrite and simplify each expression.

7. $(2 \times 7) + (2 \times 5)$

_____

_____

8. $8 \times (60 - 5)$

_____

_____

9. $(7 \times 8) - (7 \times 6)$

_____

_____

10. $(12 \times 3) + (12 \times 4)$

_____

_____

Use the Distributive Property to simplify each expression.

11. 3×27 _____

12. 5×43 _____

13. 8×59 _____

14. 7×61 _____

15. 5×84 _____

16. 6×53 _____

17. 8×48 _____

18. 4×91 _____

19. 9×38 _____

Review 20

A number is **divisible** by a second number if the second number divides into the first with no remainder. Here are some rules.

Last Digit of a Number	The Number Is Divisible by	Examples
any	1	any number
0, 2, 4, 6, 8	2	10; 24; 32; 54; 106; 138
0, 5	5	10; 25; 70; 915; 1,250
0	10	10; 20; 90; 500; 4,300

The Sum of the Digits	The Number Is Divisible by	Examples	
is divisible by 3	3	$843 \rightarrow$ $8 + 4 + 3 = 15$ and $15 \div 3 = 5$	281 R0 $3\overline{)843}$
is divisible by 9	9	$2,898 \rightarrow$ $2 + 8 + 9 + 8 = 27$ and $27 \div 9 = 3$	322 R0 $9\overline{)2,898}$

Circle the numbers that are divisible by the number at the left.

1. 2   8   15   26   42   97   105   218

2. 5   14   10   25   18   975   1,005   2,340

3. 10   100   75   23   60   99   250   655

4. 3   51   75   12   82   93   153   274

5. 9   27   32   36   108   126   245   387

Use mental math to determine if the first number is divisible by the second.

6. 185; 5 _____

7. 76,870; 10 _____

8. 461; 1 _____

9. 456; 3 _____

10. 35,994; 2 _____

11. 6,791; 3 _____

12. 12,866; 9 _____

13. 151,002; 9 _____

14. 55,340; 5 _____

15. 6,888; 2 _____

16. 31,067; 5 _____

17. 901,204; 3 _____

18. 2,232; 3 _____

19. 45,812; 9 _____

20. 3,090; 10 _____

21. 312; 9 _____

22. 1,933; 3 _____

23. 28,889; 2 _____

Test each number for being divisible by 2, 5, or 10. Some numbers may be divisible by more than one number.

24. 800 _____

25. 65 _____

26. 1,010 _____

Review 21

Prime Numbers and Prime Factorization

A *prime number* has exactly two factors, the number itself and 1.

$$5 \times 1 = 5$$
5 is a prime number.

A *composite number* has more than two factors.

$$1 \times 6 = 6$$
$$2 \times 3 = 6$$

1, 2, 3, and 6 are factors of 6.
6 is a composite number.

The number 1 is neither prime nor composite.

Every composite number can be written as a product of prime numbers.

$$6 = 2 \times 3$$
$$8 = 2 \times 2 \times 2$$
$$12 = 2 \times 2 \times 3$$

Factors that are prime numbers are called *prime factors.* You can use a *factor tree* to find prime factors. This one shows the prime factors of 50.

$50 = 2 \times 5 \times 5$ *is the prime factorization* of 50.

Tell whether each number is prime or composite. Explain.

1. 21

2. 43

3. 53

4. 74

_____

5. 54

6. 101

7. 67

8. 138

_____

9. 83

10. 95

11. 41

12. 57

_____

Complete each factor tree.

13.

14.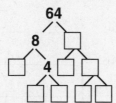

15.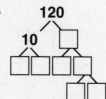

Find the prime factorization of each number.

16. 21

17. 48

18. 81

19. 56

_____

20. 63

21. 100

22. 103

23. 155

_____

Review 22

Greatest Common Factor

You can find the *greatest common factor (GCF)* of 12 and 18 using a division ladder, factor trees, or by listing the factors. Two of these methods are shown.

① List the factors of 12 and 18.

　　12: 1, 2, 3, 4, 6, 12
　　18: 1, 2, 3, 6, 9, 18

② Find the common factors.

　　12: ①,②,③, 4,⑥, 12
　　18: ①,②,③,⑥, 9, 18

　The common factors are 1, 2, 3, and 6.

③ Name the greatest common factor: 6.

① Draw factor trees.

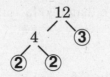

② Write each prime factorization. Identify common factors.

　　12: ②× 2 ×③
　　18: ②×③× 3

③ Multiply the common factors. $2 \times 3 = 6$. The GCF of 12 and 18 is 6.

List the factors to find the GCF of each set of numbers.

1. 10: _____

　　15: _____

　　GCF: _____

2. 14: _____

　　21: _____

　　GCF: _____

3. 9: _____

　　21: _____

　　GCF: _____

4. 12: _____

　　13: _____

　　GCF: _____

5. 15: _____

　　25: _____

　　GCF: _____

6. 15: _____

　　18: _____

　　GCF: _____

7. 36: _____

　　48: _____

　　GCF: _____

8. 24: _____

　　30: _____

　　GCF: _____

Find the GCF of each set of numbers.

9. 21, 60 _____

10. 15, 45 _____

11. 32, 40 _____

12. 54, 60 _____

13. 20, 50 _____

14. 21, 63 _____

15. 36, 40 _____

16. 48, 72 _____

17. 90, 150 _____

Review 23

Equivalent fractions are fractions that name the same amount.

To find equivalent fractions, multiply or divide the numerator and denominator by the same number.

$$\frac{2}{5} \overset{\times 2}{=} \frac{4}{10} \qquad \frac{4}{10} \overset{\div 2}{=} \frac{2}{5}$$

So, $\frac{2}{5} = \frac{4}{10}$.

To write a fraction in *simplest form,* divide the numerator and denominator by their greatest common factor.

Example: Write $\frac{8}{12}$ in simplest form.

① Find the greatest common factor.

8: 1, 2, **4**, 8
12: 1, 2, 3, **4**, 6, 12

The GCF is 4.

② Divide the numerator and denominator by the GCF.

$$\frac{8}{12} \overset{\div 4}{=} \frac{2}{3}$$

$\frac{8}{12}$ in simplest form is $\frac{2}{3}$.

Write two fractions equivalent to each fraction.

1. $\frac{5}{6}$ _____

2. $\frac{3}{7}$ _____

3. $\frac{7}{8}$ _____

4. $\frac{3}{11}$ _____

5. $\frac{3}{6}$ _____

6. $\frac{1}{5}$ _____

State whether each fraction is in simplest form. If it is not, write it in simplest form.

7. $\frac{12}{15}$ _____

8. $\frac{8}{15}$ _____

9. $\frac{9}{21}$ _____

10. $\frac{15}{22}$ _____

11. $\frac{14}{30}$ _____

12. $\frac{25}{70}$ _____

Write each fraction in simplest form.

13. $\frac{12}{24}$ _____

14. $\frac{10}{200}$ _____

15. $\frac{56}{64}$ _____

16. $\frac{3}{9}$ _____

17. $\frac{130}{170}$ _____

18. $\frac{12}{16}$ _____

19. $\frac{7}{49}$ _____

20. $\frac{22}{33}$ _____

21. $\frac{30}{225}$ _____

22. There are 420 girls out of 1,980 people attending a state fair. In simplest form, what fraction of the people attending are girls?

_____

Review 24

Mixed Numbers and Improper Fractions

To write a mixed number as an *improper fraction:*

① Multiply the whole number by the denominator.

② Add this product to the numerator.

③ Write this sum over the denominator.

$$3\frac{5}{8} = \frac{29}{8}$$

To write an improper fraction as a *mixed number:*

① Divide the numerator by the denominator.

$$\frac{20}{8} = 2 \text{ remainder } 4$$

② Write the remainder over the denominator.

$$= 2\frac{4}{8}$$

③ Simplify, if possible.

$$= 2\frac{1}{2}$$

$$\frac{20}{8} = 2\frac{1}{2}$$

Write each mixed number as an improper fraction.

1. $2\frac{2}{7}$ _____

2. $5\frac{3}{4}$ _____

3. $6\frac{1}{2}$ _____

4. $6\frac{5}{8}$ _____

5. $3\frac{4}{10}$ _____

6. $4\frac{3}{5}$ _____

7. $9\frac{1}{3}$ _____

8. $4\frac{4}{5}$ _____

9. $1\frac{7}{8}$ _____

10. $3\frac{3}{8}$ _____

11. $2\frac{3}{7}$ _____

12. $8\frac{1}{6}$ _____

On a separate sheet of paper, draw a model of a 4-inch ruler marked off in eighths. Find and label each measurement on your ruler.

13. $3\frac{5}{8}$

14. $2\frac{6}{8}$

15. $3\frac{1}{2}$

16. $1\frac{3}{4}$

17. $2\frac{1}{2}$

18. $3\frac{1}{4}$

Write each improper fraction as a mixed number in simplest form.

19. $\frac{9}{8}$ _____

20. $\frac{7}{2}$ _____

21. $\frac{12}{5}$ _____

22. $\frac{8}{3}$ _____

23. $\frac{14}{8}$ _____

24. $\frac{6}{5}$ _____

25. $\frac{20}{3}$ _____

26. $\frac{17}{5}$ _____

27. $\frac{18}{4}$ _____

28. $\frac{9}{5}$ _____

29. $\frac{29}{8}$ _____

30. $\frac{24}{9}$ _____

Review 25

Find the *least common multiple (LCM)* of 8 and 12.

① Begin listing multiples of each number.

8: 8, 16, 24, 32, 40

12: 12, 24

② Continue the lists until you find the first multiple that is common to both lists. That is the LCM.

The least common multiple of 8 and 12 is 24.

List multiples to find the LCM of each pair of numbers.

1. 4: _____

5: _____

LCM: _____

2. 6: _____

7: _____

LCM: _____

3. 9: _____

15: _____

LCM: _____

4. 10: _____

25: _____

LCM: _____

5. 8: _____

24: _____

LCM: _____

6. 8: _____

12: _____

LCM: _____

7. 4: _____

7: _____

LCM: _____

8. 15: _____

25: _____

LCM: _____

9. 15: _____

20: _____

LCM: _____

10. 4: _____

9: _____

LCM: _____

Use prime factorization to find the LCM of each set of numbers.

11. 9, 21 _____

12. 6, 8 _____

13. 18, 24 _____

14. 40, 50 _____

15. 42, 49 _____

16. 6, 12 _____

Review 26

To compare and order fractions, use the *least common denominator (LCD)*.
The LCD is the least common multiple (LCM) of the original denominators.

Compare Fractions	**Order Fractions**

Compare Fractions

Example 1: Compare $\frac{3}{4}$ and $\frac{7}{10}$.

① Find the LCD of the denominators 4 and 10:

$$4 = 2 \times 2$$
$$10 = 2 \times 5$$
$$LCD = 2 \times 2 \times 5 = 20$$

② Write equivalent fractions:

$$\frac{3}{4} \overset{\times 5}{\underset{\times 5}{=}} \frac{15}{20} \qquad \frac{7}{10} \overset{\times 2}{\underset{\times 2}{=}} \frac{14}{20}$$

③ Compare: $\frac{15}{20} > \frac{14}{20}$, or

$$\frac{3}{4} > \frac{7}{10}$$

Order Fractions

Example 2: Order from least to greatest: $\frac{2}{3}, \frac{5}{8}, \frac{3}{4}$.

① Find the LCD of the denominators 3, 8, and 4:

$$3 = 3$$
$$8 = 2 \times 2 \times 2$$
$$4 = 2 \times 2$$
$$LCD = 2 \times 2 \times 2 \times 3 = 24$$

② Write equivalent fractions:

$$\frac{2}{3} \overset{\times 8}{\underset{\times 8}{=}} \frac{16}{24} \qquad \frac{5}{8} \overset{\times 3}{\underset{\times 3}{=}} \frac{15}{24} \qquad \frac{3}{4} \overset{\times 6}{\underset{\times 6}{=}} \frac{18}{24}$$

③ Order:

$$15, 16, 18$$
$$\frac{15}{24} < \frac{16}{24} < \frac{18}{24}, \text{ or } \frac{5}{8} < \frac{2}{3} < \frac{3}{4}$$

Compare each pair of numbers using <, =, or >.

1. $\frac{2}{9} \ \square \ \frac{1}{3}$

2. $\frac{5}{6} \ \square \ \frac{7}{8}$

3. $\frac{7}{20} \ \square \ \frac{3}{10}$

4. $\frac{3}{6} \ \square \ \frac{4}{11}$

5. $\frac{2}{3} \ \square \ \frac{4}{6}$

6. $\frac{4}{8} \ \square \ \frac{2}{8}$

7. $\frac{3}{7} \ \square \ \frac{5}{8}$

8. $\frac{1}{3} \ \square \ \frac{3}{9}$

9. $\frac{1}{2} \ \square \ \frac{3}{7}$

10. $\frac{4}{5} \ \square \ \frac{7}{9}$

11. $\frac{2}{3} \ \square \ \frac{7}{10}$

12. $2\frac{5}{9} \ \square \ 2\frac{3}{5}$

Order each set of numbers from least to greatest.

13. $\frac{3}{4}, \frac{5}{8}, \frac{1}{2}$ _____

14. $\frac{5}{8}, \frac{5}{6}, \frac{2}{3}$ _____

15. $\frac{1}{2}, \frac{5}{12}, \frac{2}{3}$ _____

16. $\frac{3}{5}, \frac{2}{3}, \frac{7}{12}$ _____

17. $\frac{1}{2}, \frac{3}{5}, \frac{3}{8}$ _____

18. $\frac{7}{8}, \frac{3}{4}, \frac{13}{16}$ _____

19. Suzanne swims $1\frac{1}{9}$ miles. Eugene swims $1\frac{5}{12}$ miles. Who swims farther? Show your work.

_____

Name _____ Class _____ Date _____

Review 27

Fractions and Decimals

Example 1: Write 0.320 as a fraction in simplest form.

① Read.   "320 thousandths"

② Write. $\frac{320}{1,000}$

③ Simplify. $\frac{320}{1,000} = \frac{320 \div 40}{1,000 \div 40} = \frac{8}{25}$

$0.320 = \frac{8}{25}$

Example 2: Write 6.95 as a mixed number in simplest form.

① Read.   "6 and 95 hundredths"

② Write. $6\frac{95}{100}$

③ Simplify. $6\frac{95}{100} = 6\frac{19}{20}$

$6.95 = 6\frac{19}{20}$

Example 3: Write $\frac{1}{5}$ and $\frac{2}{3}$ as decimals.

Divide the numerator by the denominator. Insert zeros if needed.

$$\begin{array}{r} 0.2 \\ 5\overline{)1.0} \end{array} \qquad \begin{array}{r} 0.666 \\ 3\overline{)2.0000} \\ -1\,8 \\ \hline 20 \\ -18 \\ \hline 2 \end{array} \leftarrow \begin{array}{l} \text{The digits} \\ \text{repeat} \\ \text{because} \\ \text{the} \\ \text{remainder} \\ \leftarrow \text{repeats.} \end{array}$$

$\frac{1}{5} = 0.2 \qquad \frac{2}{3} = 0.666 \ldots = 0.\overline{6}$

0.2 is a *terminating decimal* because there is no remainder.

0.666 . . . is a repeating decimal because the remainder repeats. Write it as $0.\overline{6}$.

Write each decimal as a fraction or mixed number in simplest form.

1. 0.8 _____
2. 0.55 _____
3. 1.25 _____
4. 1.75 _____
5. 3.375 _____
6. 0.125 _____
7. 1.32 _____
8. 0.34 _____
9. 0.084 _____
10. 0.006 _____
11. 0.65 _____
12. 4.95 _____

Write each fraction or mixed number as a decimal.

13. $\frac{13}{20}$ _____
14. $\frac{1}{6}$ _____
15. $\frac{7}{20}$ _____
16. $2\frac{3}{5}$ _____
17. $\frac{19}{25}$ _____
18. $\frac{4}{9}$ _____
19. $\frac{7}{11}$ _____
20. $1\frac{5}{8}$ _____
21. $1\frac{2}{9}$ _____
22. $2\frac{2}{8}$ _____
23. $\frac{1}{25}$ _____
24. $\frac{5}{12}$ _____

State whether each fraction is less than, equal to, or greater than 0.50. Show your work.

25. $\frac{1}{3}$ _____
26. $\frac{20}{40}$ _____
27. $\frac{1}{6}$ _____
28. $\frac{7}{8}$ _____
29. $\frac{11}{13}$ _____
30. $\frac{8}{20}$ _____

© Pearson Education, Inc. All rights reserved.

Review 28

Problem Solving: Try, Check, and Revise

Lincoln Middle School needs new smoke alarms. The school has $415 to spend. Alarms with escape lights cost $18, and alarms with a false-alarm silencer cost $11. The school wants 4 times as many escape-light alarms as silencer alarms. How many of each kind can the school purchase?

Read and Understand   What facts are needed to solve the problem? *You need the costs of the alarms, $18 and $11; the amount to be spent, $415; and the fact that 4 times as many escape-light alarms as silencer alarms will be bought.*

Plan and Solve   You can try, check, and revise to solve this problem.

Try: Buy 12 escape-light alarms and 3 silencer alarms.

Check: $12 \times \$18 = \$216$
$3 \times \$11 = \underline{\$\ 33}$
Add: $\$249$

$249 is a lot less than the $415 that the school has to spend. Revise with different combinations until you solve the problem.

Buy 20 escape-light alarms and 5 silencer alarms.

Check: $20 \times \$18 = \$360$
$5 \times \$11 = \underline{\$\ 55}$
Add: $\$415$

Look Back and Check   Check to see whether your answer agrees with the information in the problem. *Is the total amount spent $415, or slightly less? Are there 4 times as many escape-light alarms as silencer alarms?*

Solve each problem by trying, checking, and revising.

1. Tina needs batteries. AA batteries cost $3 per pack. D batteries cost $4 per pack. If she has $26 to spend and buys 3 times as many packs of AA batteries as D batteries, how many packs of each does she buy?

2. Ian needs CDs for his CD burner. One package of 3 CDs sells for $5. Another pack of 2 costs $4. If Ian has $19 and buys 11 CDs, how many packs of each kind does he buy?

3. Hyugen has $50 to spend on CDs. New ones cost $9 and used ones cost $7. He wants to buy more new CDs than used. How many of each can he buy?

4. Frank has $41 to spend on computer disks. A pack of 10 ES brand disks costs $13, and a pack of 11 CW brand disks costs $14. How many packs of each can he buy if he spends all his money?

Review 29

Estimate sums and differences of fractions by using a benchmark. A **benchmark** is a number that is close to a fraction and is easy to use when you estimate.

Estimate: $\frac{4}{5} + \frac{3}{8}$ by using the benchmarks $0, \frac{1}{2}$, or 1.

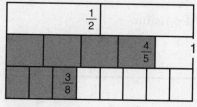

$\frac{4}{5} \approx 1$

$\frac{3}{8} \approx \frac{1}{2}$

$1 + \frac{1}{2} = 1\frac{1}{2}$

$\frac{4}{5} + \frac{3}{8} \approx 1\frac{1}{2}$

Estimate sums and differences of mixed numbers by rounding to the nearest whole number.

Subtract: $3\frac{1}{6} - 1\frac{9}{10}$

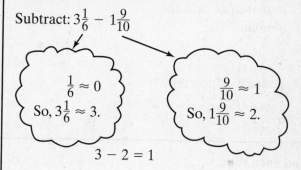

$\frac{1}{6} \approx 0$

So, $3\frac{1}{6} \approx 3$.

$\frac{9}{10} \approx 1$

So, $1\frac{9}{10} \approx 2$.

$3 - 2 = 1$

$3\frac{1}{6} - 1\frac{9}{10} \approx 1$

Estimate each sum or difference. Use the benchmarks $0, \frac{1}{2}$, and 1.

1. $\frac{7}{8} + \frac{1}{16}$ _____

2. $\frac{9}{10} + \frac{4}{5}$ _____

3. $\frac{15}{16} - \frac{1}{9}$ _____

4. $\frac{5}{8} - \frac{3}{7}$ _____

5. $\frac{21}{25} + \frac{1}{6}$ _____

6. $\frac{1}{2} + \frac{1}{18}$ _____

7. $\frac{4}{10} - \frac{2}{15}$ _____

8. $\frac{6}{7} + \frac{4}{5}$ _____

9. $\frac{7}{10} + \frac{3}{24}$ _____

10. $\frac{5}{9} + \frac{1}{15}$ _____

11. $\frac{1}{10} + \frac{1}{8}$ _____

12. $\frac{1}{18} + \frac{2}{10}$ _____

13. $\frac{6}{7} + \frac{2}{3}$ _____

14. $\frac{11}{12} - \frac{9}{10}$ _____

15. $\frac{13}{14} - \frac{4}{7}$ _____

16. $6\frac{1}{8} + 2\frac{9}{10}$ _____

17. $1\frac{1}{5} - \frac{9}{10}$ _____

18. $3\frac{8}{9} + 4\frac{8}{9}$ _____

19. $8\frac{1}{12} - \frac{8}{10}$ _____

20. $5\frac{8}{9} + 3\frac{2}{13}$ _____

21. $6\frac{9}{11} - 1\frac{1}{8}$ _____

22. $12\frac{7}{8} - \frac{11}{12}$ _____

23. $9\frac{7}{9} - \frac{9}{10}$ _____

24. $15\frac{3}{8} + 1\frac{1}{9}$ _____

25. $17\frac{2}{7} + \frac{8}{11}$ _____

26. $7\frac{1}{4} - \frac{15}{16}$ _____

27. $5\frac{1}{8} + \frac{13}{16}$ _____

Solve.

28. Katrina has a $7\frac{1}{2}$-foot roll of ribbon. She needs 2 strips of ribbon that each measure $3\frac{5}{6}$-feet long. Does she need more ribbon?

_____

29. Ricardo jogs $3\frac{3}{4}$ miles on Monday and $2\frac{1}{5}$ miles on Wednesday. Estimate the total number of miles he jogs.

_____

Review 30

Fractions With Like Denominators

Add: $\frac{1}{6} + \frac{3}{6}$

① Combine numerators over the denominator.

② Add numerators.

③ Simplify, if possible.

$\frac{1}{6} + \frac{3}{6} = \frac{1+3}{6}$

$= \frac{4}{6}$

$= \frac{2}{3}$

$\frac{1}{6} + \frac{3}{6} = \frac{2}{3}$

Subtract: $\frac{7}{10} - \frac{2}{10}$

① Combine numerators over the denominator.

② Subtract numerators.

③ Simplify, if possible.

$\frac{7}{10} - \frac{2}{10} = \frac{7-2}{10}$

$= \frac{5}{10}$

$= \frac{1}{2}$

$\frac{7}{10} - \frac{2}{10} = \frac{1}{2}$

Find each sum.

1. $\frac{1}{5} + \frac{3}{5}$ _____

2. $\frac{4}{6} + \frac{1}{6}$ _____

3. $\frac{3}{12} + \frac{3}{12}$ _____

4. $\frac{6}{10} + \frac{5}{10}$ _____

5. $\frac{3}{10} + \frac{2}{10}$ _____

6. $\frac{6}{12} + \frac{3}{12}$ _____

7. $\frac{5}{8} + \frac{1}{8}$ _____

8. $\frac{3}{8} + \frac{9}{8}$ _____

9. $\frac{3}{8} + \frac{6}{8}$ _____

Find each difference.

10. $\frac{6}{8} - \frac{3}{8}$ _____

11. $\frac{9}{10} - \frac{3}{10}$ _____

12. $\frac{3}{4} - \frac{1}{4}$ _____

13. $\frac{7}{12} - \frac{1}{12}$ _____

14. $\frac{8}{10} - \frac{6}{10}$ _____

15. $\frac{4}{6} - \frac{2}{6}$ _____

16. $\frac{5}{10} - \frac{1}{10}$ _____

17. $\frac{7}{12} - \frac{6}{12}$ _____

18. $\frac{9}{10} - \frac{4}{10}$ _____

Find each sum or difference.

19. $\frac{2}{7} + \frac{2}{7} - \frac{1}{7}$

20. $\frac{10}{100} + \frac{20}{100} + \frac{90}{100}$

21. $\frac{2}{5} - \frac{2}{5} + \frac{5}{5}$

22. $\frac{10}{11} - \left(\frac{2}{11} + \frac{4}{11} \right)$

23. $\frac{8}{10} - \frac{2}{10} - \frac{1}{10}$

24. $\frac{62}{80} - \frac{10}{80} - \frac{5}{80}$

25. For school photos, $\frac{1}{5}$ of the students choose to have a blue background, $\frac{2}{5}$ of the students choose to have a purple background, and $\frac{1}{5}$ of the students choose to have a gray background. What portion of the students choose to have another background color?

_____

Review 31

To add or subtract fractions with unlike denominators, you can use equivalent fractions.

Find $\frac{5}{6} + \frac{1}{2}$.

① Find the least common denominator of 6 and 2.

    The LCD is 6.

② Write equivalent fractions using the LCD.

$$\frac{5}{6} = \frac{5}{6} \qquad \frac{1}{2} = \frac{1 \times 3}{2 \times 3} = \frac{3}{6}$$

③ Add. Write the sum in simplest form.

$$\frac{5}{6} + \frac{1}{2} = \frac{5}{6} + \frac{3}{6}$$
$$= \frac{5 + 3}{6}$$
$$= \frac{8}{6}$$
$$= \frac{4}{3}$$
$$= 1\frac{1}{3}$$

$$\frac{5}{6} + \frac{1}{2} = 1\frac{1}{3}$$

Find $\frac{4}{5} - \frac{1}{3}$.

① Find the least common denominator of 5 and 3.

    The LCD is 15.

② Write equivalent fractions using the LCD.

$$\frac{4}{5} = \frac{4 \times 3}{5 \times 3} = \frac{12}{15} \qquad \frac{1}{3} = \frac{1 \times 5}{3 \times 5} = \frac{5}{15}$$

③ Subtract. Write the difference in simplest form.

$$\frac{4}{5} - \frac{1}{3} = \frac{12}{15} - \frac{5}{15}$$
$$= \frac{12 - 5}{15}$$
$$= \frac{7}{15}$$

$$\frac{4}{5} - \frac{1}{3} = \frac{7}{15}$$

Find each sum or difference.

1. $\frac{1}{2} + \frac{3}{4}$ _____

2. $\frac{11}{16} - \frac{5}{16}$ _____

3. $\frac{1}{6} + \frac{1}{3}$ _____

4. $\frac{7}{8} - \frac{1}{2}$ _____

5. $\frac{9}{10} + \frac{1}{2}$ _____

6. $\frac{2}{3} + \frac{5}{9}$ _____

7. $\frac{1}{2} + \frac{7}{10}$ _____

8. $\frac{3}{4} - \frac{5}{12}$ _____

9. $\frac{5}{8} + \frac{1}{4}$ _____

10. $\frac{15}{16} - \frac{1}{4}$ _____

11. $\frac{7}{12} - \frac{1}{3}$ _____

12. $\frac{5}{6} + \frac{1}{3}$ _____

13. $\frac{7}{8} - \frac{1}{4}$ _____

14. $\frac{3}{5} + \frac{1}{6}$ _____

15. $\frac{1}{12} + \frac{1}{10}$ _____

16. $\frac{7}{8} - \frac{3}{10}$ _____

17. $\frac{2}{6} + \frac{3}{4}$ _____

18. $\frac{3}{8} - \frac{1}{3}$ _____

19. $\frac{5}{8} + \frac{2}{3}$ _____

20. $\frac{3}{5} - \frac{1}{2}$ _____

21. $\frac{1}{8} + \frac{1}{5}$ _____

22. $\frac{7}{10} - \frac{3}{5}$ _____

23. $\frac{9}{10} - \frac{1}{2}$ _____

24. $\frac{1}{10} + \frac{4}{5}$ _____

Review 32

Some mixed numbers can be added mentally.

Find $5\frac{1}{4} + 2\frac{1}{8}$.

① Add the whole numbers.

$$5 + 2 = 7$$

② Add the fractions.

$$\frac{1}{4} + \frac{1}{8} = \frac{2}{8} + \frac{1}{8} = \frac{3}{8}$$

③ Combine the two parts.

$$7 + \frac{3}{8} = 7\frac{3}{8}$$

$$5\frac{1}{4} + 2\frac{1}{8} = 7\frac{3}{8}$$

Or, you can follow these steps.

Find $4\frac{4}{5} + 2\frac{9}{10}$.

① Write with a common denominator.

$$4\frac{4}{5} + 2\frac{9}{10} = 4\frac{8}{10} + 2\frac{9}{10}$$

② Add the whole numbers. $= 6\frac{17}{10}$
Add the fractions.

③ Rename $6\frac{17}{10}$ as $7\frac{7}{10}$. $= 7\frac{7}{10}$

$$4\frac{4}{5} + 2\frac{9}{10} = 7\frac{7}{10}$$

Find each sum.

1. $4\frac{4}{7} + 1\frac{1}{7}$

2. $1\frac{1}{3} + 3\frac{1}{3}$

3. $2\frac{1}{2} + 4$

4. $8\frac{2}{5} + 4\frac{1}{10}$

5. $7\frac{3}{4} + 2\frac{1}{8}$

6. $2\frac{7}{10} + 3\frac{1}{5}$

7. $7\frac{2}{9} + 1\frac{4}{9}$

8. $8\frac{3}{14} + 2\frac{1}{7}$

9. $9\frac{3}{8} + 2\frac{1}{2}$

10. $1\frac{3}{4} + 4\frac{7}{8}$

11. $7\frac{2}{3} + 8\frac{5}{6}$

12. $1\frac{2}{5} + 9\frac{2}{3}$

13. $6\frac{3}{4} + 8\frac{4}{5}$

14. $3\frac{2}{3} + 5\frac{5}{6}$

15. $4\frac{2}{5} + 6\frac{7}{10}$

16. $6 + 3\frac{2}{5}$

17. $9\frac{1}{6} + 1\frac{1}{3}$

18. $8\frac{1}{16} + 4\frac{5}{8}$

Review 33

Subtracting Mixed Numbers

Some mixed numbers can be subtracted mentally.

Find $5\frac{2}{3} - 2\frac{1}{6}$.

① Subtract the whole numbers.

$$5 - 2 = 3$$

② Then, subtract the fractions.

$$\frac{2}{3} - \frac{1}{6} = \frac{4}{6} - \frac{1}{6} = \frac{3}{6} = \frac{1}{2}$$

③ Combine the two parts.

$$3 + \frac{1}{2} = 3\frac{1}{2}$$

$$5\frac{2}{3} - 2\frac{1}{6} = 3\frac{1}{2}$$

Sometimes you must rename the first fraction before subtracting.

Find $6\frac{1}{2} - 2\frac{3}{4}$.

Cannot subtract $\frac{1}{2} - \frac{3}{4}$.

① Write with a common denominator.

$$6\frac{1}{2} - 2\frac{3}{4} = 6\frac{2}{4} - 2\frac{3}{4}$$

② Rename $6\frac{2}{4}$. $= 5\frac{6}{4} - 2\frac{3}{4}$

③ Subtract the whole numbers. $= 3\frac{3}{4}$
Then, subtract the fractions.
Simplify, if necessary.

$$6\frac{1}{2} - 2\frac{3}{4} = 3\frac{3}{4}$$

Find each difference.

1. $7\frac{7}{10} - 2\frac{3}{10}$

_____

2. $3\frac{3}{4} - 1\frac{1}{2}$

_____

3. $6\frac{2}{3} - 2\frac{1}{6}$

_____

4. $9\frac{7}{8} - 7\frac{3}{4}$

_____

5. $8\frac{1}{2} - 3\frac{1}{4}$

_____

6. $14\frac{1}{3} - 8\frac{1}{4}$

_____

7. $12\frac{1}{3} - 9\frac{2}{3}$

_____

8. $6\frac{5}{8} - 2\frac{3}{4}$

_____

9. $7\frac{5}{7} - 4\frac{13}{14}$

_____

10. $10\frac{2}{3} - 7\frac{5}{6}$

_____

11. $5\frac{7}{16} - 1\frac{1}{2}$

_____

12. $8\frac{2}{5} - 3\frac{2}{3}$

_____

13. $6\frac{1}{8} - 3\frac{1}{16}$

_____

14. $9\frac{5}{12} - 5\frac{3}{4}$

_____

15. $12\frac{3}{4} - 6\frac{1}{8}$

_____

16. $7\frac{2}{5} - 2\frac{1}{4}$

_____

17. $15\frac{5}{12} - 8\frac{1}{3}$

_____

18. $4\frac{1}{10} - 2\frac{4}{5}$

_____

Review 34

You can use mental math to solve addition and subtraction equations that involve fractions or mixed numbers. To solve equations involving fractions with unlike denominators, you need to change the fractions to equivalent fractions with like denominators.

Solve $x - \frac{3}{8} = \frac{5}{16}$.

$$x - \frac{3}{8} = \frac{5}{16}$$
$$\underline{+ \frac{3}{8} \quad + \frac{3}{8}} \qquad \text{Add } \tfrac{3}{8} \text{ to each side.}$$
$$x = \frac{5}{16} + \frac{3}{8} \qquad \text{Write the sum.}$$
$$= \frac{5}{16} + \frac{6}{16} \qquad \text{The LCD is 16. Write } \tfrac{3}{8} \text{ as } \tfrac{6}{16}.$$
$$= \frac{11}{16} \qquad \text{Simplify.}$$

Solve each equation.

1. $x + \frac{1}{5} = \frac{4}{5}$

    What number plus $\frac{1}{5}$ equals $\frac{4}{5}$? _____ So, $x =$ _____.

    Show that the equation is true. _____

2. $x - \frac{1}{3} = \frac{2}{9}$

    What is the least common multiple of 3 and 9? _____

    Rewrite the equation using like denominators. _____

    What number minus $\frac{3}{9}$ equals $\frac{2}{9}$? _____ So, $x =$ _____.

    Show that the equation is true. _____

Solve each equation.

3. $\frac{1}{4} + x = \frac{3}{4}$ $x =$ _____

4. $y - \frac{5}{8} = \frac{1}{8}$ $y =$ _____

5. $\frac{7}{10} - c = \frac{2}{5}$ $c =$ _____

6. $\frac{5}{12} + r = \frac{7}{3}$ $r =$ _____

7. $\frac{1}{12} + b = \frac{1}{4}$ $b =$ _____

8. $s - \frac{1}{2} = \frac{1}{6}$ $s =$ _____

9. $d + \frac{1}{3} = \frac{7}{12}$ $d =$ _____

10. $\frac{5}{6} - f = \frac{7}{12}$ $f =$ _____

11. $s + \frac{3}{8} = \frac{3}{4}$ $s =$ _____

12. $t - \frac{3}{10} = \frac{5}{8}$ $t =$ _____

Review 35

Find the elapsed time between 6:15 A.M. and 11:10 A.M.

1. Set up as subtraction.

$$\begin{array}{r} 11:10 \\ -6:15 \\ \hline \end{array}$$

2. Rename 11:10 as 10:70.

$$\begin{array}{r} 11:10 \rightarrow 10:70 \\ -6:15 \rightarrow -6:15 \\ \hline \end{array}$$

3. Subtract.

$$\begin{array}{r} 10:70 \\ -6:15 \\ \hline 4:55 \end{array}$$

The elapsed time is 4 hours 55 minutes.

You can find elapsed time from a schedule.

Leave	Arrive
Boston 7:09 A.M.	New York 11:02 A.M.

For travel time, find the elapsed time between 7:09 A.M. and 11:02 A.M.

11:02 − 7:09 = 3 hours 53 minutes

For each time, write an equivalent time using only the smaller unit.

Example: 4 hours 55 minutes = 4 × 60 + 55 = 295 minutes

1. 3 hours 25 minutes

_____

2. 2 hours 17 minutes

_____

3. 2 hours 48 minutes

_____

4. 5 hours 18 minutes

_____

5. 6 hours 13 minutes

_____

6. 5 hours 39 minutes

_____

Find the elapsed time between each pair of times.

7. 6:45 P.M. and 9:20 P.M.

_____

8. 9:36 A.M. and 11:50 A.M.

_____

9. 5:45 A.M. and 11:30 A.M.

_____

10. 3:11 P.M. and 10:40 P.M.

_____

11. 8:15 A.M. and 10:09 P.M.

_____

12. 1:00 A.M. and 7:28 P.M.

_____

Use the schedule to answer the following questions.

13. How much time do you have to get to the game?

_____

Leave for game	6:15 P.M.
Game begins	7:35 P.M.
Game ends	10:20 P.M.

14. How long is the game?

_____

Review 36

Yori found that each time a ball bounces, it returns to one half its previous height. If she drops the ball from 40 feet, how many feet will it have traveled when it hits the ground the fourth time?

Read and Understand

What does the problem ask?
Find the total distance the ball will travel up and down by the time it hits the ground the fourth time.

Plan and Solve

You can draw a diagram. How many feet will the first segment represent?
The first segment will represent 40 feet.

Draw a diagram to represent the problem.

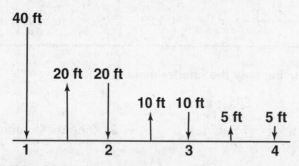

Add to solve. 40 + 20 + 20 + 10 + 10 + 5 + 5 = 110 feet

Look Back and Check

How can you be sure that the solution solves the problem?
Count the number of times the ball hits the ground; check that each bounce is one half the height of the previous bounce.

Solve each problem by drawing a diagram.

1. Yori drops a ball from 64 feet. How far will it travel until it hits the ground the fourth time if it also returns to one half the height of its previous bounce?

2. Yori drops a ball from the same height in Exercise 1. She allows it to bounce 4 times before stopping it. If it returns to $\frac{1}{4}$ its dropped height, how much less will it travel than the ball in Exercise 1?

3. A ball returns to one half its dropped height. By the time it hits the ground the fourth time, it has traveled 66 feet. From what height was it dropped?

4. When a ball bounces, it returns to a height $\frac{3}{4}$ its previous height. After it hits the ground the second time, it bounces up 9 feet. From what height was it dropped?

Review 37

You can model $\frac{2}{3}$ of $\frac{1}{4}$.

① Show $\frac{1}{4}$.

② Divide into thirds.

③ Shade $\frac{2}{3}$ of the $\frac{1}{4}$.

$\frac{2}{3}$ of $\frac{1}{4} = \frac{2}{12} = \frac{1}{6}$

Or you can use multiplication.

$$\frac{2}{3} \text{ of } \frac{1}{4} = \frac{2}{3} \times \frac{1}{4}$$

$$= \frac{2 \times 1}{3 \times 4}$$

$$= \frac{2}{12}$$

$$= \frac{1}{6}$$

Write the multiplication problem each model represents.

1.

2.

_____   _____

Find each product.

3. $\frac{1}{9}$ of $\frac{2}{3}$

4. $\frac{2}{7} \times \frac{1}{2}$

5. $\frac{5}{8} \cdot 6$

6. $\frac{3}{4} \cdot \frac{4}{7}$

_____   _____   _____   _____

7. $\frac{7}{10}$ of $\frac{1}{3}$

8. $\frac{5}{6} \times \frac{3}{4}$

9. $\frac{3}{8}$ of $\frac{7}{10}$

10. $\frac{3}{4} \times \frac{1}{9}$

_____   _____   _____   _____

11. $\frac{2}{9}$ of 8

12. $\frac{1}{3}$ of 2

13. $\frac{5}{9}$ of 4

14. $\frac{3}{4} \cdot \frac{2}{5}$

_____   _____   _____   _____

15. Every day you eat $\frac{1}{4}$ cup of cereal. Your brother eats 5 times as much. How many cups of cereal does your brother eat? _____

Review 38

Multiplying Mixed Numbers

Example 1: Multiply: $2\frac{1}{7} \times 2\frac{2}{5}$

① Change to improper fractions. $\frac{15}{7} \times \frac{12}{5}$

② Simplify. $\frac{\overset{3}{\cancel{15}}}{7} \times \frac{12}{\cancel{5}_{1}}$

③ Multiply. $\frac{36}{7} \leftarrow 3 \times 12$ $\leftarrow 7 \times 1$

④ Simplify. $5\frac{1}{7}$

$2\frac{1}{7} \times 2\frac{2}{5} = 5\frac{1}{7}$

Example 2: Multiply: $\frac{2}{3} \times 5\frac{1}{4}$

$\frac{2}{3} \times \frac{21}{4}$

$\frac{\overset{1}{\cancel{2}}}{\underset{1}{\cancel{3}}} \times \frac{\overset{7}{\cancel{21}}}{\cancel{4}_{2}}$

$\frac{7}{2} \leftarrow 1 \times 7$ $\leftarrow 1 \times 2$

$3\frac{1}{2}$

$\frac{2}{3} \times 5\frac{1}{4} = 3\frac{1}{2}$

Find each product.

1. $1\frac{1}{4} \times 2\frac{2}{3}$

2. $2\frac{2}{5} \times 4\frac{1}{2}$

3. $3\frac{1}{7} \times 2\frac{4}{5}$

4. $\frac{1}{5} \times 2\frac{7}{9}$

5. $12\frac{1}{2} \times 2\frac{2}{5}$

_____ _____ _____ _____ _____

6. $2\frac{1}{8} \times 2\frac{2}{3}$

7. $5\frac{1}{3} \times 1\frac{7}{8}$

8. $\frac{1}{2} \times 3\frac{3}{5}$

9. $2\frac{1}{7} \times 4\frac{2}{3}$

10. $1\frac{1}{2} \times 2\frac{6}{7}$

_____ _____ _____ _____ _____

11. $1\frac{5}{6} \times 2\frac{1}{4}$

12. $5\frac{1}{4} \times 2\frac{2}{7}$

13. $\frac{1}{4} \times 1\frac{3}{5}$

14. $\frac{1}{7} \times 1\frac{3}{4}$

15. $\frac{2}{9} \times 2\frac{1}{4}$

_____ _____ _____ _____ _____

16. $3\frac{1}{3} \times 3\frac{3}{10}$

17. $1\frac{2}{3} \times 3\frac{1}{2}$

18. $1\frac{2}{5} \times 4\frac{1}{3}$

19. $\frac{1}{7} \times 1\frac{3}{5}$

20. $\frac{3}{5} \times 8\frac{1}{2}$

_____ _____ _____ _____ _____

21. $3\frac{2}{5} \times 2\frac{1}{2}$

22. $1\frac{2}{3} \times 7\frac{1}{2}$

23. $1\frac{3}{10} \times 2\frac{6}{7}$

24. $\frac{3}{16} \times 1\frac{1}{7}$

25. $2\frac{6}{7} \times 1\frac{2}{5}$

_____ _____ _____ _____ _____

Solve.

26. Estimate the area of a window pane that has dimensions $6\frac{1}{8}$ by $11\frac{1}{4}$ inches.

_____

27. A hamster is $2\frac{1}{2}$ inches long. A rabbit is $3\frac{1}{2}$ times as long as the hamster. How long is the rabbit?

_____

Review 39

Find $8 \div \frac{4}{5}$.

① The *reciprocal* of $\frac{4}{5}$ is $\frac{5}{4}$.

$$\frac{4}{5} \diagup\!\!\!\!\diagdown \frac{5}{4}$$

② Multiply 8 by the reciprocal.

$$8 \div \frac{4}{5} = 8 \times \frac{5}{4} = \frac{\overset{2}{8}}{1} \times \frac{5}{\underset{1}{4}} = \frac{2 \times 5}{1 \times 1} = 10$$

$$8 \div \frac{4}{5} = 10$$

Find $\frac{4}{9} \div \frac{8}{15}$.

① The *reciprocal* of $\frac{8}{15}$ is $\frac{15}{8}$.

$$\frac{8}{15} \diagup\!\!\!\!\diagdown \frac{15}{8}$$

② Multiply $\frac{4}{9}$ by the reciprocal.

$$\frac{4}{9} \div \frac{8}{15} = \frac{4}{9} \times \frac{15}{8} = \frac{\overset{1}{4}}{\underset{3}{9}} \times \frac{\overset{5}{15}}{\underset{2}{8}} = \frac{1 \times 5}{3 \times 2} = \frac{5}{6}$$

$$\frac{4}{9} \div \frac{8}{15} = \frac{5}{6}$$

Write the reciprocal of each number.

1. $\frac{1}{4}$ _____

2. $\frac{5}{3}$ _____

3. $\frac{1}{20}$ _____

4. $\frac{8}{9}$ _____

5. 14 _____

6. 18 _____

7. $\frac{5}{9}$ _____

8. $\frac{3}{11}$ _____

9. $\frac{9}{7}$ _____

10. $\frac{11}{12}$ _____

11. $\frac{2}{7}$ _____

12. $\frac{3}{15}$ _____

Find each quotient.

13. $2 \div \frac{2}{3}$ _____

14. $7 \div \frac{7}{8}$ _____

15. $9 \div \frac{3}{4}$ _____

16. $6 \div \frac{2}{5}$ _____

17. $5 \div \frac{2}{3}$ _____

18. $14 \div \frac{5}{6}$ _____

19. $\frac{4}{5} \div \frac{4}{7}$ _____

20. $\frac{7}{8} \div \frac{7}{9}$ _____

21. $\frac{4}{7} \div 2$ _____

22. $\frac{7}{8} \div \frac{2}{3}$ _____

23. $\frac{1}{2} \div 4$ _____

24. $\frac{2}{5} \div \frac{3}{4}$ _____

25. $\frac{9}{10} \div 3$ _____

26. $\frac{3}{5} \div 5$ _____

27. $\frac{5}{8} \div 10$ _____

28. $\frac{3}{4} \div \frac{7}{8}$ _____

29. $\frac{5}{6} \div \frac{1}{3}$ _____

30. $\frac{11}{12} \div \frac{3}{4}$ _____

Review 40

Dividing Mixed Numbers

Example 1: Estimate $36\frac{1}{3} \div 5\frac{7}{8}$.

$36\frac{1}{3} \div 5\frac{7}{8}$ Round mixed numbers to nearest whole number.

$\downarrow$ $\downarrow$

$36 \div 6 = 6$ Find the quotient of the rounded values.

Example 2: Find $5\frac{1}{3} \div 2\frac{2}{5}$.

① Write each mixed number as an improper fraction.

$$5\frac{1}{3} \div 2\frac{2}{5} = \frac{16}{3} \div \frac{12}{5}$$

② The *reciprocal* of $\frac{12}{5}$ is $\frac{5}{12}$.

$$\frac{12}{5} \diagdown \frac{5}{12}$$

③ Multiply $\frac{16}{3}$ by the reciprocal.

$$\frac{16}{3} \div \frac{12}{5} = \frac{\overset{4}{16}}{3} \times \frac{5}{\underset{3}{12}} = \frac{4 \times 5}{3 \times 3} = \frac{20}{9} = 2\frac{2}{9}$$

$$5\frac{1}{3} \div 2\frac{2}{5} = 2\frac{2}{9}$$

Estimate each quotient.

1. $14\frac{8}{9} \div 5\frac{1}{5}$ _____

2. $19\frac{2}{3} \div 3\frac{8}{9}$ _____

3. $50\frac{2}{3} \div 2\frac{6}{7}$ _____

4. $5\frac{1}{3} \div 2\frac{2}{3}$ _____

5. $6\frac{1}{4} \div 2\frac{1}{2}$ _____

6. $9 \div 3\frac{1}{3}$ _____

7. $12 \div 6\frac{1}{2}$ _____

8. $5 \div 1\frac{1}{5}$ _____

9. $2\frac{7}{10} \div \frac{4}{5}$ _____

10. $6\frac{1}{2} \div 2\frac{1}{6}$ _____

11. $5\frac{2}{3} \div 1\frac{3}{4}$ _____

12. $5\frac{7}{8} \div 2\frac{1}{2}$ _____

Find each quotient.

13. $2\frac{1}{2} \div \frac{1}{4}$ _____

14. $100\frac{1}{8} \div 6\frac{1}{4}$ _____

15. $3\frac{2}{3} \div 1\frac{1}{2}$ _____

16. $6\frac{1}{8} \div 2\frac{2}{4}$ _____

17. $75\frac{1}{2} \div 5\frac{1}{2}$ _____

18. $1\frac{1}{6} \div 2\frac{2}{3}$ _____

19. $10\frac{2}{3} \div 4\frac{1}{3}$ _____

20. $18\frac{2}{9} \div 1\frac{1}{2}$ _____

21. $1\frac{1}{10} \div 1\frac{5}{6}$ _____

Review 41

Solving Fraction Equations by Multiplying

• •

When solving multiplication equations, it may help to first find the numerator of the missing value and then the denominator. If the equation includes whole numbers or mixed numbers, you may need to rewrite these numbers as fractions.

Solve: $\frac{2}{5}x = \frac{4}{25}$.

① Think: What number times $\frac{2}{5}$ equals $\frac{4}{25}$? $\boxed{2 \times 2 = 4}$

② Then use mental math to find the numerator. $\frac{2}{5} \times \frac{?}{?} = \frac{4}{25}$

③ Use mental math to find the denominator. $\frac{2}{5} \times \frac{2}{?} = \frac{4}{25}$

$\boxed{5 \times 5 = 25}$

④ Check to see that the equation is true. $\frac{2}{5} \times \frac{2}{5} = \frac{4}{25}$ ✓

So, $x = \frac{2}{5}$.

Solve each equation. Check the solution.

1. $\frac{2}{3}x = \frac{8}{15}$

   $x = $ _____

2. $\frac{3}{4}x = \frac{9}{20}$

   $x = $ _____

3. $\frac{1}{3}x = 4$

   $x = $ _____

4. $\frac{3}{8}x = \frac{18}{16}$

   $x = $ _____

5. $\frac{3}{2}x = \frac{6}{10}$

   $x = $ _____

6. $\frac{9}{5}x = \frac{9}{25}$

   $x = $ _____

7. $\frac{8}{3}x = \frac{16}{27}$

   $x = $ _____

8. $\frac{5}{4}x = \frac{35}{48}$

   $x = $ _____

9. $\frac{9}{7}x = \frac{27}{35}$

   $x = $ _____

10. $\frac{10}{3}x = \frac{20}{27}$

   $x = $ _____

11. A wrestler weighed $112\frac{1}{2}$ pounds before the state meet. After the meet, the wrestler weighed $\frac{49}{50}$ of his original weight. How much did the wrestler weigh after the meet?

   _____

12. A number divided by 4 equals 10.125. What is the number?

   _____

Review 42

Problem Solving: Solve a Simpler Problem

A mystery game has 3 rooms. Each room has 3 desks. Each desk has 3 drawers, and each drawer has 3 dollars. If you are able to collect all the money, how many dollars would this be?

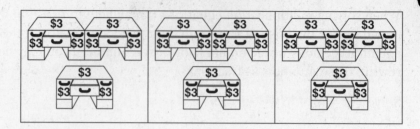

Read and Understand

What is the object of the game?
The object is to collect all the money.
What does the problem ask you to find?
Find how much money is hidden in all 3 rooms.

Plan and Solve

If you cannot solve the entire problem at once, how can you break it down into simpler problems?
Find the amount of money in one room.
Then multiply by 3.

For one room multiply:
3 (desks) × 3 (drawers) × 3 (dollars).
There is $27 in one room. 3 × $27 = $81. There is $81 in all three rooms.

Look Back and Check

How does solving a simpler problem help find the solution to the original problem?
The strategy allows you to work with easier numbers.

Solve each problem by first solving a simpler problem.

1. Another game has 7 rooms, each with 7 paintings. Behind each painting are 7 safes. Inside each safe are 7 security boxes, each with $70. How much money is hidden in the house?

   _____

2. If someone enters one of the 7 rooms while you are there collecting the money, you must give that person the contents of the safe. Suppose this happens to you in all 7 rooms. How much would you have at the end of the game?

   _____

3. Six students are playing a game. Each student plays the game once with each of the other students. How many games are played?

   _____

4. Twelve students each have 2 bookbags. Each bookbag contains 4 books. Each book costs $10.95. How much do the books cost altogether?

   _____

Review 43

Choose an appropriate customary unit of measure to describe the following:

length of a train engine You need a unit to measure length. A train engine will be quite long, so choose feet or yards.	weight of a train engine You need a unit to measure weight. Since a train engine will be quite heavy, choose tons.
amount of liquid in a large bucket You need a unit to measure capacity. A bucket is likely to contain quite a bit of water, so choose quarts or gallons.	length of a CD case You need a unit to measure length. A CD case is quite small, so choose inches.
weight of a bale of straw You need a unit to measure weight. A bale of straw is heavy, so choose pounds.	amount of liquid in a bottle of eye drops You need a unit to measure capacity. Since a bottle of eye drops will be very small, so choose fluid ounces.

Choose an appropriate unit for each measurement. Explain.

1. the length of a garden

_____

_____

2. the length of a hummingbird

_____

_____

Choose an appropriate unit for each weight. Explain.

3. the weight of a letter

_____

_____

4. the weight of steel girders

_____

_____

Choose an appropriate unit for each capacity. Explain.

5. a pitcher of juice

_____

_____

6. the water in an aquarium

_____

_____

Compare using <, ≈, or >.

7. weight of a tank ⬚ 100 pounds

8. length of a TV remote ⬚ 5 inches

Review 44

Complete the statement: $5\frac{5}{8}$ c = __?__ fl oz

① Find the relationship between cups and fluid ounces: 1 c = 8 fl oz

② Since there are 8 fluid ounces in each cup, multiply the number of cups by 8.

$$5\frac{5}{8} \times 8 = \frac{45}{8} \times 8$$

$$= \frac{45}{\overset{}{\underset{1}{8}}} \times \frac{\overset{1}{8}}{1}$$

$$= 45$$

$$5\frac{5}{8} \text{ c} = 45 \text{ fl oz}$$

Subtract: 9 ft 8 in. − 2 ft 11 in.

① Find the relationship between feet and inches: 1 ft = 12 in.

② Use the relationship to rename 9 feet 8 inches. as 8 feet 20 inches.

③ Subtract.

$$\begin{array}{ll} 9 \text{ ft} \quad 8 \text{ in.} & \longrightarrow \quad 8 \text{ ft} \quad 20 \text{ in.} \\ - 2 \text{ ft} \; 11 \text{ in.} & \qquad \underline{- 2 \text{ ft} \; 11 \text{ in.}} \\ & \qquad \qquad 6 \text{ ft} \quad 9 \text{ in.} \end{array}$$

9 ft 8 in. − 2 ft 11 in. = 6 ft 9 in.

To compare amounts, first change them to the same unit.

Compare: 25 fl oz __?__ 3 c ⟶ 25 fl oz __?__ 24 fl oz

25 fl oz > 24 fl oz

25 fl oz > 3 c

Complete each statement.

1. 12 ft = __?__ yd _____

2. 32 qt = __?__ gal _____

3. $1\frac{1}{2}$ mi = __?__ ft _____

4. 15 pt = __?__ qt _____

5. 440 yd = __?__ mi _____

6. $2\frac{1}{2}$ t = __?__ lb _____

7. $9\frac{1}{4}$ c = __?__ fl oz _____

8. 40 oz = __?__ lb _____

9. $8\frac{1}{4}$ ft = __?__ in. _____

Add or subtract.

10. $\quad$ 3 pt 1 c
$\underline{+ 4 \text{ pt } 1 \text{ c}}$

11. $\quad$ 4 yd 1 ft
$\underline{- 1 \text{ yd } 2 \text{ ft}}$

12. $\quad$ 5 lb 20 oz
$\underline{+ 8 \text{ lb } 12 \text{ oz}}$

Use <, =, or > to complete each statement.

13. 43 in. ☐ 4 ft

14. $8\frac{1}{2}$ gal ☐ 136 c

15. 108 in. ☐ $3\frac{1}{2}$ yd

16. $2\frac{1}{2}$ lb ☐ 40 oz

17. 7,000 lb ☐ $3\frac{1}{4}$ t

18. $5\frac{1}{2}$ pt ☐ 3 qt

19. A semi-truck can hold 8,500 pounds of cargo. How many tons can it hold?

_____

Review 45

Ratios

A *ratio* is a comparison of two numbers by division. Each number in a ratio is called a *term*. You can write a ratio in three different ways. For example, the ratio 4 to 5 can be written:

4 to 5

4 : 5

$\frac{4}{5}$

Equal ratios name the same number. They have the same *simplest form*.

- To find equal ratios, multiply *or* divide both the numerator and denominator of a ratio by the same number.

Find a ratio equal to $\frac{4}{7}$.

$$\frac{4}{7} = \frac{4 \times 2}{7 \times 2} = \frac{8}{14}$$

$\frac{8}{14}$ is equal to $\frac{4}{7}$.

Find the simplest form for the ratio $\frac{16}{20}$.

$$\frac{16}{20} = \frac{16 \div 4}{20 \div 4} = \frac{4}{5}$$

$\frac{4}{5}$ is the simplest form for $\frac{16}{20}$.

Write three different ratios equal to each ratio.

1. $\frac{2}{5}$ **2.** 1 : 3   **3.** 3 to 4   **4.** 5 : 8

_____   _____   _____   _____

5. 2 to 7   **6.** $\frac{1}{5}$ **7.** 12 to 20   **8.** 6 : 16

_____   _____   _____   _____

Write each ratio in simplest form.

9. 32 : 16   **10.** $\frac{14}{24}$ **11.** $\frac{36}{50}$ **12.** 60 : 25

_____   _____   _____   _____

13. $\frac{25}{40}$ **14.** 60 : 180   **15.** $\frac{75}{120}$ **16.** 80 : 20

_____   _____   _____   _____

Find the value that makes the ratios equal.

17. 3 : 4, _?_ : 16   **18.** 20 to 25, 40 to _?_   **19.** 9 to 12, 81 to _?_

_____   _____   _____

20. 7 : 10, _?_ : 100   **21.** 1 to 8, _?_ to 24   **22.** 30 : 120, 90 : _?_

_____   _____   _____

23. 5 : 100, 25 : _?_   **24.** $\frac{7}{56}, \frac{?}{280}$ **25.** $\frac{6}{12}, \frac{36}{?}$

_____   _____   _____

Review 46

Unit Rates

A *rate* is a ratio that compares quantities that are measured in different units. Suppose a sprinter runs 100 yards in 10 seconds.

$\dfrac{100 \text{ yd}}{10 \text{ s}}$ compares yards to seconds.

A *unit rate* compares a quantity to one unit of another quantity.

You can find the unit rate by dividing by the denominator.

$\dfrac{100 \text{ yd} \div 10}{10 \text{ s} \div 10} = \dfrac{10 \text{ yd}}{1 \text{ s}}$

10 yards per second is the sprinter's unit rate.

Find the unit rate for each situation.

1. $70 for 10 shirts

2. $150 for 3 games

3. $20 for 5 toys

_____ _____ _____

4. $120 for 6 shirts

5. $45 for 5 boxes

6. $132 for 3 books

_____ _____ _____

7. $100 for 5 rackets

8. $56 for 7 hours

9. $1.98 for 6 cans

_____ _____ _____

Write the unit rate as a ratio. Then find an equal ratio.

10. The cost is $4.25 for 1 item. Find the cost of 5 items. _____

11. There are 7 cheerleaders in a squad. Find the number of cheerleaders on 12 squads. _____

12. The cost if $10.10 for 1 item. Find the cost of 10 items. _____

13. There are 2.54 centimeters per one inch. Find the number of centimeters in 5 inches. _____

14. The cost is $8.50 for 1 item. Find the cost of 3 items. _____

For Exercises 15–20, tell which unit rate is greater.

15. Dillan scores 24 points in 2 games. Eric scores 40 points in 4 games. _____

16. A fern grows 4 inches in 2 months. A tree grows 6 inches in 4 months. _____

17. Tyler jogs 4 miles in 32 minutes. Joey jogs 2 miles in 18 minutes. _____

18. Dixie drinks 2 cups of water in 5 minutes. Dale drinks 10 cups of water in 12 minutes. _____

Review 47

A *proportion* is an equation stating that two ratios are equal.

Does $\frac{4}{10} = \frac{6}{15}$?

First, simplify each fraction.

$\frac{4}{10} = \frac{2}{5}$, and $\frac{6}{15} = \frac{2}{5}$

So, $\frac{4}{10} = \frac{6}{15}$.

You can use mental math to solve proportions.

Use mental math to solve $\frac{3}{5} = \frac{15}{?}$.

$3 \times 5 = 15$, so $5 \times 5 = 25$

So, $\frac{3}{5} = \frac{15}{25}$.

Do the ratios in each pair form a proportion?

1. $\frac{25}{100}, \frac{4}{16}$

2. $\frac{15}{20}, \frac{4}{5}$

3. $\frac{35}{40}, \frac{45}{50}$

4. $\frac{54}{9}, \frac{36}{6}$

5. $\frac{7}{11}, \frac{49}{77}$

6. $\frac{18}{24}, \frac{24}{30}$

7. $\frac{3}{5}, \frac{5}{3}$

8. $\frac{9}{10}, \frac{19}{20}$

9. $\frac{8}{24}, \frac{1}{3}$

Find the value that completes each proportion.

10. $\frac{6}{10} = \frac{3}{?}$

11. $\frac{8}{16} = \frac{4}{?}$

12. $\frac{9}{21} = \frac{?}{7}$

13. $\frac{2}{?} = \frac{10}{50}$

14. $\frac{11}{?} = \frac{33}{15}$

15. $\frac{?}{25} = \frac{14}{50}$

16. $\frac{6}{30} = \frac{?}{90}$

17. $\frac{45}{9} = \frac{25}{?}$

18. $\frac{18}{?} = \frac{2}{9}$

19. A basketball player bounces the ball one time for every three steps. How many times will the player bounce the ball for twelve steps?

20. Four laps around the track equals one mile. How many miles does sixteen laps equal?

Review 48

If two ratios are equal, they form a *proportion*.

$$\frac{1}{5} = \frac{2}{10}$$

Equal ratios have equal cross products.

$$\frac{1}{5} \diagdown \frac{2}{10} \quad \begin{array}{l} 5 \times 2 = 10 \\ 1 \times 10 = 10 \end{array}$$

Equal cross products also show that a proportion is true.

$$\frac{1}{6} \diagdown \frac{3}{18} \quad \begin{array}{l} 6 \times 3 = 18 \\ 1 \times 18 = 18 \end{array}$$

The cross products are equal, so the ratios are equal and form a proportion.

You can find the missing term in a proportion by using *cross products*.

Solve $\frac{4}{7} = \frac{12}{n}$.

1. Write the cross products. $\quad 4 \times n = 7 \times 12$

2. Simplify. $\quad 4n = 84$

3. Divide by 4. $\quad \frac{4n}{4} = \frac{84}{4}$

4. Simplify. $\quad n = 21$

Does each pair of ratios form a proportion?

1. $\frac{4}{7}, \frac{8}{14}$

2. $\frac{5}{2}, \frac{10}{4}$

3. $\frac{6}{8}, \frac{3}{5}$

4. $\frac{15}{3}, \frac{10}{2}$

_____

5. $\frac{15}{45}, \frac{25}{60}$

6. $\frac{12}{16}, \frac{15}{20}$

7. $\frac{9}{10}, \frac{19}{20}$

8. $\frac{32}{12}, \frac{8}{3}$

_____

9. $\frac{56}{8}, \frac{1}{7}$

10. $\frac{4}{7}, \frac{14}{21}$

11. $\frac{40}{50}, \frac{8}{10}$

12. $\frac{5}{15}, \frac{9}{27}$

_____

Solve each proportion.

13. $\frac{n}{5} = \frac{2}{10}$

14. $\frac{9}{n} = \frac{27}{3}$

15. $\frac{30}{6} = \frac{a}{9}$

16. $\frac{42}{12} = \frac{x}{4}$

_____

17. $\frac{t}{24} = \frac{3}{8}$

18. $\frac{16}{12} = \frac{r}{18}$

19. $\frac{18}{32} = \frac{27}{m}$

20. $\frac{48}{30} = \frac{32}{e}$

_____

21. $\frac{5}{6} = \frac{h}{36}$

22. $\frac{60}{24} = \frac{w}{12}$

23. $\frac{11}{14} = \frac{33}{y}$

24. $\frac{90}{25} = \frac{x}{5}$

_____

25. $\frac{10}{5} = \frac{6}{t}$

26. $\frac{9}{a} = \frac{3}{5}$

27. $\frac{b}{2} = \frac{16}{4}$

28. $\frac{12}{16} = \frac{n}{4}$

_____

Review 49

The *scale drawing* at the right shows a game field at Weld Middle School. The *scale* is a ratio that compares length on a drawing to the actual length. Here, every inch equals 36 yards on the actual field.

You can write the scale as a ratio in fraction form:

$$\frac{\text{drawing (in.)}}{\text{actual (yd)}} = \frac{1}{36}$$

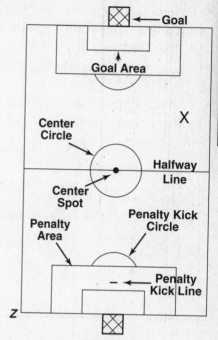

scale: 1 in. : 36 yd

To find the actual length of the field:

① Measure the scale drawing.   3 in.

② Write the scale as a ratio. $\frac{1}{36}$

③ Use the scale ratio in a proportion. $\frac{1}{36} = \frac{3}{n}$

④ Write cross products. $1 \times n = 3 \times 36$

⑤ Solve for *n*. $n = 108$

The actual length is 108 yards.

Use the scale drawing above to find the actual size.

1. Find the width of the field.

 _____

2. Find the perimeter of the field.

 _____

3. Find the measure of the shorter side of the penalty area.

 _____

4. Find the distance from the center spot to the front of the goal.

 _____

5. Brian kicks the ball from the penalty kick line to the opposite goal area. About how far does he kick the ball?

 _____

6. Kaitlin makes a direct kick from the spot marked X. She scores by getting the ball into the goal nearest her. About how far does she kick the ball?

 _____

Write each scale as a ratio.

7. a 12-inch model of a 60-foot boat

 _____

8. a 6-inch drawing of an 18-inch TV

 _____

9. a 4-centimeter model of a 28-centimeter hammer

 _____

10. a 9-inch drawing of a 54-foot garden

 _____

Review 50

Percents, Fractions, and Decimals

- To *write a percent as a fraction* in simplest form, first write a fraction with a denominator of 100. Then simplify.

$$74\% = \frac{74}{100} = \frac{37}{50}$$

- To *write a percent as a decimal,* first write a fraction with a denominator of 100. Then write the decimal.

$$74\% = \frac{74}{100} = 0.74$$

- To *write a decimal as a percent,* move the decimal point two places to the right.

$$0.23 = 23\%$$

Here are two ways to *write a fraction as a percent.*

- Write an equivalent fraction with a denominator of 100, then write the percent.

$$\frac{3}{20} = \frac{15}{100} = 15\%$$

- Divide the numerator by the denominator.

$$\frac{3}{8} = \begin{array}{r} 0.375 \\ 8\overline{)3.000} \\ -2\,4 \\ \hline 60 \\ -56 \\ \hline 40 \\ -40 \\ \hline 0 \end{array} = 37.5\%$$

↑

Move the decimal point two places to the right.

So, $\frac{3}{8} = 37.5\%$.

Write each percent as a decimal and as a fraction in simplest form.

1. 30%

2. 14%

3. 16%

4. 5%

_____

_____

_____

_____

5. 92%

6. 80%

7. 21%

8. 38%

_____

_____

_____

_____

Write each fraction or decimal as a percent.

9. $\frac{17}{25}$

10. 0.85

11. 0.16

12. $\frac{5}{40}$

_____

_____

_____

_____

13. $\frac{7}{200}$

14. $\frac{1}{10}$

15. 0.64

16. 0.008

_____

_____

_____

_____

17. $\frac{9}{20}$

18. $\frac{6}{15}$

19. 0.32

20. 0.07

_____

_____

_____

_____

21. $\frac{13}{100}$

22. $\frac{45}{50}$

23. 0.010

24. 0.60

_____

_____

_____

_____

Review 51

You can find 70% of 90 using different methods.

Use mental math.

① Write the percent as a fraction in simplest form.

$$70\% = \frac{70}{100} = \frac{7}{10}$$

② Multiply by the fraction.

$$\frac{7}{10} \times \frac{90}{1} = \frac{630}{10} = 63$$

70% of 90 = 63.

Use a proportion.

① Write a proportion.

$$\frac{70}{100} = \frac{c}{90}$$

② Write cross products and simplify.

$$100 \times c = 70 \times 90$$
$$100c = 6,300$$

③ Solve.

$$c = \frac{6,300}{100}$$
$$c = 63$$

70% of 90 = 63.

Find each answer using mental math.

1. 45% of 60

2. 60% of 160

3. 15% of 220

_____

4. 90% of 80

5. 35% of 60

6. 70% of 350

_____

Find each answer using a proportion.

7. 40% of 60

8. 85% of 300

9. 15% of 160

_____

10. 22% of 500

11. 37% of 400

12. 68% of 250

_____

Find each answer.

13. 25% of 100

14. 70% of 70

15. 10% of 70

_____

16. 75% of 40

17. 80% of 50

18. 12% of 60

_____

19. 24% of 80

20. 45% of 90

21. 60% of 72

_____

22. 55% of 120

23. 95% of 180

24. 16% of 80

_____

Review 52

You can estimate a percent of a number using mental math.

Example: Estimate 19% of $83.

① Round to convenient numbers.

20% of 80

② Find 10% of 80.

10% of 80 = 8.

③ 20% of 80 is 2 times as much.

20% of 80 is 2 × 8, or 16.

19% of 83 is about 16.

Estimate each amount.

1. 50% of 41

2. 20% of 99

3. 10% of 73

_____

_____

_____

4. 40% of 59

5. 1% of 94

6. 5% of 313

_____

_____

_____

7. 70% of 498

8. 15% of 172

9. 25% of 154

_____

_____

_____

10. 90% of 81

11. 30% of 60

12. 15% of 401

_____

_____

_____

13. 40% of 23

14. 20% of 178

15. 75% of 21

_____

_____

_____

16. 25% of 216

17. 50% of 77

18. 15% of 39

_____

_____

_____

19. 3% of 887

20. 70% of 419

21. 80% of 69

_____

_____

_____

22. A baseball glove is on sale for 75% off the original price of
$96.25. Estimate the sale price of the glove.

_____

Review 53

You can organize information needed to solve a problem by *writing an equation*. Equations are useful when modeling a situation.

Example: Franklin has $25. He needs to buy diapers for $12.99. He wants to buy as much baby formula as he can. Each jar of formula costs $.79. How many jars of formula can he buy?

First, you know Frank must buy diapers for $12.99, and he has $25. You need to find out how much money he has left to spend on formula.

Frank has $25 − $12.99, or $12.01. You can write an equation to solve the problem.

Let *j* = the number of jars of formula Frank can buy.

$$0.79 \times j = 12.01 \quad \text{Then, solve for } j.$$

$$j = \frac{12.01}{0.79}$$

$$j = 15.20$$

Since jars are sold in whole containers, Frank can buy 15 jars of formula.

Solve each problem by writing an equation.

1. A printer is on sale for $129.99. This is 25% off the regular price. What is the regular price of the printer?

   _____

2. Janie sold 250 magazine subscriptions for school this year. The number is down 12% from last year. How many subscriptions did Janie sell last year?

   _____

3. Barbara needs to buy a math book and some paper. She has $50. The math book costs $35, and paper costs $3.50 per package. How many packages of paper can Barbara buy?

   _____

4. Ice skates on sale for 25% off cost $45. What is the regular price of the skates?

   _____

5. Your homemade chili has 12 fewer fat grams than your favorite restaurant's chili. This is 10% less fat than the restaurant's chili. How many fat grams does the restaurant's chili have?

   _____

Course 1 Topics

Review 54

Mean, Median, and Mode

- The *mean* of a set of data is the sum of the values divided by the number of data items.

  $74 + 77 + 80 + 81 + 85 + 87 + 94 + 94 = 672$

  $672 \div 8 = 84$

  The mean math test grade is 84.

Math Test Grades	
Sharon	81
Rashid	94
Durrin	77
Nicole	80
Terry	74
Mei-lin	94
Kevin	87
Carlos	85

- The *median* of a data set is the middle value when the data are arranged in numerical order. When the grades are arranged in order from least to greatest, there are two middle numbers.

  74, 77, 80, 81, 85, 87, 94, 94

  To find the median, add the two middle numbers and divide the total by 2.

  $81 + 85 = 166$

  $166 \div 2 = 83$

  The median grade is 83.

- The *mode* of a data set is the item in the data set that appears most often. For this data, 94 is the mode.

Find the mean of each data set.

1. 8, 6, 5, 9, 7, 13

2. 12, 10, 16, 14, 8, 24

3. 9, 12, 14, 6, 8, 5

_____

4. 104, 126, 128, 100, 97

5. 86, 68, 70, 48, 66, 76

6. 65, 50, 95, 35, 75, 100

_____

Find the median of each data set.

7. 5, 4, 7, 9, 8

8. 12, 16, 19, 14, 14, 18

9. 9, 19, 21, 13

_____

10. 46, 38, 22, 48, 61

11. 60, 57, 53, 78, 44, 51

12. 8, 6, 6, 5, 8, 9

_____

Find the mode of each data set.

13. 3, 4, 5, 5, 3, 5, 4, 2

14. 1, 2, 1, 1, 2, 2, 3, 1

15. 6, 8, 3, 8, 3, 9, 3

_____

16. 33, 35, 34, 33, 35, 33

17. 98, 97, 98, 98, 97

18. 110, 121, 121, 110, 115, 117, 119

_____

Review 55

Sixteen students were asked to name their favorite school day. A *frequency table* can be used to organize their responses.

Favorite School Day	Tally	Frequency
Monday	III	3
Tuesday	II	2
Wednesday	III	3
Thursday	IIII	4
Friday	IIII	4

To make a frequency table:

① List all the choices.

② Mark a tally for each student's response.

③ Total the tallies for each choice.

Students compared the number of books they carry to school. A *line plot* can be used to show this data. Each ✗ represents one student.

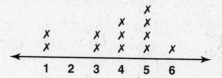

Number of Books Carried to School

To use a line plot to find the *range:*

① Subtract the least value from the greatest value along the horizontal line.

② The range is 6 − 1 or 5 books.

Organize each set of data by making a frequency table.

1. first letters of students' names:
A, A, B, D, F, F, H, J, J, J, J

First Letter	Tally	Frequency
A		
B		
D		
F		
H		
J		

2. birthday months: March, May, April, June, July, June, May, May, May, July, March, May

Month	Tally	Frequency
March		
April		
May		
June		
July		

Make a line plot for each set of data. Find the range.

3. ages of middle school students:
11, 12, 12, 12, 12, 12, 13, 13, 13, 13, 13, 13, 14, 14, 14

4. questions answered correctly on a quiz: 9, 9, 8, 7, 10, 9, 6, 7, 9, 9, 10, 8, 8, 8, 7, 6, 10, 10

The range is _____.

The range is _____.

Review 56

Some problems contain many pieces of data.

Read and Understand A stadium sells buttons, pins, and pennants. The prices are $1.25 for a button, $.54 for a pin, and $4.39 for a pennant. Audrey wants to buy an equal number of each. What is the greatest number she can buy without spending more than $20.00?

Plan and Solve To solve the problem, it may help to make an organized list of prices. Stop when the total is close to but not more than $20.00.

	1	2	3	4
Buttons	$1.25	$2.50	$3.75	$5.00
Pins	$.54	$1.08	$1.62	$2.16
Pennants	$4.39	$8.78	$13.17	$17.56
Total	$6.18	$12.36	**$18.54**	$24.72

Audrey can buy 3 of each without spending more than $20.00.

Look Back and Check You can estimate to check whether your answer is reasonable.
$4 + $2 + $13 is less than $20.

Solve each problem by making an organized list.

1. On day one at your new babysitting job, you earn $2. On each day after that you will earn $.50 more than you did the day before. On what day will you earn $6.50?

   _____

2. How many ways can you make $.50 using nickels and dimes?

   _____

3. A bakery has four types of bread, A B, C, and D and four types of meat, E, F, G, and H. How many bread-meat combinations can a customer choose from? Only one meat per bread type can be selected.

   _____

4. A library charges $.50 the first day and $.05 each additional day a book is overdue. Sonja paid an overdue fee of $2.15. How many days was the book overdue?

   _____

Review 57

A *bar graph* uses vertical or horizontal bars to display numerical information. The length of the bars tell you the numbers they represent. To read the graph at the right, first read the horizontal axis. Then read from the top of a bar to the vertical axis. This graph shows that in September, an English class read 25 books. A *histogram* is a bar graph that shows the frequency of each data item.

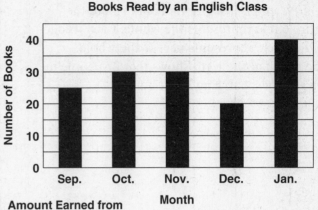

Books Read by an English Class

A *line graph* is a graph that uses a series of line segments to show changes in data. Usually, a line graph shows changes over time. For example, it may show a pattern of increase, decrease, or no change over time.

Amount Earned from After-School Job

Use the bar graph above for Exercises 1–4.

1. How many books were read in December?

   _____

2. In which month did students read the most books?

   _____

3. How many more books were read in January than in October?

   _____

4. In which two months did students read the same number of books?

   _____

Use the tables at the right for Exercises 5–6.

5. Would you use a bar graph, a histogram, or a line graph to display the data in the Sports table? Explain your choice.

   _____

   _____

Favorite Sports	
Sport	**Number Answering**
Wrestling	290
Football	50
Basketball	520
Baseball	130

6. Would you use a bar graph, a histogram, or a line graph for the Population data? Explain.

   _____

   _____

Population of Springdale	
Year	**Population**
1970	45,000
1980	62,000
1990	68,000

Course 1 Topics

Review 58

A *circle graph* is a graph of data where the entire circle represents the whole. Each wedge in the circle represents part of the whole. The graph at the right shows that 27 people in the survey speak English at home.

Languages Spoken at Home

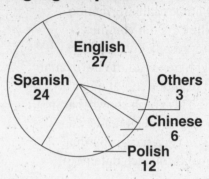

English 27
Spanish 24
Others 3
Chinese 6
Polish 12

Use the circle graph above for Exercises 1–4.

1. Which 2 languages did most people surveyed speak?

_____

2. How many people spoke Polish?

_____

3. How many more people spoke Spanish than Polish?

_____

4. Did more people speak Polish or Chinese?

_____

Sketch a circle graph for the given percents.

5. 65%, 35%

6. 26%, 62%, 12%

7. 16%, 51%, 33%

8. 10%, 90%

9. 30%, 50%, 20%

10. 15%, 15%, 70%

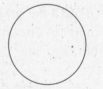

Shade the circle graph with a section equal to the given fraction.

11. $\frac{1}{4}$

12. $\frac{2}{3}$

13. $\frac{4}{5}$

Review 59

Party Pals has party equipment for rent. The company uses a *spreadsheet* to keep track of the number of hours its equipment is rented.

	A	B	C	D	E	F
1	Machine	Fri.	Sat.	Sun.	Total	Mean Rental Time
2	Party Popcorner	4	8	6		
3	Juice Fountain	0	3	3		
4	Soft Ice Cream Machine	8	9	4		
5	Pretzel Oven	1	6	5		

- A *cell* is a box in a spreadsheet where a particular row and column meet. In column C, you find the cells C1, C2, C3, and so on. C2 shows 8. Its value is 8 hours.

- Missing values can be found by telling the spreadsheet what calculation to do. The value for cell E3 can be found by using the formula = B3 + C3 + D3.

Use the spreadsheet above for Exercises 1–13. Identify the cell(s) that indicate each category.

1. machines rented

   _____

2. rental times for Saturday

   _____

3. total rental hours for the Popcorner

   _____

4. mean rental time for the pretzel oven

   _____

Write the value for the given cell.

5. B5

   _____

6. C4

   _____

7. D3

   _____

8. B3

   _____

9. D5

   _____

Wrie a formula to find each quantity.

10. the total in cell E4

    _____

11. the total in cell E5

    _____

12. the total in cell E2

    _____

13. the mean score in cell F5

    _____

Review 60

Stem-and-Leaf Plots

A *stem-and-leaf plot* is a graph that uses the digits of each number to show the shape of the data. Each data value is broken into a "stem" on the left and a "leaf" on the right. A vertical segment separates the stems from the leaves. To read the data, combine the stem with each leaf in the same row.

Example: Make a stem-and-leaf diagram of the data showing minutes spent eating lunch.

Minutes Spent Eating Lunch
46, 35, 12, 37, 28, 10, 22, 54, 19, 13, 46, 51

① Decide what the stem of the diagram will represent. Since these data are two-digit numbers, the stem will be the tens digits and the leaves will be the ones digits.

② Write the tens digits in order in the lefthand column of the diagram. Then write each leaf at the right of its stem as they occur in the problem.

③ Complete the second stem-and-leaf diagram, with the leaves in order from least to greatest.

②

Stem	Leaf
1	2 0 9 3
2	8 2
3	5 7
4	6 6
5	4 1

③

Stem	Leaf
1	0 2 3 9
2	2 8
3	5 7
4	6 6
5	1 4

For Exercises 1–4, use the stem-and-leaf plot at the right.

1. What does 1 | 8 represent?

   _____

2. How many entries have a value of 25?

   _____

3. How many people were older than 40?

   _____

4. How many people were at the poetry reading?

   _____

5. Make a stem-and-leaf plot for the data showing the monthly attendance at the teen club.

Ages of People Attending a Poetry Reading

Stem	Leaf
0	5 8 8 9
1	8 8 9 9
2	3 5 5 6 8 8 9
3	2 2 7
4	0 1 3
5	2 8
6	4 4 6 7 8

Key 0 | 8 means 8 years old

Attendance at Teen Club
489, 527, 479, 519, 514, 480, 493, 523, 508, 504

Stem	Leaf

Review 61

Misleading Graphs and Statistics

Data can be displayed on graphs in ways that are misleading.

The horizontal scales make these line graphs seem different.

As the numbers are moved farther apart, it appears that the change over time is less.

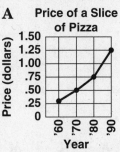

A Price of a Slice of Pizza

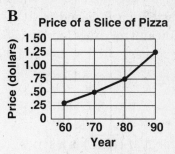

B Price of a Slice of Pizza

These bar graphs may seem different because of how the vertical scales are drawn.

The break in the vertical scale makes the differences seem greater than they really are.

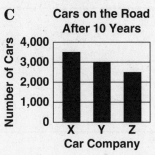

C Cars on the Road After 10 Years

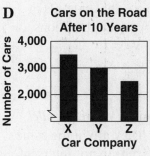

D Cars on the Road After 10 Years

Use the graphs above for Exercises 1–4.

1. Which graph might be used to convince someone that the price of pizza has risen too quickly over the years?

   _____

2. Which graph might be used to convince someone that pizza makers should raise their prices?

   _____

3. Which graph would Car Company X use to show that its cars last longer than the competition?

   _____

4. Which graph of cars still on the road after 10 years would Car Company Z prefer?

   _____

5. On a science exam, six students scored a mean of 75. Their scores were 88, 90, 12, 85, 87, and 88. Why might the mean be misleading?

   _____

   _____

   _____

Review 62

Each *point F, G,* and *H,* indicates an exact location in space.

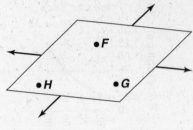

Plane FGH is flat and extends indefinitely as suggested by the arrows.

Line KM ($\overleftrightarrow{KM}$) is a series of points that extends in two opposite directions without end.

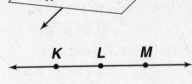

Segment LM ($\overline{LM}$) is part of $\overrightarrow{KM}$. The points *L* and *M* are endpoints of $\overline{LM}$.

Ray LM ($\overrightarrow{LM}$) is part of a line. Point *L* is its only endpoint.

$\overleftrightarrow{ST}$ and $\overleftrightarrow{UV}$ are *parallel lines.* They are in the same plane but do not intersect. They have no points in common.

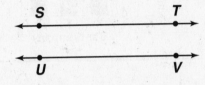

Points on the same line are *collinear.* Points *S* and *T* are collinear.

Skew lines are neither parallel nor intersecting.

Read each statement. Write *true* or *false*.

1. A line has two endpoints.

   _____

2. A plane has only two points.

   _____

3. A segment is part of a line.

   _____

4. A plane is flat.

   _____

5. Collinear points lie on different lines.

   _____

6. A ray has two endpoints.

   _____

7. A ray has no beginning or end.

   _____

8. A plane contains only one line.

   _____

9. Parallel segments do not intersect.

   _____

10. Skew lines intersect.

   _____

Match each figure with its name.

11. _____ 12. _____

13. _____ 14. _____

a. ray

b. plane

c. line

d. segment

Review 63

You can classify an *angle* according to its measure in degrees.

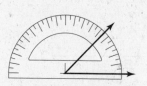 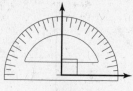 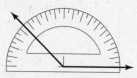 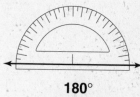

between 0° and 90°
acute angle

90°
right angle

between 90° and 180°
obtuse angle

180°
straight angle

Classifying can help you estimate and measure the size of ∠*RST*.

∠*RST* is an obtuse angle.
It is greater than 90° but less than 180°.
A good estimate is 135°.

To find the measure of ∠*RST*:

① Extend the sides so they reach the scales on the *protractor*.

② Place the protractor over the angle as shown. $\overrightarrow{ST}$ is on zero.

③ Read the inner scale.

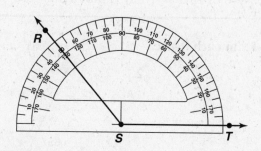

The measure of ∠*RST* is 130°. Since ∠*RST* is obtuse, it cannot be 50°.

Classify each angle as *acute*, *right*, *obtuse*, or *straight*.

1.
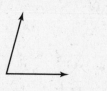

_____

2.

_____

3.
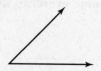

_____

4.

_____

Use a protractor to measure each angle.

5.

_____

6.

_____

7.
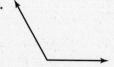

_____

8.

_____

Review 64

Special Pairs of Angles

Complementary angles:
sum of measures = 90°.

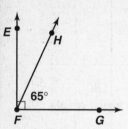

Example 1: Find the complement of ∠HFG.

$x + 65° = 90°$

$x = 25°$

∠EFH has a measure of 25°.

Supplementary angles:
sum of measures = 180°.

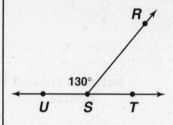

Example 2: Find the supplement of ∠USR.

$x + 130° = 180°$

$x = 50°$

∠RST has a measure of 50°.

Congruent angles
have the same measure.

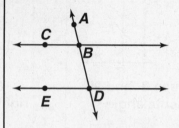

Example 3: ∠ABC and ∠BDE have the same measure; they are congruent.

Find the value of x in each figure.

1.

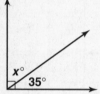

_____

2.

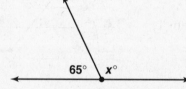

_____

3.

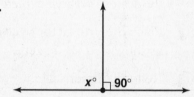

_____

Use the diagram at the right. Complete each sentence with *complementary,* *supplementary,* or *congruent.* Some exercises use more than one word.

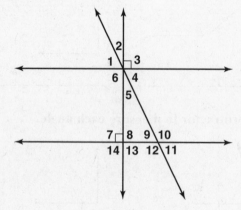

4. Angles 1 and 2 are

   _____.

5. Angles 9 and 10 are

   _____.

6. Angles 3 and 7 are

   _____.

7. Angles 4 and 5 are

   _____.

8. Angles 10 and 11 are

   _____.

9. Angles 7 and 14 are

   _____.

Review 65

Triangles can be classified by the measures of their angles.

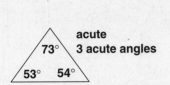
acute
3 acute angles
73° 53° 54°

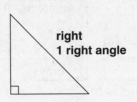
right
1 right angle

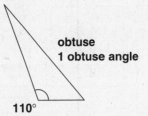
obtuse
1 obtuse angle
110°

Triangles can be classified by the number of congruent sides.

equilateral
all congruent sides
2 2 2

isosceles
2 congruent sides
3 3 1.8

scalene
no congruent sides
2.5 1 2

Classify each triangle as *acute*, *right*, or *obtuse*.

1.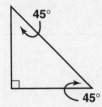
45°
45°

2.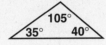
105°
35° 40°

3.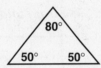
80°
50° 50°

4.
60° 60°
60°

_____   _____   _____

Classify each triangle by its angles.

5. 90°, 40°, 50°   6. 38°, 72°, 70°   7. 115°, 30°, 35°   8. 70°, 60°, 50°

_____   _____   _____   _____

Classify each triangle by its sides.

9.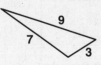
9
7 3

10.
5 5
3

11.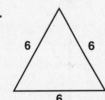
6 6
6

12.
4
7 7

_____   _____   _____   _____

Name _____ Class _____ Date _____

Review 66

A *polygon* is a closed figure formed by three or more line segments that do not cross.

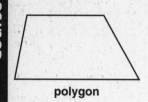
polygon

not closed

not a line segment

segments
cross

not polygons

Polygons can be named according to the number of sides.

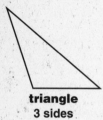
triangle
3 sides

quadrilateral
4 sides

pentagon
5 sides

hexagon
6 sides

octagon
8 sides

decagon
10 sides

Write all the possible names for each quadrilateral. Choose from
parallelogram, rhombus, square, **and** *trapezoid.*

1.

2.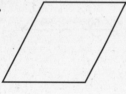

3.

4.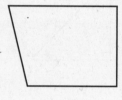

_____ _____ _____ _____

_____ _____ _____ _____

Identify each polygon according to the number of sides.

5.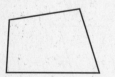

6.

7.

8.

_____ _____ _____ _____

9.

10.

11.

12.

_____ _____ _____ _____

Review 67

Daniel, Sandy, Rita, and Joseph mixed up their class schedules. Each student has math class during a different period, and the schedules show math in period A, B, C, or D. Daniel knows he eats lunch during period C. Sandy sees Daniel arrive for math class just as she is leaving. Rita goes to math after eating lunch with Daniel. Which schedule belongs to each student?

Read and Understand

There are four different schedules for four students. Clues are given about which schedule belongs to each student. The goal is to match each student with a schedule.

Plan and Solve

Make a table. Label the schedules A, B, C, and D for the periods in which math appears. Use the clues to determine whether or not a student has a given schedule.

- Daniel eats lunch during period C. Write "No" in the box for Daniel and schedule C.

- Rita goes to math after eating lunch with Daniel. Rita must have math during period D.

- Sandy sees Daniel arrive for math just as she is leaving. To have math before Daniel, Sandy must go to math in period A. Daniel has math in period B.

- Complete the table. Joseph must have math in period C.

	A	B	C	D
Daniel	No	Yes	No	No
Sandy	Yes	No	No	No
Rita	No	No	No	Yes
Joseph	No	No	Yes	No

Look Back and Check

Reread the problem. Make sure your solution matches all the facts given.

Solve each problem using logical reasoning.

1. Patrick, Tony, and Neil live in a row of three houses on the same street. Walking past their houses, they pass a white house first, then a green house, then a blue house. Patrick lives next door to the green house. Tony does not live next door to his friend who lives in the blue house. Who lives in each house?

_____

_____

2. A landscaper is planting five types of flowers in a row. The daisies are not planted at either end of the row. The snapdragons are planted at one of the ends and are next to the daffodils. The tulips are only next to the hyacinths. The hyacinths are second in the row. In what order did the landscaper plant the flowers?

_____

_____

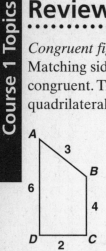

Course 1 Topics

Review 68

Congruent and Similar Figures

Congruent figures have the same size and shape. Matching sides and matching angles are congruent. These are corresponding parts. Here, quadrilaterals *ABCD* and *EFGH* are congruent.

Similar figures have the same shape, but may not be the same size. They have congruent corresponding angles and proportional corresponding sides. Here, triangles *RST* and *UVW* are similar.

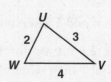

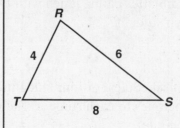

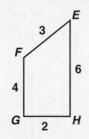

For each triangle, tell whether it is congruent to triangle *RST*.

1.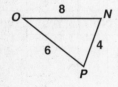

2.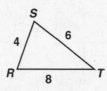

3.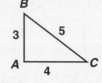

_____   _____   _____

4. List the figures that are similar to the figure shown.

a.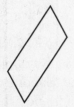

b.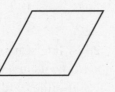

c.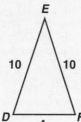

_____

Tell whether the figures are *congruent* or *similar*.

5.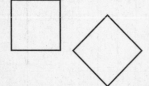

6.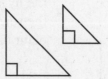

7.

_____   _____   _____

Review 69

Line Symmetry

A figure has *line symmetry* if you can fold it in half so that the two halves match exactly. The line is called a *line of symmetry*.

This figure has line symmetry.
Trace the figure and the line through it.
Cut out the figure and fold it on the line.
The two halves match exactly.

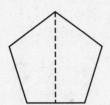

This figure *does not have* line symmetry.
Trace the figure and the line through it.
Cut out the figure and fold it on the line (or on any other line). The two halves do not match exactly.

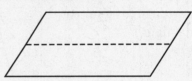

Some figures have many lines of symmetry. Draw a circle and try to find all the lines of symmetry.

Does the figure have line symmetry? Write *yes* or *no*. If yes, trace the figure and draw all the lines of symmetry.

1.

_____

2.

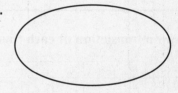

_____

3.

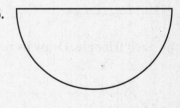

_____

4.

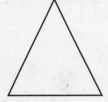

_____

5.

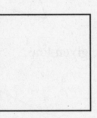

_____

6.

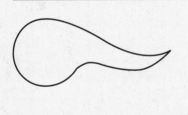

_____

Can you find a line of symmetry for each word? Write *yes* or *no*. If yes, copy the word and draw the line of symmetry.

7. DAD

8. HAH

9. DAY

10. COB

_____   _____   _____   _____

Review 70

In a *translation,* or slide, every point of a figure moves the same distance and in the same direction.

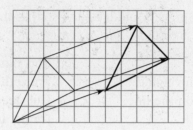

In a *reflection,* or flip, a figure is flipped across a line. The new figure is a mirror image of the original figure.

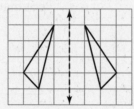

In a *rotation,* a figure is turned, or rotated about a point. You can describe a rotation in terms of degrees. The triangle has been rotated 90° clockwise.

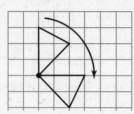

Draw a translation of each triangle.

1.
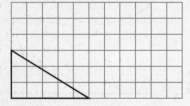

2.
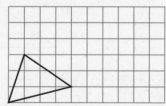

Copy each triangle. Draw its reflection over the given line.

3.
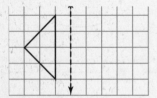

4.
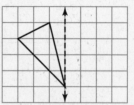

Circle all rotations of the first shape. State the number of degrees you must rotate the shape.

5.   a.   b.   c.

Review 71

The standard unit of length in the metric system is the *meter*.

millimeter (mm)	= 0.001 meter
centimeter (cm)	= 0.01 meter
meter (m)	= 1 meter
kilometer (km)	= 1,000 meters

A length can be named using different metric units. The point marked on the ruler is 2.7 centimeters.

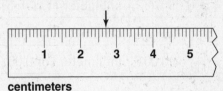

centimeters

Since each centimeter is 10 millimeters, the point is also 27 millimeters.

In the metric system, solids can be measured in units of *mass*.

milligram (mg)	= 0.001 gram
gram (g)	= 1 gram
kilogram (kg)	= 1,000 grams

The standard unit of mass is the *gram*.
- The mass of a vitamin pill may be measured in milligrams.
- A thumbtack has a mass of about 1 gram.
- A full liter bottle of soda has a mass of about 1 kilogram.

Liquids are measured in units of *capacity*.

milliliter (mL)	= 0.001 liter
liter (L)	= 1 liter
kiloliter (kL)	= 1,000 liters

The standard unit of capacity is the *liter*.
- The capacity of a soup spoon is measured in milliliters.
- A 1-liter soda bottle can fill about four average-sized glasses.
- Water in a river is measured in kiloliters.

Choose an appropriate metric unit of length.

1. distance across the end of a pencil _____

2. length of a thumb _____

3. distance from your home to Australia _____

4. width of a swimming pool _____

Choose an appropriate metric unit of mass.

5. the mass of a tooth _____

6. the mass of a puppy _____

Choose an appropriate metric unit of capacity.

7. the capacity of a bucket of water _____

8. the amount of water in a pond _____

Review 72

The most common metric units use the prefixes *kilo-*, *centi-*, and *milli-*.

Prefix	Meaning	Examples
kilo-	1,000	kilometer (1,000 m), kilogram (1,000 g), kiloliter (1,000 L)
centi-	$\frac{1}{100}$ or 0.01	centimeter (or 0.01 m), centigram (or 0.01 g), centiliter (or 0.01 L)
milli-	$\frac{1}{1,000}$ or 0.001	millimeter (or 0.001 m), milligram (or 0.001 g), milliliter (or 0.001 L)

Multiply to convert from larger units to smaller units.

Convert 4.7 kilometers to meters.

- A kilometer is larger than a meter. Multiply.

- Since 1 km = 1,000 m, multiply by 1,000.

$4.7 \times 1,000 = 4,700$
$4.7 \text{ km} = 4,700 \text{ m}$

- Or use mental math. Multiply by 1,000 by moving the decimal point three places to the *right*.

$4.7 \rightarrow 4,700$

Divide to convert from smaller units to larger units.

Convert 347 milliliters to liters.

- A milliliter is smaller than a liter. Divide.

- Since 1,000 mL = 1 L, divide by 1,000.

$347 \div 1,000 = 0.347$
$347 \text{ mL} = 0.347 \text{ L}$

- Or use mental math. Divide by 1,000 by moving the decimal point three places to the *left*.

$347 \rightarrow 0.347$

Convert each measurement to meters.

1. 2.5 km _____

2. 371 cm _____

3. 490 mm _____

4. 48 cm _____

5. 4 km _____

6. 1,500 mm _____

Convert each measurement to liters.

7. 0.6 kL _____

8. 799 cL _____

9. 0.9 mL _____

10. 35.6 mL _____

11. 0.006 kL _____

12. 1.8 cL _____

Convert each measurement to grams.

13. 4 kg _____

14. 661 cg _____

15. 1,500 mg _____

16. 2 cg _____

17. 1.95 kg _____

18. 2.3 mg _____

Convert each measurement.

19. 19 mL = _____ L

20. 5.5 kg = _____ g

21. 4.9 cL = _____ L

22. 730 mg = _____ g

23. 0.06 kL = _____ L

24. 2,540 mm = _____ cm

Review 73

Perimeters and Areas of Rectangles

Perimeter

The *perimeter* of a figure is the sum of the lengths of its sides. Opposite sides of a rectangle are equal. To find the perimeter, add the 2 lengths (ℓ) and the 2 widths (w).

$$P = \ell + \ell + w + w \text{ or } P = 2\ell + 2w$$

Find the perimeter.

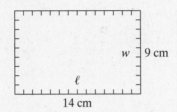

14 cm

$$\begin{aligned}
P &= 2\ell + 2w \\
&= 2(14) + 2(9) \\
&= 28 + 18 = 46
\end{aligned}$$

The perimeter is 46 centimeters.

Area

The *area* of a figure is the number of square units needed to cover the figure. To find the area of a rectangle, multiply the length (ℓ) and the width (w).

$$A = \ell \times w$$

Find the area.

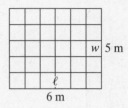

6 m

$$\begin{aligned}
A &= \ell \times w \\
&= 6 \times 5 \\
&= 30
\end{aligned}$$

The area is 30 square meters.

Estimate the area of each figure. Each square represents 1 square inch.

1.   _____

2.   _____

3.   _____

Find the perimeter and area of each rectangle or square.

4. $\ell = 12$ cm, $w = 2$ cm

_____

5. $\ell = 9$ ft, $w = 7.5$ ft

_____

6. $\ell = 2.5$ m, $w = 2.5$ m

_____

7. $\ell = 5.5$ in., $w = 5.5$ in.

_____

8. $\ell = 6.2$ in., $w = 3.4$ in.

_____

9. $\ell = 4.5$ ft, $w = 0.75$ ft

_____

10. $\ell = 8$ cm, $w = 8$ cm

_____

11. $\ell = 10.5$ m, $w = 5.2$ m

_____

12. $\ell = 22$ in., $w = 9$ in.

_____

13. What is the area of a square with a perimeter of 60 meters?

_____

Review 74

Areas of Parallelograms and Triangles

Parallelogram

To find the area of a parallelogram, multiply base times height.

$$A = b \times h$$

Find the area of the parallelogram.

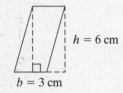

$h = 6$ cm

$b = 3$ cm

$$A = b \times h$$
$$= 3 \times 6$$
$$= 18$$

The area is 18 square centimeters.

Triangle

The area of a triangle is $\frac{1}{2}$ times the base times the height.

$$A = \frac{1}{2}b \times h$$

Find the area of the triangle.

$h = 6$ cm

$b = 3$ cm

$$A = \frac{1}{2} \times b \times h$$
$$= \frac{1}{2} \times 3 \times 6$$
$$= 9$$

The area is 9 square centimeters.

Find the area of each parallelogram.

1. $b = 6$ ft, $h = 8$ ft

2. $b = 12$ in, $h = 9$ in.

3. $b = 6$ yd, $h = 12$ yd

_____

4. $b = 2.8$ in., $h = 3.4$ in.

5. $b = 31$ yd, $h = 19$ yd

6. $b = 4.5$ m, $h = 4.5$ m

_____

7. $b = 15$ cm, $h = 7$ cm

8. $b = 8.3$ ft, $h = 11.7$ ft

9. $b = 14.4$ m, $h = 6.5$ m

_____

Find the area of each triangle.

10. $b = 8$ cm, $h = 14$ cm

11. $b = 7$ in., $h = 18$ in.

12. $b = 11$ m, $h = 4.6$ m

_____

13. $b = 6.4$ ft, $h = 3.5$ ft

14. $b = 104$ in., $h = 55$ in.

15. $b = 5.9$ cm, $h = 4.2$ cm

_____

16. $b = 1.7$ m, $h = 3.3$ m

17. $b = 5.8$ yd, $h = 5.8$ yd

18. $b = 8.6$ in., $h = 0.8$ in.

_____

Review 75

Parts of a Circle

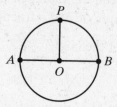

Point O is the center of the *circle*.
$\overline{AB}$ is a *diameter*.
$\overline{OA}$ is a *radius*. $\overline{OP}$ is also a radius.

In any circle, the length of the diameter is twice the length of the radius.

$$d = 2r$$

The radius is half the diameter.

$$r = \frac{d}{2}$$

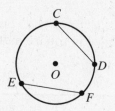

$\overline{CD}$ and $\overline{EF}$ are *chords*.
A diameter of a circle is the longest chord.

Circumference of a Circle

Circumference is the distance around a circle.

To find circumference:

- Multiply π times the diameter.

$$C = \pi d$$

- Or multiply π times twice the radius.

$$C = 2\pi r$$

To estimate the circumference of a circle, use 3 for π.

Estimate the circumference of a circle.

$$C \approx 3d$$
$$= 3 \times 8$$
$$= 24$$

The circumference is about 24 centimeters.

List each of the following for circle Q.

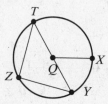

1. one diameter

_____

2. two chords

_____

3. three radii

_____

Find the unknown length for a circle with the given dimension.

4. $r = 8$ cm

$d = $ _____

5. $d = 110$ in.

$r = $ _____

6. $d = 48$ ft

$r = $ _____

Use 3 for π to estimate the circumference of a circle with the given radius or diameter.

7. $r = 12$ in. _____

8. $d = 15$ yd _____

9. $d = 7$ m _____

10. $d = 13$ ft _____

11. $r = 21$ yd _____

12. $r = 19$ cm _____

Review 76 ....

The formula for the *area of a circle* is:

$$Area = \pi \times radius \times radius$$

$$A = \pi \times r \times r$$

$$A = \pi r^2$$

Find the area of the circle.

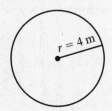

$$A = \pi r^2$$
$$= \pi \times 4^2$$
$$= \pi \times 4 \times 4$$
$$= \pi \times 16$$
$$\approx 50.27$$

The area is about 50.27 square meters.

Use $\frac{22}{7}$ for π when the radius or diameter of a circle is a multiple of 7 or a fraction.

Find the area of the circle.

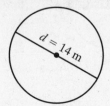

$$d = 14 \text{ m, so } r = 7 \text{ m}$$
$$A = \pi r^2$$
$$\approx \frac{22}{7} \times 7^2$$
$$= \frac{22}{7} \times 7 \times 7$$
$$= \frac{22}{7} \times 7^1 \times 7$$
$$= 154$$

The area is about 154 square meters.

Find the area of each circle. Round to the nearest tenth or use $\frac{22}{7}$ for π where appropriate.

1.
3 m

2.
2 m

3.
12 m

_____ _____ _____

4. $r = 8$ cm **5.** $r = 13$ in. **6.** $d = 28$ m **7.** $d = 24$ ft

_____ _____ _____ _____

8. $r = 3\frac{1}{2}$ m **9.** $d = 13$ cm **10.** $r = 1\frac{3}{11}$ ft **11.** $d = 29$ in.

_____ _____ _____ _____

Find the area of each circle to the nearest tenth. Use 3.14 for π.

12. $d = 23$ ft **13.** $r = 2.5$ yd **14.** $d = 48$ in. **15.** $r = 19$ cm

_____ _____ _____ _____

Review 77

Prisms and pyramids are three-dimensional figures. Their parts have special names.

- *Faces*—flat surface on a prism or pyramid

- *Edge*—segment where two faces meet

- *Vertex*—point where edges meet

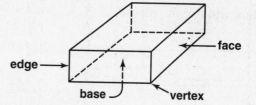

Prisms and pyramids can be named by the shape of their bases.

Prism	**Pyramid**
- has two *bases* congruent and parallel to one another	- has one base; other faces are triangles

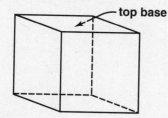

6 faces
12 edges
8 vertices

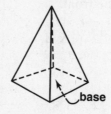

5 faces
8 edges
5 vertices

The bases are rectangles.
This prism is a *rectangular prism*.

The base is a square.
This pyramid is a *square pyramid*.

Name each three-dimensional figure.

1.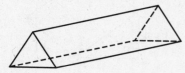

_____

2.

_____

3.

_____

4.

_____

5. How many faces, edges, and vertices does a pentagonal prism have?

_____

Name _____ Class _____ Date _____

Review 78

The *surface area* of a rectangular prism is the sum of the areas
of the faces. You can use nets to find surface area.

Find the surface area of the prism.

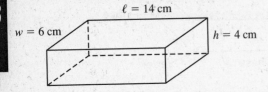

$\ell = 14$ cm

$w = 6$ cm $h = 4$ cm

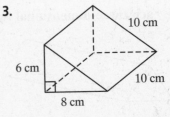

14 cm

Top   6 cm

Left side   Front   Right side

6 cm   Bottom

4 cm   Back   4 cm

area of top = area of bottom
area of front = area of back
area of right side = area of left side

① Find the area of
the top.
$A = \ell \times w$
$= 14 \times 6$
$= 84$ cm^2

② Find the area of
the front.
$A = \ell \times h$
$= 14 \times 4$
$= 56$ cm^2

③ Find the area of
the right side.
$A = w \times h$
$= 6 \times 4$
$= 24$ cm^2

④ Add.
$84 + 84 + 56 + 56 + 24 + 24 = 328$

The surface area of the prism is 328 square centimeters.

Find the surface area of each prism.

1.

4 m   4 m   4 m

_____

2.

2 cm   2 cm

6 cm

_____

3.

10 cm   6 cm   10 cm   8 cm

_____

Find the surface area of each cylinder. (*Hint:* The net of a cylinder is
two circles and a rectangle.)

4. 6 cm

4 cm

_____

5.

4 cm

4 cm

_____

Name _____ Class _____ Date _____

Review 79

Volumes of Rectangular Prisms and Cylinders

Volume is the number of cubic units needed to fill the space inside a three-dimensional figure. It is measured in cubic units.

Find the volume of the rectangular prism.

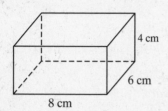

Volume = Area of base × height

$$V = B \times h$$
$$= \ell \times w \times h$$
$$= 8 \times 6 \times 4$$
$$= 192$$

The volume is 192 cubic centimeters.

Find the volume of the cylinder

$$V = B \times h$$

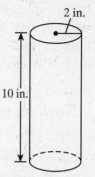

① Find the area of the base.

$$B = \pi \times r^2$$
$$= \pi \times 2^2$$
$$\approx 12.57$$

② Find the volume.

$$V = B \times h$$
$$= 12.57 \times 10$$
$$= 125.7$$

The volume is 125.7 cubic inches.

Find the volume of each rectangular prism.

1.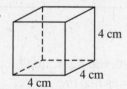

_____

2.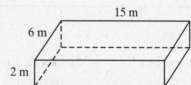

_____

3.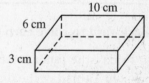

_____

Find the volume of each rectangular prism with the given dimensions.

4. $\ell = 6$ in., $w = 9$ in., $h = 3$ in.

_____

5. $\ell = 3.5$ cm, $w = 1.5$ cm, $h = 7$ cm

_____

6. $\ell = 16$ mm, $w = 18$ mm, $h = 2.5$ mm

_____

7. $\ell = 5$ m, $w = 6.2$ m, $h = 3.9$ m

_____

Find the volume of each cylinder. Round to the nearest tenth.

8. $r = 8$ m, $h = 9$ m

_____

9. $r = 12$ m, $h = 2$ m

_____

Review 80

Problem Solving: Work Backward

The store manager recorded 80 greeting cards sold on Friday. The day before she had sold one-half that number. On Wednesday, she sold 25 more than on Thursday. On Monday and Tuesday she sold a total of twice what she sold on Wednesday. How many cards did she sell during the 5 days?

Read and Understand

What does the problem ask you to find? *You need to find the total number of cards sold during the 5 days.*

Plan and Solve

How can you find the number sold on each day? *Use the information given in the problem. Work backward from that information to find the number sold on Thursday, then Wednesday, and finally, the total on Tuesday and Monday.*

Work backward.

Cards sold on Friday	80
80 ÷ 2 sold on Thursday	40
40 + 25 sold on Wednesday	65
2 × 65 sold on Monday and Tuesday	+ 130
	315

She sold 315 cards.

Look Back and Check

Write the number of cards sold as a mathematical expression. Solve by using the order of operations.

$$80 + (80 ÷ 2) + (40 + 25) + (2 × 65) = 315$$

Work backward to solve each problem.

1. On Friday, the diner served 56 ears of corn. On Thursday, the diner served one-half as much corn as on Friday. On Wednesday, the diner served two times as much as on Thursday. On Tuesday, the diner served one-half of what it had served on Wednesday. How much corn did the diner serve during the 4 days?

   _____

2. On Thursday, the diner served 42 pounds of green beans. On Wednesday, the diner served one-third that amount. On both Tuesday and Monday, the diner served one-half the amount it had served on Wednesday. How many pounds of beans did the diner serve during the 4 days?

   _____

3. On Friday, the diner served 60 baked potatoes. On both Tuesday and Thursday, the diner served one-fifth that amount. On both Monday and Wednesday, it served one-sixth of Thursday's amount. How many baked potatoes were served during the 5 days?

   _____

4. The diner served 32 pounds of salad on Saturday night. On both Friday and Thursday, one-half that amount was served. On Wednesday, one-eighth of Saturday's amount was served. How many pounds of salad did the diner serve during the 4 days?

   _____

Review 81

The numbers . . . $-3, -2, -1, 0, +1, +2, +3,$ . . . are *integers.*
Integers are the set of positive whole numbers, their opposites, and 0.

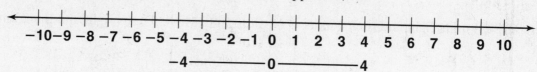

The absolute value of a number is its distance from 0 on a number
line. $|-4| = 4$. *Opposite integers,* like -4 and 4, are the same distance
from 0.

Compare -2 and 1.

For two integers on a number line, the greater integer is farther to the
right.

① Locate -2 and 1 on the number line.

② Find that 1 is farther to the right.

③ Write $1 > -2$ (1 is greater than -2),
   or $-2 < 1$ (-2 is less than 1.)

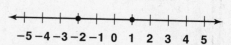

Name the opposite of each integer.

1. 7 _____

2. -212 _____

3. 49 _____

4. 1,991 _____

5. -78 _____

6. 16 _____

Compare using < or >.

7. 6 ☐ 3

8. 2 ☐ 8

9. -2 ☐ 2

10. 9 ☐ -9

11. 0 ☐ 5

12. -9 ☐ -5

13. 0 ☐ 10

14. -5 ☐ -2

15. 7 ☐ -9

16. -5 ☐ -1

17. 6 ☐ -6

18. -12 ☐ 0

19. 8 ☐ -3

20. -1 ☐ -2

21. -5 ☐ 4

22. -3 ☐ -2

Find each absolute value.

23. $|-2|$

24. $|-100|$

25. $|-16|$

_____

_____

_____

26. $|8|$

27. $|-25|$

28. $|-250|$

_____

_____

_____

29. $|16|$

30. $|12|$

31. $|75|$

_____

_____

_____

Name _____ Class _____ Date _____

Review 82

You can add integers on a number line.

Example 1: Find $4 + 3$.

Start at 0. Move 4 units right and then 3 units right.

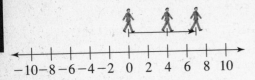

$4 + 3 = 7$

Example 2: Find $-3 + -2$.

Start at 0. Move 3 units left and then 2 units left.

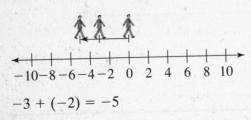

$-3 + (-2) = -5$

Example 3: Find $5 + (-3)$

Start at 0. Move 5 units right and then 3 units left.

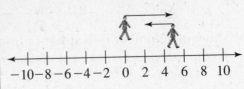

$5 + (-3) = 2$

Example 4: Find $-4 + 1$.

Start at 0. Move 4 units left and then 1 unit right.

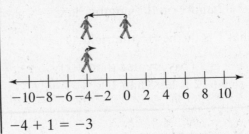

$-4 + 1 = -3$

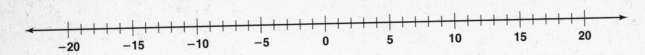

Use the number line to find each sum.

1. $3 + 2$ _____

2. $6 + 4$ _____

3. $-4 + (-1)$ _____

4. $-4 + (-8)$ _____

5. $4 + (-1)$ _____

6. $-6 + 8$ _____

7. $-7 + 3$ _____

8. $-5 + 8$ _____

9. $3 + 5$ _____

10. $-3 + (-5)$ _____

11. $3 + (-5)$ _____

12. $-3 + 5$ _____

Find each sum.

13. $-6 + (-4)$ _____

14. $7 + (-2)$ _____

15. $-1 + (-6)$ _____

16. $9 + (-2)$ _____

17. $-6 + (-6)$ _____

18. $13 + 3$ _____

19. $-14 + (-5)$ _____

20. $5 + (-12)$ _____

21. $-9 + 9$ _____

22. $18 + (-18)$ _____

23. $0 + (-4)$ _____

24. $6 + 0$ _____

25. $15 + (-15)$ _____

26. $-12 + 0$ _____

27. $-9 + 10$ _____

28. $12 + (-11)$ _____

29. $-12 + 11$ _____

30. $2 + (-10)$ _____

Name _____ Class _____ Date _____

Review 83

To subtract an integer, add the opposite.

Example 1: Subtract $5 - 8$.

Add the opposite: $5 + (-8)$

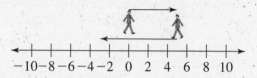

$5 - 8 = -3$

Example 2: Subtract $2 - (-4)$.

Add the opposite: $2 + 4$

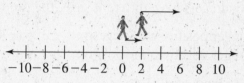

$2 - (-4) = 6$

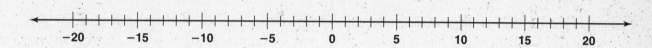

Use a number line. Find each difference.

1. $3 - (-6)$ _____

2. $2 - (-4)$ _____

3. $-1 - 2$ _____

4. $-3 - (-5)$ _____

5. $-8 - (-3)$ _____

6. $4 - (-4)$ _____

7. $-8 - 2$ _____

8. $8 - (-2)$ _____

9. $-8 - (-2)$ _____

10. $-7 - 4$ _____

11. $-10 - 2$ _____

12. $-5 - (-5)$ _____

13. $-5 - 6$ _____

14. $9 - (-3)$ _____

15. $-11 - (-6)$ _____

Find each difference.

16. $15 - (-4)$ _____

17. $-12 - 3$ _____

18. $21 - (-7)$ _____

19. $3 - (-12)$ _____

20. $-2 - 10$ _____

21. $-13 - 13$ _____

22. $5 - (-5)$ _____

23. $18 - (-10)$ _____

24. $-7 - (-13)$ _____

25. $14 - 16$ _____

26. $3 - 15$ _____

27. $-6 - (-9)$ _____

28. $-12 - 6$ _____

29. $15 - (-9)$ _____

30. $7 - 19$ _____

Solve each equation.

31. $12 + s = -10$ _____

32. $x - 8 = -3$ _____

33. $b + 18 = 12$ _____

34. $x - 21 = -2$ _____

35. $s - 25 = -100$ _____

36. $y + 5 = 9$ _____

37. $-5 + c = -10$ _____

38. $x + 30 = 5$ _____

39. $15 + b = 10$ _____

Review 84

When two integers have like signs, the product will always be positive.

Both integers are positive: $3 \times 4 = 12$
Both integers are negative: $-3 \times (-4) = 12$

When two integers have different signs, the product will always be negative.

One integer positive, one negative: $3 \times (-4) = -12$
One integer negative, one positive: $-3 \times 4 = -12$

Example 1: Find -8×3.

① Determine the product.
$8 \times 3 = 24$

② Determine the sign of the product. Since one integer is negative and one is positive, the product is negative.

③ So, $-8 \times 3 = -24$.

Example 2: Find $(-10) \times (-20)$.

① Determine the product.
$10 \times 20 = 200$

② Determine the sign of the product. Since both integers are negative, the product is positive.

③ So, $(-10) \times (-20) = 200$.

Find each product.

1. $7 \times (-4)$

_____

2. $-5 \times (-9)$

_____

3. -11×2

_____

4. $8 \times (-9)$

_____

5. $15 \times (-3)$

_____

6. $-7 \times (-6)$

_____

7. -12×6

_____

8. $13 \times (-5)$

_____

9. $-10 \times (-2)$

_____

10. A dog lost 2 pounds three weeks in a row. What integer expresses the total change in the dog's weight? _____

Find each quotient.

11. $18 \times (-6)$

_____

12. $-35 \times (-7)$

_____

13. -15×3

_____

14. $28 \times (-4)$

_____

15. $25 \times (-5)$

_____

16. $-27 \times (-9)$

_____

17. -12×4

_____

18. $33 \times (-11)$

_____

19. $-50 \times (-2)$

_____

Review 85

When two integers have like signs, the quotient will always be positive.

Both integers are positive: $8 \div 2 = 4$
Both integers are negative: $-8 \div (-2) = 4$

When two integers have different signs, the quotient will always be negative.

One integer positive, one negative: $8 \div (-2) = -4$
One integer negative, one positive: $-8 \div 4 = -2$

Example 1: Find $-24 \div 8$.

① Determine the quotient.
$24 \div 8 = 3$

② Determine the sign of the quotient. Since one integer is negative and one is positive, the quotient is negative.

③ So, $-24 \div 8 = 3$.

Example 2: Find $35 \div (-7)$.

① Determine the quotient.
$35 \div 7 = 5$

② Determine the sign of the quotient. Since one integer is positive and one is negative, the quotient is negative.

③ So, $35 \div (-7) = -5$.

Find each quotient.

1. $18 \div (-6)$

_____

2. $-35 \div (-7)$

_____

3. $-15 \div 3$

_____

4. $28 \div (-4)$

_____

5. $25 \div (-5)$

_____

6. $-27 \div (-9)$

_____

7. $-12 \div 4$

_____

8. $33 \div (-11)$

_____

9. $-50 \div (-25)$

_____

Solve each equation.

10. $-2y = 12$

_____

11. $\frac{p}{10} = -6$

_____

12. $-10y = -100$

_____

13. $7x = -28$

_____

14. $-6x = 36$

_____

15. $\frac{s}{-2} = -14$

_____

16. $\frac{x}{8} = -12$

_____

17. $4x = -24$

_____

18. $3x = 30$

_____

19. A ship sank at a rate of 90 feet in 10 seconds.
Represent the rate of change with an integer. _____

Course 1 Topics

Review 86

Example: Graph $(2, -4)$.

- 2 is the *x-coordinate*. It tells how far to move left or right from the origin.

- -4 is the *y-coordinate*. It tells how far to move up or down from the origin.

Find the coordinates of point *A*.

① Start at the origin.

② How far left or right? *3 left*
The *x-coordinate* is -3.

③ How far up or down? *5 up*
The *y-coordinate* is 5.

The coordinates of point *A* are $(-3, 5)$.

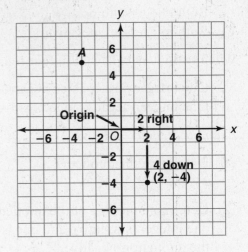

Graph each point in a coordinate plane.

1. $B(1, 6)$

2. $C(-4, -3)$

3. $D(0, 5)$

4. $E(-2, 2)$

5. $F(-1, -5)$

6. $G(6, -4)$

7. $H(5, 5)$

8. $J(4, 0)$

9. $K(-4, -4)$

10. $L(2, -3)$

11. $M(-2, 0)$

12. $N(5, -1)$

13. $P(0, -3)$

14. $Q(-4, 0)$

Find the coordinates of each point.

15. R _____

16. S _____

17. T _____

18. U _____

Look at the coordinate grid above.

19. If you travel 7 units down from *S*, at which point will you be located?

_____

20. If you travel 4 units right from *T* and 2 units down, at which point will you be located?

_____

Review 87

To find a *balance*, add the income (positive number) and the expenses (negative number). The sum is the balance.

Balance Sheet for Lunch Express		
Month	Income	Expenses
January	$1,095	−$459
February	$1,468	−$695
March	$1,773	−$700
April	$602	−$655

- To find the balance for February, add

  $1,468 + (−695) = 773$.

  Lunch Express made a profit of $773.

- To find the balance for April, add

  $602 + (−655) = −53$.

  Lunch Express had a loss of $53.

To look for a trend in the data, draw a line graph of the monthly balances.

- Balances range from −$53 to $1,073. Make the vertical scale from −$200 to $1,100. Use intervals of $100.

- Use the horizontal scale for the months.

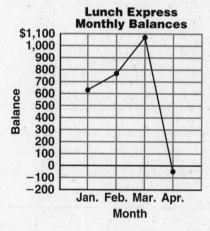

The trend was for increasing balances— until April.

Find each sum or difference.

1. −$9 + $17

_____

2. $51 − $83

_____

3. $42 − (−$18)

_____

4. −$77 + $92

_____

5. −$109 + $109

_____

6. $28 − $4310

_____

7. −$156 + $429

_____

8. $232 − (−$97)

_____

9. −$401 − $582

_____

10. $1,874 − (−$1,892)

_____

11. $6,012 + (−$3,933)

_____

12. −$4,401 − (−$1,560)

_____

13. A company earned $2,357 in January. The company earned $2,427 in February and $1,957 in March. The company's total expenses for the first quarter were $4,594. What was the company's profit?

_____

14. Your bank account is overdrawn $31. The bank charges $20 for being overdrawn. You deposit $100. What is the balance of your bank account?

_____

Course 1 Topics

Review 88

A table or a graph can show how the input and output of a *function* are related.

Make a table to show how number of feet is a function of number of yards.

Input (yards)	Output (feet)
1	3
2	6
3	9
4	12
5	15

The table shows that for every yard, there are 3 feet. You multiply the number of yards by 3 to find the number of feet.

Use the values in the table to draw a graph of the function.

① Locate the points from the table: $(1, 3), (2, 6), (3, 9), (4, 12), (5, 15)$

② Draw a line through the points.

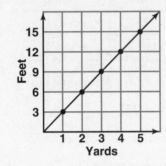

Complete the table.

1.

Input	Output
1	4
2	5
3	6
4	
5	

2.

Input	Output
4	2
6	4
8	6
10	
12	

3.

Input	Output
2	10
3	15
4	20
5	
6	

Complete each table given the rule. Then graph the function.

4. cups as a function of quarts

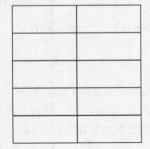
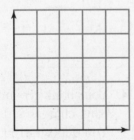

5. days as a function of weeks

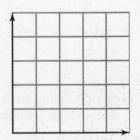

Review 89

Make a Graph

Stuart is from Australia, where speed limits are measured in kilometers per hour. While visiting the United States, Stuart drives along a road with a speed limit of 50 miles per hour (mph). Stuart would like to know the equivalent speed in kilometers per hour (kph). He remembers that 15 mph = 25 kph, and 30 mph = 50 kph.

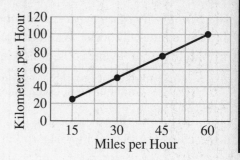

Read and Understand 15 mph = 25 kph, and 30 mph = 50 kph. You need to approximate 50 miles per hour in kilometers per hour.

Plan and Solve You can approximate 50 miles per hour in kilometers per hour by *making a line graph*. Stuart knows two pairs of equivalent speeds. Plot the points (15, 25) and (30, 50) on a coordinate plane and connect them with a line.

Look Back and Check "50 miles per hour is about 83 kilometers per hour" can be written as (50, 83). You can see that this point is on the line drawn.

Solve each problem by making a graph.

1. The federal minimum wage in 1965 was $1.25 per hour. In 1980, the minimum wage was $3.10 per hour. In 2000, it was $5.50 per hour. Estimate the minimum wage in 1990.

2. In 1989, there were 960,000 civilians working for the military. In 1993, this number decreased to 850,000. How many civilians were working for the military in 1991?

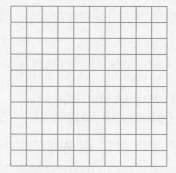

Review 90

The *probability of an event* is a number that describes how likely it is that the event will occur. When the outcomes are equally likely, the probability of an event is the following ratio.

$$P(\text{event}) = \frac{\text{number of favorable outcomes}}{\text{total number of outcomes}}$$

Find the probability of choosing the red chip if the chips are placed in a bag and mixed.

$$P(\text{red}) = \frac{\text{number of favorable outcomes}}{\text{total number of outcomes}} = \frac{1}{5}$$

The probability of choosing the red chip is $\frac{1}{5}$.

- If an event is impossible, its probability is 0. The probability of drawing an 11 from cards numbered 1 to 10 is impossible.

- If an event is unlikely, equally likely, or likely, its probability is between 0 and 1. The probability that you will draw a 2 or a 4 from cards numbered 1 to 10 is likely.

- If an event is certain, its probability is 1. The probability that you will draw a card from 1 to 10 from a set of cards numbered 1 to 10 is certain.

Find the probability of each event.

1. You pick a vowel from the letters in EVENT. _____

2. You pick a weekend day from days of the week. _____

3. You pick a month that begins with the letter J. _____

4. A spinner is labeled 1–6. You spin 1 or 5. _____

5. You pick an odd number from 75 to 100. _____

6. You pick a word with four letters from this sentence. _____

7. You have a birthday on February 30. _____

8. A number cube is tossed. You toss a 1, 3, or 5. _____

Each of the 26 letters in the English alphabet is put on a slip of paper. One slip is selected at random. Classify each event as *impossible, unlikely, likely,* or *certain*.

9. $P(\text{consonant})$

10. $P(\text{a letter from A to Z})$

11. $P(\text{vowel})$

_____

_____

_____

12. $P(\text{B})$

13. $P(10)$

14. $P(*)$

_____

_____

_____

Review 91

A *fair* game generates equally likely outcomes. To decide whether a game is fair:

① Make a list of all the possible outcomes of the game.

② Determine whether each player has about the same probability of winning.

The Spinner Game
Spin a spinner with equal-size sections numbered 1–8. Player A wins on a multiple of 2 or 3. Player B wins on any other number. Is this game fair?

① Possible outcomes: 1, 2, 3, 4, 5, 6, 7, 8.

② Player A wins with a 2, 3, 4, 6, and 8. Player B wins with a 1, 5, 7.

P(A winning) $= \frac{5}{8}$, P(B winning) $= \frac{3}{8}$

The game is not fair.

You can use the results of playing a game to find the *experimental probability* of each player winning.

Example: Two players played a game 25 times. Player A won 15 times and player B won 10 times.

P(A wins) $= \frac{\text{number of times A won}}{\text{total games played}}$

$\qquad = \frac{15}{25}$

$\qquad = \frac{3}{5}$

P(B wins) $= \frac{\text{number of times B won}}{\text{total games played}}$

$\qquad = \frac{10}{25}$

$\qquad = \frac{2}{5}$

You and your friend play a game. You win if you roll a number cube and it lands on 5. Your friend wins if she rolls a number cube and it lands on a factor of 6.

1. What is the probability that you win? _____

2. What is the probability that your friend wins? _____

3. Is the game fair? Explain your reasoning.

_____

The line plot shows the results of rolling a number cube 20 times. Find the experimental probability.

4. P(6) _____

5. P(less than 4) _____

6. P(greater than 3) _____

7. P(even number) _____

8. P(prime number) _____

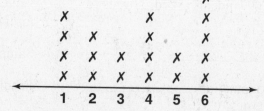

Review 92

Making Predictions From Data

Sometimes you cannot survey an entire *population.* Instead, you survey a *sample*—a part of the population that can be used to make predictions about the entire population.

A city has 5,000 sixth graders. To estimate the number of sixth graders who ride bicycles to school, a random sample was used. Of the 200 sixth graders chosen, 40 said they ride bicycles to school. Predict the number of sixth graders out of 5,000 who ride bicycles to school.

① Write a proportion. $\frac{40}{200} = \frac{n}{5,000}$

② Solve. $200 \times n = 40 \times 5,000$

$$200n = 200,000$$

$$n = \frac{200,000}{200}$$

$$n = 1,000$$

The sample suggests that 1,000 sixth graders ride bikes to school.

Identify the sample size. Then make a prediction for the population.

1. How many in a class of 100 students prefer banana yogurt to other flavors? Of 10 students asked, 6 prefer banana.

   Sample size _____

   Prediction for population _____

2. How many of the 1,900 joggers seen at the park like to run at 6 A.M.? Of 190 joggers asked, 35 like to run at 6 A.M.

   Sample size _____

   Prediction for population _____

3. Of 600 first graders in the school district, 109 are not yet reading. How many first graders out of 180,000 in the entire state are not yet reading?

   Sample size _____

   Prediction for population _____

4. Out of 300 families, 150 read the morning newspaper. There are 2,400 families in town. How many read the morning newspaper?

   Sample size _____

   Prediction for population _____

5. How many in a town of 500 students walk to school? Of 100 students asked, 32 walked to school.

   Sample size _____

   Prediction for population _____

6. Out of 150 families, 16 drive sport utility vehicles (SUVs). How many of the 4,500 families in the county drive SUVs?

   Sample size _____

   Prediction for population _____

Review 93

Problem Solving: Simulate a Problem

You have six different-color pairs of loose socks in a drawer. You reach into the drawer without looking and take out two socks. What is the probability you will pick a matched pair?

Read and Understand

How many socks are in the drawer? 12

How many different colors are there? 6

What are the possible results of picking two socks? *You can pick two socks of the same color or two socks of different colors.*

What are you trying to find? *The probability of picking two socks of the same color.*

Plan and Solve

You can simulate the problem by making a spinner like the one at the right. Each number stands for one of the six colors. Spin the spinner twice to find the colors of the two socks. Record whether the colors are the same or different.

Repeat the simulation many times. Divide the number of times the colors were the same by the total number of simulations to find the experimental probability of getting a matched pair.

Look Back and Check

What other methods could you use to simulate the problem? *Randomly pick two cards from six matched pairs of cards.*

Simulate and solve each problem. Show all your work.

1. You have four pairs of different-color loose socks in a drawer. You pick 2 socks without looking. What is the probability that you will get a matched pair? Use a spinner with 8 equal sections. Let each section represent one sock.

2. You have 5 different-color pens and 2 different-color pencils in your pocket. You pick a pen and a pencil without looking. What is the probability that you will pick the red pen and red pencil? Use real pens and pencils to simulate this event.

3. Each day a restaurant offers a special sandwich made with one of three different meats and one of three different cheeses. Your favorite is salami with American cheese. What is the probability that your favorite is the special of the day? Use two spinners, each with three equal sections: one spinner for the meats and one for the cheeses.

4. In the refrigerator, you have 3 different juices in bottles and 4 different sodas in cans. Your favorites are the orange juice and the ginger ale. If you pick a juice and a soda without looking, what is the probability that you will get both your favorites? Use one spinner with three sections and one with four. Let the first spinner represent the bottles and the second, the cans.

Review 94

Your choices for your new car are an exterior color of white, blue, or black, and an interior of fabric or leather.

A *tree diagram* shows all possible choices. Each branch shows one choice.

color	interior	outcome
white	fabric	white fabric
	leather	white leather
blue	fabric	blue fabric
	leather	blue leather
black	fabric	black fabric
	leather	black leather

The tree diagram shows 6 choices. Choosing your car at random, the probability of picking a white car with leather interior is

$$P(\text{white, leather}) = \frac{1}{6}.$$

You can use the *counting principle* to find the total number of choices.

> When there are m ways of making one choice and n ways of making a second choice, then there are $m \times n$ ways to make the first choice followed by the second choice.

Exterior choices		Interior choices		Total
3	×	2	=	6

There are 6 possible choices for your car.

Draw a tree diagram to find each probability. Show your work.

1. Marva can have a small, medium, or large salad. She can have Italian, French, or Russian dressing on it. Find the probability that she choses a small salad with French dressing.

   _____

2. You flip a coin two times. Find the probability of getting tails on both tosses.

   _____

Use the counting principle to find the total number of outcomes.

3. There are 4 kinds of fruit, 2 kinds of cereal, and 2 kinds of milk. How many ways can a bowl of cereal, fruit, and milk be chosen?

   _____

4. There are 4 choices for skis, 2 choices for bindings, and 5 choices for boots. How many ways can skis, bindings, and boots be chosen?

   _____

5. There are 3 pairs of jeans, 2 vests, and 5 shirts. How many ways can jeans, a vest, and a shirt be chosen?

   _____

6. There are 10 yogurt flavors, 4 syrups, and 5 toppings. How many ways can one flavor, one syrup, and one topping be chosen?

   _____

Review 95

An arrangement of items in a particular order is a *permutation*.

Find the number of permutations for lining up Leah, Brian, and Ahmad for a photograph. You can use these different methods.

- Draw a tree diagram.

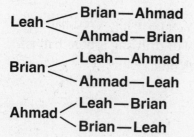

- Use the counting principle.

  In how many ways can the first person be chosen? *3 ways*

  In how many ways can the middle person be chosen? *2 ways*

  In how many ways can the remaining person be chosen? *1 way*

  $$3 \times 2 \times 1 = 6$$

- Make an organized list.
  Leah, Brian, and Ahmad
  Leah, Ahmad, and Brian
  Brian, Leah, and Ahmad
  Brian, Ahmad, and Leah
  Ahmad, Leah, and Brian
  Ahmad, Brian, and Leah

There are 6 permutations of Leah, Brian, and Ahmad.

Make an organized list or a tree diagram to find the permutations of each set of numbers or letters. Use each item exactly once.

1. the letters COW

_____

2. the numbers 2, 3, and 8

_____

3. the letters IF

_____

4. the numbers 7 and 9

_____

Use a tree diagram, a list, or the counting principle to find the number of permutations of each set.

5. A basketball team has 5 starting players. In how many ways can their names be announced before the game?

_____

6. In how many ways can 8 songs on a CD be played if you use the shuffle feature on your CD player?

_____

7. Three students are waiting for the cafeteria to open. In how many ways can they enter the food line?

_____

8. For how many consecutive baseball games can the manager use a different batting order for 9 players?

_____

Review 96

Events are *independent* when the occurrence of one event does not affect the other event. If two events are independent, the probability that both will occur is the product of their probabilities.

Example 1: A ball is drawn from the bag, its color noted, and then put back into the bag. Then another ball is drawn. Are the two events independent?

The events are independent because the color of the first ball drawn does not affect the color of the next ball drawn.

A *compound event* consists of two or more separate events.

Example 2: Find the probability that a red ball is drawn, replaced, and then a blue ball is drawn at random.

- Probability of drawing a red ball is $\frac{2}{5}$.
- Probability of drawing a blue ball is $\frac{1}{5}$.
  $P(\text{red}) \times P(\text{blue})$
  $$= \frac{2}{5} \times \frac{1}{5}$$
  $$= \frac{2}{25}$$

The probability of drawing a red ball, replacing it, and then drawing a blue ball at random is $\frac{2}{25}$.

Decide whether or not the events are independent. Write *yes* or *no*.

1. You pick a green ball from the bag above. You keep the ball out, and pick a red ball. _____

2. You toss five coins. _____

3. You get three 4's on three rolls of a number cube. _____

4. You select a colored marker from a package of colored markers. Your teacher selects one after you. _____

Find the probability for each situation.

5. A letter is chosen from the words BABY GIRL and then replaced.

   Find $P(\text{Y and R})$.

   _____

6. A letter is chosen from the words BABY BOY and then replaced.

   Find $P(\text{B and B})$.

   _____

A number cube is rolled and a coin is tossed. Find the probability of each event.

7. the number 6 and tails _____

8. an even number and heads _____

9. a number less than 1 and heads _____

10. an odd number and tails _____

11. A coin is tossed three times. Find the probability that the coin lands on tails, then heads, then tails. _____

Review 97

Some equations contain two operations. To solve them, use inverse operations to get the variable alone on one side of the equation. Begin by undoing addition or subtraction. Then undo multiplication or division.

Example: Solve $2d + 1 = 9$.

$$2d + 1 = 9$$

$2d + 1 - \mathbf{1} = 9 - \mathbf{1}$ Subtract 1 from each side to undo the addition.

$\dfrac{2d}{\mathbf{2}} = \dfrac{8}{\mathbf{2}}$ Divide each side by 2 to undo the multiplication.

$d = 4$ Simplify.

                 Check your work by substituting 4 for d

$2 \cdot 4 + 1 \stackrel{?}{=} 9$ in the equation and solving.

$9 = 9$ Since $9 = 9$, the solution is correct.

---

1. Solve $7x - 5 = 16$.

  a. What must you first do to both sides? _____

  b. What must you next do to both sides? _____

  c. What is the solution? _____

2. Solve $12 = \frac{t}{5} + 8$.

  a. What must you first do to both sides? _____

  b. What must you next do to both sides? _____

  c. What is the solution? _____

Solve each equation. Check the solution.

3. $7y - 6 = 8$ **4.** $81 = 3x - 6$

_____   _____

5. $\frac{c}{8} + 10 = 15$ **6.** $2f - 6 = 4$

_____   _____

7. $4k + 20 = 24$ **8.** $\frac{e}{5} + 100 = 120$

_____   _____

Review 98

An *inequality* contains $<$, $>$, $\leq$, $\geq$, or $\neq$. Unlike the equations you have worked with, an inequality may have many solutions.

The *solutions of an inequality* are the values that make the inequality true. They can be graphed on a number line. An open circle shows that the number below it is not a solution. A closed circle shows that the number below it is a solution.

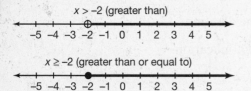

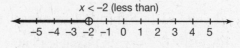

Example: Graph the inequality $x > 4$.

The inequality is read as "x is greater than 4." Since all numbers to the right of 4 are greater than 4, you can draw an arrow from 4 to the right. Since 4 is not greater than itself, use an open circle on 4.

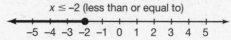

---

1. Graph the inequality $x \leq -4$.

   a. Write the inequality in words. _____

   b. Will the circle at -4 be open or closed? _____

   c. Graph the solution.

   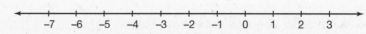

2. Graph the inequality $x \geq -1$.

   a. Write the inequality in words. _____

   b. Will the circle at -1 be open or closed? _____

   c. Graph the solution.

   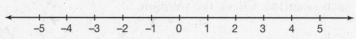

3. Graph the inequality $x < 4$.

   a. Write the inequality in words. _____

   b. Will the circle at 4 be open or closed? _____

   c. Graph the solution.

   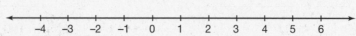

Review 99

Solving One-Step Inequalities

You can solve an inequality by using inverse operations to get the variable alone.

Example 1: Solve $x - 7 \leq 2$. Then check the solution.

$$x - 7 \leq 2$$
$$x - 7 + 7 \leq 2 + 7 \quad \text{Add 7 to both sides.}$$
$$x \leq 9$$

Check. Test a number greater than 9 and another number less than 9.

Try 11. $11 - 7 \leq 2$ Try 5. $5 - 7 \leq 2$
          $4 \leq 2$ false $-2 \leq 2$ true

Example 2: Solve $a + 15 > 10$. Then check the solution.

$$a + 15 > 10$$
$$a + 15 - 15 > 10 - 15 \quad \text{Subtract 15 from both sides.}$$
$$a > -5$$

Test a number greater than -5 and another number less than -5.

Try 0. $0 + 15 > 10$ Try -6. $-6 + 15 > 10$
         $15 > 10$ true $9 > 10$ false

Solve each inequality.

1. $x + 8 < 15$

_____

2. $y + 2 > 8$

_____

3. $a - 5 \geq -1$

_____

4. $x - 10 \leq -11$

_____

5. $y - 7 \geq 2$

_____

6. $d - 18 \geq 2$

_____

7. $13 + c \leq 33$

_____

8. $-12 + b \geq 4$

_____

9. $4 + w \geq 18$

_____

10. $x + 15 < -9$

_____

Review 100

You can sometimes draw a diagram or write an equation to solve a problem.

Example Kristin staked out a rectangular garden that has one side measuring 6 ft. If the area of the garden is 48 ft, what are the dimensions of the garden?

Read and Understand

The area of a rectangular garden is 48 ft^2. One side is 6 ft long.

Plan and Solve

Method 1: Draw a diagram.

Draw a row of 6 equal squares to represent one side of the garden.

← 6 ft →

Add rows to the diagram until you have 48 total squares.

The rectangle is 6 squares long and 8 squares wide, so the garden is 6 ft × 8 ft.

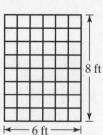
8 ft
← 6 ft →

Method 2: Write and solve an equation.

Use the formula for the area of a rectangle.

$$l \cdot w = A$$
$$6 \cdot w = 48$$
$$w = 8$$

The garden is 6 ft × 8 ft.

Look Back and Check

The length times the width of the garden must equal the area of the garden.

$6 \cdot 8 \stackrel{?}{=} 48$

$48 = 48$ The answer checks.

Choose a strategy and solve each problem.

1. Carlos is packing mugs in a box with a bottom that is 56 cm by 72 cm. In order to prevent the mugs from breaking, Carlos needs a square with area 64 cm^2 for each mug. Assuming he doesn't stack the mugs, how many mugs can he fit in the box?

    _____

2. Agatha is hiking along a 150-mile trail. She hikes 10% of the trail the first day and 15% of the trail the second day. How many miles of the trail are left?

    _____

3. Beth uses one-foot wide square tiles to cover a rectangular area. The rectangle has 16 tiles on one side, and she uses 192 tiles to cover the area. What are the dimensions of the rectangle?

    _____

4. Todd is stacking boxes against a wall that is 12 m high. If he has stacked 3 boxes and the pile reaches halfway to the ceiling, what is the height of each box?

    _____

Review 101

Exploring Square Roots and Rational Numbers

A *perfect square* is the square of a whole number. The number 81 is a perfect square because it is the square of 9.

You can also say that 9 is the *square root* of 81, or $\sqrt{81} = 9$. The square root of a given number is a number that, when multiplied by itself, is the given number. You can use a calculator to find square roots.

Example 1

a. Find $\sqrt{4}$.

Since $2 \times 2 = 4$, $\sqrt{4} = 2$.

b. Find $\sqrt{75}$.

$\sqrt{75} \approx 8.6602540$

You can estimate square roots using perfect squares.

Example 2

Tell which two consecutive whole numbers $\sqrt{52}$ is between.

$49 < 52 < 64$	Find perfect squares close to 52.
$\sqrt{49} < \sqrt{52} < \sqrt{64}$	Write the square roots in order.
$7 < \sqrt{52} < 8$	Simplify.

$\sqrt{52}$ is between 7 and 8.

Determine if each number is a perfect square.

1. 24 _____
2. 36 _____
3. 49 _____
4. 121 _____

Find each square root.

5. $\sqrt{9}$ _____
6. $\sqrt{25}$ _____
7. $\sqrt{4}$ _____

8. $\sqrt{100}$ _____
9. $\sqrt{400}$ _____
10. $\sqrt{2,500}$ _____

Use a calculator to tell whether each number is a perfect square.

11. 576 _____
12. 1,200 _____
13. 2,401 _____

14. 900 _____
15. 1,521 _____
16. 1,875 _____

Tell which two consecutive whole numbers the square root is between.
Use a calculator to find each square root to the nearest tenth.

17. $\sqrt{42}$ _____
18. $\sqrt{88}$ _____
19. $\sqrt{63}$ _____

20. $\sqrt{75}$ _____
21. $\sqrt{30}$ _____
22. $\sqrt{97}$ _____

Name _____ Class _____ Date _____

Review 102

The *hypotenuse* of a right triangle is the side opposite the right angle and is the longest side. The other two sides are called *legs*. In the shown triangle, sides a and b are the legs. Side c is the hypotenuse.

The *Pythagorean Theorem* states that the sum of the squares of the lengths of the legs of a right triangle is equal to the square of the length of the hypotenuse. This can be written algebraically as $a^2 + b^2 = c^2$.

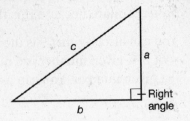

Example

Find the missing length.

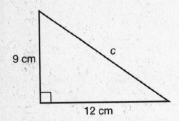

$a^2 + b^2 = c^2$ Use the Pythagorean Theorem to find the length of side c.

$9^2 + 12^2 = c^2$ Substitute 9 for a and 12 for b.

$81 + 144 = c^2$ Square 9 and 12.

$225 = c^2$ Add.

$15 = c$ Find $\sqrt{225}$.

The length of the hypotenuse is 15 cm.

Find the missing side length of each right triangle.

1.
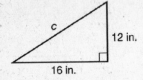

_____

2.
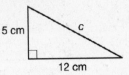

_____

3.

_____

4.
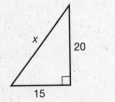

_____

5.

_____

6.
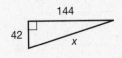

_____

7.
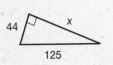

_____

8.

_____

9.

_____

10. An 8-ft ladder is leaning against a building. If the bottom of the ladder is 3 ft from the base of the building, how far is it up the building from the bottom of the ladder to the top of the ladder? Round to the nearest tenth of a foot. _____

© Pearson Education, Inc.

Review 103

One way to estimate a sum, difference, or product is to round
numbers to the nearest whole number. Then add, subtract,
multiply or divide.

Round to the largest nearest whole number	**Round to the largest nearest whole number**
$1.6 \rightarrow 2$	$17.2 \rightarrow 20$
$+ 4.4 \rightarrow + 4$	$\times\ 7.3 \rightarrow \times\ 7$
6 Estimate	**140** Estimate

You can get a quick estimate if you use *compatible numbers* to
compute mentally.

$$\begin{array}{r} \$24.27 \\ -\ \ \ 8.79 \end{array} \longrightarrow \begin{array}{r} \$24.00 \\ -\ \ 9.00 \\ \hline \$15.00 \ \text{Estimate} \end{array}$$

Estimate each sum, difference, product or quotient.

Estimate   Estimate

1. $\begin{array}{r} 9.265 \\ +6.840 \end{array}$ $\rightarrow$ $\underline{\quad}$
    $\rightarrow$ $+\ \underline{\quad}$

2. $\begin{array}{r} 12.91 \\ -\ 7.80 \end{array}$ $\rightarrow$ $\underline{\quad}$
    $\rightarrow$ $-\ \underline{\quad}$

3. $\begin{array}{r} \$16.49 \\ -\ \ 5.25 \end{array}$ $\rightarrow$ $\underline{\quad}$
    $\rightarrow$ $-\ \underline{\quad}$

4. $\begin{array}{r} 2.362 \\ +\ 0.815 \end{array}$ $\rightarrow$ $\underline{\quad}$
    $\rightarrow$ $+\ \underline{\quad}$

5. $\begin{array}{r} 2.4 \\ \times\ 5.2 \end{array}$ $\rightarrow$ $\underline{\quad}$
    $\rightarrow$ $\times\ \underline{\quad}$

6. $\begin{array}{r} 6.5 \\ \times\ 0.9 \end{array}$ $\rightarrow$ $\underline{\quad}$
    $\rightarrow$ $\times\ \underline{\quad}$

7. $\begin{array}{r} \$12.09 \\ -\ 10.55 \end{array}$ $\rightarrow$ $\underline{\quad}$
    $\rightarrow$ $-\ \underline{\quad}$

8. $\begin{array}{r} 6.147 \\ +\ 0.715 \end{array}$ $\rightarrow$ $\underline{\quad}$
    $\rightarrow$ $+\ \underline{\quad}$

9. $\begin{array}{r} 65.4 \\ -\ 22.2 \end{array}$ $\rightarrow$ $\underline{\quad}$
    $\rightarrow$ $-\ \underline{\quad}$

10. $\begin{array}{r} 27.14 \\ \times\ \ 3.1 \end{array}$ $\rightarrow$ $\underline{\quad}$
    $\rightarrow$ $\times\ \underline{\quad}$

11. $\begin{array}{r} 9.21 \\ \div\ 3.95 \end{array}$ $\rightarrow$ $\underline{\quad}$
    $\rightarrow$ $\div\ \underline{\quad}$

12. $\begin{array}{r} 110.2 \\ \div\ 10.8 \end{array}$ $\rightarrow$ $\underline{\quad}$
    $\rightarrow$ $\div\ \underline{\quad}$

Course 2 Topics

Review 104

Add 3.19 + 6.098 + 2.67.

① Round to estimate.

$$3.19 \rightarrow 3$$
$$6.098 \rightarrow 6$$
$$\underline{+\ 26.7 \rightarrow +\ 27}$$
$$36$$

② Line up the decimal points.

$$3.19$$
$$6.098$$
$$\underline{+\ 26.700}$$

③ Add zeros. Then add.

$$3.190$$
$$6.098$$
$$\underline{+\ 26.700}$$
$$35.988$$

Compare to make sure your answer is reasonable: 35.988 is close to 36.

Subtract 8.7 − 4.97.

① Round to estimate.

$$8.7 \rightarrow 9$$
$$\underline{-\ 4.97 \rightarrow -\ 5}$$
$$4$$

② Line up the decimal points.

$$8.7$$
$$\underline{-\ 4.97}$$

③ Add zeros. Then subtract.

$$8.70$$
$$\underline{-\ 4.97}$$
$$3.73$$

Compare to make sure your answer is reasonable: 3.73 is close to 4.

Estimate first. Then find each sum or difference.

1. $\quad 46.2$ $\quad \underline{-\ 34.09}$	**2.** $\quad 3.31$ $\quad \underline{+\ 9.075}$	**3.** $\quad 9.06$ $\quad \underline{-\ 7.2}$
4. $\quad 84.32$ $\quad \underline{+\ 6.94}$	**5.** $\quad 8.037$ $\quad \underline{+\ 1.9}$	**6.** $\quad 10.6$ $\quad \underline{-\ 4.59}$

Find each sum or difference.

7. $4.102 + 7.7$

8. $5.4 - 1.6$

9. $7.09 + 4.3 + 20.1$

_____ _____ _____

10. $0.392 - 0.26$

11. $15.64 - 8.5$

12. $8.709 + 3.2$

_____ _____ _____

13. $6 + 0.497$

14. $95.1 + 6$

15. $0.004 - 0.0005$

_____ _____ _____

16. $0.2408 - 0.051$

17. $0.36 + 4.7 + 6$

18. $5.306 - 0.78$

_____ _____ _____

Course 2 Topics

Review 105

Multiplying and Dividing Decimals

Multiply 5.43 × 1.8.

(1) Multiply as if the numbers were whole numbers.

$$5.43 \quad \}\ \textbf{3 decimal}$$
$$\underline{\times\ 1.8} \quad \textbf{places}$$
$$4344$$
$$\underline{+\ 543}$$

(2) Count the total number of decimal places in the factors.

$$9.774 \leftarrow \textbf{3 decimal places}$$

(3) Place the decimal point in the product.

Multiply 38.25 ÷ 1.5.

(1) Rewrite the problem with a whole number divisor.

$$1.5\overline{)38.25}$$
$$\downarrow$$

(2) Place the decimal point in the quotient.

$$1.5.\overline{)38.2.5}$$

Move 1 place each.

(3) Divide. Then check.

$$\begin{array}{r} 25.5 \\ 15\overline{)382.5} \\ -30 \\ \hline 82 \\ -75 \\ \hline 7\,5 \\ -7.5 \\ \hline 0 \end{array}$$

$$25.5 \times 15 = 382.5\ \checkmark$$
Multiply to check.

Course 2 Topics

Find each product.

1. $\begin{array}{r} 1.42 \\ \underline{\times\ 7.2} \end{array}$

2. $\begin{array}{r} 2.2 \\ \underline{\times\ 4.1} \end{array}$

3. $\begin{array}{r} 5.11 \\ \underline{\times\ 0.3} \end{array}$

4. $\begin{array}{r} 3.68 \\ \underline{\times\ 5.8} \end{array}$

5. 2.8×0.05

6. $1.45 \cdot 0.7$

7. $(2.07)(4.9)$

_____ _____ _____

8. $9.3(0.56)$

9. $0.006(3.75)$

10. 3.8×912

_____ _____ _____

Rewrite each problem so the divisor is a whole number.

11. $5.1\overline{)351.9}$ _____

12. $1.8\overline{)14.9}$ _____

13. $0.32\overline{)39.68}$ _____

14. $0.06\overline{)0.948}$ _____

15. $0.8\overline{)2.112}$ _____

16. $0.49\overline{)9.457}$ _____

Find each quotient.

17. $2\overline{)15.8}$

18. $0.4\overline{)2.2}$

19. $0.09\overline{)0.99}$

20. $2.7\overline{)12.15}$

21. $0.14\overline{)28.14}$

22. $0.08\overline{)0.64}$

Review 106

The **metric system** of measurements uses *prefixes* to describe amounts that are much larger or smaller than the base unit. The base units for measuring length, mass, and volume are shown in the table below.

÷ 1000	÷ 100	÷ 10	base unit	× 10	× 100	× 1000
kilo-	hecto-	deca-	meter gram liter	deci-	centi-	milli-
× 1000	× 100	× 10	base unit	÷ 10	÷ 100	÷ 1000

To change a unit in the metric system, you multiply or divide by a power of 10.

① Change 34,000 mL to L.   34,000 mL = ? L

② Look at the table. To convert mL to L, $34,000 ÷ 1,000 = 34$
   divide by 1,000.

③ Answer: 34,000 mL = 34 L

Write the number that makes each statement true.

1. 16 grams = _?_ milligrams

   Are you converting from a smaller unit to a larger unit or a larger unit to a smaller unit?

   _____

   Will you multiply or divide?

   _____

   What number will you multiply or divide by?

   _____

   16 grams = _____ milligrams

2. 1,600 meters = _?_ kilometers

   Are you converting from a smaller unit to a larger unit or a larger unit to a smaller unit?

   _____

   Will you multiply or divide?

   _____

   What number will you multiply or divide by?

   _____

   1,600 meters = _____ kilometers

3. 6 meters = _____ centimeters

4. 162 kilograms = _____ grams

5. 4000 milliliters = _____ liters

6. 25,000 millimeters = _____ meters

Choose a reasonable estimate.

7. width of a dime:
   1 m, 1 cm, 1 mm

   _____

8. height of a building
   50 m, 50 cm, 50 mm

   _____

Course 2 Topics

Review 107

The three-step problem-solving plan is a step-by-step approach you can use to solve problems.

Step 1: Read and Understand the problem
Step 2: Plan how to solve the problem. **Solve** it.
Step 3: Look back and **check** to see if your answer makes sense.

A volunteer organization finds that on the average, 2.87 of every 100 families need advice from the agency. About how many families can they expect to advise in a town of 966 families?

Read and Understand

What are you asked to find?

About how many families need advice from the volunteer organization?

Do you need to find an exact answer or an estimate?

Estimate.

Plan and Solve

Use compatible numbers to estimate about how many 100s there are in 966. Write an equation.

1,000 ÷ 100 = 10

What number sentence shows about how many families need advice?

10 × 3

About how many families need advice?

30 families

Look Back and Check

What strategy can you use to check your answer? Show an example.

Make a table.

3	6	9	12	15	18	21	24	27	30
100	200	300	400	500	600	700	800	900	1,000

Use the problem-solving plan to solve each problem.

1. In the seventh grade at Howard Middle School, 2.14 out of every 100 students play the trumpet. There are 400 seventh graders at Howard. About how many students play the trumpet? _____

2. Tyrone, Brett, Gabe, and Mario compete in a softball throwing contest. Tyrone won the contest with a distance of 79.25 meters. Brett threw 10.65 meters less than Mario. Gabe threw 6.9 meters further than Brett but 2.75 meters less than Tyrone. How many meters did Mario throw the softball? _____

Review 108

The numbers 2 and −2 are opposites. The numbers 7 and −7 are opposites.
Integers are the set of positive whole numbers, their opposites, and zero.

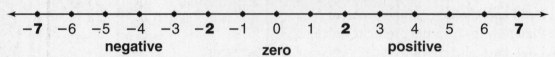

You can use the number line to compare integers.

−2 is less than 0.　　　　　　　　　　　　　7 is greater than 2.
　　−2 < 0　　　　　　　　　　　　　　　　　　7 > 2

Numbers to the left are less. −2 is farther left than 0.	Numbers to the right are greater. 7 is farther right than 2.

The **absolute value** of an integer is its distance from zero on the
number line. Distance is always positive.

The absolute value of −5 is 5.　　　　　　The absolute value of 3 is 3.
　　$|-5| = 5$　　　　　　　　　　　　　　　　$|3| = 3$

Compare using <, >, or =.

1. 4 ☐ 2　　　　　　　2. −3 ☐ −2　　　　　　3. 3 ☐ −4

4. −1 ☐ −2　　　　　　5. 0 ☐ 5　　　　　　　6. 0 ☐ −4

7. −6 ☐ 4　　　　　　　8. −8 ☐ −2　　　　　　9. 3 ☐ 0

10. −7 ☐ −10　　　　　11. −10 ☐ 10　　　　　12. 1 ☐ −1

Find each absolute value.

13. $|-6| =$ _____　　　14. $|3| =$ _____　　　15. $|-8| =$ _____

16. $|9| =$ _____　　　17. $|-5| =$ _____　　　18. $|0| =$ _____

19. $|6| =$ _____　　　20. $|-10| =$ _____　　　21. $|-20| =$ _____

Order the numbers from least to greatest.

22. −4, 5, −2, 0, 1　　　　　　　　　23. 6, −3, −5, 4, −6

_____　　　　　　　_____

24. 3, −5, 4, −4, −7, 0　　　　　　　25. 1, 3, −7, −6, 5, −2

_____　　　　　　　_____

Review 109

Use these rules to add and subtract integers.

Adding Integers

Same Sign ◄————————————————► Different Signs

• The sum of two positive integers is positive.
  Example: 6 + 16 = 22
• The sum of two negative integers is negative
  Example: −9 + (−3) = −12
	• First find the absolute values of each
	  number.
	• Then subtract the lesser absolute value from
	  the greater.
	• The sum has the sign of the integer with the
	  greater absolute value.
	  Example: −10 + 9 = −1

Subtracting Integers

↓

• To subtract integers, add the opposite.
• Then following the rules for adding integers.
  Example: 6 − (−3) = 6 + 3 = 9

Find each sum.

1. 8 + (−2) _____

2. −9 + 4 _____

3. 3 + (−2) _____

4. −1 + 11 _____

5. 12 + 13 _____

6. −9 + 5 _____

7. 7 + 2 _____

8. −1 + (−7) _____

9. −3 + 0 _____

10. −1 + (−1) _____

11. 6 + 5 _____

12. 3 + (−2) _____

Complete.

13. −3 −4   Change to addition: −3 + _____ = _____

14. 5 −2   Change to addition: 5 + _____ = _____

15. −6 − (−10)   Change to addition: −6 + _____ = _____

16. 8 − (−2)   Change to addition: 8 + _____ = _____

Find each difference.

17. 4 −5 _____

18. −5 −4 _____

19. −8 − (−7) _____

20. 19 − (−6) _____

21. −10 −12 _____

22. −12 −10 _____

23. −4 − (−5) _____

24. −2 − (−3) _____

25. 9 − (−7) _____

26. 0 −3 _____

27. 6 −8 _____

28. 0 − (−10) _____

Review 110

Course 2 Topics

To multiply integers:

- If the signs are alike, the product is positive.

$$2 \cdot 3 = 6$$
$$-2 \cdot -3 = 6$$

- If the signs are different, the product is negative.

$$2 \cdot -3 = -6$$
$$-2 \cdot 3 = -6$$

To divide integers:

- If the signs are alike, the quotient is positive.

$$6 \div 3 = 2$$
$$-6 \div -3 = 2$$

- If the signs are different, the quotient is negative.

$$6 \div -3 = -2$$
$$-6 \div 3 = -2$$

Study these four examples. Write positive or negative to complete each statement.

$$7 \cdot 3 = 21 \qquad\qquad 7 \cdot -3 = -21$$
$$-7 \cdot -3 = 21 \qquad\qquad -7 \cdot 3 = -21$$

1. When both integers are positive, the product is _____.

2. When one integer is positive and one is negative, the product is _____.

3. When both integers are negative, the product is _____.

$$21 \div 3 = 7 \qquad\qquad -21 \div -3 = 7$$
$$21 \div -3 = -7 \qquad\qquad -21 \div 3 = -7$$

4. When both integers are positive, the quotient is _____.

5. When both integers are negative, the quotient is _____.

6. When one integer is positive and one is negative, the quotient is _____.

Tell whether each product or quotient will be *positive* or *negative.*

7. $4 \cdot 7$

8. $-4 \cdot 7$

9. $-4 \cdot -7$

10. $4 \cdot -7$

_____   _____   _____   _____

11. $-28 \div 4$

12. $28 \div 4$

13. $-28 \div -7$

14. $28 \div -7$

_____   _____   _____   _____

15. $10 \cdot -4$

16. $-25 \div 5$

17. $-2 \cdot -2$

18. $100 \div 10$

_____   _____   _____   _____

Review 111

Order of Operations and the Distributive Property

You can remember the order of operations using this phrase:

Please, **M**y **D**ear **A**unt **S**ally

Parentheses **M**ultiply **D**ivide **A**dd **S**ubtract

① First, do operations within parentheses.

$7 + 8 \cdot \boxed{(5 + 3)} - 1$ 　　　　$3 \div \boxed{(5 - 2)} + 36$

$7 + 8 \cdot \quad 8 \quad - 1$ 　　　　$3 \div \quad 3 \quad + 36$

② Next, multiply and divide from left to right.

$7 + \boxed{8 \cdot 8} - 1$ 　　　　$\boxed{3 \div 3} + 36$

$7 + \quad 64 \quad - 1$ 　　　　$1 \quad + 36$

③ Then, add and subtract from left to right.

$\boxed{7 + 64} - 1$ 　　　　$\boxed{1 + 36}$

$71 \quad - 1$ 　　　　37

70

Complete.

1. $3 + 2 \cdot 4$

   $3 +$ _____

   _____

2. $5 \cdot 4 + 3 \cdot 2$

   _____ $+$ _____

   _____

3. $(5 \cdot 4) + 3 - 2$

   _____

   _____

4. $5 + 7 \cdot 2$

   $5 +$ _____

   _____

5. $8 \cdot 6 + 4 \cdot 4$

   _____ $+$ _____

   _____

6. $(6 \cdot 2) + (12 \div 2)$

   _____ $+$ _____

   _____

Find the value of each expression.

7. $8 + 5 \cdot 6 + 2$

   _____

8. $7 - 4 + 5 \cdot 3$

   _____

9. $9 + 3 \cdot 7 - 5$

   _____

10. $(15 + 9) \div (8 - 2)$

   _____

11. $80 - 6 \cdot 7$

   _____

12. $15 \div (5 - 2)$

   _____

Find the missing numbers. Then simplify.

13. $8(5 + 2) = \boxed{}(5) + \boxed{}(2) = \boxed{}$

14. $\boxed{}(5.6) = 4(6.0) - 4(\boxed{}) = \boxed{}$

15. $\boxed{}(3.4 + 7) = 5(3.4) + 5(7) = \boxed{}$

16. $4(6 + 7) = \boxed{}(6) + \boxed{}(7) = \boxed{}$

17. $9(3 + 6) = 9(\boxed{}) + 9(\boxed{}) = \boxed{}$

18. $\boxed{}(10 - 5) = 4(10) - 14(5) = \boxed{}$

Review 112

Alexis, Rita, Ming, Mario, and Jewel are in the Library Club.
During the summer they read the following numbers of books.

11, 6, 11, 8, 3

To find the **mean,** or average, number of books read
by the Library Club members:

① Find the sum of the numbers of books read.

② Divide the sum by the number of readers, 5.

$11 + 6 + 11 + 8 + 3 = 39$

$39 \div 5 = 7.8$

The mean is 7.8 books.

To find the **median,** or middle value, of the data set:

① Arrange the numbers in order.

② Find the middle number.

3; 6, **8**, 11, 11

↑

8 is the middle number.

The median is 8 books.

The **mode** is the number that occurs most often.
In this data set, 11 occurs twice. The mode is 11.

3, 6, 8, **11, 11**

Use the table to complete Exercises 1–4.

1. Jerry plays basketball. What number would
   you divide by to find the mean number of
   points Jerry scored per game? _____

2. What is the mean number of points Jerry scored?

   _____

3. Write the data in order. Then find the median number of points
   Jerry scored.

   _____

4. What is the mode of the data? _____

Game Points Scored by Jerry		
10	11	15
18	9	16
10	12	10

Find the mean, median, and mode for each situation.

5. the miniature golf scores for 7 friends:

   23, 30, 39, 32, 35, 14, 23

   mean _____ median _____ mode _____

6. the scores for a geography quiz:

   7 8 6 9 9 8 10 6 9 8 9 7

   mean _____ median _____ mode _____

Review 113

Evaluating and Writing Algebraic Expressions

To evaluate an *expression*, substitute a value for the *variable* and compute.

Evaluate $5y - 8$ for $y = 7$.

$5y - 8$

$5 \times 7 - 8$ ← **Substitute *y* with 7.**

$35 - 8 = 27$ ← **Compute.**

You can use key words to write a word phrase for an algebraic expression.

$a + 5$ → *a* plus 5
    or *a* increased by 5

$2n$ → the product of 2 and *n*
    or 2 times *n*

Evaluate each expression using the values $m = 3$ and $x = 8$.

1. $4m + 9$

   Substitute *m*: $4 \times$ _____ $+ 9$

   Compute: _____ $+ 9 =$ _____

2. $4x - 7$

   Substitute *x*: $4 \times$ _____ $- 7$

   Compute: _____ $- 7 =$ _____

3. $5x + x$

   Substitute *x*: $5 \times$ _____ $+$ _____

   Compute: _____ $+$ _____ $=$ _____

4. $x + 2m$

   Substitute *x* and *m*: _____ $+ 2 \times$ _____

   Compute: _____ $+$ _____ $=$ _____

Evaluate each expression using the values $y = 4$, $z = 8$, and $p = 10$.

5. $3y + 6 =$ _____

6. $4z - 2 =$ _____

7. $p + 2p =$ _____

8. $3z \times z =$ _____

9. $5z - y =$ _____

10. $2p + y =$ _____

11. $8p - p =$ _____

12. $3y + 2z =$ _____

Write a word phrase for each algebraic expression.

13. $9 + x$

   _____

14. $6x$

   _____

15. $x - 8$

   _____

16. $\frac{x}{5}$

   _____

Write an algebraic expression for each word phrase.

17. x newspapers plus 10

   _____

18. 4 less than x teabags

   _____

19. 3 more than x envelopes

   _____

20. 6 times x school buses

   _____

Course 2 Topics

Review 114

One way to solve some equations is to use mental math.

Solve $t + 9 = 13$.	Solve $y - 7 = 15$.
Ask yourself, what number added to 9 is 13?	Ask yourself, what number minus 7 is 15?
$4 + 9 = 13$ So, $t = 4$.	$22 - 7 = 15$ So, $y = 22$.
Solve $\frac{a}{3} = 9$	Solve $3y = 15$.
Ask yourself, what number divided by 3 equals 9?	Ask yourself, what number multiplied by 3 is 15?
$\frac{27}{9} = 3$ So, $a = 27$.	$3 \cdot 5 = 15$ So, $y = 5$.

Solve each equation using mental math.

1. $4t = 24$

_____

2. $3w = 45$

_____

3. $p + 8 = 16$

_____

4. $a + 2 = 11$

_____

5. $\frac{h}{3} = 7$

_____

6. $\frac{g}{4} = 7$

_____

7. $y - 7 = 15$

_____

8. $d - 6 = 14$

_____

Solve each equation using mental math or estimation.

9. $d + 7 = 21$

_____

10. $c - 21 = 4$

_____

11. $a + 9 = 50$

_____

12. $q - 43.94 = 400.12$

_____

13. $3 + b = -6$

_____

14. $91 + r = 100$

_____

15. $28 - n = 20$

_____

16. $16.3 + s = 36.94$

_____

Course 2 Topics

Review 115

Solving Equations by Adding or Subtracting

Follow these steps to solve equations.

$$\text{Solve:} \quad n + (-2) = 11 \qquad\qquad \text{Solve:} \quad n - 6 = -36$$

① Use the inverse
operation on both sides $\quad n + (-2) - (-2) = 11 - (-2) \qquad n - 6 + 6 = -36 + 6$
of the equation.

② Simplify. $\qquad\qquad\qquad\qquad n = 13 \qquad\qquad\qquad\qquad n = -30$

③ Check. $\qquad\qquad\qquad\qquad n + (-2) = 11 \qquad\qquad\qquad n - 6 = -36$
$\qquad\qquad\qquad\qquad\qquad 13 + (-2) \overset{?}{=} 11 \qquad\qquad -30 - 6 \overset{?}{=} -36$
$\qquad\qquad\qquad\qquad\qquad\qquad 11 = 11 \;\checkmark \qquad\qquad\qquad -36 = -36 \;\checkmark$

Solve each equation. Check each answer.

1. $n + 6 = 8$

$n + 6 - 6 = 8 - \underline{\hspace{1.5cm}}$

$n = \underline{\hspace{1.5cm}}$

2. $n - 3 = 20$

$n - 3 + \underline{\hspace{1.5cm}} = 20 + 3$

$n = \underline{\hspace{1cm}}$

3. $n - (-3) = -1$

$n - (-3) + \underline{\hspace{1.5cm}} = -1 + \underline{\hspace{1.5cm}}$

$n = \underline{\hspace{1.5cm}}$

4. $-2 = n + 5$

$-2 - \underline{\hspace{1.5cm}} = n + 5 - \underline{\hspace{1.5cm}}$

$\underline{\hspace{1.5cm}} = n$

5. $n - (-4) = -2$

$n - (-4) + \underline{\hspace{1.5cm}} = -2 + \underline{\hspace{1.5cm}}$

$n = \underline{\hspace{1.5cm}}$

6. $n - 16 = -23$

$n - 16 + \underline{\hspace{1.5cm}} = -23 + \underline{\hspace{1.5cm}}$

$n = \underline{\hspace{1.5cm}}$

Use a calculator, pencil and paper, or mental math. Solve each equation.

7. $n + 1 = 17$

_____

8. $n - (-6) = 7$

_____

9. $n - 8 = -12$

_____

10. $n - 19 = 34$

_____

11. $61 = n + 29$

_____

12. $n + 84 = 131$

_____

13. $-13 = n + 9$

_____

14. $-18 = n - (-5)$

_____

15. In track practice Jesse ran a mile in 7 minutes. His mile time was $2\frac{1}{2}$ minutes faster than Michael's time. Write and solve an equation to calculate Michael's mile time.

_____

Review 116

Solving Equations by Multiplying or Dividing

Follow these steps to solve equations.

Solve: $\frac{t}{5} = -7$ Solve: $-2x = 8$

① Use the inverse operation on both sides of the equation.

$$(5)\frac{t}{5} = (5)(-7) \qquad \frac{-2x}{-2} = \frac{8}{-2}$$

② Simplify.

$$t = -35 \qquad\qquad x = -4$$

③ Check.

$$\frac{t}{5} = -7 \qquad\qquad -2x = 8$$

$$\frac{-35}{5} \overset{?}{=} -7 \qquad\qquad -2(-4) \overset{?}{=} 8$$

$$-7 = -7 ✔ \qquad\qquad 8 = 8 ✔$$

Solve and check each equation.

1. $-5n = 30$

$$\frac{-5n}{\boxed{}} = \frac{30}{\boxed{}}$$

$n =$ _____

2. $\frac{a}{2} = -16$

$$\left(\boxed{}\right)\frac{a}{2} = \left(\boxed{}\right)(-16)$$

$a =$ _____

3. $-2w = -4$

$$\frac{-2w}{\boxed{}} = \frac{-4}{\boxed{}}$$

$w =$ _____

4. $8t = 32$

$$\frac{8t}{\boxed{}} = \frac{32}{\boxed{}}$$

$t =$ _____

5. $5 = \frac{g}{6}$

$$\left(\boxed{}\right)(5) = \left(\boxed{}\right)\frac{g}{6}$$

_____ $= g$

6. $\frac{n}{-3} = -5$

$$\left(\boxed{}\right)\frac{n}{-3} = \left(\boxed{}\right)(-5)$$

$n =$ _____

Use a calculator, pencil and paper, or mental math. Solve each equation.

7. $\frac{x}{4} = -1$

_____

8. $-5w = 125$

_____

9. $\frac{m}{-8} = 10$

_____

10. $-2 = \frac{x}{-4}$

_____

11. $3y = 12$

_____

12. $-4t = -64$

_____

13. $9w = -81$

_____

14. $21 = -3z$

_____

15. $\frac{a}{-4} = 12$

_____

16. $-6b = 42$

_____

17. $-3 = \frac{c}{-8}$

_____

18. $5 = \frac{d}{7}$

_____

19. $2t = 38$

_____

20. $-9 = 9q$

_____

21. $n \div 6 = -3$

_____

22. $-8k = -40$

_____

Course 2 Topics

Review 117

You can change a word expression into an algebraic expression by converting the words to variables, numbers, and operation symbols.

To write a two-step algebraic expression for *seven more than three times a number,* follow these steps.

① Define the variable.

② Ask yourself are there any key words?

③ Write an algebraic expression.

④ Simplify.

Let n represent the number.

"More than" means add and "times" means multiply.

$7 + 3 \cdot n$

$7 + 3n$

Define a variable and write an algebraic expression for each phrase.

1. 3 inches more than 4 times your height

   _____

2. 4 less than 6 times the weight of a turkey

   _____

3. 8 more than one-half the number of miles run last week

   _____

4. twice the cost plus 30

   _____

Solve.

5. Three friends pay $4 per hour to rent a paddleboat plus $5 for snacks. Write an expression for the total cost of rental and snacks. Then evaluate the expression for 2 hours.

   _____

6. A lawn care service charges $10 plus $15 per hour to mow and fertilize lawns. Write an expression for the total cost of having your lawn mowed and fertilized. Then evaluate the expression for 4 hours.

   _____

Solve each equation using number sense.

7. $2s + 6 = 12$

   _____

8. $\frac{f}{10} - 1 = 2$

   _____

9. $4r - 7 = 9$

   _____

10. $4x - 10 = 30$

    _____

11. $2n - 7 = 13$

    _____

12. $\frac{s}{3} + 2 = 4$

    _____

Review 118

The marbles and boxes represent this equation.

$$2x + 3 = 7$$

The variable x stands for the number of marbles (unseen) in each box.

To solve the equation, follow these steps.

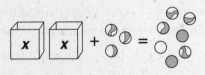

There are the same number of marbles on each side and the same number of marbles in each box.

Step 1

Subtract the extra marbles from both sides.

$$2x + 3 - 3 = 7 - 3$$
$$2x = 4$$

Step 2

Divide the number of marbles by 2, the number of boxes.

$$\frac{2x}{2} = \frac{4}{2}$$
$$x = 2$$

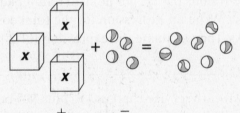

Write and solve an equation for each situation.

1.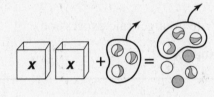

_____ + _____ = _____

$x =$ _____

2.

_____ + _____ = _____

$x =$ _____

Complete to solve each equation.

3. $5x + 7 = 2$

$5x + 7 -$ _____ $= 2 -$ _____

$\dfrac{5x}{\Box} = \dfrac{-5}{\Box}$

$x =$ _____

4. $2x - 1 = 9$

$2x - 1 +$ _____ $= 9 +$ _____

$\dfrac{2x}{\Box} = \dfrac{10}{\Box}$

$x =$ _____

Solve each equation.

5. $4x + 7 = 15$ _____

6. $3b - 5 = 13$ _____

7. $5t - 2 = -17$ _____

8. $3z + 1 = 16$ _____

9. $7h - 9 = -2$ _____

10. $2k + 12 = -2$ _____

Review 119

The cost for a car and driver on a car ferry is $15. Each additional passenger is $2. If Brett pays a toll of $21, how many additional passengers does he have?

Read and Understand

What information are you given? *You know the cost for the car and driver, the cost for each passenger and the total toll paid.* What are you asked to find? *You want to find the number of additional passengers.*

Plan and Solve

You are given a relationship between numbers. So, an equation may help solve the problem. The toll is $15 for the car and driver plus $2 for each passenger (*p*).

$$15 + 2p = \text{toll}$$
$$15 + 2p = 21$$

Solve the equation for *p*.

$$15 + 2p = 21$$
$$15 - 15 + 2p = 21 - 15 \qquad \leftarrow \textbf{Subtract 15.}$$
$$2p = 6 \qquad \leftarrow \textbf{Simplify.}$$
$$\frac{2p}{2} = \frac{6}{2} \qquad \leftarrow \textbf{Divide by 2.}$$
$$p = 3 \qquad \leftarrow \textbf{Simplify.}$$

There are 3 passengers.

Look Back and Check

$15 for car + $2 × 3 additional passengers = $21.

Solve each problem by writing an equation.

1. A jacket costs $28 more than twice the cost of a pair of slacks. If the jacket costs $152, how much do the slacks cost?

2. Jennifer has $22.75 in her bank. She saves quarters and half dollars. She has $10.50 in half dollars. How many quarters does she have?

3. The monthly fee for cable is $25 plus $4.50 per movie channel. Eugene paid $56.50 in May for his cable bill. How many movie channels does he get?

4. Eric and Wyatt collect football cards. Eric has seven cards more than four times as many as Wyatt. Wyatt has 20 cards. How many cards does Eric have?

Review 120

Two expressions separated by an inequality sign form an **inequality.** An inequality shows that the two expressions *are not* equal. Unlike the equations you have worked with, an inequality has many solutions.

The **solutions of an inequality** are the values that make the inequality true. They can be graphed on a number line. Use a closed circle (●) for ≤ and ≥ and an open circle (**O**) for > and <. For example:

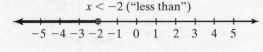

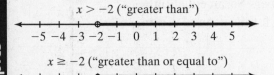

Graph the inequality $x > 4$.

The inequality is read as "x is greater than 4." Since all numbers to the right of 4 are greater than 4, you can draw an arrow from 4 to the right. Since 4 is not greater than itself, use an open circle on 4.

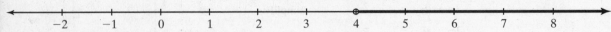

1. **Graph the inequality $x \le -3$.**

   a. Write the inequality in words. _____

   b. Will the circle at -3 be open or closed? _____

   c. Graph the solution.
   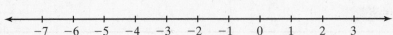

2. **Graph the inequality $x \ge -1$.**

   a. Write the inequality in words. _____

   b. Will the circle at -1 be open or closed? _____

   c. Graph the solution.
   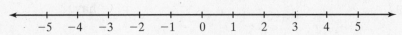

3. **Graph the inequality $x < 3$.**

   a. Write the inequality in words. _____

   b. Will the circle at 3 be open or closed? _____

   c. Graph the solution.
   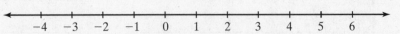

Course 2 Topics

Name _____ Class _____ Date _____

Review 121

Solving Inequalities by Adding or Subtracting

To solve an inequality you can add the same number to or subtract it from each side of the inequality.

Solve $x + 5 \geq 9$.   Graph the solution.

$x + 5 \geq 9$
$x + 5 - 5 \geq 9 - 5$ Subtract 5 from each side.
$\quad x \geq 4$ Simplify.

Solve $y - 3 < 2$.   Graph the solution.

$y - 3 < 2$
$y - 3 + 3 < 2 + 3$ Add 3 to each side.
$y < 5$ Simplify.

Graph:

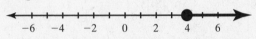

Graph:

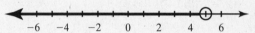

Solve each inequality. Graph the solution.

1. $2 + a > 6$ _____

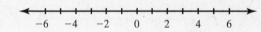

2. $-4 + w \leq 0$ _____

3. $3 + a \geq 8$ _____

4. $w + 1 \leq 4$ _____

5. $y + 3 < 5$ _____

6. $6 + g \geq 12$ _____

7. $2 + x > 7$ _____

8. $2 + r < 8$ _____

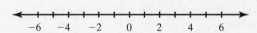

© Pearson Education, Inc. All rights reserved.

Course 2 Topics

121

Review 122

Solving Inequalities by Multiplying or Dividing

To solve an inequality you can multiply or divide each side by the same number. However, if the number is negative, you must also reverse the direction of the inequality sign.

Solve $-4y \geq 16$. Graph the solution.

$$-4y \geq 16$$
$$\frac{-4y}{-4} \leq \frac{16}{-4} \quad \text{Divide each side by } -4.$$
$$\text{Reverse the direction}$$
$$\text{of the inequality symbol.}$$
$$y \leq -4 \quad \text{Simplify.}$$

Solve $\frac{w}{3} > 2$. Graph the solution.

$$\frac{w}{3} > 2$$

$$(3)\frac{w}{3} > 2(3) \quad \text{Multiply each side by 3.}$$
$$w > 6 \quad \text{Simplify.}$$

Graph:

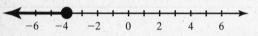

Graph:

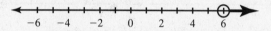

Solve each inequality. Graph the solution.

1. $2a > 10$ _____

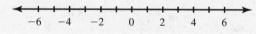

2. $-4w < 16$ _____

3. $\frac{r}{2} \geq -2$ _____

4. $18 \leq 9a$ _____

5. $\frac{a}{3} < 1$ _____

6. $6g < 6$ _____

7. $-3x \geq -6$ _____

8. $\frac{m}{-2} > 0$ _____

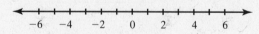

Review 123

You can use a shortcut to indicate repeated multiplication. The **exponent** tells how many times the **base** is used as a factor.

5^4 is called an **exponential expression** and 625 is the **value of the expression**.

$$5 \times 5 \times 5 \times 5 = 5^4 = 625$$

exponent

base

You can use this sentence ⟶ **P**lease **E**xcuse **M**y **D**ear **A**unt **S**ally. to remember the order of operations for expressions with exponents.

$2^2 + 4(7 - 3) + 6 = 2^2 + 4(4) + 6$

$= 4 + 4(4) + 6$

$= 4 + 16 + 6$

$= 26$

P	Do all operations within **P**arentheses first.
E	Evaluate any terms with **E**xponents.
M-D	**M**ultiply and **D**ivide in order from left to right.
A-S	**A**dd and **S**ubtract in order from left to right.

Write each expression using exponents.

1. $6 \times 6 \times 6 \times 6 \times 6$ _____

2. $0.2 \times 0.2 \times 0.2$ _____

3. $9 \times 9 \times 9 \times 9$ _____

4. $12 \times 12 \times 12 \times 12 \times 12$ _____

Write each expression as a product of its factors. Then evaluate each expression.

5. 12^2

_____

6. 8^3

_____

7. $(0.4)^3$

_____

8. 5^5

_____

9. 3^6

_____

10. 1.4^2

_____

Simplify each expression.

11. $7^2 + 3^3$

12. $8 + 4^2$

13. $5(0.2 + 0.8)^{10}$

14. $(9 - 7)^2$

_____ _____ _____ _____

15. $(8^2 + 16) \div 2$

16. $5^3 + 100$

17. $(4 + 7)^2 - 8$

18. $(9 - 3)^2 + 6 \times 2$

_____ _____ _____ _____

Course 2 Topics

Review 124

Scientific notation is an efficient way to write very large numbers. A number is written as the product of a number between 1 and 10 and a power of 10.

Write 4,000,000,000 in scientific notation.

① Count the number of places that you need to move the decimal point to the left to get a factor between 1 and 10.

$$4,\underbrace{000,000,000}_{\text{9 places}} \to 4.000\ 000\ 000$$

② Use the number of places as the exponent of 10.

$$4,000,000,000 = 4 \times 10^9$$

To change a number from scientific notation to standard form, undo the steps at the left.

Write 3.5×10^8 in standard form.

① Note the exponent of 10. (Here it is 8.)

② Move the decimal point to the right the number of places that is equal to the exponent.

$$3.5 \times 10^8 \to \underset{\text{8 places}}{350,000,000}$$

$$3.5 \times 10^8 = 350,000,000$$

Write in scientific notation.

1. 3,500

Move the decimal point _____ places

to the _____.

3,500 = _____ × _____

2. 1,400,000

Move the decimal point _____ places

to the _____.

1,400,000 = _____ × _____

3. 93,000,000 _____

4. 1,200,000 _____

5. 17,000 _____

6. 750,000 _____

7. 2,400 _____

8. 6,532,000 _____

9. 560,000,000,000 _____

10. 34,800,000 _____

Write in standard form.

11. 2.58×10^3 _____

12. 8×10^6 _____

13. 4.816×10^5 _____

14. 8.11×10^2 _____

15. 1.85×10^7 _____

16. 3.7509×10^3 _____

17. 8.003×10^1 _____

18. 5.66×10^9 _____

19. 4.23×10^2 _____

20. 9.992×10^{10} _____

Review 125

One integer is **divisible** by another if the remainder is 0 when you divide the larger number by the smaller number.

Divisibility Tests for 2, 3, 4, 5, 8, 9, and 10.

An integer is divisible by
- 2 if it ends in 0, 2, 4, 6, or 8.
- 3 if the sum of its digits is divisible by 3.
- 4 if the number formed by the last two digits is divisible by 4.
- 5 if it ends in 0 or 5.
- 8 if the number formed by the last three digits is divisible by 8.
- 9 if the sum of its digits is divisible by 9.
- 10 if it ends in zero.

Is the first number divisible by the second?

a. 1,256 by 2   Yes, 1,256 is even.

b. 287 by 3   No, $2 + 8 + 7 = 17$, which is not divisible by 3.

c. 1,536 by 4   Yes, 36 is divisible by 4.

d. 922 by 5   No, 922 does not end in 5 or 0.

e. 30,780 by 8   No, 780 is not divisible by 8.

f. 4,518 by 9   Yes, $4 + 5 + 1 + 8 = 18$, which is divisible by 9.

g. 541 by 10   No, 541 does not end in zero.

Is the first number divisible by the second? Explain.

1. 2,336 by 8

2. 580 by 10

3. 722 by 5

4. 2,505 by 3

5. 225,325 by 9

6. 421 by 4

Tell whether each number is divisible by 2, 3, 4, 5, 8, 9, or 10. Some numbers may be divisible by more than one number.

7. 526

8. 1,325

9. 888

10. 981

11. 62,810

12. 565,852

Review 126

Course 2 Topics

A **prime number** has exactly
two factors, 1 and itself.
2 and 7 are prime numbers.
2 is the smallest prime number.

$2 \times 1 = 2 \qquad 7 \times 1 = 7$

Every **composite number** can be
written as a product of two or more
prime numbers. This is called the
prime factorization of the number.

$60 = 2 \cdot 2 \cdot 3 \cdot 5 = 2^2 \cdot 3 \cdot 5$
$40 = 2 \cdot 2 \cdot 2 \cdot 5 = 2^3 \cdot 5$

You can use a *factor tree* and division to find the prime factorization
of a number.

① Divide by a factor other than 1 and
the number itself. Record the divisor
and the quotient in the factor tree.

② Continue dividing until all the
factors are prime numbers.

③ Use exponents to write the
prime factorization.

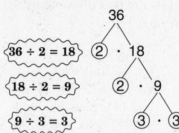

$36 = 2^2 \cdot 3^2$

**Complete each factor tree. Then write the prime factorization using
exponents where possible.**

1.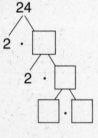

2.

3.

_____   _____   _____

**Write the prime factorization of each number. Use exponents where
possible.**

4. 20 = _____   5. 54 = _____   6. 40 = _____

7. 48 = _____   8. 56 = _____   9. 150 = _____

Review 127

A fraction is in **simplest form** when the numerator and denominator have no common factors other than 1.

To write $\frac{18}{24}$ in the simplest form:

(1) Divide the numerator and denominator $\frac{18 \div 2}{24 \div 2} = \frac{9}{12}$ by a common factor.

(2) Continue dividing by common factors $\frac{9 \div 3}{12 \div 3} = \frac{3}{4}$ until the only common factor is 1. The only factor common to 3 and 4 is 1.

In simplest form $\frac{18}{24}$ is $\frac{3}{4}$.

You can use the greatest common factor (GCF) to write a fraction in simplest form. Divide the numerator and the denominator by the GCF.

The GCF of 18 and 24 is 6.

$\frac{18}{24} = \frac{18 \div 6}{24 \div 6} = \frac{3}{4}$

Complete to write each fraction in simplest form.

1. $\frac{10}{20} = \frac{10 \div}{20 \div 2} = \frac{\div}{10 \div} =$ _____

2. $\frac{24}{60} = \frac{24 \div 6}{60 \div} = \frac{\div}{10 \div} =$ _____

Find the GCF of the numerator and denominator of each fraction. Then write each fraction in simplest form.

3. $\frac{12}{14} =$ _____

   GCF = _____

4. $\frac{9}{15} =$ _____

   GCF = _____

5. $\frac{35}{42} =$ _____

   GCF = _____

6. $\frac{40}{50} =$ _____

   GCF = _____

Write each fraction in simplest form.

7. $\frac{42}{60} =$ _____

8. $\frac{20}{36} =$ _____

9. $\frac{18}{20} =$ _____

10. $\frac{9}{27} =$ _____

11. $\frac{42}{56} =$ _____

12. $\frac{16}{72} =$ _____

13. $\frac{24}{40} =$ _____

14. $\frac{18}{32} =$ _____

15. $\frac{25}{75} =$ _____

16. $\frac{65}{75} =$ _____

17. $\frac{40}{60} =$ _____

18. $\frac{50}{95} =$ _____

Review 128

Course 2 Topics

Follow these steps to *compare* $\frac{2}{5}$ and $\frac{3}{10}$ (unlike denominators).

① Find the **least common denominator** (LCD).

The denominators are 5 and 10. The LCD of 5 and 10 is their least common multiple.

② Write the equivalent fractions using the LCD.

$\frac{2}{5} = \frac{4}{10}$ and $\frac{3}{10} = \frac{3}{10}$

③ Compare the numerators.

$4 > 3$

So, $\frac{4}{10} > \frac{3}{10}$ and $\frac{2}{5} > \frac{3}{10}$.

Follow these steps to *order* the fractions $\frac{1}{2}, \frac{3}{5}$, and $\frac{2}{3}$.

① Find the LCD.

The LCD of 2, 5, and 3 is 30.

② Write equivalent fractions using the LCD.

$\frac{1}{2} = \frac{1 \cdot 15}{2 \cdot 15} = \frac{15}{30}$

$\frac{3}{5} = \frac{3 \cdot 6}{5 \cdot 6} = \frac{18}{30}$

$\frac{2}{3} = \frac{2 \cdot 10}{3 \cdot 10} = \frac{20}{30}$

③ Order the fractions using their numerators.

$\frac{15}{30} < \frac{18}{30} < \frac{20}{30}$

So, $\frac{1}{2} < \frac{3}{5} < \frac{2}{3}$.

Find each missing number. Then compare the fractions.
Use <, >, or =.

1. $\frac{2}{3}$ and $\frac{3}{5}$

   a. $\frac{2}{3} = \frac{\Box}{15}, \frac{3}{5} = \frac{\Box}{15}$

   b. $\frac{2}{3} \Box \frac{3}{5}$

2. $\frac{1}{2}$ and $\frac{5}{8}$

   a. $\frac{1}{2} = \frac{\Box}{8}, \frac{5}{8} = \frac{\Box}{8}$

   b. $\frac{1}{2} \Box \frac{5}{8}$

3. $\frac{3}{4}$ and $\frac{9}{12}$

   a. $\frac{3}{4} = \frac{\Box}{12}, \frac{9}{12} = \frac{\Box}{12}$

   b. $\frac{3}{4} \Box \frac{9}{12}$

Compare each pair of fractions. Use <, >, or =.

4. $\frac{3}{5} \Box \frac{4}{5}$

5. $\frac{3}{4} \Box \frac{7}{8}$

6. $\frac{8}{12} \Box \frac{2}{3}$

7. $\frac{1}{2} \Box \frac{9}{16}$

8. $\frac{2}{3} \Box \frac{1}{2}$

9. $\frac{5}{9} \Box \frac{10}{18}$

10. $\frac{6}{7} \Box \frac{5}{6}$

11. $\frac{3}{8} \Box \frac{3}{5}$

Order from least to greatest.

12. $\frac{1}{2}, \frac{4}{5}, \frac{1}{4}$ _____

13. $\frac{2}{3}, \frac{3}{8}, \frac{1}{2}$ _____

14. $\frac{5}{6}, \frac{7}{8}, \frac{1}{4}$ _____

15. $\frac{1}{2}, \frac{5}{8}, \frac{5}{6}$ _____

16. $\frac{7}{10}, \frac{2}{3}, \frac{1}{5}$ _____

17. $\frac{2}{3}, \frac{1}{4}, \frac{11}{12}$ _____

Review 129

Problem Solving: Solve a Simpler Problem and Look for a Pattern

When solving a problem it may be helpful to look for a pattern.

Look at the three drawings of boxes. How many boxes should there be in the next drawing?

Read and Understand Think about the information you are given. You know there are 2 boxes in the first drawing, 4 boxes in the second, and 8 boxes in the third.

 2 boxes

 4 boxes

Plan and Solve You know the number of boxes in each drawing. It makes sense to look for a pattern. There is a pattern. The number of boxes doubles each time. The next drawing should have 16 boxes.

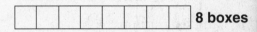 8 boxes

Look Back and Check Is there another pattern possible?

For Exercises 1–2, describe each pattern and draw the next arrangement of boxes.

1.

   Pattern: _____

2. How many diagonals can you draw in a 12-sided regular polygon?

   _____

3. Look for a pattern to find the value of $(-1)^{100}$.

   a. $(-1)^1 =$ _____   b. $(-1)^2 =$ _____   c. $(-1)^3 =$ _____

   d. $(-1)^4 =$ _____   e. $(-1)^{100} =$ _____

4. Describe the pattern you used in Exercise 3.

   _____

5. A winter coat is on sale. Look for a pattern in the prices to predict the price of the coat on the tenth day.

   _____

Winter Coat Sale Price	
Day 1—$129.00	Day 2—$124.50
Day 3—$120.00	Day 4—$115.50

Course 2 Topics

Review 130
Mixed Numbers and Improper Fractions

An **improper fraction** is greater than or equal to 1. Its numerator is greater than or equal to its denominator.

Improper fractions

$\frac{6}{4}$ $\frac{8}{8}$ $\frac{10}{8}$ $\frac{7}{2}$

A mixed number is the sum of a whole number and a fraction.

Mixed numbers

$1\frac{2}{3}$ $5\frac{4}{9}$ $3\frac{1}{2}$

To write a mixed number as an improper fraction:

① Write the mixed number as a sum.

$3\frac{1}{2} = 3 + \frac{1}{2}$

② Write both numbers as fractions.

$= \frac{6}{2} + \frac{1}{2}$

③ Add the fractions.

$= \frac{7}{2}$

To write an improper fraction as a mixed number:

① Divide the numerator by the denominator.

$\frac{7}{2}$ Think: $7 \div 2$

$$\begin{array}{r} 3 \\ 2\overline{)7} \\ \underline{-6} \\ 1 \end{array}$$

② Write the whole number, then the remainder over the divisor.

$\frac{7}{2} = 3\frac{1}{2}$

Write each mixed number as an improper fraction.

1. $3\frac{1}{4} =$ _____

2. $2\frac{2}{3} =$ _____

3. $1\frac{3}{8} =$ _____

4. $5\frac{2}{7} =$ _____

5. $6\frac{3}{4} =$ _____

6. $1\frac{1}{9} =$ _____

7. $4\frac{1}{2} =$ _____

8. $3\frac{4}{5} =$ _____

9. $5\frac{1}{6} =$ _____

10. $3\frac{1}{3} =$ _____

11. $5\frac{7}{8} =$ _____

12. $4\frac{1}{8} =$ _____

Write each improper fraction as a mixed number in simplest form.

13. $\frac{14}{4} =$ _____

14. $\frac{12}{2} =$ _____

15. $\frac{22}{5} =$ _____

16. $\frac{16}{3} =$ _____

17. $\frac{47}{8} =$ _____

18. $\frac{56}{7} =$ _____

19. $\frac{17}{4} =$ _____

20. $\frac{21}{6} =$ _____

21. $\frac{13}{5} =$ _____

22. $\frac{23}{4} =$ _____

23. $\frac{13}{9} =$ _____

24. $\frac{14}{2} =$ _____

Course 2 Topics

Review 131

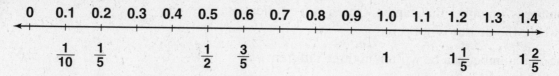

To change a fraction to a decimal, divide the numerator by the denominator.

$\frac{3}{5}$ ⟨ Think: 3 ÷ 5 ⟩

$$\begin{array}{r} 0.6 \\ 5\overline{)3.0} \\ -30 \\ \hline 0 \end{array}$$

$\frac{3}{5} = 0.6$

To change a decimal to a fraction:

① Read the decimal to find the denominator. Write the decimal digits over 10, 100, or 1,000.

0.65 is 65 *hundredths* → $\frac{65}{100}$

② Use the GCF to write the fraction in simplest form.

The GCF of 65 and 100 is 5.

$\frac{65}{100} = \frac{65 \div 5}{100 \div 5} = \frac{13}{20}$

Write each fraction as a decimal.

1. $\frac{4}{5}$ = _____

2. $\frac{3}{4}$ = _____

3. $\frac{1}{6}$ = _____

4. $\frac{1}{4}$ = _____

5. $\frac{2}{3}$ = _____

6. $\frac{7}{10}$ = _____

7. $\frac{5}{9}$ = _____

8. $\frac{1}{5}$ = _____

9. $\frac{3}{8}$ = _____

Write each decimal as a mixed number or fraction in simplest form.

10. 0.4 = _____

11. 0.75 = _____

12. 1.5 = _____

13. 0.35 = _____

14. 2.7 = _____

15. 1.8 = _____

16. 0.625 = _____

17. 0.78 = _____

18. 0.88 = _____

Order from least to greatest.

19. $2.\overline{6}, \frac{13}{6}, 2\frac{5}{6}$

20. $2.\overline{02}, 2\frac{1}{200}, 2.0202$

21. $\frac{5}{4}, 1\frac{4}{5}, 1.\overline{4}$

_____

_____

_____

Review 132

Rational Numbers

A **rational number** is a number that can be written as a quotient of two integers, where the divisor is not zero.

A negative rational number can be written in three different ways.

$$-\frac{2}{3} = \frac{-2}{3} = \frac{2}{-3}$$

Comparing Negative Rational Numbers

Compare $-\frac{2}{3}$ and $-\frac{1}{4}$.

Method 1 Use a number line. Graph both points on a number line and see which is farther to the left.

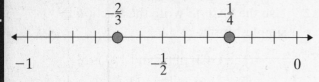

Since $-\frac{2}{3}$ is farther to the left, $-\frac{2}{3} < -\frac{1}{4}$.

Method 2 Use the lowest common denominator.

$$-\frac{2}{3} = \frac{-2}{3} = \frac{-2 \times 4}{3 \times 4} = \frac{-8}{12} \qquad -\frac{1}{4} = \frac{-1}{4} = \frac{-1 \times 3}{4 \times 3} = \frac{-3}{12}$$

Since $\frac{-8}{12} < \frac{-3}{12}$, then $-\frac{2}{3} < -\frac{1}{4}$.

Compare. Use <, >, or =.

1. $-\frac{4}{9}$ ☐ $-\frac{2}{3}$

2. -1 ☐ $-\frac{4}{5}$

3. $-\frac{7}{8}$ ☐ $-\frac{1}{8}$

4. $-\frac{1}{3}$ ☐ $-\frac{5}{6}$

5. $-\frac{2}{5}$ ☐ $-\frac{1}{10}$

6. $-\frac{2}{8}$ ☐ $-\frac{1}{4}$

Order from least to greatest.

7. $-\frac{1}{3}, 0.3, -0.35, -\frac{3}{10}$

8. $\frac{1}{5}, -0.25, 0.21, \frac{3}{10}$

_____

_____

9. $-6.25, 2\frac{8}{9}, \frac{-5}{12}, 2.1$

10. $\frac{-9}{11}, -0.5\overline{5}, \frac{-3}{4}, \frac{-12}{25}$

_____

_____

11. You and your brother invested an equal amount of money in a college savings plan. In the last quarter your investment was worth $1\frac{5}{6}$ of its original value. Your brother's investment was worth 1.85 of its original value. Whose investment is worth more?

_____

Course 2 Topics

Review 133

Estimating with Fractions and Mixed Numbers

You can estimate sums, differences, and products by using benchmarks.
A *benchmark* is a value that can be used as a reference point.

- You can use the benchmarks to estimate fractions.

- Round mixed numbers to the nearest whole number.

Estimate the sum:

$\frac{5}{6} + \frac{7}{12}$

$1 + \frac{1}{2} = 1\frac{1}{2}$

Estimate the difference:

$3\frac{5}{6} - 2\frac{1}{3}$

$4 - 2 = 2$

Estimate the product:

$4\frac{1}{3} \times 2\frac{2}{3}$

$4 \times 3 = 12$

You can estimate a quotient by using compatible numbers.

Estimate: $15\frac{3}{8} \div 4\frac{1}{8}$

Think: $15\frac{3}{8}$ is close to 16.

16 is divisible by 4.

$15\frac{3}{8} \div 4\frac{1}{8} \approx 16 \div 4 = 4$

Course 2 Topics

Circle the better estimate.

1. $\frac{1}{2} + \frac{3}{8}$ 1 or $\frac{1}{2}$

2. $\frac{9}{10} - \frac{7}{8}$ 0 or $\frac{1}{2}$

3. $\frac{5}{8} + \frac{3}{7}$ $\frac{1}{2}$ or 1

4. $\frac{8}{9} - \frac{1}{9}$ $\frac{1}{2}$ or 1

5. $\frac{5}{8} + \frac{8}{9}$ 1 or $1\frac{1}{2}$

6. $\frac{5}{6} + \frac{11}{12}$ $1\frac{1}{2}$ or 2

Estimate each sum or difference.

7. $\frac{1}{2} + \frac{3}{7}$ _____

8. $\frac{5}{9} - \frac{3}{7}$ _____

9. $4\frac{2}{3} - \frac{1}{2}$ _____

10. $6\frac{7}{8} + 4\frac{4}{9}$ _____

11. $5\frac{8}{9} + 3\frac{1}{3}$ _____

12. $11\frac{1}{5} - 4\frac{1}{12}$ _____

Circle the better choice to estimate each product or quotient.

13. $5\frac{1}{4} \cdot 2\frac{1}{8}$

$5 \cdot 2$ or $5 \cdot 3$

14. $13\frac{1}{4} \div 3\frac{7}{8}$

$12 \div 4$ or $15 \div 3$

15. $6\frac{3}{4} \cdot 8\frac{7}{8}$

$7 \cdot 8$ or $7 \cdot 9$

16. $21\frac{1}{2} \div 4\frac{1}{4}$

$20 \div 4$ or $24 \div 4$

17. $4\frac{13}{15} \cdot 7\frac{2}{9}$

$5 \cdot 7$ or $4 \cdot 8$

18. $38\frac{5}{6} \div 5\frac{1}{3}$

$35 \div 5$ or $40 \div 5$

Estimate each product or quotient.

19. $6\frac{1}{4} \cdot 3\frac{5}{6}$ _____

20. $9\frac{1}{2} \div 2\frac{5}{8}$ _____

21. $2\frac{1}{7} \cdot 3\frac{5}{7}$ _____

22. $9\frac{4}{5} \cdot 4\frac{5}{6}$ _____

23. $15\frac{1}{2} \div 3\frac{5}{7}$ _____

24. $11\frac{1}{9} \cdot 2\frac{7}{8}$ _____

Review 134

Adding and Subtracting Fractions

Follow these steps to add or subtract fractions with different denominators.

Add: $\frac{1}{3} + \frac{1}{6}$ Subtract: $\frac{11}{12} - \frac{1}{6}$

① Write the fractions with the same denominator.

$\frac{2}{6} + \frac{1}{6}$ $\frac{11}{12} - \frac{2}{12}$

② Add or subtract the numerators.

$\frac{2}{6} + \frac{1}{6} = \frac{3}{6}$ $\frac{11}{12} - \frac{2}{12} = \frac{9}{12}$

③ Simplify the fraction.

$\frac{3}{6} = \frac{1}{2}$ $\frac{9}{12} = \frac{3}{4}$

Complete to find each sum or difference.

1. $\frac{3}{10} + \frac{2}{5}$

$\frac{3}{10} + \frac{\square}{10} = \frac{\square}{\square}$

2. $\frac{1}{4} + \frac{3}{6}$

$\frac{\square}{12} + \frac{\square}{12} = \frac{\square}{\square} = \frac{\square}{\square}$

3. $\frac{5}{8} + \frac{1}{4}$

$\frac{5}{8} + \frac{\square}{8} = \frac{\square}{\square}$

4. $\frac{3}{4} - \frac{1}{2}$

$\frac{3}{4} - \frac{\square}{4} = \frac{\square}{\square}$

5. $\frac{5}{9} - \frac{1}{3}$

$\frac{5}{9} - \frac{\square}{9} = \frac{\square}{\square}$

6. $\frac{3}{5} - \frac{1}{3}$

$\frac{\square}{15} - \frac{\square}{15} = \frac{\square}{\square}$

Find each sum or difference. Write it in simplest form.

7. $\frac{4}{5} + \frac{4}{5}$

8. $\frac{7}{8} - \frac{5}{8}$

9. $\frac{5}{6} - \frac{2}{3}$

10. $\frac{5}{12} - \frac{1}{4}$

11. $\frac{7}{8} + \frac{1}{4}$

12. $\frac{3}{4} - \frac{1}{8}$

13. $\frac{2}{5} + \frac{1}{10}$

14. $\frac{7}{12} - \frac{1}{3}$

15. $\frac{3}{5} + \frac{7}{15}$

16. $\frac{1}{2} + \frac{9}{10}$

17. $\frac{5}{6} - \frac{1}{4}$

18. $\frac{9}{10} - \frac{1}{2}$

19. $\frac{5}{8} + \frac{1}{2}$

20. $\frac{2}{5} - \frac{3}{10}$

21. $\frac{5}{6} - \frac{7}{12}$

Review 135

Adding and Subtracting Mixed Numbers

Follow these steps to add or subtract mixed numbers with different denominators.

Add: $2\frac{2}{5} + 1\frac{3}{4}$ Subtract: $4\frac{1}{3} - 2\frac{5}{6}$

① Write the equivalent fractions with the LCD.

$2\frac{8}{20} + 1\frac{15}{20}$ $4\frac{2}{6} - 2\frac{5}{6}$

② Rename, if necessary.

$4\frac{2}{6} = 3 + 1\frac{2}{6} = 3\frac{8}{6}$

③ Add or subtract the whole numbers. Add or subtract the fractions.

$2\frac{8}{20} + 1\frac{15}{20} = 3\frac{23}{20}$ $3\frac{8}{6} - 2\frac{5}{6} = 1\frac{3}{6}$

④ Simplify.

$3\frac{23}{20} = 4\frac{3}{20}$ $1\frac{3}{6} = 1\frac{1}{2}$

Complete to find each sum or difference.

1. $4\frac{3}{4} - 2\frac{3}{8}$

$4\frac{\square}{8} - 2\frac{\square}{8} = \square\frac{\square}{\square}$

2. $4\frac{7}{12} + 2\frac{5}{6}$

$4\frac{\square}{12} + 2\frac{\square}{\square} = \square\frac{\square}{\square}$

$= \square\frac{\square}{\square}$

3. $4\frac{1}{3} - 1\frac{3}{5}$

$4\frac{\square}{15} - 1\frac{\square}{15}$

$= \square\frac{\square}{\square} - \square\frac{\square}{\square}$

$= \square\frac{\square}{\square}$

Find each sum or difference. Write it in simplest form.

4. $2\frac{3}{5} + 1\frac{1}{10}$ _____

5. $2\frac{5}{6} + 3\frac{4}{9}$ _____

6. $5 - 3\frac{7}{10}$ _____

7. $3\frac{1}{6} - 2\frac{1}{3}$ _____

8. $4\frac{3}{4} - 1\frac{2}{3}$ _____

9. $3\frac{1}{2} + 4\frac{1}{3}$ _____

10. $3\frac{3}{10} + 1\frac{3}{5}$ _____

11. $6\frac{1}{3} + 7\frac{1}{4}$ _____

12. $4\frac{3}{5} + 6\frac{7}{10}$ _____

13. $7\frac{15}{16} - 2\frac{3}{8}$ _____

14. $4 - 2\frac{3}{10}$ _____

15. $5\frac{1}{4} - 1\frac{3}{8}$ _____

16. $2\frac{1}{2} + 5\frac{3}{5}$ _____

17. $7\frac{1}{4} - 3\frac{3}{5}$ _____

18. $5 - 2\frac{5}{8}$ _____

19. $9\frac{3}{5} + 1\frac{7}{10}$ _____

20. $6 - 5\frac{5}{6}$ _____

21. $4\frac{7}{10} + 4\frac{1}{2}$ _____

22. Shea cut $2\frac{1}{8}$ in. material off of the bottom of a $21\frac{1}{4}$ in. skirt. How long is the skirt now?

_____

Course 2 Topics

Review 136

Multiplying Fractions and Mixed Numbers

Follow these steps to multiply fractions and mixed numbers.

Multiply: $\frac{3}{4} \cdot \frac{2}{5}$ Multiply: $2\frac{2}{3} \cdot 1\frac{5}{8}$

① Write the mixed numbers as improper fractions if necessary.

$\frac{8}{3} \cdot \frac{13}{8}$

② Multiply numerators. Multiply denominators.

$\frac{3 \cdot 2}{4 \cdot 5} = \frac{6}{20}$ $\frac{8 \cdot 13}{3 \cdot 8} = \frac{104}{24}$

③ Simplify, if necessary.

$\frac{6}{20} = \frac{3}{10}$ $\frac{104}{24} = 4\frac{1}{3}$

Complete to find each product.

1. $\frac{1}{5} \cdot \frac{2}{3}$

$\frac{1 \cdot 2}{5 \cdot 3} = \dfrac{\boxed{}}{\boxed{}}$

Product _____

2. $\frac{1}{4} \cdot 4\frac{1}{8}$

$\frac{1}{4} \cdot \dfrac{\boxed{}}{8} = \dfrac{\boxed{}}{32}$

Product _____

3. $2\frac{3}{4} \cdot 1\frac{2}{3}$

$\dfrac{\boxed{}}{4} \cdot \dfrac{\boxed{}}{3} = \dfrac{\boxed{}}{12}$

Product _____

Find each product. Write the product in simplest form.

4. $\frac{5}{8} \cdot \frac{2}{5}$ _____

5. $\frac{2}{3} \cdot 9$ _____

6. $\frac{5}{12} \cdot \frac{3}{10}$ _____

7. $\frac{3}{4} \cdot 1\frac{4}{5}$ _____

8. $\frac{1}{2} \cdot 5\frac{1}{6}$ _____

9. $3\frac{4}{5} \cdot \frac{1}{6}$ _____

10. $1\frac{2}{3} \cdot 5$ _____

11. $1\frac{3}{4} \cdot 3\frac{1}{7}$ _____

12. $2\frac{3}{5} \cdot \frac{1}{4}$ _____

13. $2\frac{3}{5} \cdot \frac{7}{8}$ _____

14. $4\frac{1}{5} \cdot \frac{5}{7}$ _____

15. $\frac{1}{2} \cdot 2\frac{1}{8}$ _____

16. $3\frac{5}{6} \cdot 2\frac{1}{4}$ _____

17. $2\frac{5}{7} \cdot 1\frac{1}{3}$ _____

18. $7\frac{2}{3} \cdot 2\frac{1}{7}$ _____

19. $5\frac{1}{2} \cdot 2\frac{2}{3}$ _____

20. $\frac{5}{6} \cdot 3\frac{3}{5}$ _____

21. $7\frac{3}{4} \cdot 2$ _____

Review 137

Dividing Fractions and Mixed Numbers

To find the **reciprocal** of a fraction, interchange the numerator and the denominator.

Examples: The reciprocal of $\frac{1}{4}$ is $\frac{4}{1}$. The reciprocal of $\frac{7}{5}$ is $\frac{5}{7}$.

Follow these steps to divide fractions and mixed numbers.

		Divide: $\frac{2}{3} \div \frac{1}{4}$	Divide: $3\frac{3}{4} \div 1\frac{2}{5}$
①	Rewrite mixed numbers as improper fractions as needed.		$\frac{15}{4} \div \frac{7}{5}$
②	Multiply by the reciprocal of the divisor.	$\frac{2}{3} \cdot \frac{4}{1}$	$\frac{15}{4} \cdot \frac{5}{7}$
③	Multiply numerators. Multiply denominators.	$\frac{2 \cdot 4}{3 \cdot 1} = \frac{8}{3}$	$\frac{15 \cdot 5}{4 \cdot 7} = \frac{75}{28}$
④	Simplify.	$\frac{8}{3} = 2\frac{2}{3}$	$\frac{75}{28} = 2\frac{19}{28}$

Course 2 Topic

Find the reciprocal of each number.

1. $\frac{7}{8}$ _____

2. $\frac{1}{6}$ _____

3. $\frac{8}{3}$ _____

4. $\frac{9}{10}$ _____

Write each mixed number as an improper fraction. Then find the reciprocal.

5. $1\frac{1}{2}$ _____

6. $2\frac{1}{3}$ _____

7. $1\frac{4}{5}$ _____

8. $2\frac{3}{4}$ _____

Complete to find each quotient. Write the quotient in simplest form.

9. $\frac{2}{3} \div \frac{3}{8}$

$\frac{2}{3} \cdot \dfrac{\boxed{}}{3} = \dfrac{\boxed{}}{9}$

Quotient _____

10. $10 \div \frac{7}{8}$

$\dfrac{\boxed{}}{1} \div \frac{7}{8} = \dfrac{\boxed{}}{1} \cdot \dfrac{\boxed{}}{\boxed{}}$

$= \dfrac{\boxed{}}{7}$

Quotient _____

11. $3\frac{3}{5} \div 1\frac{1}{5}$

$\dfrac{\boxed{}}{5} \div \dfrac{\boxed{}}{5} = \dfrac{\boxed{}}{5} \cdot \dfrac{\boxed{}}{\boxed{}}$

$= \dfrac{\boxed{}}{30}$

Quotient _____

12. $\frac{1}{5} \div \frac{1}{2}$ _____

13. $\frac{3}{8} \div \frac{2}{3}$ _____

14. $8 \div \frac{4}{5}$ _____

15. $6 \div \frac{3}{4}$ _____

16. $1\frac{1}{8} \div 2\frac{2}{5}$ _____

17. $3\frac{1}{5} \div 2\frac{2}{3}$ _____

Review 138

To solve equations, remember to use inverse operations.

$n + 4\frac{1}{4} = 5\frac{3}{4}$ ←   **Addition equation: use subtraction to solve.**

$n + 4\frac{1}{4} - 4\frac{1}{4} = 5\frac{3}{4} - 4\frac{1}{4}$ ←   **Subtract $4\frac{1}{4}$ from each side.**

$n = 1\frac{2}{4} = 1\frac{1}{2}$ ←   **Simplify.**

$n - 1\frac{3}{4} = \frac{1}{2}$ ←   **Subtraction equation: use addition to solve.**

$n - 1\frac{3}{4} + 1\frac{3}{4} = \frac{1}{2} + 1\frac{3}{4}$ ←   **Add $1\frac{3}{4}$ to each side.**

$n = \frac{2}{4} + 1\frac{3}{4}$ ←   **Find a common denominator.**

$n = 1\frac{5}{4} = 2\frac{1}{4}$ ←   **Simplify.**

Complete to solve each equation.

1. $x + \frac{1}{5} = \frac{3}{5}$

    $x + \frac{1}{5} - \underline{\hspace{1cm}} = \frac{3}{5} - \underline{\hspace{1cm}}$

          $x = \underline{\hspace{1cm}}$

2. $\frac{1}{4} + t = 1\frac{3}{4}$

    $\frac{1}{4} - \underline{\hspace{1cm}} + t = 1\frac{3}{4} - \underline{\hspace{1cm}}$

         $t = \underline{\hspace{1cm}} = \underline{\hspace{1cm}}$

3. $\frac{7}{8} = w - \frac{3}{8}$

    $\frac{7}{8} + \underline{\hspace{1cm}} = w - \frac{3}{8} + \underline{\hspace{1cm}}$

    $\underline{\hspace{1cm}} = \underline{\hspace{1cm}} = w$

4. $h - 2\frac{1}{3} = \frac{2}{3}$

    $h - 2\frac{1}{3} + \underline{\hspace{1cm}} = \frac{2}{3} + \underline{\hspace{1cm}}$

         $h = \underline{\hspace{1cm}}$

Solve each equation.

5. $a + 1\frac{2}{5} = 4\frac{4}{5}$ _____

6. $2\frac{3}{4} = f - \frac{1}{4}$ _____

7. $\frac{5}{9} + k = 1\frac{7}{9}$ _____

8. $z - \frac{3}{5} = \frac{9}{10}$ _____

9. $4\frac{2}{3} + s = 6$ _____

10. $\frac{5}{8} = b - \frac{1}{8}$ _____

11. $3\frac{5}{6} + m = 10\frac{2}{3}$ _____

12. $n - 1\frac{1}{3} = \frac{1}{2}$ _____

13. $\frac{3}{5} = t + \frac{1}{3}$ _____

14. $z + 1\frac{2}{7} = 2\frac{5}{7}$ _____

15. $r - 3\frac{1}{2} = 4\frac{3}{8}$ _____

16. $x + \frac{7}{9} = 2\frac{2}{3}$ _____

17. $3\frac{5}{9} = r + 2\frac{1}{6}$ _____

18. $k - 2\frac{3}{10} = \frac{4}{5}$ _____

19. $2\frac{1}{4} = m + 1\frac{1}{6}$ _____

20. $\frac{6}{7} = a + \frac{2}{3}$ _____

Review 139

Problem Solving: Try, Check, Revise and Work Backward

Ramón began his shopping trip by cashing his paycheck. While shopping, he noted what he spent. At the end of the day, he had $49.50 left. What was the amount of his paycheck?

Videotape	$13.95
Sweater	45.99
Shirt	17.99
Pants	32.45

Read and Understand What information are you given? *You know how much Ramón had left and how much he spent.*

Plan and Solve It makes sense to *work backward* to find the amount Ramón began with.

Add the amount spent to the amount left. Ramón's paycheck was for $159.88.

Amount left	$49.50
Amount spent	32.45
	17.99
	45.99
	13.95
	$159.88

Look Back and Check You can check your answer by *working forward*. Begin with $159.88. Subtract each amount Ramón spent.

Solve each problem by using either of the methods in the lesson. Check each answer in the original problem.

1. Madeline took her month's allowance to the amusement park. She had $1.50 left at the end of the day. She made a list of her expenses.

Rides	$3.50
Food	2.50
Admission	1.50
Toss-a-ring	2.00

   How much was her allowance?

   Allowance: _____

2. Dana left nuts out for the chipmunks. She kept track of how many each chipmunk took.

Curlytail	15
Whitefoot	22
Squeaker	19
Stripes	32

   If there were 12 nuts left, how many did she start with?

   Total nuts: _____

3. Suzy multiplied her age by 2, subtracted 5, divided by 3, and added 9. The result was 20. How old is she?

   _____

4. Each time a ball bounces it returns to a height $\frac{2}{3}$ the height of the previous bounce. After the third bounce, the ball returns to a height of 4 ft. From what height was it dropped?

   _____

Course 2 Topics

Review 140

Length	Weight	Capacity
12 inches (in.) = 1 foot (ft)	16 ounces (oz) = 1 pound (lb)	8 fluid ounces (fl oz) = 1 cup (c)
3 ft = 1 yard (yd)	2,000 lb = 1 ton (t)	2 c = 1 pint (pt)
5,280 ft = 1 mile (mi)		2 pt = 1 quart (qt)
		4 qt = 1 gallon (gal)

To change to a *larger* unit, divide.

66 in. = _?_

1 ft is larger than 1 in.
12 in. = 1 ft

$66 \div 12 = \frac{66}{12} = 5\frac{6}{12} = 5\frac{1}{2}$

66 in. = $5\frac{1}{2}$ ft

To change to a *smaller* unit, multiply.

$3\frac{1}{2}$ qt = _?_ pt

1 pt is smaller than 1 qt.
1 qt = 2 pt

$3\frac{1}{2} \cdot 2 = \frac{7}{2} \cdot \frac{2}{1} = \frac{14}{2} = 7$

$3\frac{1}{2}$ qt = 7 pt

Multiply to change to a smaller unit. Write the fact you used.

1. $3\frac{1}{2}$ ft = _____

2. $1\frac{1}{2}$ c = _____

3. 5 lb = _____

4. $5\frac{1}{2}$ qt = _____

5. $3\frac{1}{4}$ gal = _____

6. 4 pt = _____

7. 2 mi = _____

8. 6 qt = _____

9. $1\frac{1}{2}$ t = _____

Divide to change to a larger unit. Write the fact you used.

10. 24 oz = _____

11. 32 oz = _____

12. 10 qt = _____

13. 3 c = _____

14. 4,000 lb = _____

15. 17 oz = _____

16. 7 pt = _____

17. 27 ft = _____

18. 30 in. = _____

19. The Missouri River is 4,470,400 yards long. Express this measurement in miles. _____

Review 141

The precision of a measurement refers to its degree of exactness. The smaller the unit of measure, the more precise the measurement. If the same unit is used in two measurements, then the measurement to the smallest decimal place is more precise.

Determine which measurement in each set is more precise.

a. 3 yd, 110 in.

Since the units of measure are different, the measurement with the smaller unit of measure is more precise. An inch is smaller than a yard, so 110 in. is more precise than 3 yd.

b. 45.12 cm, 45.2 cm

Since the units of measure are the same, the measurement with the smaller decimal place is more precise. Since 45.12 has the smaller decimal place, 45.12 cm is more precise than 45.2 cm.

Write the more precise measurement.

1. 1.6 mi, 8,448 ft

2. 8.9 km, 8.87 km

3. 2 ft, 13 in.

4. 5.64 cm, 56.2 cm

5. 4.3 yd, 2 mi

6. 17.33 mm, 17 mm

7. 100 ft, 56.5 ft

8. 6.2 km, 3.25 km

Compute. Round your answer appropriately.

9. 2,100 cm − 418 cm

10. 41.3 in. × 84 in.

11. 2.3 in. + 6.31 in.

12. 17.2 cm × 5 cm

13. 4 cm × 7.70 cm

14. 19.65 ft − 4.3 ft

15. 24 mm − 16.1 mm

16. 2.25 yd × 6 yd

Review 142

A ratio is a comparison of two numbers by division. You can write a ratio three ways.

Compare the number of red tulips to the number of yellow tulips.

| **red tulips** | **yellow tulips** | **orange mums** | **white mums** |

6 to 2, 6 : 2, or $\frac{6}{2}$

To find equal ratios, multiply or divide each part of the ratio by the same nonzero number.

$\frac{6}{2} = \frac{6 \times 2}{2 \times 2} = \frac{12}{4}$ ← **Multiply by 2.**

The ratio $\frac{3}{1}$ is in **simplest form.**

$\frac{6}{2} = \frac{6 \div 2}{2 \div 2} = \frac{3}{1}$ ← **Divide by 2.**

Use the drawings at the top of the page. Write each ratio in three ways.

1. yellow tulips to red tulips

   _____

2. white mums to orange mums

   _____

3. red tulips to orange mums

   _____

4. yellow tulips to white mums

   _____

5. red tulips to all flowers

   _____

6. orange mums to all flowers

   _____

7. tulips to mums

   _____

8. white mums to tulips

   _____

9. yellow tulips to all flowers

   _____

10. yellow tulips to orange mums

   _____

Write two ratios equal to the given ratio.

11. $\frac{5}{10}$ _____

12. 2:5 _____

13. 18 to 30 _____

Write each ratio in simplest form.

14. $\frac{8}{16}$ _____

15. 8 to 2 _____

16. 10 : 15 _____

17. $\frac{48}{24}$ _____

18. $\frac{6}{100}$ _____

19. 8 : 18 _____

Review 143

A **rate** is a ratio that compares two quantities measured in different units.

The cost for 10 copies is $1.50.

The rate is $1.50/10 copies ($1.50 per 10 copies).

A **unit rate** is a rate that has a denominator of 1. You can compare using unit rates.

To find the unit rate for 10 copies:

$$\$1.50/10 \text{ copies} = \frac{\$1.50}{10}$$
$$= \frac{\$1.50 \div 10}{10 \div 10}$$
$$= \frac{\$.15}{1}$$

The unit rate is $.15 per copy. This is also the *unit price*.

COPY CENTER	
Color Copies	
1 copy	$.25
10 copies	$1.50
25 copies	$2.50
50 copies	$4.50
100 copies	$6.00

For the better buy, compare unit rates.

The unit price for 10 copies is $.15/copy.

The unit price for 1 copy is $.25/copy.

Since $.15 < $.25, the 10-copy price is the better buy.

Use the Copy Center chart. Find the unit rate.

1. 25 copies

    $\dfrac{\$2.50}{25} = \dfrac{\$2.50 \div \boxed{}}{25 \div \boxed{}} =$

    _____

2. 100 copies

    $\dfrac{\$6.00}{100} = \dfrac{\$6.00 \div \boxed{}}{100 \div \boxed{}} =$

    _____

3. 50 copies

    $\dfrac{\$4.50}{50} = \dfrac{\$4.50 \div \boxed{}}{50 \div \boxed{}} =$

    _____

Write the unit rate for each situation.

4. drive 1,800 mi in 30 h

    _____

5. 390 mi on 15 gal of

    gasoline _____

6. jog 4,000 m in 12 min

    _____

7. $25.50 for 17 tickets

    _____

8. 456 mi on 12 gal of

    gasoline _____

9. 54 c of flour for 12

    cakes _____

Find each unit price. Then determine the better buy.

10. juice: 18 oz for $1.26
        8 oz for $.70

    _____

11. cloth: 2 yd for $3.15
        6 yd for $7.78

    _____

12. socks: 2 pairs for $3.50
        6 pairs for $9.00

    _____

13. pecans: 1 lb for $4.80
        2 oz for $1.00

    _____

Review 144

Problem Solving: Draw a Diagram and Solve a Simpler Problem

If a problem has large numbers or many steps, try to solve a similar, but simpler, problem or drawing a diagram.

Read and Understand	The coach needs 24 jump ropes for his physical education students. He has a rope long enough to be cut into 24 jump ropes. How many cuts are needed?
What are you asked to do?	*Find out how many cuts are needed to make a rope into 24 jump ropes.*
Plan and Solve	Try solving a similar problem, but with simpler numbers.

A rope is long enough to be cut into 2 jump ropes.   1 cut
A rope is long enough to be cut into 3 jump ropes.   2 cuts
A rope is long enough to be cut into 4 jump ropes.   3 cuts

What pattern do you see?	*The number of cuts is 1 less than the number of pieces. So, it would take 24 − 1, or 23 cuts to create 24 jump ropes.*
Look Back	How could you check your answer? *Try solving the problem another way. You can draw a diagram.*

Solve each problem by either drawing a diagram or solving a simpler problem.

1. You are hand-numbering the pages of a report. If there are 238 numbered pages, how many digits will you write?

   _____

2. A square flower garden is enclosed with 7 posts on each side. How many posts are there in all?

   _____

3. Martin is planning to bike 160 miles in a road race. On the first day he biked $\frac{1}{2}$ of the distance. On the next day he biked $\frac{1}{4}$ of the remaining distance. How far did he have left to go?

   _____

4. A landscape design company is planning a large outdoor display. They planted 60 plants in the first row, 62 plants in the second row, 64 in the third row, and 66 in the fourth row. At this rate, how many plants will be planted in the sixteenth row?

   _____

5. The county closes a section of road to repair the road and replace a bridge. The detour is west for 4 miles, south for 6 miles, east for 2 miles, north for 2 miles and east for 2 miles. How many miles long is the closed section of road?

   _____

Review 145

A **proportion** is an equation stating that two ratios are equal.

Consider $\frac{2}{10}$ and $\frac{5}{25}$.

$\frac{2}{10} = \frac{2 \div 2}{10 \div 2} = \frac{1}{5}$

$\frac{5}{25} = \frac{5 \div 5}{25 \div 5} = \frac{1}{5}$

Both ratios are equal to $\frac{1}{5}$, the ratios are proportional.

If two ratios form a proportion, the **cross products** are equal.

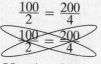

$100 \cdot 4 = 200 \cdot 2$

$400 = 400$

Complete the cross products to determine which pairs of ratios could form a proportion. Then write *yes* or *no*.

1. $\frac{3}{10} \overset{?}{=} \frac{6}{20}$

$3 \cdot 20 =$ _____

$10 \cdot 6 =$ _____

_____

2. $\frac{12}{24} \overset{?}{=} \frac{2}{4}$

$12 \cdot 4 =$ _____

$24 \cdot \boxed{} =$ _____

_____

3. $\frac{8}{5} \overset{?}{=} \frac{16}{8}$

$8 \cdot \boxed{} =$ _____

$5 \cdot \boxed{} =$ _____

_____

Can the pair of ratios form a proportion? Write *yes* or *no*.

4. $\frac{7}{5}, \frac{21}{15}$

_____

5. $\frac{16}{3}, \frac{5}{1}$

_____

6. $\frac{12}{9}, \frac{4}{3}$

_____

7. $\frac{4}{24}, \frac{2}{6}$

_____

8. $\frac{15}{5}, \frac{6}{2}$

_____

9. $\frac{9}{3}, \frac{27}{9}$

_____

Determine if the ratios in each pair are proporational.

10. $\frac{25}{35}, \frac{5}{7}$

_____

11. $\frac{15}{3}, \frac{10}{2}$

_____

12. $\frac{9}{3}, \frac{12}{4}$

_____

13. $\frac{2}{5}, \frac{6}{15}$

_____

14. $\frac{3.6}{200}, \frac{1.8}{100}$

_____

15. $\frac{6}{12}, \frac{4}{8}$

_____

16. $\frac{16}{11}, \frac{96}{24}$

_____

17. $\frac{3}{7}, \frac{2}{5}$

_____

18. $\frac{2}{22}, \frac{1}{11}$

_____

Review 146

Solving a proportion means finding a missing part of the proportion. You can use unit rates to solve a proportion. First find the unit rate. Then multiply to solve the proportion.

Shawn filled 8 bags of leaves in 2 hours. At this rate, how many bags would he fill in 6 hours?

① Find a unit rate for the number of bags per hour. Divide by the denominator.

$$\frac{8 \text{ bags}}{2 \text{ hours}} = \frac{8 \text{ bags} \div 2}{2 \text{ hours} \div 2} = \frac{4 \text{ bags}}{1 \text{ hour}}$$ The unit rate is 4 bags per hour.

② Multiply the unit rate by 6 to find the number of bags he will fill in 6 hours.

Unit rate	Number of hours	Total
↓	↓	↓
4	× 6 =	24

At this rate, Shawn can fill 24 bags in 6 hours.

If two ratios form a proportion, the **cross products** are equal.

Solve. $\frac{5}{15} = \frac{n}{3}$

① Write the cross products. $5 \cdot 3 = 15 \cdot n$

② Simplify. $15 = 15n$

③ Solve the equation. $n = 1$

Solve.

1. The bookstore advertises 5 notebooks for $7.75. At this rate, how much will 7 notebooks cost? _____

2. Leroy can lay 144 bricks in 3 hours. At this rate, how many bricks can he lay in 7 hours? _____

Solve each proportion using cross products.

3. $\frac{4}{24} = \frac{n}{6}$

   $4 \cdot$ _____ $= 24 \cdot$ _____

   $n =$ _____

4. $\frac{30}{5} = \frac{6}{n}$

   _____ $=$ _____

   $n =$ _____

5. $\frac{n}{6} = \frac{27}{9}$

   _____ $=$ _____

   $n =$ _____

Solve each proportion.

6. $\frac{50}{70} = \frac{n}{7}$ _____

7. $\frac{14}{7} = \frac{6}{n}$ _____

8. $\frac{n}{15} = \frac{2}{5}$ _____

9. $\frac{4}{10} = \frac{n}{15}$ _____

10. $\frac{4}{200} = \frac{n}{100}$ _____

11. $\frac{6}{n} = \frac{5}{10}$ _____

12. $\frac{32}{22} = \frac{96}{n}$ _____

13. $\frac{6}{3} = \frac{n}{5}$ _____

14. $\frac{2}{n} = \frac{4}{10}$ _____

Review 147

Two polygons are **similar,** if

- corresponding angles have the same measure, and

- the lengths of corresponding sides are proportional.

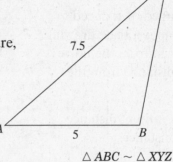

$\triangle ABC \sim \triangle XYZ$

You can use proportions to find missing lengths in similar ($\sim$) figures.

① Find corresponding sides.

$\overline{AB}$ corresponds to $\overline{XY}$.
$\overline{AC}$ corresponds to $\overline{XZ}$.
$\overline{BC}$ corresponds to $\overline{YZ}$.

② Write ratios of their lengths in a proportion.

$\dfrac{AB}{XY} = \dfrac{AC}{XZ}$

③ Substitute the information you know.

$\dfrac{5}{2} = \dfrac{7.5}{n}$

④ Write cross products. Solve for n.

$5n = 2 \cdot 7.5$
$n = 3$

The length of $\overline{XZ}$ is 3 units.

The figures are similar. Find the corresponding sides. Then complete the proportion and solve for n.

1. $\overline{AB}$ corresponds to _____ .

   $\overline{BC}$ corresponds to _____ .

   $\overline{CA}$ corresponds to _____ .

2. $\dfrac{CA}{SQ} = \dfrac{\boxed{}}{RS}$

   $\dfrac{8}{20} = \dfrac{\boxed{}}{\boxed{}}$

   $n = $ _____

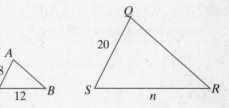

The pairs of figures below are similar. Find the value of each variable.

3. _____

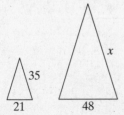

4. _____

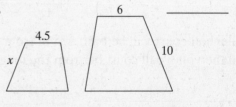

Course 2 Topics

Review 148

A **scale drawing** is an enlarged or reduced drawing of an object. A map is a scale drawing. On this map, the pool is 3 cm from the horse corral. What is the actual distance from the corral to the pool?

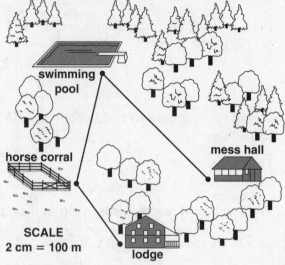

Silver Lake Camp

swimming pool

horse corral

mess hall

**SCALE
2 cm = 100 m**

lodge

① Use the scale. Write a ratio of distance on the map to actual distance.

$$\frac{\text{map (cm)}}{\text{actual (m)}} = \frac{2}{100}$$

② Write a proportion using the scale.

$$\frac{\text{map (cm)}}{\text{actual (m)}} = \frac{2}{100} = \frac{3}{n}$$

③ Use cross products. Solve for n.

$$2n = 100 \cdot 3$$
$$n = 150 \text{ m}$$

The pool is 150 m from the corral.

Use the information on the map. Write and solve a proportion to find the distance.

1. On the map, the mess hall is 4 cm from the pool. What is the actual distance from the pool to the mess hall?

$$\frac{\text{map}}{\text{actual}} = \frac{\square}{100} = \frac{\square}{n}$$

$$n = \underline{\hspace{1cm}}$$

2. The lodge is 2 cm from the horse corral on the map. What is the actual distance from the corral to the lodge?

$$\frac{\text{map}}{\text{actual}} = \frac{\square}{100} = \frac{\square}{n}$$

$$n = \underline{\hspace{1cm}}$$

3. The pool is actually 225 m from the lodge. How far would the pool be from the lodge on the map?

$$\frac{\text{map}}{\text{actual}} = \frac{\square}{100} = \frac{\square}{n}$$

$$n = \underline{\hspace{1cm}}$$

4. The mess hall is 150 m from the lodge. How far would the mess hall be from the lodge on the map?

$$\frac{\text{map}}{\text{actual}} = \frac{\square}{100} = \frac{\square}{n}$$

$$n = \underline{\hspace{1cm}}$$

5. A volleyball court will be built 175 m from the lodge. How far would the volleyball court be from the lodge on the map?

_____

Review 149

A **percent** is a ratio that compares a number to 100. The figure at the right contains 25 squares.

$\frac{9}{25}$ of the squares are shaded.

To write $\frac{9}{25}$ as a percent, follow these steps.

① Write a ratio with a denominator of 100 that is equal to $\frac{9}{25}$.

$$\frac{9}{25} = \frac{9 \cdot 4}{25 \cdot 4} = \frac{36}{100}$$

② Write the ratio as a percent.

$$\frac{36}{100} = 36\%$$

36% of the squares are shaded.

Write a percent for each shaded figure.

1.

_____

2.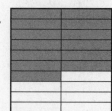

_____

3.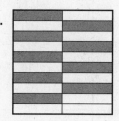

_____

4.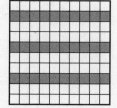

_____

5.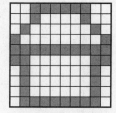

_____

6.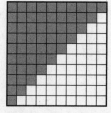

_____

Write each ratio as a percent.

7. $\frac{3}{5}$ _____

8. $\frac{17}{100}$ _____

9. $\frac{18}{25}$ _____

10. $\frac{13}{20}$ _____

11. $\frac{8}{10}$ _____

12. $\frac{1}{4}$ _____

13. $\frac{17}{50}$ _____

14. $\frac{11}{25}$ _____

15. $\frac{7}{20}$ _____

16. $\frac{21}{25}$ _____

17. $\frac{3}{10}$ _____

18. $\frac{16}{25}$ _____

19. $\frac{2}{5}$ _____

20. $\frac{99}{100}$ _____

21. $\frac{11}{20}$ _____

22. $\frac{13}{25}$ _____

23. $\frac{1}{10}$ _____

24. $\frac{39}{50}$ _____

25. $\frac{19}{20}$ _____

26. $\frac{6}{25}$ _____

Review 150

To write a percent as a fraction, write a fraction with 100 as the denominator.

$45\% = \dfrac{45}{100}$ ← **Denominator 100**

$= \dfrac{45 \div 5}{100 \div 5} = \dfrac{9}{20}$ ← **Simplify.**

$45\% = \dfrac{9}{20}$

To write a decimal as a percent, multiply by 100.	To write a percent as a decimal, divide by 100.
Write 0.85 as a percent.	Write 46% as a decimal.
$0.85 \cdot 100 = 85$	$46 \div 100 = 0.46$
$0.85 = 85\%$	$46\% = 0.46$

Write each fraction as a percent.

1. $\dfrac{3}{4}$

2. $\dfrac{12}{25}$

3. $\dfrac{4}{5}$

4. $\dfrac{23}{4}$

Write each percent as a fraction in simplest form.

5. 45%

6. 60%

7. 16%

8. 25%

9. 37.5%

10. 99%

11. 40%

12. 86%

Write each percent as a decimal or each decimal as a percent.

13. 35%

14. 48%

15. 116%

16. 8%

17. 12%

18. 5.5%

19. 400%

20. 0.6%

21. 0.39

22. 0.735

23. 0.86

24. 0.34

25. 0.4

26. 0.6

27. 0.004

28. 6

Review 151

You can express a percent that is less than 1% or greater than 100% as a decimal and as a fraction. A percent that is less than 1% is a quantity that is less than $\frac{1}{100}$. A percent that is greater than 100% is a quantity that is greater than 1.

- Write 0.5% as a decimal and as a fraction.

Move the decimal point two places to the left to write a percent as a decimal. Add zeros as needed.

$00.5\% = 0.005$

Since percent means per 100, you can write the percent as a fraction with a denominator of 100.

$0.5\% = \frac{0.5}{100}$

Then rewrite the numerator as a whole number. Since $10 \times 0.5 = 5$, multiply the numerator and the denominator by 10. Then simplify.

$\frac{0.5}{100} = \frac{0.5 \times 10}{100 \times 10} = \frac{5}{1,000} = \frac{1}{200}$

So, $0.5\% = 0.005 = \frac{1}{200}$.

- Write 125% as a decimal and as a fraction.

Move the decimal point two places to the left to write a percent as a decimal. Add zeros as needed.

$125\% = 1.25.$

Since percent means per 100, you can write the percent as a fraction with a denominator of 100.

$125\% = \frac{125}{100}$

Then simplify.

$\frac{125}{100} = \frac{125 \div 25}{100 \div 25} = \frac{5}{4} = 1\frac{1}{4}$

So, $125\% = 1.25 = 1\frac{1}{4}$.

Write each percent as a fraction and a decimal.

1. 0.01%

_____

2. 0.45%

_____

3. 0.2%

_____

4. 0.67%

_____

5. 150%

_____

6. 225%

_____

7. 186%

_____

8. 201%

_____

Review 152

		Find 12% of 50.	Find 150% of 90.
①	Write the percent as a decimal.	0.12	1.5
②	Multiply.	$0.12 \cdot 50 = 6$	$1.5 \cdot 90 = 135$
		12% of 50 is 6.	150% of 90 is 135.

Complete to find each answer.

1. 15% of 80

15% = _____

_____ · 80 = _____

2. 4% of 70

4% = _____

_____ · 70 = _____

3. 70% of 20

70% = _____

_____ · 20 = _____

Find each answer.

4. 10% of 80

_____

5. 20% of 80

_____

6. 50% of 80

_____

7. 75% of 80

_____

8. 9% of 70

_____

9. 2% of 66

_____

10. 28% of 50

_____

11. 75% of 20

_____

12. 16% of 35

_____

13. 94% of 22

_____

14. 33% of 50

_____

15. 40% of 45

_____

16. 120% of 30

_____

17. 110% of 70

_____

18. 160% of 200

_____

19. 180% of 250

_____

20. 145% of 78

_____

21. 187% of 40

_____

22. 164% of 350

_____

23. 125% of 230

_____

Solve.

24. Pablo's weekly salary is $105. Each week he saves 60% of his salary. How much does he save each week?

_____

25. The sixth-grade class is selling magazine subscriptions to raise money for charity. They will give 55% of the money they raise to the homeless. If they raise $2,670, how much do they give to the homeless?

_____

Course 2 Topics

Review 153

Solving Percent Problems Using Proportions

You can use proportions to solve percent problems. Remember, the percent is compared to 100.

Finding the part:

10% of 40 is __?__ .

$$\frac{10}{100} = \frac{n}{40}$$

$100 \cdot n = 10 \cdot 40$

$n = 4$

10% of 40 is 4.

Finding the whole:

20% of __?__ is 8.

$$\frac{20}{100} = \frac{8}{n}$$

$20 \cdot n = 100 \cdot 8$

$n = 40$

20% of 40 is 8.

Finding the percent:

__?__ % of 25 is 20.

$$\frac{n}{100} = \frac{20}{25}$$

$25 \cdot n = 100 \cdot 20$

$n = 80$

80% of 25 is 20.

Complete to solve for n.

1. 75% of __?__ is 12.

$$\frac{75}{100} = \frac{12}{n}$$

$75 \cdot \_\_\_\_ = 100 \cdot \_\_\_\_$

$n = \_\_\_\_$

2. 20% of __?__ is 82.

$$\frac{20}{100} = \frac{82}{\Box}$$

$75 \cdot \_\_\_\_ = 100 \cdot \_\_\_\_$

$n = \_\_\_\_$

3. 5% of __?__ is 9.

$$\frac{5}{100} = \frac{\Box}{n}$$

$\_\_\_\_ = \_\_\_\_$

$n = \_\_\_\_$

4. 60 is 5% of n.

$$\frac{5}{100} = \frac{n}{\Box}$$

$5n = 100 \cdot \_\_\_\_$

$n = \_\_\_\_$

5. 6% of n is 4.8.

$6n = \_\_\_\_ \cdot 4.8$

$n = \_\_\_\_$

6. 51 is 170% of n.

$\_\_\_\_ = \_\_\_\_$

$n = \_\_\_\_$

Use a proportion to solve.

7. 12% of n is 9.

_____

8. 49% of n is 26.95.

_____

9. 18% of n is 27.

_____

10. What is 210% of 44?

_____

11. What is 30% of 200?

_____

12. 64 is what percent of 80?

_____

Review 154

You can write equations to solve percent problems by substituting amounts into the statement: "_____ % of _____ is _____?"

- 64% of 50 is what number?

  ① Choose a variable for the unknown amount. Let n = unknown number.

  ② Reword the statement, _____ % of _____ is _____. 64% of 50 is n

  ③ Write an equation. $64\% \cdot 50 = n$

  ④ Write the percent as a decimal. $0.64 \cdot 50 = n$

  ⑤ Multiply to solve for n. $32 = n$

  ⑥ So, 64% of 50 is 32.

- What percent of 36 is 18?

  ① Choose a variable for the unknown amount. Let p = unknown percent.

  ② Reword the statement, _____ % of _____ is _____. $p\%$ of 36 is 18.

  ③ Write an equation. $36 \cdot p = 18$

  ④ Divide each side by 36. $36 \cdot \frac{p}{36} = \frac{18}{36}$

  ⑤ Simplify and write the decimal as a percent. $p = 0.5 = 50\%$

  ⑥ So, 18 is 50% of 36.

Answer each question.

1. Write an equation for: 9% of 150 is what number. _____ · _____ = n

2. Solve the equation to find 9% of 150 is what number? _____

3. 48% of 250 is what number? _____

4. 82% of 75 is what number? _____

5. 16% of 50 is what number? _____

6. 32% of 800 is what number? _____

7. Reword the statement: What percent of 75 is 12? _____ % of _____ is _____

8. Use the statement to find what percent of 75 is 12. _____

9. What percent of 60 is 18? _____

10. What percent of 50 is 35? _____

Review 155

Finding Sales Tax

sales tax = percent of tax · purchase price

Find the amount of sales tax on a television that costs $350 with an 8% sales tax.

sales tax = 8% · $350
sales tax = 0.08 · 350
sales tax = 28

The sales tax is $28.

How much does the television cost with sales tax?

$350 + $28 = $378

Finding a Commission

commission = commission rate · sales

Find the commission earned with a 3% commission rate on $3,000 in sales.

commission = 3% · $3,000
commission = 0.03 · 3,000
commission = 90

The commission earned is $90.

How much do you earn if you have a base salary of $500 plus 3% commission on sales of $3,000?

$90 + $500 = $590

Find each payment.

1. $10.00 with a 4% sales tax

   _____

2. $8.75 with a 5.25% sales tax

   _____

3. $61.00 with an 7% sales tax

   _____

4. $320.00 with a 6.5% sales tax

   _____

5. $6.30 with a 8% sales tax

   _____

6. $26.75 with a 7.5% sales tax

   _____

Find each commission.

7. 6% on $3,000 in sales

   _____

8. 1.5% on $400,000 in sales

   _____

9. 8% on $1,200 in sales

   _____

10. 5.5% on $2,400 in sales

    _____

Course 2 Topics

Review 156

Percent of change is the percent something increases or decreases from its original amount.

	Find the percent of increase from 12 to 18.	Find the percent of decrease from 20 to 12.
① Subtract to find the amount of change.	$18 - 12 = 6$	$20 - 12 = 8$
② Write a proportion. $\dfrac{\text{change}}{\text{original}} = \dfrac{\text{percent}}{100}$	$\dfrac{6}{12} = \dfrac{n}{100}$ $6 \cdot 100 = 12n$	$\dfrac{8}{20} = \dfrac{n}{100}$ $8 \cdot 100 = 20n$
③ Solve for n.	$n = 50$	$n = 40$
	The percent of increase is 50%.	The percent of decrease is 40%.

State whether the change is an *increase* or *decrease*. Complete to find the percent of change.

1. 40 to 60

$$60 - 40 = \underline{\hspace{1cm}}$$

$$\frac{\boxed{}}{40} = \frac{n}{100}$$

$$\underline{\hspace{1.5cm}} \cdot 100 = 40n$$

$$n = \underline{\hspace{1cm}}$$

_____

2. 15 to 9

$$15 - 9 = \underline{\hspace{1cm}}$$

$$\frac{\boxed{}}{15} = \frac{n}{100}$$

$$\underline{\hspace{1.5cm}} \cdot 100 = 15n$$

$$n = \underline{\hspace{1cm}}$$

_____

3. 0.4 to 0.9

$$0.9 - 0.4 = \underline{\hspace{1cm}}$$

$$\frac{\boxed{}}{0.4} = \frac{n}{\boxed{}}$$

$$\underline{\hspace{1.5cm}} = 0.4n$$

$$n = \underline{\hspace{1cm}}$$

_____

Find the percent of *increase*.

4. 16 to 40

5. 22 to 66

6. 4 to 8

7. 20 to 22

_____ _____ _____ _____

8. 9 to 18

9. 28 to 35

10. 80 to 112

11. 150 to 165

_____ _____ _____ _____

Find the percent of *decrease*.

12. 20 to 15

13. 100 to 57

14. 52 to 26

15. 90 to 45

_____ _____ _____ _____

16. 140 to 126

17. 75 to 72

18. 1000 to 990

19. 420 to 357

_____ _____ _____ _____

Course 2 Topics

Review 157

The cost for a car and driver on a car ferry is $15. Each additional passenger is $2. If Brett pays a toll of $21, how many additional passengers does he have?

Read and Understand   What information are you given? *You know the cost for the car and driver, and the cost for each passenger.* What are you asked to find? *You want to find the number of additional passengers.*

Plan and Solve   You are given a relationship between numbers. So, an equation may help solve the problem. The toll is $15 for the car and driver plus $2 for each passenger ($p$).

$$15 + 2p = \text{toll}$$

$$15 + 2p = 21$$

Solve the equation for p.

$$15 + 2p = 21$$

$$15 - 15 + 2p = 21 - 15 \qquad \leftarrow \textbf{Subtract 15.}$$

$$2p = 6 \qquad \leftarrow \textbf{Simplify.}$$

$$\frac{2p}{2} = \frac{6}{2} \qquad \leftarrow \textbf{Divide by 2.}$$

$$p = 3 \qquad \leftarrow \textbf{Simplify.}$$

There are 3 passengers.

Look Back and Check $15 for car + 2×3 additional passengers = $21.

Write and solve an equation for each problem.

1. Mia is 8 years older than Kenji. Mia is 26 years old. How old is Kenji?

   _____

2. The perimeter of a rectangle is 100 in. The width is 18 in. Find the length.

   _____

3. A jacket costs $28 more than twice the cost of a pair of slacks. If the jacket costs $152, how much do the slacks cost?

   _____

4. Jennifer has $22.75 in her bank. She saves quarters and half dollars. She has $10.50 in half dollars. How many quarters does she have?

   _____

5. One number is 6 less than another number. Their sum is 20. Find the greater number.

   _____

6. Sari has 11 more markers than Sam. Together they have 61 markers. How many markers does Sam have?

   _____

Course 2 Topics

Name _____ Class _____ Date _____

Review 158

Lines and Planes

A plane is an infinite flat surface. A line is a series of points that extends in two opposite directions without end. Lines in a plane that never meet are called **parallel** lines. Lines that intersect to form a right angle (90°) are called **perpendicular** lines. Intersecting lines have exactly one common point.

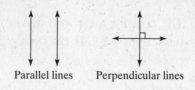
Parallel lines   Perpendicular lines

A line segment is formed by two endpoints and all the points between them.

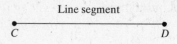
Line segment
C ———————— D

Course 2 Topics

• Use the figure to name a line segment, a point, two intersecting lines, and a pair of parallel lines.

Two endpoints are *S* and *U,* so they form a line segment, $\overline{SU}$.

There are 5 points, *R, S, M, U, T.*

Intersecting lines have exactly one point in common. So, $\overleftrightarrow{RU}$ and $\overline{SU}$ are intersecting lines.

Line $\overleftrightarrow{TU}$ never intersects line $\overleftrightarrow{RS}$, so $\overleftrightarrow{TU}$ and $\overleftrightarrow{RS}$ are parallel lines.

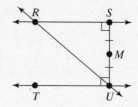

Write *parallel* or *perpendicular* to describe the lines formed by this book.

1. Top and bottom sides _____ 2. Top and left sides _____

Use the figure to name each of the following.

3. a line segment _____

4. a point _____

5. two pairs of intersecting lines _____

6. a pair of parallel lines _____

7. Sketch a rectangle to represent a bulletin board.

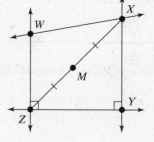

   a. Write *parallel* or *perpendicular* to describe the lines formed by the left and right sides of a bulletin board.

   b. Write *parallel* or *perpendicular* to describe the lines that meet at a corner of the bulletin board.

   _____   _____

Use a straightedge to draw each figure.

8. $\overleftrightarrow{AB}$ 9. $\overline{BC}$ 10. $\overrightarrow{MN}$

© Pearson Education, Inc. All rights reserved.

Review 159

An **angle** is made up of two rays (the *sides* of the angle) with a common endpoint (the *vertex* of the angle).

You can name this angle $\angle A$, $\angle BAC$, or $\angle CAB$.

$\angle A$ is an **acute** angle because its measure is less than 90°. If an angle has a measure greater than 90° and less than 180°, it is an **obtuse** angle.

You can measure an angle using a protractor. Write the measure of $\angle A$ as $m\angle A$.

To measure an angle:

① Place the center point of your protractor on the vertex of the angle.

② Line up one side of the angle with zero on the protractor scale.

③ Read the scale at the second side of the angle. Since $\angle A$ is an acute angle, read 80° and not 100°.

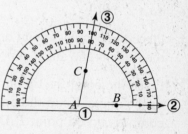

acute
less than 90°

obtuse
greater than 90°
less than 180°

$m\angle A = 80°$

Measure each angle. Then circle *acute* or *obtuse*.

1.

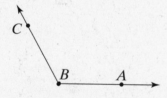

$m\angle B =$ _____

acute   obtuse

2.

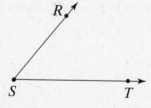

$m\angle S =$ _____

acute   obtuse

3.

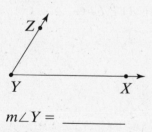

$m\angle Y =$ _____

acute   obtuse

4.

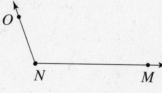

$m\angle N =$ _____

acute   obtuse

Classify each angle with the given measure as *acute* or *obtuse*.

5. 45° _____

6. 148° _____

7. 4° _____

8. 106° _____

9. 65° _____

10. 179° _____

11. 23° _____

12. 115° _____

Review 160

To bisect $\overline{AB}$:

① Open the compass more than half the length of $\overline{AB}$. With the compass tip on A, draw an arc.

② Without changing the opening, move the compass tip to B. Draw another arc.

③ Draw $\overleftrightarrow{CD}$ through the intersections of the arcs. $\overleftrightarrow{CD}$ is the bisector of $\overline{AB}$. Point M is the midpoint of $\overline{AB}$.

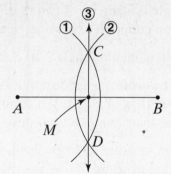

To bisect $\angle ABC$:

① Place the compass point on vertex B. Draw an arc intersecting the sides of the angle at points P and M.

② Place the compass tip on point M. Draw an arc in the interior of the angle. Keep the opening the same and place the compass tip on point P. Draw a second arc intersecting the first at point Q.

③ Draw $\overrightarrow{BQ}$. $\overrightarrow{BQ}$ is the bisector of $\angle ABC$.

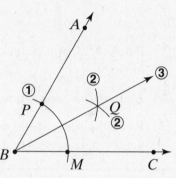

Complete each construction to bisect the figure.

1.

Bisect $\overline{ST}$.

2.

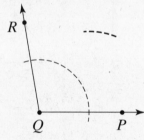

Bisect $\angle RQP$.

3.

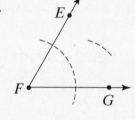

Bisect $\angle EFG$.

Bisect each figure.

4.

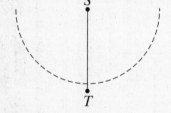

5.

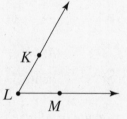

6.

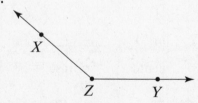

Review 161

Classifying Triangles by Angles	Classifying Triangles by Sides
Acute triangle: three acute angles	**Equilateral triangle:** three congruent sides
Right triangle: one right angle	**Isosceles triangle:** at least two congruent sides
Obtuse triangle: one obtuse angle	**Scalene triangle:** no congruent sides

The sum of the measures of the angles of a triangle is 180°.

Find the value of x in the triangle at the right.

$$x = m\angle A$$
$$m\angle A + 40° + 78° = 180°$$
$$m\angle A + 118° = 180°$$
$$m\angle A = 180° - 118°$$
$$m\angle A = 62°$$
$$x = 62°$$

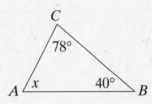

Classify each triangle by its sides and then by its angles.

1.

_____

2.

_____

3.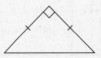

_____

4.

_____

5.

_____

6.

_____

Find the value of x in each triangle.

7.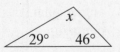

_____

8.

_____

9.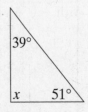

_____

Review 162

You name polygons by the number of sides. A **quadrilateral** is a polygon with four sides. The table shows the names and properties of some special quadrilaterals.

Special Quadrilaterals

Quadrilateral	Figure	Only 1 Pair of Parallel Sides	2 Pairs of Parallel Sides	All Sides Must be Congruent	Opposite Sides Are Congruent	All Angles Must Be Right Angles
Square			✔	✔	✔	✔
Rectangle			✔		✔	✔
Rhombus			✔	✔	✔	
Parallelogram			✔		✔	
Trapezoid		✔				

Look at the rhombus. It is also a parallelogram, but the name rhombus is best because it gives the most information about the figure.

Write the best name for each quadrilateral.

1.

2.

3.

4.

_____   _____   _____   _____

Draw each of the following.

5. a trapezoid with a right angle

6. a quadrilateral with opposite sides parallel and a right angle

7. a regular octagon

8. an irregular pentagon

Course 2 Topics

Review 163

One acute angle of a right triangle is 35°. What is the measure of the other acute angle?

Read and Understand What kind of triangle is given? *A right triangle is given.* What do you know about a right triangle? *It has one 90° angle and two acute angles.* What are you given? *You are given one acute angle that measures 35°.* What do you want to find? *You want to find the measure of the other acute angle.*

Plan and Solve A good strategy for this problem is to draw a diagram. Show a right triangle with the acute angle labeled and the right angle marked.

Remember that the sum of the angle measures of a triangle is 180°. The diagram reminds you that the right angle measures 90°.

$$180° - (90° + 35°) = 180° - 125°$$
$$= 55°$$

The measure of the third angle is 55°.

Look Back and Check Check by adding: 55° + 35° + 90° = 180°

Solve each problem by drawing a diagram.

1. One acute angle of a right triangle is 42°. What is the measure of the other acute angle?

2. One of the two equal angles of an isosceles triangle is 48°. What are the measures of the other two angles?

_____

3. A square garden is enclosed by a fence that has 9 posts on each side. How many posts are there in all?

4. A piece of string is cut in half. Then each piece is cut in half. Each of those pieces is cut in half. How many cuts were made?

_____

5. You planned to bike 120 mi on your vacation. On the first day you biked $\frac{1}{2}$ of the distance. On the next day you biked $\frac{1}{4}$ of the remaining distance. How far did you have left to go?

6. Newtown is 522 km west of Jamesburg. Pottsville is 356 km east of Jamesburg and 928 km east of Mayfield. How far and in what direction is Newtown from Mayfield?

_____

Review 164

Congruent polygons have congruent sides and angles. These are called the *corresponding parts* of the congruent figures.

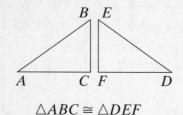

$\triangle ABC \cong \triangle DEF$

Corresponding Angles	Corresponding Sides
$\angle A \cong \angle D$	$BC \cong EF$
$\angle B \cong \angle E$	$CA \cong FD$
$\angle C \cong \angle F$	$AB \cong DE$

Complete each congruence statement.

1. $\triangle LMN \cong \triangle RPQ$

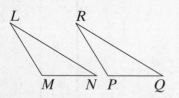

$\overline{MN} \cong \overline{PQ}$ $\angle M \cong \angle P$

$\overline{NL} \cong$ _____ $\angle L \cong$ _____

2. $\triangle FGJ \cong \triangle YWX$

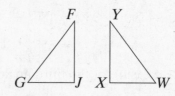

$\overline{JF} \cong \overline{XY}$ $\angle G \cong \angle W$

$\overline{FG} \cong$ _____ $\angle J \cong$ _____

3. $\triangle ABC \cong \triangle DEF$ **a.** $\angle A \cong$ _____   **b.** $\angle B \cong$ _____   **c.** $\angle C \cong$ _____

d. $\overline{AC} \cong$ _____   **e.** $\overline{BC} \cong$ _____   **f.** $\overline{AB} \cong$ _____

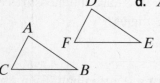

Are the figures below *congruent* or *not congruent*? Explain.

4.

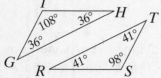

_____

_____

_____

5.

_____

_____

_____

Review 165

A **circle** is the set of points in a plane that are all the same distance from a point, called the *center*. This circle is called circle *A*.

$\overline{AB}$ is a **radius** of circle *A*. It is a segment that has one endpoint on the circle and the other at the center. $\overline{AC}$ and $\overline{AD}$ are also *radii* of circle *A*.

$\overline{DC}$ is a **diameter** of circle *A*. It is a segment that passes through the center of the circle and has both endpoints on the circle.

$\overline{DE}$ is a chord of circle *A*. A **chord** is a segment that has both endpoints on the circle.

$\overarc{DB}$ is an arc of circle *A*. An **arc** is part of a circle.

$\angle DAB$ is a **central angle** of circle *A*. It is an angle with its vertex at the center of the circle.

$\overarc{DEC}$ is a **semicircle.** A semicircle is an arc that is half a circle.

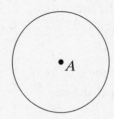 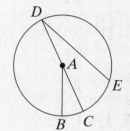

Name each of the following for circle *P*.

1. all radii _____

2. all chords _____

3. 3 arcs _____

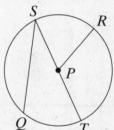

Name each of the following shown for circle *M*.

4. all diameters

   _____

5. 3 central angles

   _____

6. all chords

   _____

7. 2 semicircles

   _____

8. two radii

   _____

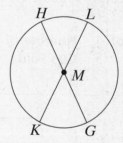

Review 166

Use the information in the table to create a circle graph.

The class took a survey of what time students usually go to sleep.
To make a circle graph:

① Find the total number of students.

② Use a proportion to find the measure of each central angle. Round to the nearest degree.

③ Use a compass. Draw a circle. Use a protractor. Draw the central angles. Label each sector.

Time Students Go to Sleep

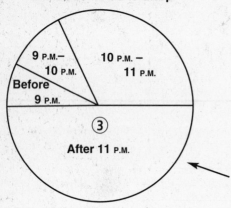

Time Students Go to Sleep	Number of Students	② Central Angle Measure
Before 9 P.M.	2	$\frac{2}{28} = \frac{a}{360°}$ $a \approx 26°$
9 P.M.–10 P.M.	3	$\frac{3}{28} = \frac{b}{360°}$ $b \approx 39°$
10 P.M.–11 P.M.	9	$\frac{9}{28} = \frac{c}{360°}$ $c \approx 116°$
After 11 P.M.	14	$\frac{14}{28} = \frac{d}{360°}$ $d \approx 180°$
① Total	28	

The central angle measures add to 361° because of rounding, but the difference does not show in the graph.

Complete the table. Draw a circle graph of the data.

Tuesday's Music CD Sales

Type of Music	Number of CDs Sold	Central Angle Measure
Country	10	
Rock	8	
Jazz	16	
Rap	14	
Total		

Tuesday's Music CD Sales

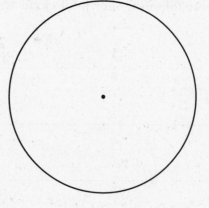

Course 2 Topics

Review 167

To choose a reasonable estimate determine if the measurement is
small like inches or centimeters or big like feet, yards, or meters.

Choose a reasonable estimate. Explain your choice.

• Which is a better estimate for the height of an office building? 20 in. or 20 yd?

The height of an office building is tall, so 20 yd is the better estimate.

• To estimate the area of a figure, estimate the number of square units contained in the figure.

Each square unit represents 1 ft^2.
Estimate the area.

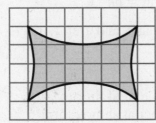

12 whole squares
partial squares ≈ 2 whole squares

12 + 2 = 14

The area is about 14 ft^2.

Estimate the length of the line segment by each number in inches.

1.

   _____

2. ⊢————⊣

   _____

Estimate the length of the line segment by each number in centimeters.

3. ⊢—————⊣

   _____

4. ⊢———⊣

   _____

Choose a reasonable estimate. Explain your choice.

5. height of a refrigerator: 6 in. or 6 ft

   _____

   _____

6. height of a stop sign: 8 ft or 8 yd

   _____

   _____

**Each square on the grids below represents 10 mi^2. Estimate the area
of each region.**

7.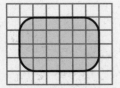

   _____

8.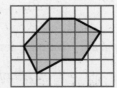

   _____

Review 168

Areas of Parallelograms and Triangles

You can use the area of a rectangle to find the area of a parallelogram.

① Draw a perpendicular segment from one vertex to the opposite side to form a triangle.

② Move the triangle to the right side of the parallelogram to form a rectangle.

③ Find the area of the rectangle.
A = length $\times$ width = base $\times$ height = bh

The parallelogram has the same base, height, and area as the rectangle.

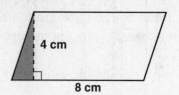

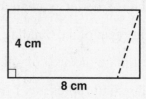

$$A = bh$$
$$= 8 \cdot 4$$
$$= 32 \text{ cm}^2$$

You can use the area of a parallelogram to find the area of a triangle. Two identical triangles, together as shown, form a parallelogram. Each triangle has half the area of the parallelogram.

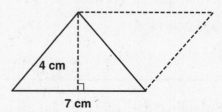

Area of parallelogram: $A = bh$

Area of triangle: $\quad = \frac{1}{2}bh = \frac{1}{2} \cdot 7 \cdot 4 = 14 \text{ cm}^2$

Find the area of each figure.

1.

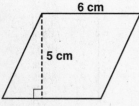

_____

2.

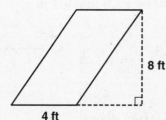

_____

3.

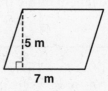

_____

4.

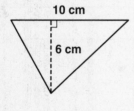

_____

5.

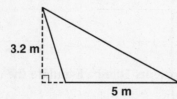

_____

6.

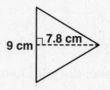

_____

Find the area of a parallelogram with base length b and height h.

7. $b = 7$ in., $h = 4$ in.

8. $b = 9$ m, $h = 1.5$ m

9. $b = 1.25$ cm, $h = 2$ cm

_____   _____   _____

Course 2 Topics

Review 169

Trapezoid

Two identical trapezoids, together as shown, form a parallelogram. The trapezoid has half the area of the parallelogram.

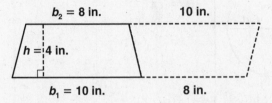

Area of parallelogram: $A = (b_1 + b_2)h$

Area of trapezoid: $A = \frac{1}{2}h(b_1 + b_2)$

$= \frac{1}{2}(4)(10 + 8)$

$= 2(18) = 36 \text{ in.}^2$

Irregular Figures

Not all geometric figures are shapes with which you are familiar. Some of them, however, can be divided into familiar shapes.

Find the area of the figure.

Use the area formulas to find the areas of the triangle and the rectangle.

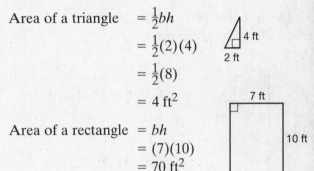

Area of a triangle $= \frac{1}{2}bh$

$= \frac{1}{2}(2)(4)$

$= \frac{1}{2}(8)$

$= 4 \text{ ft}^2$

Area of a rectangle $= bh$

$= (7)(10)$

$= 70 \text{ ft}^2$

Find the total area by adding the area of each figure.

Total area = area of triangle + area of rectangle

$= 4 + 70$

$= 74$

The total area is 74 ft^2.

Find the area of each figure.

1.

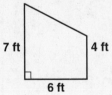

2.

3.

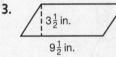

4.

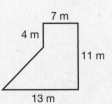

5.

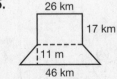

6.

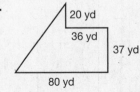

Review 170

The **circumference** of a circle is the distance around it. To find the circumference of a circle with radius r and diameter d, use either the formula $C = 2\pi r$ or $C = \pi d$. Use 3.14 for π.

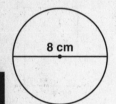

$$d = 8 \text{ cm}$$
$$C = \pi d$$
$$\approx 3.14 \cdot 8$$
$$= 25.12 \text{ cm}$$

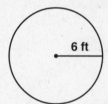

$$r = 6 \text{ ft}$$
$$C = 2\pi r$$
$$\approx 2 \cdot 3.14 \cdot 6$$
$$= 37.68 \text{ ft}$$

To the nearest centimeter, the circumference is 25 cm.

To the nearest foot, the circumference is 38 ft.

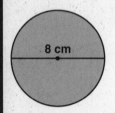

To find the area of a circle, use $A = \pi r^2$.
The diameter of the circle is 8 cm, so the radius is 4 cm.

$$A = \pi r^2$$
$$\approx 3.14 \cdot 4 \cdot 4$$
$$= 50.24 \text{ cm}^2$$

To the nearest square centimeter, the area is 50 cm^2.

Find the circumference and area of each circle. Round your answer to the nearest whole unit.

1.

7 cm

_____

2.

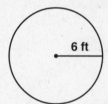

2 in.

_____

3.

10 m

_____

4.

2 cm

_____

5.

3 ft

_____

6.

8 yd

_____

Course 2 Topics

Review 171

The number 25 is a **perfect square.**

It is the square of the whole number 5. $\quad 5^2 = 25$

5 is the **square root** of 25. $\quad\quad\quad\quad 5 = \sqrt{25}$

You can find the length of a side of a square
by finding the square root of the area.

$$s^2 = A = 225$$
$$s = \sqrt{A} = \sqrt{225} = 15$$

The length of each side is 15 in.

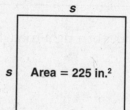

s

s | Area = 225 in.²

You can use patterns to find the square roots
of some larger numbers.

$$9^2 = 81 \rightarrow 90^2 = 8{,}100$$
$$9 = \sqrt{81} \rightarrow 90 = \sqrt{8{,}100}$$

A **rational number** is a ratio of two integers, $\frac{a}{b}$, where $b \neq 0$. Since
terminating decimals and repeating decimals can be written as ratios,
they are rational. Irrational numbers are numbers that cannot be
written as ratios. Decimals that do not end or repeat are irrational
numbers.

Find each of the following.

1. $\sqrt{144}$ _____

2. $\sqrt{36}$ _____

3. $\sqrt{100}$ _____

4. $\sqrt{2{,}500}$ _____

5. $\sqrt{324}$ _____

6. $\sqrt{400}$ _____

Find the length of a side of a square with the given area.

7. $A = 49 \text{ cm}^2$
side $= \sqrt{49} =$ _____

8. $A = 81 \text{ in.}^2$
side $= \sqrt{81} =$ _____

9. $A = 144 \text{ cm}^2$
side $= \sqrt{144} =$ _____

10. $A = 625 \text{ in.}^2$ _____

11. $A = 676 \text{ ft}^2$ _____

12. $A = 3{,}600 \text{ yd}^2$ _____

Identify each number as rational or irrational.

13. $1\frac{1}{3}$ _____

14. $\sqrt{15}$ _____

15. 7 _____

16. $\sqrt{144}$ _____

Review 172

Course 2 Topics

Pythagorean Theorem

$$a^2 + b^2 = c^2$$

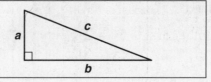

If you know the lengths of two sides of a right triangle, you can find the length of the third side.

Find the length of *a*.

$$a^2 + b^2 = c^2$$
$$a^2 + 12^2 = 13^2$$
$$a^2 + 144 = 169$$
$$a^2 = 169 - 144$$
$$a^2 = 25$$
$$a = 5$$

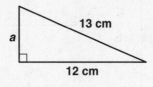

If $a^2 + b^2 = c^2$, then the triangle is a right triangle.

Is this triangle a right triangle?

$\underline{3^2 + 4^2} = 9 + 16 = 25 = \underline{5^2}$

Yes, the triangle is a right triangle.

Find each missing length. Round your answer to the nearest tenth of a unit.

1.

_____

2.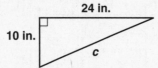

_____

3.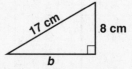

_____

4.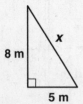

_____

5.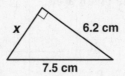

_____

6.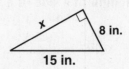

_____

7. A ladder leans against a wall 6 ft above the ground. The base of the ladder is 3 ft from the wall. How long is the ladder?

_____

8. A small rectangular tray measures 16 cm by 18 cm. How long is the diagonal?

_____

Review 173

A **prism** is a three-dimensional figure with two parallel and congruent polygonal **bases.** It is named by the shape of a base.

Rectangular prism
The bases are rectangles.

rectangular
prism

Triangular prism
The bases are triangles.

triangular
prism

Hexagonal prism
The bases are hexagons.

hexagonal
prism

A **pyramid** is a three-dimensional figure with only one base.

Triangular pyramid
The base is a triangle.

triangular
pyramid

Square pyramid
The base is a square.

square
pyramid

The **cylinder, cone,** and **sphere** are also three-dimensional figures.

cylinder   cone   sphere

Give the best name for each figure.

1.

_____

2.

_____

3.

_____

4.

_____

5.

_____

6.

_____

7.

_____

8.

_____

9.

_____

Course 2 Topics

Review 174

The **surface area** of a prism is the sum of the areas of its faces. You can use a **net,** or pattern, for the prism to help you find its surface area.

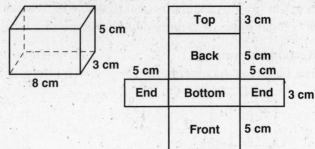

• Add the areas of all the surfaces.

Surface Area
= front + back + top + bottom + end + end
= $(8 \cdot 5) + (8 \cdot 5) + (8 \cdot 3) + (8 \cdot 3) + (5 \cdot 3) + (5 \cdot 3)$
= $40 + 40 + 24 + 24 + 15 + 15$
= 158 cm^2

• To find the surface area of a cylinder, add the area of the rectangle and the areas of the bases. Use $\pi = 3.14$.

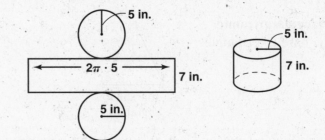

Surface area
= top + bottom + side (rectangle)
= $(\pi \cdot 5 \cdot 5) + (\pi \cdot 5 \cdot 5) + (2\pi \cdot 5 \cdot 7)$
= $(25\pi) + (25\pi) + (70\pi)$
≈ $120(3.14) = 376.8 \text{ in.}^2$

Use the net to find the surface area. Round your answers to the nearest whole unit.

1.

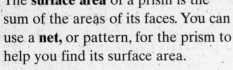

_____

2.

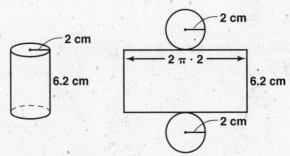

_____

Draw a net for each figure. Then find the surface area to the nearest tenth of a unit.

3.

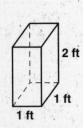

_____

4.

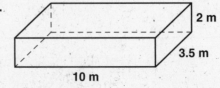

_____

Course 2 Topics

Review 175

The **volume** of a three-dimensional figure is the number of cubic units needed to fill the space inside the figure. A **cubic unit** is a cube whose edges are 1 unit long. You can find the volume of a prism or a cylinder by finding the *area of the base* (*B*) and multiplying by the *height* (*h*). Use $\pi = 3.14$.

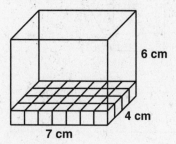

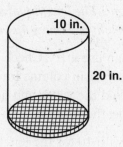

$B = lw$
$B = 7 \cdot 4 = 28 \text{ cm}^2$
$V = Bh$
$V = 28 \cdot 6 = 168 \text{ cm}^3$
The volume is 168 cubic centimeters.

$B = \pi r^2$
$B \approx 3.14 \cdot 10 \cdot 10 = 314 \text{ in.}^2$
$V = Bh$
$V \approx 314 \cdot 20 = 6{,}280 \text{ in.}^3$
The volume is 6,280 cubic inches.

Complete to find the volume to the nearest tenth of a unit.

1.

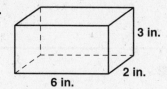

$V = Bh = lwh$

$= \underline{\hspace{1cm}} \cdot \underline{\hspace{1cm}} \cdot \underline{\hspace{1cm}}$

$= \underline{\hspace{2cm}}$

2.

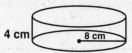

$V = Bh = \pi r^2 h$

$\approx 3.14 \cdot \underline{\hspace{1cm}} \cdot \underline{\hspace{1cm}} \cdot \underline{\hspace{1cm}}$

$= \underline{\hspace{2cm}}$

Find the volume. Round to the nearest cubic unit.

3.

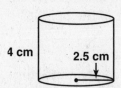

4.

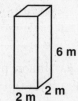

5.

_____   _____   _____

Name _____ Class _____ Date _____

Review 176

The length and width of a rectangular prism are equal and the height is 2 times that amount. If the volume of the prism is 3,456 m³, what are the dimensions of the rectangle?

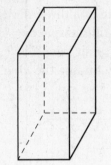

Read and Understand

What is the volume of the prism? What do you know about the dimensions? *The volume is 3,456 m³. The length and width are the same. The height is 2 times that dimension.*

Plan and Solve

You can use a Try, Check, and Revise strategy and the prism volume formula. Try the length, then find the width and height. Multiply to find volume, then check.

① Start with 10 for the length. The width would be 10 and the height 20. Volume of 2,000 is not enough.

② Try 15 for the length. The width would be 15 and the height 30. Volume of 6,750 is too much.

③ Try 12 m. A length of 12 m gives the correct volume.

Length	Width	Height	Volume
① 10	10	20	2,000
② 15	15	30	6,750
③ 12	12	24	3,456

Look Back and Check

The guesses of 10 and 15 helped you make the next guess of 12.

Use Try, Check, and Revise, or write an equation to solve each problem.

1. The product of two numbers is 2,250. Their difference is 5. What are the two numbers?

   _____

2. The length of a rectangle is twice the width. The area of the rectangle is 648 ft². How long is the rectangle?

   _____

3. Kevin opened a book. The product of the 2 page numbers was 7,832. What are the page numbers?

   _____

4. The base of a triangle is 8 cm and the area is 36 cm². What is the height?

   _____

5. One leg of a right triangle measures 8 m. The other leg measures 6 m. Find the length of the hypotenuse.

   _____

6. Jason purchased three pennants for $5.60, two sweatshirts, and 1 ball hat for $15.50. He paid the cashier $100 and received $49.90 in change. If the sweatshirts were the same price, how much was one sweatshirt?

   _____

Review 177

Graphs can help you visualize the relationship between data. A graph includes two scales, the horizontal axis and the vertical axis. An interval is the distance between the values on a scale.

Graph the data in the table.

Step 1 Choose the scales and intervals.

Graph the data in the first column on the horizontal axis. Graph the data in the second column on the vertical axis.

Choose the interval for the scale on the horizontal axis. The greatest number of hours worked is 9. If each interval is 1 hour, then the number of intervals is $9 \div 1 = 9$.

Choose the interval for the scale on the vertical axis. The greatest amount of money earned is $74.25. If each interval is $5, then the number of intervals is $74.25 \div 5 = 14.85$, or 15 intervals.

Step 2 Draw the graph and plot the data. Estimate the position of data points that fall between intervals.

Hours Worked	Money Earned
5	$41.25
6	$49.50
7	$57.75
8	$66.00
9	$74.25

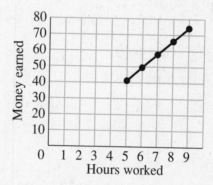

Graph the data in each table.

1.

Hours	Miles Run
2	10
2.8	14
3.2	16
3.6	18

2.

Gallons of Gas	Miles Driven
0.5	13
1.5	39
2.5	65
3	78

Review 178

A set of numbers that follows a pattern forms a **sequence.** The numbers 2, 4, 6, 8, . . . form a sequence. The three dots ". . ." tell you that the pattern continues. The numbers 2, 4, 6, 8, and so on are the **terms** of the sequence.

Course 2 Topics

Arithmetic Sequence

Add the same number to each term to get the next term. In the sequence 2, 4, 6, 8, . . . , you add 2 to each term to get the next term.

Write a rule to describe this sequence, and find the next three terms.
5, 10, 15, 20, . . .

$$5 \quad 10 \quad 15 \quad 20$$
$$\underset{+5}{\smile} \quad \underset{+5}{\smile} \quad \underset{+5}{\smile}$$

Start with 5 and add 5 repeatedly.

To find the next three terms, add 5.

$$20 + 5 = 25$$
$$25 + 5 = 30$$
$$30 + 5 = 35$$

The next three terms are 25, 30, and 35.

Geometric Sequence

Multiply each term by the same number to get the next term. In the sequence 1, 4, 16, 64, . . . , you multiply each term by 4 to get the next term.

Write a rule to describe this sequence, and find the next three terms.
2 , 4, 8, 16, . . .

$$2 \quad 4 \quad 8 \quad 16$$
$$\underset{\times 2}{\smile} \quad \underset{\times 2}{\smile} \quad \underset{\times 2}{\smile}$$

Start with 2 and multiply by 2 repeatedly.

To find the next three terms, multiply by 2.

$$16 \times 2 = 32$$
$$32 \times 2 = 64$$
$$64 \times 2 = 128$$

The next three terms are 32, 64, and 128.

Write a rule for each arithmetic sequence. Then find the next three terms.

1. 4, 7, 10, 13, . . .

2. 2, 4, 6, 8, . . .

3. 20, 35, 50, . . .

_____

_____

_____

Write a rule for each geometric sequence. Then find the next three terms.

4. 5, 25, 125, 625, . . .

5. 7, 49, 343, 2,401, . . .

6. 0.3, 0.9, 2.7, 8.1, . . .

_____

_____

_____

Review 179

A table can help you write a variable expression that describes a sequence.

Give the next two terms in this sequence: 6, 12, 18, 24, 30 . . .

Term number	1	2	3	4	5
Term	6	12	18	24	30

The rule is *"multiply the term number by 6."*

So, the next two terms will be 36 and 42.

Give the next two terms in this sequence: 4, 8, 12, 16, 20, . . .

1. What will you multiply the term number by to find the corresponding term? _____

2. Let n = term number. Write an expression that shows this relationship. _____

3. How will you find the sixth term in the sequence? the seventh term? _____

4. What are the sixth and seventh terms?

   _____

Give the next two terms in this sequence: 5, 7, 9, 11, 13, . . .

5. If n equals the term number, circle the expression that gives the rule for this sequence.

   $2n + 1$ $\qquad\qquad$ $n - 3$ $\qquad\qquad$ $2n + 3$ $\qquad\qquad$ $n + 3$

6. How will you find the sixth term in the sequence? the seventh term?

   _____

7. What are the sixth and seventh terms?

   _____

Let n equal the term number. Circle the expression that gives the rule for each sequence.

8. 2, 5, 8, 11, 14 . . . $\qquad$ $2n - 1$ $\qquad\qquad$ $3n - 1$ $\qquad\qquad$ $3n + 1$

9. 1, 4, 9, 25, 36, . . . $\qquad$ $n + 5$ $\qquad\qquad$ n^2 $\qquad\qquad$ $n^2 - 1$

10. 5, 10, 15, 20, 25 . . . $\qquad$ $5n$ $\qquad\qquad$ n^5 $\qquad\qquad$ $n + 5$

Review 180

The function table shows the relationship between inputs and outputs.
A function rule for this table is:

output = 4 · input

Input	Output
1	4
2	8
3	12

You can use the function rule $y = 2x + 3$ to find y when $x = 0, 1, 2,$ and 3.
Replace x with $0, 1, 2,$ and 3.

x	y = 2x + 3
0	2(0) + 3 = 3
1	2(1) + 3 = 5
2	2(2) + 3 = 7
3	2(3) + 3 = 9

Write input-output function rules for each table of values.

1.

Input	Output
3	6
4	8
5	10
6	12

_____

2.

Input	Output
1	3
2	4
3	5
4	6

_____

3.

Input	Output
1	45
2	90
3	135
4	180

_____

Make a table for the function represented by each rule. Find y when $x = 0, 1, 2,$ and 3.

4. $y = 10x$

x	y
0	
1	
2	
3	

5. $y = x - 4$

x	y
0	
1	
2	
3	

6. $y = 2x + 4$

x	y
0	
1	
2	
3	

7. $y = 3x - 1$

x	y
0	
1	
2	
3	

8. A printer can print 9 black and white pages per minute.

a. Write a function rule to represent the relationship between the number of black and white printed pages and the time it takes to print them. _____

b. How many black and white pages can be printed in 15 minutes? _____

c. How long would it take to print a 75 page black and white report? _____

Review 181

If you ride a bicycle at 12 mi/h, the distance you ride is a **function** of time. For each input value (time), there is exactly one output value (distance).

- You can represent the relationship between time and distance with a table.

Input (hours)	1	2	3	4
Output (miles)	12	24	36	48

- You can represent the relationship, or function, with a rule.

  output $= 12 \cdot$ input
  distance $= 12 \cdot$ time

- You can represent the relationship, or function, with a graph.

① Graph the points from the table.
(1, 12), (2, 24), (3, 36), (4, 48)

② Draw a line through the points.

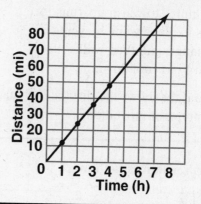

Graph the equation $y = -2x$.

1. Complete the table of values for the equation $y = -2x$. Then write each pair of values as ordered pairs.

Table of values   Ordered pairs

x	y
-2	
0	
1	
3	
4	

→ _____

→ _____

→ _____

→ _____

→ _____

2. Plot the points on the coordinate grid. Then connect the points.

Review 182

You can describe a situation shown by a graph.

- An airplane ascends to its cruising altitude of 20,000 ft in 20 min. After 50 min it begins its descent into Atlanta. The descent takes 15 min.

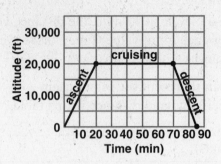

The graph at the right shows time and altitude for the airplane trip. Each part of the trip is labeled.

You can sketch a graph to describe a situation.

- When Ahmad goes out for a run, he walks for a few minutes to warm up, runs for a while, jogs in place while he waits for a light to change, and then walks the rest of the way to cool down.

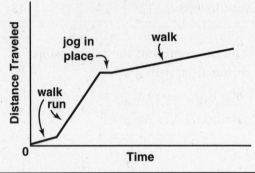

The graph at the right shows the distance Ahmad travels and each type of movement.

Match each graph with its situation.

A.

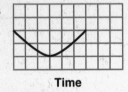

B.

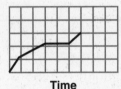

C.

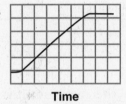

1. A car travels 10 mph for 5 min, 50 mph for 27 min, and then is stopped for 10 min.

   _____

2. Total rainfall over a 24-hour period

   _____

3. Water level in a bay

   _____

Sketch a graph for the situation. Include labels.

4. You walk to a park, visit with a friend for few minutes, and then jog home.

5. You climb up a ladder, then climb down the ladder.

Review 183

Simple and Compound Interest

When you deposit money in a bank, the bank pays interest.
Simple interest is interest paid only on the amount you deposited,
called the **principal. Compound interest** is paid on the original
principal and on any interest that has been left in the account.

Simple Interest

To find simple interest, use this formula.

Interest = principal · rate · time in years

$$I = p \cdot r \cdot t$$

Find the simple interest on $1,800
invested at 5% annual interest for
3 years.

$$
\begin{aligned}
I &= p \cdot r \cdot t \\
&= 1{,}800 \cdot 0.05 \cdot 3 \leftarrow \textbf{Use 0.05 for 5\%.} \\
&= 270
\end{aligned}
$$

The interest is $270. (The balance will be
$1,800 + $270, or $2,070.)

Compound Interest

To find compound interest, use this formula.

Balance = principal · (1 + rate)$^{\text{time in years}}$

$$B = p(1 + r)^t$$

You put $1,800 in the bank. The interest
rate is 5% compounded annually. How
much will be in the account after 3 years?

$$
\begin{aligned}
B &= p(1 + r)^t \\
&= 1{,}800(1 + 0.05)^3 \quad \leftarrow \textbf{Use 0.05 for 5\%.} \\
&= 1{,}800 \cdot (1.05)^3 \\
&\approx 2{,}083.73
\end{aligned}
$$

The balance is $2,083.73.

Find the simple interest earned by each account.

1. $800 principal
   4% interest rate
   5 years
   $I = p \cdot r \cdot t$

   = _____ · _____ · _____

   = _____

2. $1,200 principal
   5.5% interest rate
   25 years
   $I = p \cdot r \cdot t$

   = _____ · _____ · _____

   = _____

3. $800 principal
   3% interest
   4 years

   _____

4. $1,900 principal
   4.5% interest
   20 years

   _____

5. $20,000 principal
   3.5% interest
   15 years

   _____

Find the balance of each account earning compound interest.

6. $600 principal, 6% interest rate,
   3 years
   $B = p(1 + r)^t$

   = _____ (1+ _____)^3

   = _____

7. $9,000 principal, 5% interest rate,
   4 years
   $B = p(1 + r)^t$

   = _____ (1+ _____)—

   = _____

Review 184

You can use your equation-solving abilities to help you solve real-world problems.

Cory wants to buy new track shoes that cost $75. So far, she has saved $25. She usually earns $10 each week cutting lawns. How many weeks will it take her to earn the rest of the money needed to buy the shoes?

You can often use these three steps to help you solve problems.

Read and Understand: Choose a variable to represent what you want to find.
Let w = the number of weeks.

Plan and Solve: Write an equation to show the information in the problem.

Cost of shoes = Money saved + Money earned

$$\downarrow \qquad\qquad \downarrow \qquad\qquad \downarrow$$

$$75 \quad = \quad 25 \quad + \quad 10w$$

Solve your equation.

$$75 = 25 + 10w$$
$$75 - 25 = 25 - 25 + 10w$$
$$\frac{50}{10} = \frac{10w}{10}$$
$$5 = w$$

Look Back and Check: Answer the question in the problem.
It will take Cory 5 weeks to earn the money.

Solve.

1. The area of Jared's computer room floor is 168 ft^2. The formula for area of a rectangle is $A = l \times w$. If the length of the room is 14 feet, what is the width? Let w = width.

   Write an equation. Use the formula to help you. _____

   Solve the equation. w = _____

   Answer the question. _____

2. A skirt costs $15 more than a blouse. The skirt costs $48. What is the price of the blouse? Write an equation. Then solve the problem.

   _____

3. Mary ate one of the muffins she baked and had 12 left. How many muffins did Mary bake? Write an equation. Then solve the problem.

   _____

Course 2 Topics

Review 185

A **formula** such as $I = prt$ states the relationship among unknown quantities represented by the variables $I, p, r,$ and t. It means that *interest* equals the *principal* times the *rate* times the *time*.

You can use a formula by **substituting** values for the variables. Some formulas have numbers that do not vary, such as this formula for finding the perimeter of a square: $P = 4s$. The number 4 is a **constant.**

A Boeing 747 airplane traveled at 600 mi/hr. At this speed how many hours did it take to travel 2,100 miles?

$d = r \cdot t$	Use the formula $d = rt$.
$2,100 = 600 \cdot t$	Substitute the known values.
$3.5 = t$	Divide to find the unknown value.

The Boeing 747 airplane traveled 2,100 miles in 3.5 hours.

---

1. Lisa rides her bike for 2 hours and travels 12 miles. Find her rate of speed.

   a. Which formula should you use to find the rate? _____

   b. What is the rate of speed? _____

Solve each formula for the values given.

2. $A = lw$ for A, given $l = 35$ m and $w = 22$ m

   _____

3. $P = 2l + 2w$ for l given $P = 30$ in. and $w = 7$ in.

   _____

4. $r = \frac{d}{t}$ for t, given $d = 366$ mi and $r = 30.5$ mi/hr

   _____

5. $C = 2\pi r$ for $r = 10$ cm. Use 3.14 for π.

   _____

6. $V = lwh$ for l given $V = 60$ ft^3, $w = 3$ ft, and $h = 5$ ft

   _____

7. $I = prt$ for $p = \$100$, $r = 0.05$, and $t = 2$ years

   _____

Course 2 Topics

Review 186

The intersection of a horizontal number line and a vertical number line forms the **coordinate plane.** The coordinate plane below shows point *A* for the **ordered pair** $(3, -4)$.

To graph point *A* with **coordinates** $(3, -4)$:

① Start at the origin, *O*. Move 3 units to the right.

② Move 4 units down for -4. Draw point *A*.

The axes form four **quadrants** in the coordinate plane.

- The point $(3, -4)$ is located in quadrant IV.

- Point *B* is located in quadrant II.

The line containing two points with the same *x*-coordinate is a vertical line. The line containing two points with the same *y*-coordinate is a horizontal line.

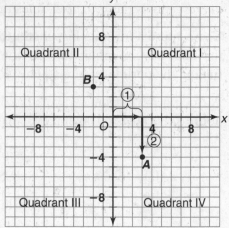

Name the point with the given coordinates.

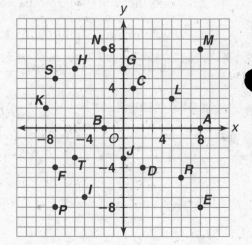

1. $(8, 0)$ _____

2. $(8, -8)$ _____

3. $(1, 4)$ _____

4. $(-7, -4)$ _____

5. $(-5, 6)$ _____

6. $(-2, 0)$ _____

7. $(6, -5)$ _____

8. $(-5, -3)$ _____

Write the coordinates of each point.

9. *D* _____

10. *G* _____

11. *I* _____

12. *J* _____

13. *K* _____

14. *L* _____

15. *M* _____

16. *S* _____

Identify the quadrant in which each point lies.

17. *F* _____

18. *C* _____

19. *D* _____

20. *H* _____

21. *N* _____

22. *P* _____

23. *S* _____

24. *R* _____

Without graphing, tell whether the line containing each pair of points is vertical or horizontal.

25. *F* and *P*

26. *H* and *G*

27. *A* and *M*

_____   _____   _____

Review 187

The **solutions** of $y = x + 3$ are the (x, y) pairs that make the equation true.

The solutions can be listed in a table.

x	$x + 3$	y	(x, y)
0	$0 + 3$	3	$(0, 3)$
1	$1 + 3$	4	$(1, 4)$
-2	$-2 + 3$	1	$(-2, 1)$

If all the solutions lie on a line, the equation is a **linear equation** and the line is its **graph.**

$y = x + 3$ is a linear equation.

The solutions can be graphed in the coordinate plane, as shown.

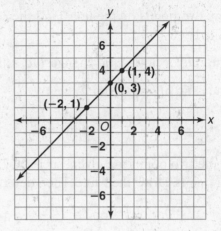

Complete each table.

1. $y = x - 4$

x	$x - 4$	y	(x, y)
2			
4			
6			

2. $y = 3x$

x	$3x$	y	(x, y)
-1			
0			
3			

3. $y = -x + 1$

x	$-x + 1$	y	(x, y)
0			
2			
-3			

Graph each linear equation.

4. $y = x - 5$

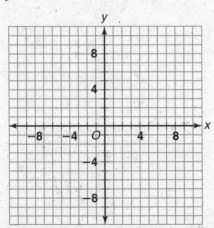

5. $y = 3x - 4$

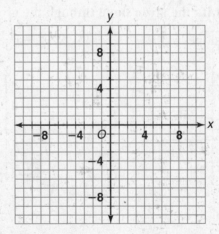

Course 2 Topics

Review 188

The steepness of a line is measured by its **slope.** To find the slope of a line, follow these steps.

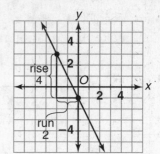

① Pick any two points on the line. Find the *rise,* or vertical change. Here, the rise is −4.

② Find the *run,* or horizontal change. Here, the run is 2.

③ Find the ratio of rise to run.

$$\text{slope} = \frac{\text{rise}}{\text{run}} = \frac{-4}{2} = -2$$

Sometimes the two points are given, such as (2, 3) and (4, 6). Graph both points. Draw their line. Then determine the slope.

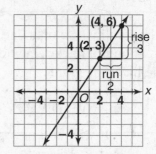

$$\text{slope} = \frac{\text{rise}}{\text{run}} = \frac{3}{2}$$

The slope of the line through (2, 3) and (4, 6) is $\frac{3}{2}$.

Course 2 Topics

Find the slope of each line.

1.

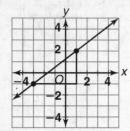

$$\text{slope} = \frac{\text{rise}}{\text{run}} = \underline{\qquad}$$

2.

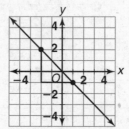

$$\text{slope} = \frac{\text{rise}}{\text{run}} = \underline{\qquad}$$

3.

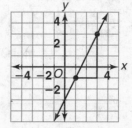

$$\text{slope} = \frac{\text{rise}}{\text{run}} = \underline{\qquad}$$

Draw a line with the given slope through the given point.

4. $B(3, 5)$, slope = 3

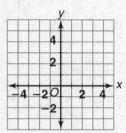

5. $Z(1, -1)$, slope = −1

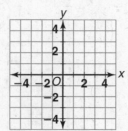

6. $S(1, -2)$, slope = 2

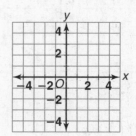

Review 189

The graph of $y = x^2 - 1$ is a U-shaped curve called a **parabola.** To graph a parabola:

① Make a table of values.

x	$x^2 - 1$	y	(x, y)
-2	$(-2)^2 - 1$	3	$(-2, 3)$
-1	$(-1)^2 - 1$	0	$(-1, 0)$
0	$0^2 - 1$	-1	$(0, -1)$
1	$1^2 - 1$	0	$(1, 0)$
2	$2^2 - 1$	3	$(2, 3)$

② Graph the points.

③ Draw the U shape.

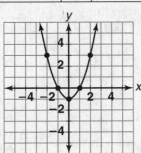

The graph of $y = 2|x|$ is called an **absolute value equation.** Its graph is V-shaped. To graph the equation:

① Make a table of values.

x	$2|x|$	y	(x, y)
-2	$2 \cdot 2$	4	$(-2, 4)$
-1	$2 \cdot 1$	2	$(-1, 2)$
0	$2 \cdot 0$	0	$(0, 0)$
1	$2 \cdot 1$	2	$(1, 2)$
2	$2 \cdot 2$	4	$(2, 4)$

② Graph the points.

③ Draw the V shape.

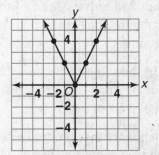

Make a table of values for each equation. Then graph each equation.

1. $y = x^2 - 2$

x	y
-2	
-1	
0	
1	
2	

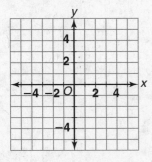

2. $y = 2x^2 - 3$

x	y
-2	
-1	
0	
1	
2	

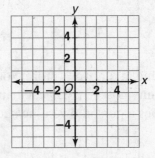

3. $y = \frac{1}{2}|x| + 1$

x	y
-4	
-2	
0	
2	
4	

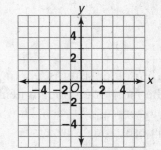

Course 2 Topics

Review 190

Problem Solving: Make a Table and Make a Graph

You can solve problems by making a table and a graph. First, use the information in the problem to make a table. Then use the table to draw a graph. You can use the graph to answer questions or make predictions.

Suppose there is a 60-in.-tall tree in your front yard. After a month the tree is 64 in. tall. After another month the tree is 66 in. tall. After the third month it is 68 in. tall. How tall is the tree after 6 months?

Read and Understand Given the tree's height after each of the first three months, find the height of the tree after 6 months.

Plan and Solve Make a table to organize the information in the problem. Then make a graph to predict the height of the tree after 6 months.

Month	Height (in.)
0	60
1	64
2	66
3	68

Use the table to create a graph. Use an interval of 1 on the *x*-axis and label it from 1 to 6 months. Use an interval of 2 on the *y*-axis and label it from 58 to 70 in.

It appears that the tree grows about 2 in. each month. So in 6 months the tree should be about 74 in. tall.

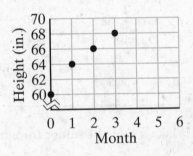

Look Back and Check Since the rate of increase is assumed to be constant, you can say that every month the tree grows 2 in.

Solve the problem by making a table and a graph.

1. The distance that an object falls when dropped from a height is given by the rule $d = \frac{1}{2}gt^2$ where $g = 32$ ft/sec/sec, and t = time. What is the distance the object has fallen after 7 seconds?

   _____

2. Your older sister is working part-time at a novelty store. Some of the most often bought items are funny noses at $.29 each and buzzers at $.79 each. How much does a person owe if he/she buys 3 noses and 4 buzzers?

   _____

Review 191

Movements of figures on a plane are called **transformations.** A translation, or slide, moves all points the same distance and direction.

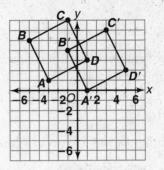

The translation $(x, y) \rightarrow (x + 4, y - 1)$ moves *each* point to the right 4 units and down 1 unit.

$A (-3, 1)$ moves to $(-3 + 4, 1 - 1)$, where point $A'(1, 0)$ is its **image.**

The square $ABCD$ moves to its image square $A'B'C'D'$.

Complete the following for the figure above.

1. $B (-5, 5) \rightarrow B' (\underline{\hspace{0.5cm}}, \underline{\hspace{0.5cm}})$

2. $C (-1, 7) \rightarrow C' (\underline{\hspace{0.5cm}}, \underline{\hspace{0.5cm}})$

3. $D(\underline{\hspace{0.5cm}}, \underline{\hspace{0.5cm}}) \rightarrow D'(\underline{\hspace{0.5cm}}, \underline{\hspace{0.5cm}})$

Graph each translation of figure *PRST*.

4. right 2 units

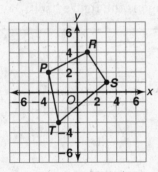

5. left 2 units, down 2 units

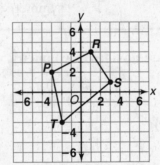

6. right 1 unit, up 3 units

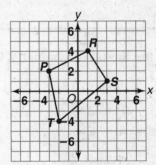

Complete the rule for each translation.

7. right 3 units, up 1 unit

$(x, y) \rightarrow$ _____

8. left 4 units, up 5 units

$(x, y) \rightarrow$ _____

9. left 1 unit, down 9 units

$(x, y) \rightarrow$ _____

Write a rule for the translation.

10. left 1 unit, down 3 units

_____

11. right 1 unit, up 2 units

_____

12. left 3 units, up 2 units

_____

Review 192

Symmetry

A figure is **symmetrical** if one side is a mirror image of the other. The line that divides a figure into two identical parts is called a **line of symmetry.**

The figure below has 2 lines of symmetry.

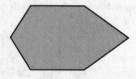

You can trace the figure and fold it along either line to see that the two halves match.

Reflections

A **reflection** is a transformation that creates a mirror image. $\triangle A'B'C'$ is the mirror image of $\triangle ABC$ across the x-axis. The x-axis is the **line of reflection.**

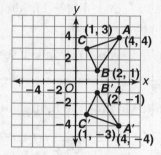

- When you reflect across the x-axis, the y-coordinates change sign.

- When you reflect across the y-axis, the x-coordinates change sign.

- When you reflect across a line of symmetry, the image is the figure itself.

Draw the line(s) of symmetry. If there are no lines of symmetry, write *none.*

1.

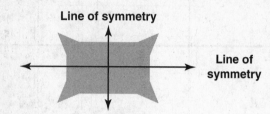

_____

2.

_____

3.

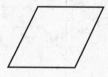

_____

$\triangle ABC$ **is shown. Draw** $\triangle A'B'C'$ **so it is a reflection of** $\triangle ABC$ **over the specified axis. Then complete each statement.**

4. over the x-axis

$A(-4, 4) \rightarrow A'$

_____

$B(-2, 0) \rightarrow B'$

_____

$C(0, 2) \rightarrow C'$

_____

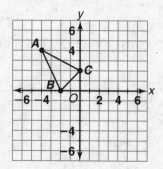

5. over the y-axis

$A(-4, 4) \rightarrow A'$

_____

$B(-2, 0) \rightarrow B'$

_____

$C(0, 2) \rightarrow C'$

_____

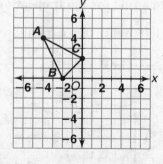

Review 193

A **rotation** is a transformation that turns a figure about a fixed point. The fixed point is called the **center of rotation.**

A figure has **rotational symmetry** it can be rotated less than 360° and fit exactly on top of the original figure.

The figure below has rotational symmetry.

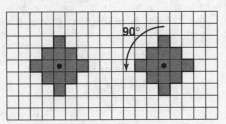

For a rotation of 90° or 180° about its center, the figure fits exactly on top of itself.

To draw a 180° rotation about point A, trace $\triangle ABC$. Place a pencil tip on point A and rotate the tracing 180°. Mark points A', B', and C'. Then draw $\triangle A'B'C'$.

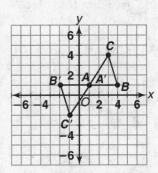

Does each figure have rotational symmetry?

1.

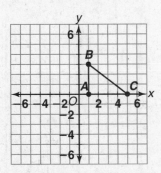

_____

2.

_____

3.

_____

Draw the image of the figure after each rotation about point O.

4. rotation of 90°

5. rotation of 180°

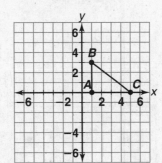

6. rotation of 270°

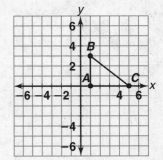

Review 194

Aimee asked students in her grade how many CDs they own. She displayed her data in a **frequency table.** Each tally stands for 1 CD.

Students' CD Collections

Number of CDs	17	18	19	20	21	22	23	24
Tally	ℍℍ I	I	ℍℍ	III	I	IIII	II	IIII
Frequency	6	1	5	3	1	4	2	4

She displayed the same data in a **line plot.** Each ✗ stands for 1 CD.

Number of CDs Students Own

```
✗
✗       ✗
✗   ✗           ✗           ✗
✗   ✗   ✗       ✗           ✗
✗   ✗   ✗       ✗       ✗   ✗
✗   ✗   ✗   ✗   ✗   ✗   ✗   ✗
17  18  19  20  21  22  23  24
```

She also made a **histogram** to show the frequencies. The bars represent intervals of equal size. The height of each bar gives the frequency of the data.

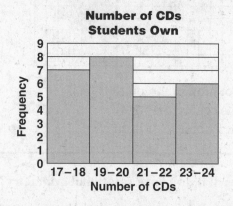

Number of CDs Students Own

Use the frequency table for Exercises 1–3.

1. Ms. Ortiz's class is planning a school garden. She asked her students how many rose bushes they want in the garden. She recorded the data in a frequency table. Complete the table.

Number of Rose Bushes	1	2	3	4	5	6
Tally	I	IIII	III	ℍℍ I	I	I
Frequency						

2. Use the frequency table to make a line plot for the data.

3. Draw a histogram of the students' data.

Review 195

A **spreadsheet** is one way to organize data.

Columns are labeled A, B, C, and so on. Rows are numbered 1, 2, 3, and so on. The box where column B and row 3 meet is called **cell** B3. The *value* in cell B3 is 10.

Weekly Butter and Margarine Sales

	A	B	C
1	Day	Butter	Margarine
2	Monday	9	7
3	Tuesday	10	9
4	Wednesday	7	6
5	Thursday	9	6
6	Friday	10	8
7	Saturday	11	9

- Spreadsheet column A gives the labels for the horizontal axis.

- Spreadsheet column B gives the heights for one set of bars and one set of points.

- Spreadsheet column C gives the heights for another set of bars and another set of points.

You can use the data from this spreadsheet to make a **double bar graph.** A double bar graph compares two sets of data. The **legend,** or key, tells what kinds of data the graph is comparing.

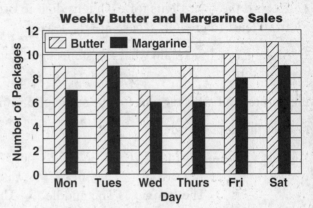

Weekly Butter and Margarine Sales

You can compare changes over time of two sets of data with a double line graph.

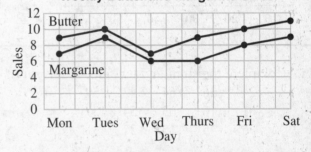

Weekly Butter and Margarine Sales

Use the data in the spreadsheet for Exercises 1–4.

1. What is the value in cell B4? cell C2?

   _____

2. In which cell is the year 2000? 1997?

   _____

Percents of Families Who Prefer Frozen and Fresh Vegetables

	A	B	C
1	Year	Frozen	Fresh
2	1997	61	39
3	1998	70	30
4	1999	78	22
5	2000	84	16

3. Make a double bar graph from the spreadsheet. Include a legend.

4. Make a double line graph from the spreadsheet. Include a legend.

Review 196

Make a **stem-and-leaf plot** of the summer earnings data.

① Make a column of the tens digits of the data in order from least to greatest. These are the stems.

② Record the ones digits for each tens digit in order from least to greatest. These are the leaves.

③ Make a *key* to explain what the stems and leaves represent.

Summer Earnings					
$35	$35	$38	$15	$52	$40
$20	$23	$56	$12	$14	$58

① stems	② leaves
1	1 | 2 4 5
2	2 | 0 3
3	3 | 5 5 8
4	4 | 0
5	5 | 2 6 8

③ 1 | 2 means 12

Make a **box-and-whisker plot** for the summer earnings data.

① List the data in order.

least value → 12 14 15 20 23 35 35 38 40 52 56 58 ← greatest value

         ↑   ↑   ↑

      The lower   The middle   The upper
quartile is 17.5.   quartile is 35.   quartile is 46.

② Use a number line to draw the box-and-whisker plot.

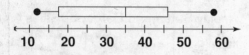

    10   20   30   40   50   60

---

1. Complete the stem-and-leaf plot of this set of data.

24	36	64	42	59
61	16	63	54	39
36	45	15	27	51

1	_ _
2	4 _
3	6 _ _
4	_ _
5	_ _ _
6	_ _ _

1 | 5 means ___

2. Brandy recorded these high temperatures for two weeks in July. Make a stem-and-leaf plot of her data.

92	86	91	90	85
82	84	78	79	83
84	89	86	87	

3. Mr. Wang recorded these test scores. Make a box-and-whisker plot for the data.

66	83	58	65	66
66	82	55	57	71
40	43	41	56	71
74	81	85	63	62

Course 2 Topics

Review 197

Problem Solving: Make a Table and Use Logical Reasoning

Travis, Seritta, Ariel, and Tess are going hiking, boating, biking, and surfing.

1. Tess does not know how to surf.

2. Ariel asked the hiker to show her a map.

3. Tess and Ariel talked with the biker and the boater.

4. Travis doesn't like water.

Tell who will do each activity.

Read and Understand
What do you need to find out? *The problem asks you to tell who will do each activity.*

	Hiker	Boater	Biker	Surfer
Travis				
Seritta				
Ariel				
Tess				no

Plan and Solve
Make a logic table. Use the clues from the problem. Write *yes* or *no* in each box.

Fact ① tells you Tess is not the surfer. Write *no* in the box where Tess and Surfer meet.

Fact ② says that Ariel is not the hiker. Write *no* for this.

	Hiker	Boater	Biker	Surfer
Travis				
Seritta				
Ariel	no	no	no	yes
Tess		no	no	no

Fact ③ says that Tess and Ariel are not the boater nor the biker. Write *no* in four boxes, leaving Ariel to be the surfer. Write yes in the box where Ariel and Surfer meet.

Look Back and Check
Complete the table. *Travis is the biker, Seritta is the boater, Ariel is the surfer, and Tess is the hiker.*

	Hiker	Boater	Biker	Surfer
Travis	no	no	yes	no
Seritta	no	yes	no	no
Ariel	no	no	no	yes
Tess	yes	no	no	no

Course 2 Topics

Complete the table to solve the problem.

Iona, Sara, Pete, and Tim went to the Northwest Coast Indian Conference. They are from the Noottka, Salish, Haida, and Tlingit families. Pete and Sara had not seen a Haida for a year. The Tlingit gave Iona and Tim a wood carving. Iona is not the Noottka. Sara joined the Noottka at the evening ceremonies. The Tlingit is not a woman. Who is the Noottka? the Salish? the Haida? the Tlingit? _____

	Iona	Sara	Pete	Tim
Noottka				
Salish				
Haida				
Tlingit				

Review 198

Carlos is curious about sports that students in his school like best. He cannot interview every student in the school. But he could interview a sample of the school **population.**

Carlos wants a **random sample.** A sample is random if everyone has an equal chance of being selected. How will Carlos get a random sample? He considers two possibilities:

- He can interview 30 students at a soccer game.

- He can interview 5 students in each of 6 class changes.

Carlos realizes that students at a soccer game probably like soccer better than other sports. That would not be a random sample. He decides on the interviews during class changes.

What question will he ask? He considers two possibilities:

- "Which sport do you prefer, football, soccer, baseball, or tennis?"

- "Which do you enjoy most, the slow sport of baseball or one of the more exciting sports like football, soccer, or tennis?"

The second question is **biased.** It makes one answer seem better than another. Carlos decides to ask the first question.

1. You want to find how many people in your community are vegetarian. Where would be the best place to take a survey?

   _____

In each question biased or fair?

2. Will you vote for the young inexperienced candidate, Mr. Soong, or the experienced candidate, Ms. Lopez? _____

3. Will you vote for Mr. Soong or Ms. Lopez? _____

You plan to survey people to see what percent own their home and what percent rent. Tell whether the following will give a random sample. Explain.

4. You interview people outside a pool supply store in the suburbs.

   _____

5. You interview people in the street near an apartment complex.

   _____

6. You mail a survey to every 20th person in the telephone book.

   _____

Review 199

Researchers tagged 100 fish in a pond and then released them back into the pond. Later they captured 60 fish and found that 3 were tagged. Estimate the number of fish in the pond.

① Write a proportion of tagged fish to total fish.

$$\frac{\text{tagged fish (pond)}}{\text{total fish (pond)}} = \frac{\text{tagged fish (sample)}}{\text{total fish (sample)}}$$

$$\frac{100}{n} = \frac{3}{60}$$

② Write cross products.

$$3n = 6{,}000$$

③ Solve.

$$n = 2{,}000$$

There are about 2,000 fish in the pond.

Complete to estimate the number of deer in the woods.

1. One year researchers tagged 80 deer. They later captured 15 deer and found 5 were tagged. Estimate the number of deer in the woods.

$$\frac{80}{n} = \frac{\square}{\square}$$

$$5n = 15 \cdot \underline{\qquad}$$

$$n = \underline{\qquad}$$

There are about _____ deer.

2. Two years later, researchers tagged 45 deer. They later captured 20 and found 3 were tagged. Estimate the number of deer in the woods then.

$$\frac{\square}{n} = \frac{\square}{20}$$

$$3n = \underline{\qquad}$$

$$n = \underline{\qquad}$$

There are about _____ deer.

Use a proportion to estimate each animal population.

3. In another project, researchers caught and tagged 85 sea lions in a bay. Later they caught and released 50 sea lions. Of those, 9 had tags. Estimate the sea lion population in the bay.

_____

4. Other researchers caught and tagged 5 spotted owls. Later they caught 7 owls. Of those, 4 were tagged. Estimate the number of spotted owls in that forest.

_____

5. An ecology class helped researchers determine the rabbit population in a nature preserve. One weekend, the students captured, tagged, and set free 32 rabbits. A month later, they captured 27 rabbits including 16 with tags. Estimate the number of rabbits in the nature preserve.

_____

6. Another ecology class helped researchers determine the pigeon population in a city park. In one day, the students captured, banded, and released 200 pigeons. Two weeks later, of the 24 pigeons they captured, 3 had bands. Estimate the pigeon population in the park.

_____

Course 2 Topics

Review 200

There are 3 ways that graphs can be drawn to be misleading.

1. The interval on the vertical axis may not start at zero.

2. There may be a break in the graph.

3. The intervals on the horizontal or vertical axis may have unequal intervals.

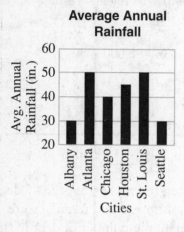

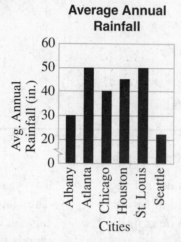

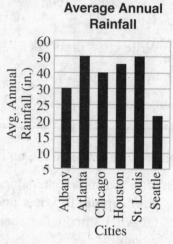

Mean, median, and mode can also be used to mislead. Consider a set of data where most of the numbers are in a certain range. There are a few numbers that are either way above or way below the range. The mean is not a good measure of the data in this case.

For each graph do the following:
(a) Tell what the graph shows. (b) What can you say about the graph?

1.

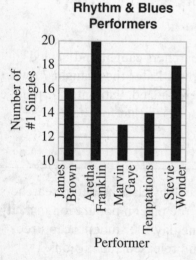

2.

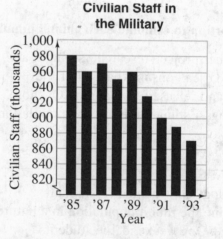

_____   _____

_____   _____

_____   _____

_____   _____

_____   _____

Name _____ Class _____ Date _____

Review 201

Gilbert is investigating the relationship between the number of credit cards a person has and the amount of credit card debt.

First, he made a table from his data.

Then he plotted the data in a scatter plot.

Credit Cards and Credit Card Debt

Number of Cards	Amount of Debt
1	$0
1	$1,000
1	$5,000
2	$3,000
2	$5,000
3	$10,000
3	$5,000
3	$8,000
4	$10,000
5	$19,000

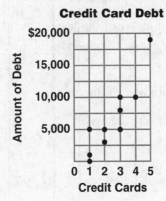

Credit Card Debt

Gilbert's scatter plot shows a **positive trend** in the data. That means as the number of credit cards goes up so does the amount of debt. As one value goes up, so does the other.

In a **negative trend,** one value goes up while the other goes down.

Complete the scatter plot for the data.

1. Dana surveyed her friends about how much TV they watch and their average test scores. Her results are shown below.

Test Scores and TV

TV Hours Per Day	Average Test Score	TV Hours Per Day	Average Test Score
1	98	3	79
1	86	3	73
2	90	3	75
2	82	4	62
2	85	5	68

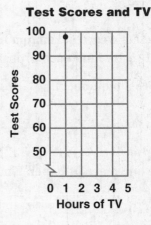

Test Scores and TV

2. Is the trend in the data negative or positive? Explain.

_____

3. Describe the relationship Dana likely found between test scores and TV time.

_____

Review 202

To find a **theoretical probability,** first list all possible **outcomes.** Then use the formula:

$$P(\text{event}) = \frac{\text{number of favorable outcomes}}{\text{total number of possible outcomes}}$$

A letter is selected at random from the letters of the word FLORIDA. What is the probability that the letter is an A?

- There are 7 letters (possible outcomes).

- There is one A, which represents a favorable outcome.

$$P(A) = \frac{\text{number of favorable outcomes}}{\text{total number of outcomes}} = \frac{1}{7}$$

The probability that the letter is an A is $\frac{1}{7}$.

Selecting a letter other than A is called *not* A and is the **complement** of the event A. The sum of the probabilities of an event and its complement equals 1, or 100%.

What is the probability of the event "*not* A"?

$$P(A) + P(\textit{not } A) = 1$$

$$\frac{1}{7} + P(\textit{not } A) = 1$$

$$P(\textit{not } A) = 1 - \frac{1}{7} = \frac{6}{7}$$

The probability of the event "*not* A," (selecting F, L, O, R, I, or D), is $\frac{6}{7}$.

Spin the spinner shown once. Find each probability as a fraction, a decimal, and a percent.

1. $P(5)$

$$\frac{\text{number of favorable outcomes}}{\text{total number of outcomes}}$$

$$= \frac{\square}{5} \underline{\hspace{2cm}}$$

2. $P(\text{odd number})$

$$\frac{\text{number of favorable outcomes}}{\text{total number of outcomes}}$$

$$= \frac{2}{\square} \underline{\hspace{2cm}}$$

You select a card at random from a box that contains cards numbered from 1 to 10. Find each probability as a fraction, a decimal, and a percent.

3. $P(\text{even number})$

4. $P(\text{number less than 4})$

5. $P(\text{not 5})$

_____   _____   _____

The letters H, A, P, P, I, N, E, S, and S are written on pieces of paper. Select one piece of paper. Find each probability.

6. $P(P)$ _____

7. $P(\text{not vowel})$ _____

8. $P(\text{not E})$ _____

A number is selected at random from the numbers 1 to 50. Find the odds in favor of each outcome.

9. selecting a multiple of 5

10. selecting a factor of 50

11. selecting a number that is not a factor of 50

_____   _____   _____

Name _____ Class _____ Date _____

Review 203

Probability measures how likely it is that an event will occur. For an **experimental probability,** you collect data through observations or experiments and use the data to state the probability.

The jar contains red, green, and blue chips. You shake the jar, draw a chip, note its color, and then put it back. You do this 20 times with these results: 7 blue chips, 5 red chips, and 8 green chips. The experimental probability of drawing a green chip is

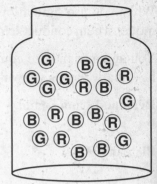

$$P(\text{green chip}) = \frac{\text{number of times "green chips" occur}}{\text{total number of trials}}$$

$$P(\text{green chip}) = \frac{8}{20} = \frac{2}{5} = 0.4 = 40\%$$

The probability of drawing a green chip is $\frac{2}{5}$, or 0.4, or 40%.

Sometimes a model, or simulation, is used to represent a situation. Then, the simulaton is used to find the experimental probability. For example, spinning this spinner can simulate the probability that 1 of 3 people is chosen for president of the student body.

Use the 20 draws above to complete each exercise.

1. What is the experimental probability of drawing a red chip? Write the probability as a fraction.

   $P(\text{red chip}) = \dfrac{}{20} =$ _____

2. What is the experimental probability of drawing a blue chip? Write the probability as a percent.

   $P(\text{blue chip}) = \dfrac{}{} =$ _____

Suppose you have a bag with 30 chips: 12 red, 8 white, and 10 blue. You shake the jar, draw a chip, note its color, and then put it back. You do this 30 times with these results: 10 blue chips, 12 red chips, and 8 white chips. Write each probability as fraction in simplest form.

3. $P(\text{red})$ _____   4. $P(\text{white})$ _____   5. $P(\text{blue})$ _____

Describe a probability simulation for each situation.

6. You guess the answers on a true/false test with 20 questions.

   _____

   _____

7. One student out of 6 is randomly chosen to be the homeroom representative.

   _____

   _____

Review 204

Problem Solving: Make an Organized List and Simulate a Problem

When you use simulation to solve a problem, you must first develop a model. Then, conduct experiments to generate data.

You and a friend are equally skilled at playing checkers. Estimate how many games you will have to play until one of you wins 6 games.

Read and Understand   What do you want to find? *Find out how many games you can expect to play until one of you wins six games.*

Plan and Solve   Instead of playing the games, develop a simulation. Toss a coin to see who wins each game. Heads means you win. Tails means your friend wins. Keep track of the results.

Show the results of the simulation in a table. You tossed the coin 10 times before either 6 heads or 6 tails appeared. So you estimate that you would have to play 10 games before one of you would win 6 games.

Tosses of a Coin	
Result	**Number**
Heads	~~HHT~~ I
Tails	IIII

Look Back and Check   Would you get the same results if you repeated the simulation?

Solve each problem by either making an organized list or by simulating the problem. Explain why you chose the method you did.

1. There is one of four symbols on the inner wrapper of energy bars. The symbols are equally distributed among the wrappers. If you collect all four symbols, you get a free bar. Estimate how many bars you need to purchase to win a free bar.

    _____

    _____

    _____

2. A bank gives away one of six baseball cards each time you make a deposit. There is an equal chance of getting any one of the cards. Estimate how many deposits you will have to make to get all six cards.

    _____

    _____

    _____

3. A bakery puts a saying in each cookie. There are 36 different sayings, and there is an equally likely chance that any one of them will be inside any cookie. Estimate how many cookies Mary would have to buy to collect all 36 sayings.

    _____

    _____

    _____

4. Your 10 pairs of socks are in the dryer. Each pair of socks is a different color. Estimate how many socks you will have to pull out without looking to get two the same color.

    _____

    _____

    _____

Review 205

The set of all possible outcomes of an experiment is called the **sample space.**

You can use a *tree diagram* or a table to show the sample space for an experiment. The tree diagram below shows the sample space for spinning the spinner and tossing a coin.

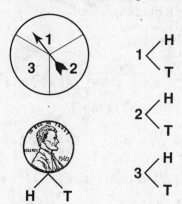

There are 6 possible outcomes: 1H, 1T, 2H, 2T, 3H, 3T. What is the probability of spinning a 3 and tossing heads? There is one favorable outcome (3H) out of 6 possible outcomes. The probabilty is $\frac{1}{6}$.

You can use the *counting principle* to find the number of possible outcomes: If there are *m* ways of making one choice and *n* ways of making a second choice, then there are *m* × *n* ways of making the first choice followed by the second.

Evelyn and Kara are planning to go skating or to a movie. Afterward they want to go out for pizza, tacos, or cheeseburgers. How many possible choices do they have?

- There are *two choices* for an activity and *three choices* for food.

- First choices × Second choices

     2   ×   3   = 6

There are 6 possible choices.

Complete the tree diagram to show the sample space.

1. Roll a number cube and toss a coin. What is the probability of getting (4, Heads)?

   1   2   3   4   5   6

   ／＼ ／＼ ／＼ ／＼ ／＼ ／＼

   __ __ __ __ __ __ __ __ __ __ __ __

   Number of outcomes _____

   $P(4, heads)$ = _____

Use the counting principle.

2. 4 kinds of yogurt and 8 toppings

   _____

3. 6 shirts and 9 pairs of slacks

   _____

4. 3 types of sandwiches and 3 flavors of juice

   _____

5. 4 types of bread and 6 different sandwich spreads

   _____

Review 206

If you toss a coin and roll a number cube, the events are **independent.** The outcome of one event does not affect the outcome of the second event.

Find the probability of tossing a heads (H) and rolling an even number (E).

Find P(H and E). H and E are independent.

① Find P(H):

$$P(H) = \frac{1 \text{ heads}}{2 \text{ sides}} = \frac{1}{2}$$

② Find P(E):

$$P(E) = \frac{3 \text{ evens}}{6 \text{ faces}} = \frac{1}{2}$$

③ $P(\text{H and E}) = P(H) \times P(E) = \frac{1}{2} \times \frac{1}{2} = \frac{1}{4}$

If the outcome of the first event affects the outcome of the second event, the events are **dependent.**

A bag contains 3 blue and 3 red marbles. Draw a marble, then draw a second marble without replacing the first marble. Find the probability of drawing 2 blue marbles.

① Find P(blue).

$$P(\text{blue}) = \frac{3 \text{ blue}}{6 \text{ marbles}} = \frac{1}{2}$$

② Find P(blue after blue).

$$P(\text{blue after blue}) = \frac{2 \text{ blue}}{5 \text{ marbles}} = \frac{2}{5}$$

③ Find P(blue, then blue)

P(blue, then blue)
$= P(\text{blue}) \times P(\text{blue after blue})$

$= \frac{1}{2} \times \frac{2}{5} = \frac{1}{5}$

In Exercises 1–6, you draw a marble at random from the bag of marbles shown. Then, you replace it and draw again. Find each probability.

1. P(blue and red)   2. P(2 reds)   3. P(2 blues)

_____   _____   _____

Next, you draw two marbles randomly *without* replacing the first marble. Find each probability.

4. P(blue and red)   5. P(2 reds)   6. P(2 blues)

_____   _____   _____

You draw two letters randomly from a box containing the letters **M, I, S, S, O, U, R,** and **I.**

7. Suppose you do not replace the first letter before drawing the second. What is P(M and I)?

_____

8. Suppose you replace the first letter before drawing the second. What is P(M and I)?

_____

Review 207

You can arrange the letters A, B, and C in different ways: ABC, ACB, and so on. An arrangement in which order is important is a **permutation.**

How many ways can the three blocks be arranged in a line?

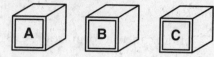

① List the ways.

② Count the number of arrangements.

There are 6 possible arrangements.

ABC   ACB
BAC   BCA
CAB   CBA

You can use the counting principle as a shortcut.

choices for 1st block		choices for 2nd block		choice for 3rd block	
3	×	2	×	1	= 6

A factorial can be used to show the product of all integers less than or equal to a number.

$$3! \quad = 3 \quad × \quad 2 \quad × \quad 1 \quad = 6$$

Complete to find the number of permutations for each.

1. In how many ways can you arrange 4 different books on a shelf?

$4 \times$ _____ $\times$ _____ $\times 1 =$ _____

2. In how many ways can the first, second, and third prizes be awarded to 10 contestants?

_____ $\times$ _____ $\times$ _____ = _____

Find the number of permutations for each.

3. In how many different ways can the four letters in BIRD be arranged?

_____

4. How many different ways can you frame two of five pictures in different frames?

_____

5. How many different seating arrangements are possible for a row of five chairs, choosing from six people?

_____

6. A basket contains five different pieces of fruit. If three people each choose one piece, in how many different ways can they make their choices?

_____

Find the number of two-letter permutations of the letters.

7. R, I, B

_____

8. H, E, L, P

_____

9. R, A, M, B, L, E

_____

10. C, A, N, D, L, E, S

_____

Find the number of three-letter permutations of the letters.

11. T, A, B

12. R, A, D, I, O

13. T, O, P, S

14. W, A, L, R, U, S

Name _____ Class _____ Date _____

Review 208

Course 2 Topics

An arrangement in which order does *not* matter is a **combination.**
For example, if you pair Raiz and Carla to play tennis, it is the same
as if you pair Carla and Raiz.

How many groups of 2 letters can you form from A, B, C, and D?

① Make an organized list.

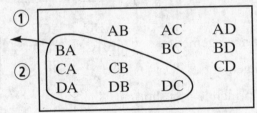

② Eliminate any duplicates.

③ List the combinations.   AB, AC, AD, BC, BD, CD

There are 6 possible combinations.

You can also get the number of combinations from the number of
permutations.

$$\text{combinations} = \frac{\text{total number of permutations}}{\text{number of permutations of smaller group}} = \frac{4 \times 3}{2 \times 1} = 6 \text{ possible combinations}$$

Use the letters C, O, M, P, U, T, E, R for Exercises 1–4.

1. How many combinations of 2 vowels are
   there? Show an organized list with no
   duplicates.

   _____

   _____

   _____

2. How many combinations of 3 consonants
   are there? Show an organized list with no
   duplicates.

   _____

   _____

   _____

3. If you use C, O, M, P, U, T, E, R, S instead
   of C, O, M, P, U, T, E, R, how many
   combinations of 2 vowels are there?

   _____

4. If you use C, O, M, P, U, T, E, R, S instead
   of C, O, M, P, U, T, E, R, how many
   combinations of 3 consonants are there?

   _____

Find the number of combinations.

5. In how many ways can Robin pick 2 different
   kinds of muffins from a choice of wheat,
   raisin, blueberry, banana, garlic, and plain?

   _____

6. Sara has 24 tapes. In how many different
   ways can she take 2 tapes to school?

   _____

7. Augusto has purple, green, black, red, and
   blue T-shirts. In how many ways can he
   choose 3 for his vacation?

   _____

8. Abdul selects three light filters from a box
   of ten different filters. How many different
   sets could he choose?

   _____

Review 209

Algebraic Expressions and the Order of Operations

A *variable* represents a number. An *algebraic expression* is formed from numbers, variables, and operations.

To evaluate an algebraic expression, substitute a number for each variable. Then follow the order of operations.

	Evaluate $4(n + 2)$ for $n = 3$.	Evaluate $n + 12 \div (3 \times m)$ for $n = 4$ and $m = 2$.
① Substitute for each variable.	$4(3 + 2)$	$4 + 12 \div (3 \times 2)$
② Work inside grouping symbols.	$= 4(5)$	$= 4 + 2 \div 6$
③ Multiply and divide from left to right.	$= 20$	$= 4 + 2$
④ Add and subtract from left to right.		$= 6$

Evaluate each expression for $g = 4$, $k = 2$, and $t = 9$.

1. $4t$

2. $3k$

3. $g + 4$

4. $5t + 7$

5. $4(g - 1)$

6. $15k + 6$

7. $3t - g$

8. $gt \div k$

9. $27 \div t \times k$

10. $g + 12 - 3 \times k$

11. $32 \div g \times k$

12. $(2t + 2) \div g$

13. $(20 \div g) \times k$

14. $4g + t - k$

15. $3(3g - t)$

16. $2g + 2 \times 3$

17. $kt - 3$

18. $10 + 4k \div 8$

19. The formula for the perimeter of a rectangle is $P = 2l + 2w$. If $l = 2$ in. and $w = 4$ in., what operation(s) would you do first?

_____

Course 3 Topics

Review 210

You can use a problem-solving plan to organize information and solve problems. Use these three steps to solve problems.

① Read and understand the problem.

② Plan how to solve the problem, and then solve it.

③ Look back and check to see if your answer makes sense.

Sarah is 2 years older than her sister Lacey.
If the sum of their ages is 14, how old is each girl?

Read and Understand   What are you asked to find? *the ages of Sarah and Lacey*

Plan and Solve   You can use the *Try, Test, and Revise* strategy and *Make a Table*.

Pick two ages that are 2 years apart and add. If the sum is too low try again. If the sum is too high, decrease your number. Keep a record of results.

	Sarah's Age	Lacey's Age	Total	
first try →	4	2	6	← too low
second try →	6	4	10	← too low
third try →	9	7	16	← too high
fourth try →	8	6	14	← Solved!

Sarah is 8 and Lacey is 6.

Look Back and Check   Is Sarah 2 years older than Lacey? *yes*
Is the sum of their ages 14? *yes*

Use the problem-solving plan to solve each problem.

1. Joe is 5 years older than Bijan. If the sum of their ages is 25, how old is each boy?

2. A chicken dinner costs $2.50 more than a spaghetti dinner. If the cost of both is $18.40, how much does each meal cost?

3. Elaine sold twice as many T-shirts as Kim. How many did each girl sell if the total number of T-shirts sold was 27?

4. There are 5 more rows of corn than rows of peas in the garden. How many rows of each are there if there are 19 rows in all?

5. Becki thinks of a number. If she multiplies her number by 8, adds 10, and then divides by 5, the result is 26. What is Becki's number?

6. Martina went shopping. She spent one-fifth of what she had in her wallet and then one-fifth of what remained. In all she spent $36. How much did she start with?

Review 211

Integers are the set of whole numbers and their opposites. Negative integers are to the left of zero on a number line. Positive integers are to the right of zero on a number line.

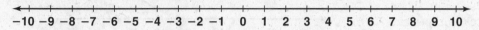

−10 −9 −8 −7 −6 −5 −4 −3 −2 −1 0 1 2 3 4 5 6 7 8 9 10

−5 is to the left of −2.   −7 is to the left of 4.   6 is to the right of 3.
−5 is less than −2. $-7 < 4$ 6 is greater than 3.
$-5 < -2$ $6 > 3$

The *absolute value* of a number is its distance from zero on a number line.
The absolute value of 5 is written as $|5|$.

−3 is 3 units from 0.   2 is 2 units from 0.   0 is 0 units from 0.
$|-3| = 3$ $|2| = 2$ $|0| = 0$

Write the integers missing from each number line.

1.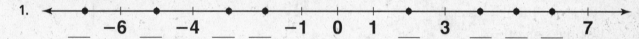

__ −6 __ −4 __ __ −1 0 1 __ 3 __ __ __ 7

2.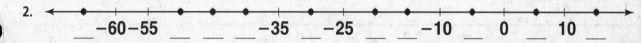

__ −60 −55 __ __ __ −35 __ −25 __ __ −10 __ 0 __ 10 __

Compare. Write <, >, or =.

3. 6 ☐ 0   4. −8 ☐ −5   5. −2 ☐ 2

6. 12 ☐ 5   7. 3 ☐ −2   8. −4 ☐ −6

9. −5 ☐ 5   10. −5 ☐ −10   11. 0 ☐ 0

12. 8 ☐ −1   13. −4 ☐ 0   14. 4 ☐ −2

Find each absolute value.

15. $|3|$ 16. $|-2|$ 17. $|10|$

_____   _____   _____

18. $|-4|$ 19. $|4|$ 20. $|0|$

_____   _____   _____

21. $|-1|$ 22. $|-18|$ 23. $|50|$

_____   _____   _____

Course 3 Topics

Review 212

A number line can help you add integers. For positive integers, move to the right. For negative integers, move to the left.

Example Add $5 + (-3)$:

First, move 5 spaces to the right.
Then move 3 spaces to the left.

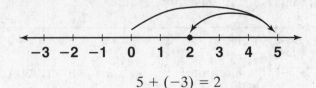

$$5 + (-3) = 2$$

- To add integers with the same sign, add absolute values and use the same sign.

  $3 + 5 = 8$ $\qquad$ $-2 + -4 = -6$

- To add integers with different signs, subtract absolute values and use the sign of the integer with the greater absolute value.

  $-7 + 3 = ?$
  $|-7| - |3| = 7 - 3 = 4$
  Use the sign of -7.
  So, $-7 + 3 = -4$.

- To subtract an integer, add its opposite.

  $3 - (-2) = 3 + 2$ $\qquad$ The opposite of -2 is 2.
  $\qquad\quad = 5$

  $3 - 4 = 3 + (-4)$ $\quad$ The opposite of 4 is -4.
  $\qquad\quad = -1$

  $-4 - (-5) = -4 + 5$ $\quad$ The opposite of -5 is 5.
  $\qquad\qquad = 1$

Simplify each expression.

1. $8 + (-4) =$ _____

2. $8 + 4 =$ _____

3. $-8 + 4 =$ _____

4. $-3 + (-3) =$ _____

5. $6 + (-2) =$ _____

6. $11 + (-16) =$ _____

7. $-7 + 11 =$ _____

8. $-4 + 16 =$ _____

9. $8 + (-12) =$ _____

10. $-9 + (-10) =$ _____

11. $23 + (-3) =$ _____

12. $-5 + 2 =$ _____

13. $9 - (-3) =$ _____

14. $18 - 14 =$ _____

15. $-6 - 7 =$ _____

16. $-3 - (-3) =$ _____

17. $-4 - 16 =$ _____

18. $8 - (-9) =$ _____

19. $-3 - 12 =$ _____

20. $6 - (-2) =$ _____

21. $10 - (-16) =$ _____

22. $-9 - (-10) =$ _____

23. $2 - (-3) =$ _____

24. $-5 - 2 =$ _____

25. $12 - 32 =$ _____

26. $42 - (-15) =$ _____

27. $-16 - 23 =$ _____

28. You owe your teacher $26 for the class trip. You give her a payment of $11. How much do you still owe?

_____

29. A golf ball is 6 inches under water. While trying to retrieve it, the golfer accidentally kicks it so that it descends another 9 inches. How far under the surface of the water is the golf ball?

_____

Course 3 Topics

Review 213

- If two integers have the same sign, the product is positive.

  $8 \cdot 7 = 56$ $\qquad$ $(-8) \cdot (-7) = 56$

- If two integers have opposite signs, the product is negative.

  $(-8) \cdot 7 = -56$ $\qquad$ $8 \cdot (-7) = -56$

- If two integers have the same sign, the quotient is positive.

  $8 \div 2 = 4$ $\qquad$ $(-8) \div (-2) = 4$

- If two integers have opposite signs, the quotient is negative.

  $(-8) \div 2 = -4$ $\qquad$ $8 \div (-2) = -4$

Determine the sign of the product.

1. $-9 \cdot 3 = \boxed{}27$

2. $80 \cdot (-2) = \boxed{}160$

3. $-23 \cdot (-20) = \boxed{}460$

4. $7 \cdot (-5) = \boxed{}35$

5. $-6 \cdot (-8) = \boxed{}48$

6. $64 \cdot 5 = \boxed{}320$

Determine the sign of the quotient.

7. $24 \div (-3) = \boxed{}8$

8. $-(24) \div (-2) = \boxed{}12$

9. $-25 \div 5 = \boxed{}5$

10. $-27 \div (-9) = \boxed{}3$

11. $160 \div 4 = \boxed{}40$

12. $90 \div (-30) = \boxed{}3$

Simplify each expression.

13. $12 \cdot (-3)$

14. $-9 \cdot (-9)$

15. $9 \cdot (-1)$

16. $(-8) \cdot (-4)$

17. $5 \cdot 70$

18. $(-8) \cdot (-3)$

19. $-10 \cdot (-5)$

20. $-9 \cdot 8$

21. $4 \cdot 7$

22. $14 \cdot (-3)$

23. $-16 \cdot (-3)$

24. $5 \cdot (-25)$

25. $\frac{30}{5}$

26. $\frac{-72}{-8}$

27. $\frac{45}{-9}$

28. $-2 \div (-2)$

29. $6 \div (-1)$

30. $40 \div 2$

31. $48 \div (-12)$

32. $-99 \div (-9)$

33. $-21 \div 3$

34. $-33 \div 3$

35. $100 \div (-5)$

36. $75 \div (-3)$

Review 214

- The *median* of this set of data is the middle value when the scores are ordered.

  23 25 25 26 26 **26 26** 26 27 27 28 29

  Since there are two middle scores, add them and divide by 2.

  $\frac{26 + 26}{2} = 26$

Number of Pages Read by Members of the Science Fiction Book Club			
25	26	28	25
26	27	27	26
26	29	26	23

- The *mean* is the sum of the scores divided by the number of scores.

  25 + 26 + 28 + 25 + 26 + 27 + 27 + 26 + 26 + 29 + 26 + 23 = 314

  $\frac{314}{12} = 26.166667$ or about 26.2 pages

- The *mode* is the score that occurs the most. The mode is 26 pages.

Find the mean, median, and mode of each set of data.

1. movies seen: 3 3 1 4 0 4 2 5 7 4 1 2

   _____

2. miles hiked: 5 10 9 12 8 4 5 7 5 13 11

   _____

3. yards earned: 0 0 −8 4 15 −9 1 −1 6 7 −10 2

   _____

4. cost of tickets:
   $3.25 $2.50 $4.00 $4.00 $3.50 $2.00 $4.00 $3.00 $2.50
   $3.00 $4.00

   _____

Which would you report to your parents—mean, median, or mode? Give your reason.

5. test scores: 89 84 79 80 81 55

   _____

   _____

6. friends' allowances: $10 $15 $12 $15 $8

   _____

   _____

Course 3 Topics

Review 215

Follow the order of operations when evaluating expressions with exponents.

Example 1 Evaluate $-(3 + 1)^2 + 5 \cdot 3^2$

① Work inside grouping symbols first. $-(3 + 1)^2 + 5 \cdot 3^2 = -(4)^2 + 5 \cdot 3^2$

② Work with exponents. $= -16 + 5(9)$

- To evaluate a power, write the factors and multiply.

$5^4 = 5 \cdot 5 \cdot 5 \cdot 5$ $(-2)^4 = (-2) \cdot (-2) \cdot (-2) \cdot (-2)$ $-2^4 = -(2 \cdot 2 \cdot 2 \cdot 2)$
$\quad = 625$ $\quad\quad = 16$ $\quad\quad = -16$

- To multiply numbers or variables with the same base, add the exponents.

Simplify. $3^2 \cdot 3^4$ Simplify. $n^3 \cdot n^4$ Simplify. $-4^3 \cdot -4^5$
$\quad 3^2 \cdot 3^4 = 3^{(2+4)}$ $\quad n^3 \cdot n^4 = n^{(3+4)}$ $\quad -4^3 \cdot -4^5 = 4^{(3+5)}$
$\quad\quad = 3^6$ $\quad\quad = n^7$ $\quad\quad = 4^8$

③ Multiply and divide from left to right. $= -16 + 45$

④ Add and subtract from left to right. $= 29$

To evaluate a variable expression with exponents, substitute a number for the variable and then evaluate as above.

Example 2 Evaluate $-2a^3$ for $a = 3$.
$$-2a^3 = (-2)(3)^3$$
$$= (-2)(27)$$
$$= -54$$

Write using exponents.

1. $7 \cdot 7 \cdot 7 = $ _____

2. $(-6) \cdot (-6) \cdot (-6) \cdot (-6) \cdot (-6) = $ _____

3. $10 \cdot 10 \cdot 10 \cdot 10 = $ _____

4. $1 \cdot 1 \cdot 1 \cdot 1 \cdot 1 \cdot 1 = $ _____

5. $(-8) \cdot (-8) \cdot (-8) \cdot (-8) \cdot (-8) = $ _____

6. $2 \cdot 2 \cdot 2 \cdot 2 \cdot 2 \cdot 2 \cdot 2 = $ _____

Simplify each expression.

7. $3^2 + 7 \cdot 9$ _____

8. $9 \cdot 3 - 2^3$ _____

9. $2 + (10 - 3)^2$ _____

10. $6 - 3^2 \cdot 4$ _____

Evaluate each expression for the given values of the variables.

11. $m^2 - 6; m = 4$ _____

12. $4c^3; c = 2$ _____

13. $-2k^2 + 3; k = -5$ _____

14. $2d^2 \div 6; d = 3$ _____

15. $-2n^2 - 4; n = 4$ _____

16. $3ab^2; a = -4, b = 2$ _____

Course 3 Topics

Review 216

Properties of numbers can help you find sums, differences, and products mentally.

Use the *Commutative Property* and the *Associative Property* to group opposites, to group negative numbers, or to make multiples of 10.

- Group opposites.

  $(-8) + (-15) + 8$

  $= (-8) + 8 + (-15)$

  $= 0 + (-15)$

  $= -15$

- Group negatives.

  $-13 + 25 + (-18) + 9$

  $= -13 + (-18) + 25 + 9$

  $= -31 + 34$

  $= 3$

- Make multiples of 10.

  $6 + (-28) + 54$

  $= 6 + 54 + (-28)$

  $= 60 + (-28)$

  $= 32$

Use the *Distributive Property* to rewrite one factor as the sum or difference of two numbers.

$3(5.9)$ ⟨ **Think: 5.9 = 6 − 0.1** ⟩ $4(8.2)$ ⟨ **Think: 8.2 = 8 + 0.2** ⟩

$3(5.9) = 3(6 - 0.1)$ $4(8.2) = 4(8 + 0.2)$

$\quad = 3(6) - 3(0.1)$ $\quad = 32 + 0.8$

$\quad = 18 - 0.3$ $\quad = 32.8$

$\quad = 17.7$

Use mental math to simplify each expression.

1. $-8 + 16 + (-2)$ _____

2. $-4 + 3 + (-26) + 7$ _____

3. $49 + 12 + 31$ _____

4. $5 + (-8) + 25 + 8$ _____

5. $55 + (-6) + 15 + 6$ _____

6. $(4)(-12)(5)$ _____

7. $20 \cdot 18 \cdot 5$ _____

8. $(-2)(9)(-5)$ _____

9. $-8(5 \cdot 7)$ _____

10. $4(36 \cdot 25)$ _____

11. $-81 + 4 + (-19)$ _____

12. $-28 + 32 + (-46) + 28$ _____

Use mental math and the distributive property to simplify.

13. $8(3.9)$

_____

14. $6(21)$

_____

15. $4(7.2)$

_____

16. $5(38)$

_____

17. $6(10.1)$

_____

18. $7(42)$

_____

Review 217

To solve one-step equations:

① Use opposite, or inverse, operations to isolate the variable.

② Simplify.

③ Check by substituting your answer for the variable.

Solve and check each equation.

$$x + 7 = 34$$
$$x + 7 - 7 = 34 - 7 \quad \leftarrow \text{Subtract 7 from each side.}$$
$$x = 27 \quad \leftarrow \text{Simplify.}$$

Check: $\quad x + 7 = 34$
$$27 + 7 \stackrel{?}{=} 34$$
$$34 = 34 \checkmark$$

$$\frac{w}{5} = 20$$
$$5 \cdot \frac{w}{5} = 5 \cdot 20 \quad \leftarrow \text{Multiply each side by 5.}$$
$$w = 100 \quad \leftarrow \text{Simplify.}$$

Check: $\quad \frac{w}{5} = 20$
$$\frac{100}{5} \stackrel{?}{=} 20$$
$$20 = 20 \checkmark$$

Show your steps to solve each equation. Then check.

1. $\quad n + 5 = 11$

$$n + 5 - \boxed{} = 11 - \boxed{}$$

$$n = \boxed{}$$

Check: $\quad n + 5 = 11$

$$\boxed{} + 5 \stackrel{?}{=} 11$$

$$\boxed{} = 11$$

2. $\quad 13 + b = 27$

$$13 + b - \boxed{} = 27 - \boxed{}$$

$$b = \boxed{}$$

Check: $\quad 13 + b = 27$

$$13 + \boxed{} \stackrel{?}{=} 27$$

$$\boxed{} = 27$$

3. $\quad y - 18 = 24$

_____

_____

Check: _____

_____

_____

4. $\quad 3x = 18$

$$\frac{3x}{\boxed{}} = \frac{18}{\boxed{}}$$

$$x = 6$$

Check: $3x = 18$

$$3 \cdot \boxed{} \stackrel{?}{=} 18$$

$$\boxed{} = 18$$

5. $\quad \frac{y}{-5} = -13$

$$\frac{y}{-5} \cdot \boxed{} = -13 \cdot \boxed{}$$

$$y = \boxed{}$$

Check: $\frac{y}{-5} = -13$

$$\frac{\boxed{}}{-5} \stackrel{?}{=} -13$$

$$\boxed{} = -13$$

6. $\quad y \cdot 8 = 24$

_____

_____

Check: $y \cdot 8 = 24$

_____

_____

7. $6 = f + 12$

$f =$ _____

8. $-18 = s + (-23)$

$s =$ _____

9. $w + 4 = \frac{1}{2}$

$w =$ _____

10. $-16 = -8x$

$x =$ _____

11. $\frac{b}{0.4} = 1.6$

$b =$ _____

12. $7.5 = 1.5c$

$c =$ _____

Course 3 Topics

Review 218

Michael bought 4 books for the same price at a fair. Admission to the fair was $5.
How much was each book if Michael spent a total of $17 at the fair?

Follow these steps to solve the two-step equation: $4b + 5 = 17$

① Add or subtract on each side. $4b + 5 - 5 = 17 - 5$

$4b = 12$

② Multiply or divide to isolate the variable. $\frac{4b}{4} = \frac{12}{4}$

$b = 3$ ← Each book cost $3.

③ Check by substituting your answer for the variable.   Check: $4b + 5 = 17$

$4 \cdot 3 + 5 \overset{?}{=} 17$

$17 = 17$ ✔

Show your steps to solve each equation. Then check.

1. $2k + 5 = 25$

$2k + 5 - \boxed{} = 25 - \boxed{}$

$\frac{2k}{\boxed{}} = \frac{20}{\boxed{}}$

$k = \boxed{}$

Check: $2k + 5 = 25$

$2 \cdot \boxed{} + 5 \overset{?}{=} 25$

$\boxed{} = 25$

2. $\frac{p}{2} - 2 = 2$

$\frac{p}{2} - 2 + \boxed{} = 2 + \boxed{}$

$\frac{p}{2} \cdot \boxed{} = 4 \cdot \boxed{}$

$p = \boxed{}$

Check: $\frac{p}{2} - 2 = 2$

$\frac{\boxed{}}{2} - 2 \overset{?}{=} 2$

$\boxed{} = 2$

3. $7y - 17 = -38$

_____

_____

_____

Check: _____

_____

_____

Solve each equation.

4. $\frac{x}{-2} + 6 = 4$

$x =$ _____

5. $14j - 7 = 91$

$j =$ _____

6. $240a - 3 = 5$

$a =$ _____

7. $2.4 + 3s = -0.6$

$s =$ _____

8. $2 + \frac{n}{-5} = 4$

$n =$ _____

9. $140 = -4 - 12e$

$e =$ _____

Review 219

A *term* is a number, a variable, or the product of a number and variable(s). The two terms in $-2x + 4y$ are $-2x$ and $4y$.

Terms with exactly the same variable factor are called *like terms*. In $-3x + 4y + 5x$, $-3x$ and $5x$ are like terms.

One way to *combine like terms* is by addition or subtraction.

- Add to combine like terms in $4y + y$.

  $4y + y = (4 + 1)y = 5y$

- Subtract to combine like terms in $2m - 5m$.

  $2m - 5m = (2 - 5)m = -3m$

To *simplify* an expression, combine its like terms. Perform as many of its operations as possible.

Simplify: $3a + 5b - a + 2b$
$= (3a - a) + (5b + 2b)$
$= 2a + 7b$

Simplify: $2(x - 4)$
$= 2x - 2(4)$
$= 2x - 8$

Combine like terms.

1. $6x + 2x = $ _____

2. $4c - c = $ _____

3. $-h - h = $ _____

4. $-3y + 4y = $ _____

5. $m - 5m = $ _____

6. $6n + n = $ _____

7. $2s - 6s = $ _____

8. $-t - 2t = $ _____

9. $3b - 9b = $ _____

10. $-2p - 5p = $ _____

11. $v + 9v = $ _____

12. $-4j + j = $ _____

Simplify each expression.

13. $8(c - 5) = $ _____

14. $4(d + 6) = $ _____

15. $5n + 3 + n = $ _____

16. $x + 2y + x + y = $ _____

17. $3(m + 4) - 5m = $ _____

18. $(v - 4)5 = $ _____

19. $4a + 2 - 8a + 1 = $ _____

20. $6s + 5 - (s - 6) = $ _____

21. $3(u + 4) - 5u = $ _____

22. $2x + y - (9 - 4x) = $ _____

23. $-5x + 3(x - y) = $ _____

24. $v + 6v - 2v = $ _____

25. $-2s + 6 - s - 4 = $ _____

26. $-x + 4(x - 2) = $ _____

27. $3(k + j) - 4k - k = $ _____

28. $4a - 6 - a + 1 = $ _____

Course 3 Topics

Review 220

Combining terms can help solve equations.

Solve: $5n + 6 + 3n = 22$

$5n + 3n + 6 = 22$ ← Commutative Property

$8n + 6 = 22$

$8n + 6 - 6 = 22 - 6$

$8n = 16$

$\frac{8n}{8} = \frac{16}{8}$

$n = 2$

Check: $5n + 6 + 3n = 22$

$5(2) + 6 + 3(2) \overset{?}{=} 22$

$22 = 22$ ✔

When an equation has a variable on both sides, add or subtract to get the variable on one side.

Solve: $-6m + 45 = 3m$

$-6m + 6m + 45 = 3m + 6m$ ← Add 6m to each side.

$45 = 9m$

$\frac{45}{9} = \frac{9m}{9}$

$5 = m$

Check: $-6m + 45 = 3m$

$-6(5) + 45 \overset{?}{=} 3(5)$

$15 = 15$ ✔

Solve each equation. Check the solution.

1. $a - 4a = 36$

$a = $ _____

2. $3b - 5 - 2b = 5$

$b = $ _____

3. $5n + 4 - 8n = -5$

$n = $ _____

4. $12k + 6 = 10$

$k = $ _____

5. $3(x - 4) = 15$

$x = $ _____

6. $y - 8 + 2y = 10$

$y = $ _____

7. $3(s - 10) = 36$

$s = $ _____

8. $-15 = p + 4p$

$p = $ _____

9. $2g + 3g + 5 = 0$

$g = $ _____

10. $6c + 4 - c = 24$

$c = $ _____

11. $3(x - 2) = 15$

$x = $ _____

12. $4y + 9 - 7y = -6$

$y = $ _____

13. $4(z - 2) + z = -13$

$z = $ _____

14. $24 = -2(b - 3) + 8$

$b = $ _____

15. $17 = 3(g + 3) - g$

$g = $ _____

16. $5(k - 4) = 4 - 3k$

$k = $ _____

17. $8 - m - 3m = 16$

$m = $ _____

18. $6n + n + 14 = 0$

$n = $ _____

19. $7(p + 1) = 9 - p$

$p = $ _____

20. $36 = 4(q - 5)$

$q = $ _____

21. $25 + 2t = 5(t + 2)$

$t = $ _____

Course 3 Topics

Review 221

Problem Solving: Draw a Diagram and Write an Equation

If a problem has many steps, try to write an equation, by first defining a variable. Drawing a diagram can help you visualize a problem.

Read and Understand   Mrs. Harris is fencing a rectangular dog kennel and has 180 feet of fencing. If she wants the length to be 15 feet longer than the width, what will be the dimensions of the kennel?

What are you asked to do?   *Find the dimensions of the dog kennel.*

Plan and Solve   Let x represent the width of the fence. The length of the kennel is 15 feet longer than the width. So, let $x + 15$ equal the length of the dog kennel.

Words | kennel width | + | kennel width | + | kennel length | + | kennel length | = 180 ft

Equation | x | + | x | + | $x + 15$ | + | $x + 15$ | = 180 ft

$$x + x + (x + 15) + (x + 15) = 180$$
$$4x + 30 = 180 \leftarrow \text{Combine like terms.}$$
$$4x = 150 \leftarrow \text{Subtract 30 from each side.}$$
$$\frac{4x}{4} = \frac{150}{4}$$
$$x = 37.5 \text{ ft the width}$$
$$x + 15 = 52.5 \text{ ft the length}$$

Look Back   How could you check your answer? *Substitute the dimensions back in the problem. Two times the width plus 2 times the length does give you 180 feet. The answer checks.*

Solve each problem by either drawing a diagram or writing an equation.

1. Tickets for an adult and three children to attend a soccer game costs $20. An adult's ticket cost $2 more than a child's ticket. Find the cost of each ticket.

   _____

2. A rectangular deck has a perimeter of 42 feet. The length is 3 feet longer than the width. What is the length and width of the deck?

   _____

3. On a family vacation, the Martins drove 842 miles in 2 days. On the second day they drove 24 more miles than the first day. How many miles did they drive each day?

   _____

4. On the third day of a school fundraiser, Nichole sold 14 bags of flower bulbs. This was twice as many as the second day. On the second day, she sold two more bags than on the first day. How many bags of flower bulbs did she sell on the first day?

   _____

Course 3 Topics

Review 222

You can graph inequality solutions on a number line.

Inequality	Graph	How to Read the Graph
$x > 2$ x is *greater than* 2	−3 −2 −1 0 1 2 3 (open dot at 2, shaded right)	An open dot at 2 shows that 2 is not included. All numbers greater than 2 are included.
$x < 2$ x is *less than* 2	−3 −2 −1 0 1 2 3 (open dot at 2, shaded left)	An open dot at 2 shows that 2 is not included. All numbers less than 2 are included.
$x \geq 2$ x is *equal to or greater than* 2	−3 −2 −1 0 1 2 3 (solid dot at 2, shaded right)	A solid dot at 2 shows that 2 is included. All numbers greater than 2 are also included.
$x \leq 2$ x is *equal to or less than* 2	−1 0 1 2 3 4 5 (solid dot at 2, shaded left)	A solid dot at 2 shows that 2 is included. All numbers less than 2 are also included.

To help solve an inequality, you can subtract the same number from
or add the same number to each side.

Solve: $x + 5 > 8$.

$$x + 5 > 8$$
$$x + 5 - 5 > 8 - 5 \quad \leftarrow \text{Subtract 5 from each side.}$$
$$x > 3 \quad \leftarrow \text{Simplify.}$$

Graph the solution:

−2 −1 0 1 2 3 4 (open dot at 3, shaded right)

Solve: $y - 4 \leq 1$.

$$y - 4 \leq 1$$
$$y - 4 + 4 \leq 1 + 4 \quad \leftarrow \text{Add 4 to each side.}$$
$$y \leq 5 \quad \leftarrow \text{Simplify.}$$

Graph the solution:

−1 0 1 2 3 4 5 (solid dot at 5, shaded left)

Graph each inequality on a number line.

1. $x > -2$

−5 −4 −3 −2 −1 0 1 2 3 4 5

2. $4 \geq a$

−5 −4 −3 −2 −1 0 1 2 3 4 5

3. $y \leq -1$

−5 −4 −3 −2 −1 0 1 2 3 4 5

4. $t \geq 0$

−5 −4 −3 −2 −1 0 1 2 3 4 5

Solve each inequality. Graph the solution.

5. $9 + a > 11$ _____

−5 −4 −3 −2 −1 0 1 2 3 4 5

6. $-4 + r < 0$ _____

−5 −4 −3 −2 −1 0 1 2 3 4 5

7. $2 > n - 1$ _____

−5 −4 −3 −2 −1 0 1 2 3 4 5

8. $1 + s \leq 5$ _____

−5 −4 −3 −2 −1 0 1 2 3 4 5

Course 3 Topics

Review 223

Solving Inequalities by Multiplying or Dividing

To help solve an inequality, you can divide or multiply each side by the same number. However, if the number is a negative number, you must also *reverse* the direction of the inequality.

Solve: $-3y \geq 6$. Graph the solution.

$-3y \geq 6$

$\dfrac{-3y}{-3} \leq \dfrac{6}{-3}$ ← Reverse the direction of the inequality.

Divide each side by 23.

$y \leq -2$ ← Simplify.

Graph:

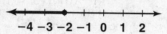

Solve: $\dfrac{a}{2} > 1$. Graph the solution.

$\dfrac{a}{2} > 1$

$2\left(\dfrac{a}{2}\right) > 1(2)$ ← Multiply each side by 2.

$a > 2$ ← Simplify.

Graph:

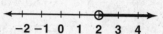

Solve each inequality and graph the solutions.

1. $2a > 8$ _____

$\leftarrow\!\!+\!\!+\!\!+\!\!+\!\!+\!\!+\!\!+\!\!+\!\!+\!\!+\!\!+\!\!\rightarrow$
$-5\,-4\,-3\,-2\,-1\;0\;1\;2\;3\;4\;5$

2. $12 < -3r$ _____

$\leftarrow\!\!+\!\!+\!\!+\!\!+\!\!+\!\!+\!\!+\!\!+\!\!+\!\!+\!\!+\!\!\rightarrow$
$-5\,-4\,-3\,-2\,-1\;0\;1\;2\;3\;4\;5$

3. $\frac{1}{3}n > 1$ _____

$\leftarrow\!\!+\!\!+\!\!+\!\!+\!\!+\!\!+\!\!+\!\!+\!\!+\!\!+\!\!+\!\!\rightarrow$
$-5\,-4\,-3\,-2\,-1\;0\;1\;2\;3\;4\;5$

4. $12 \geq 6s$ _____

$\leftarrow\!\!+\!\!+\!\!+\!\!+\!\!+\!\!+\!\!+\!\!+\!\!+\!\!+\!\!+\!\!\rightarrow$
$-5\,-4\,-3\,-2\,-1\;0\;1\;2\;3\;4\;5$

5. $\frac{m}{4} < 1$ _____

$\leftarrow\!\!+\!\!+\!\!+\!\!+\!\!+\!\!+\!\!+\!\!+\!\!+\!\!+\!\!+\!\!\rightarrow$
$-5\,-4\,-3\,-2\,-1\;0\;1\;2\;3\;4\;5$

6. $5q \geq 5$ _____

$\leftarrow\!\!+\!\!+\!\!+\!\!+\!\!+\!\!+\!\!+\!\!+\!\!+\!\!+\!\!+\!\!\rightarrow$
$-5\,-4\,-3\,-2\,-1\;0\;1\;2\;3\;4\;5$

7. $-4x \leq 8$ _____

$\leftarrow\!\!+\!\!+\!\!+\!\!+\!\!+\!\!+\!\!+\!\!+\!\!+\!\!+\!\!+\!\!\rightarrow$
$-5\,-4\,-3\,-2\,-1\;0\;1\;2\;3\;4\;5$

8. What is the least whole number solution of $-9x < -27$?

_____

9. Donna sings on average $2\frac{1}{2}$ minutes per song. If a cassette holds 20 minutes of songs, what is the greatest number of songs she can record on a cassette?

_____

Course 3 Topics

Review 224

You can solve a two-step inequality by isolating the variable on one side of the inequality symbol.

① First add or subtract the same number on each side to undo the addition or subtraction.

② Then multiply or divide both sides by the same nonzero number to undo the multiplication or division.

Solve: $4x + 5 < -27$.

$4x + 5 < -27$	← Undo addition first.	Check:
$4x + 5 - 5 < -27 - 5$	← Subtract 5 from both sides.	$4(-10) + 5 < -27$
$4x < -32$	← Then undo multiplication.	$-40 + 5 < -27$
$\frac{4x}{4} < \frac{-32}{4}$	← Divide both sides by 4.	$-35 < -27$ ✔
$x < -8$		

The solution is $x < -8$.

Solve: $\frac{x}{5} - 20 \geq 35$

$\frac{x}{5} - 20 \geq 35$	← Undo subtraction first.	Check:
$\frac{x}{5} - 20 + 20 \geq 35 + 20$	← Add 20 from both sides.	$\frac{300}{5} - 20 \geq 35$
$\frac{x}{5} \geq 55$	← Then undo division.	$60 - 20 \geq 35$
$\frac{x}{5}(5) \geq 55(5)$	← Multiply both sides by 5.	$40 \geq 35$ ✔
$x \geq 275$		

The solution is $x \geq 275$.

Solve each inequality. Check your work.

1. $3x - 10 < 20$ _____

2. $\frac{x}{5} + 3 < 63$ _____

3. $16 > 2x + 6$ _____

4. $2x - 7 \leq 35$ _____

5. $28 \leq 3x + 1$ _____

6. $9 \geq \frac{x}{8} - 2$ _____

7. $3x - 17 \geq 43$ _____

8. $\frac{x}{6} + 3 < -15$ _____

9. $\frac{1}{5}x - 9 < 16$ _____

10. $8 > \frac{x}{4} + 1$ _____

11. $2x - 0.75 \geq 3.25$ _____

12. $7.8 \leq 2x + 3.2$ _____

Course 3 Topics

Review 225

You can graph a point on a *coordinate plane*. Use an *ordered pair*
(x, y) to record the coordinates. The first number in the pair is the
x-coordinate. The second number is the *y-coordinate*.

To graph a point, start at the origin, O. Move horizontally according
to the value of x. Move vertically according to the value of y.

Example 1: $(4, -2)$
Start at O, move right 4, then down 2.

Example 2: $(-3, 2)$
Start at O, move left 3, then up 2.

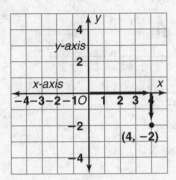

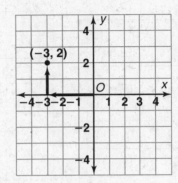

**Graph each ordered pair on the coordinate plane. Label each point
with its letter. Then connect the points in order from A to S. Connect
point S with point A to complete a picture.**

$A(7, 7)$ $J(-4, -6)$

$B(6, 3)$ $K(-7, -7)$

$C(6, 2)$ $L(-5, 1)$

$D(5, 1)$ $M(-6, 2)$

$E(7, -7)$ $N(-6, 3)$

$F(4, -6)$ $P(-7, 7)$

$G(1, -2)$ $Q(-1, 3)$

$H(0, -4)$ $R(0, 4)$

$I(-1, -2)$ $S(1, 3)$

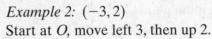

Review 226

You can use a table to help graph a *linear equation* on a coordinate plane.

① Choose a value for *x*. Solve for *y*.

② Find at least 3 such solutions.

③ Graph the solutions.

④ Draw a line through the points.

Graph $y = 2x - 1$.

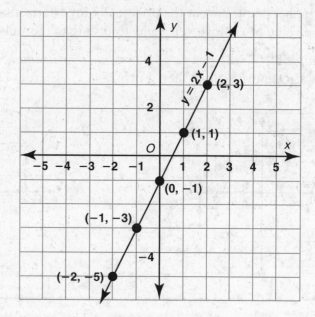

Choose *x*.	Solve for *y*. $(y = 2x - 1)$	*y*	*(x, y)*
−2	2(−2) − 1	−5	(−2, −5)
−1	2(−1) − 1	−3	(−1, −3)
0	2(0) − 1	−1	(0, −1)
1	2(1) − 1	1	(1, 1)
2	2(2) − 1	3	(2, 3)

Complete the table. Graph each *(x, y)* solution. Draw a line through the points.

1. $y = \frac{1}{2}x + 3$

x	*y*
−2	2
0	
2	
4	

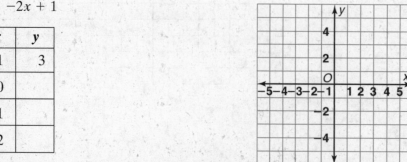

2. $y = -2x + 1$

x	*y*
−1	3
0	
1	
2	

Course 3 Topics

Name _____ Class _____ Date _____

Review 227

The *slope of a line* is $\frac{\text{change in } y}{\text{change in } x}$, found by using two points on the line.

Find the slope of the line that passes through these two points:
$(4, 3)$ and $(2, -1)$.

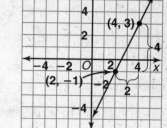

- To find the change in y, subtract one y-coordinate from the other:
  $(3 - (-1)) = 4$.

- To find the change in x, subtract one x-coordinate from the other:
  $(4 - 2) = 2$.

When you find the slope of a line, the y-coordinate you use first for the rise must belong to the same point as the x-coordinate you use for the run.

The slope of the line is: $\frac{\text{change in } y}{\text{change in } x} = \frac{3 - (-1)}{4 - 2} = \frac{4}{2} = 2$

A table of values from the graph also shows the slope.

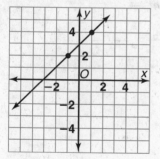

x	5	4	3	2	1
y	5	3	1	-1	-3

Compare the change in each coordinate.

$\frac{\text{change in } y}{\text{change in } x} = \frac{-2}{-1} = 2$

Find the slope of each line.

1.

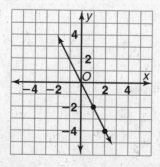

slope = _____

2.

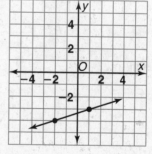

slope = _____

3.

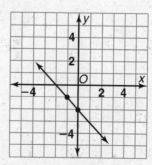

slope = _____

4.

slope = _____

Review 228

An equation of a line can be written in the *slope-intercept form:* $y = mx + b$. The slope of the line is *m* and the *y*-intercept is *b*.

The *y-intercept* is the *y*-coordinate of the point where the line crosses the *y*-axis.

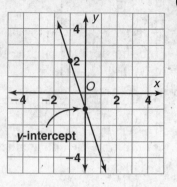

Example: For $y = -3x - 1$, the slope is -3. The *y*-intercept is -1.

Use the graph to write an equation for the line through $(-1, 2)$ and $(0, -1)$.

① Find *m:* slope $\frac{\text{change in } y}{\text{change in } x} = \frac{2 - (-1)}{-1 - 0} = \frac{3}{-1} = -3$

② Find *b:* *y*-intercept $= -1$

③ In the equation $y = mx + b$, substitute $m = -3$ and $b = -1$.

The equation for the line is $y = -3x - 1$.

Find the slope and *y*-intercept of each equation.

1. $y = 2x + 3$

$m = $ _____

$b = $ _____

2. $y = -5x - 2$

$m = $ _____

$b = $ _____

3. $y = -3x + 2$

$m = $ _____

$b = $ _____

4. $y = x - 3$

$m = $ _____

$b = $ _____

5. $y = \frac{1}{2}x - 4$

$m = $ _____

$b = $ _____

6. $y = 5x$

$m = $ _____

$b = $ _____

Write an equation for each line.

7.

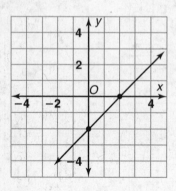

8.

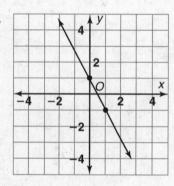

_____   _____

Review 229

Problem Solving: Write an Equation and Make a Graph

You can write an equation with two variables and make a graph to describe a real-world situation.

Suppose you are planning your sister's bridal shower at a restaurant. A buffet dinner costs $12 per person. You are going to buy a cake and bring it to the shower. The cake costs $38.

Write an equation and make a graph to describe the total cost of the bridal shower. Use the graph to estimate the number of people you can invite for $200.

Read and Understand Your goal is to estimate the number of people you can invite for $200, including your sister, you, and your family. The cake costs $38 and the buffet costs $12 per person. Assume there is no tax or tip.

Plan and Solve First, write an equation to represent the total cost of the shower. The cost of the cake is a fixed cost, but the cost per person depends on the total number of people you invite.

Words	total cost	=	cost of cake	+	cost per person	×	number of people

↓　　　Let t = the total cost　　Let p = the number of people

Equation	t	=	38	+	12	×	p

Write the equation, $t = 38 + 12p$, in slope intercept form.

$$y = mx + b$$

$$t = 12p + 38$$

↑　　↑

slope = 12　　y-intercept = 38

Graph $t = 12p + 38$.

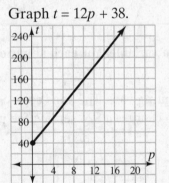

You can invite no more than 13 people to spend less than $200.

Look Back and Check

$t = 12p + 38; t = 12(13) + 38; t = \$194$

This is less than $200.

---

1. You are planning a party where it costs $200 to rent the hall and $10 per person. Write and graph an equation with two variables to model the situation. Use your equation to find the maximum number of people you can invite if you only want to spend $1,500.

_____

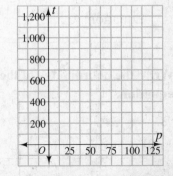

Course 3 Topics

Review 230

The accounting department is having its annual luncheon. They have budgeted $120 for the luncheon. Each table costs $10, and lunch will cost $5 per person.

You can write an equation to represent the number of tables and people who attend. Use a graph to show how the number of tables will vary with the number who attend.

- *Words* $120 = $10 × number of tables + $5 × number who attend

  Let x = number of tables and y = number who attend.

- *Equation* $120 = 10x + 5y$

① Find the coordinates of the *x-intercept* (■, 0).
Let $y = 0$ and solve for x.

$120 = 10x + 5(0)$

$120 = 10x$

$\frac{120}{10} = 10x$

$12 = x$

The coordinates of the *x*-intercept are (12, 0).

② Find the coordinates of the *y-intercept*, (■, 0).
Let $y = 0$ and solve for x.

$120 = 10(0) + 5y$

$120 = 5y$

$\frac{120}{5} = 5y$

$24 = y$

The coordinates of the *y*-intercept are (0, 20).

③ Plot the *x*- and *y*-intercepts and draw the line to graph the equation.

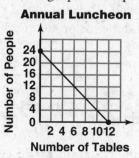

Write an equation with two variables for each situation. Then graph the equation.

1. The Nature Club is renting vans. The vans costs $6 per student. The van company also charges a $24 service fee per van. The club can spend $168.

   Equation: _____

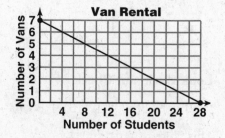

2. Kim has $30 to spend at at garden shop. Plants are $2 each and bags of potting soil are $5 each.

   Equation: _____

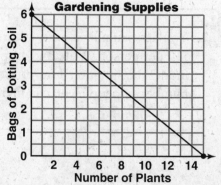

Write the coordinates of the *x*-intercept and *y*-intercept for each equation.

3. $y = 3x + 6$

   _____

4. $2x + 4y = 16$

   _____

Review 231

When two linear equations are considered together, they form a *system of linear equations*. An ordered pair that is a solution to both equations is called a *solution* of the system.

Example: Solve the system of equations by graphing $y = x - 1$ and $y = -x + 3$.

Find three solutions for each equation and graph each line. Find the point where the lines intersect.

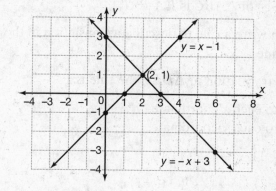

x	0	1	4
y	-1	0	3

x	0	3	6
y	3	0	-3

$y = x - 1$ $y = -x + 3$

The solution for this system of linear equations is the ordered pair (2, 1). Check the coordinates for x and y in both equations.

$y = x - 1$ $y = -x + 3$

$1 \overset{?}{=} 2 - 1$ $1 \overset{?}{=} -2 + 3$

$1 = 1$ ✔ $1 = 1$ ✔

Find three solutions for each equation. Then solve the system of equations by graphing both equations on the grid at the right.

1. $y = -x + 1$

2. $y = -\frac{1}{2}x + 2$

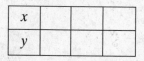

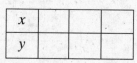

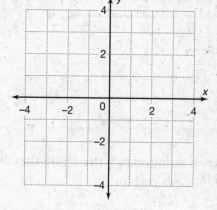

3. Solution for system of equations: _____

4. Check your solution.

_____

_____

_____

Review 232

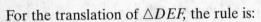

A *translation* moves every point of a figure the same distance in the same direction.

Triangle *ABC* is translated 5 units to the right and 4 units up. The *image* of △*ABC* is △*A′B′C′*.

You can write a rule to describe a translation in the coordinate plane.

For the translation of △*DEF*, the rule is:

Add 5 to each *x*-coordinate.
Add 1 to each *y*-coordinate.

$D(-4, -1) \rightarrow D'(1, 0)$

$E(-6, -2) \rightarrow E'(-1, -1)$

$F(-6, -5) \rightarrow F'(-1, -4)$

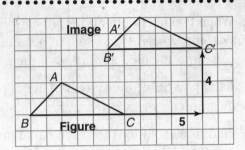

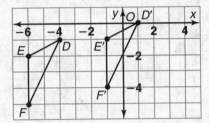

Copy each figure. Then graph the image after the given translation. Name the coordinates of the image.

1. right 5 units, up 1 unit

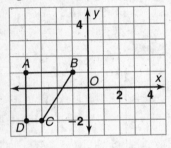

_____

_____

2. left 3 units, down 2 units

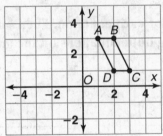

_____

_____

Use arrow notation to write a rule that describes the translation shown on each graph.

3.

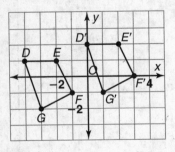

_____

_____

4.

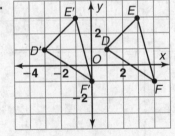

_____

_____

Review 233

A *reflection* flips a figure over a line (the *line of reflection*). Figure
$A'B'C'$ is the image of figure ABC after a reflection over the *y*-axis.

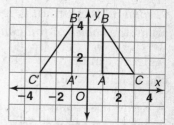

Each point of the image is the same distance from the line of
reflection as the corresponding point of the original figure.

Since A is 1 unit to the right of the *y*-axis, locate A' 1 unit to the left
of the *y*-axis.

If the image is identical to the original figure, then the figure has
reflectional symmetry and has a *line of symmetry*.

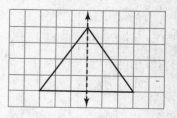

Copy each figure.

1. Reflect the figure over the *x*-axis.

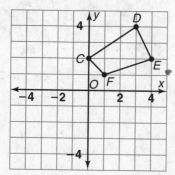

2. Reflect the figure over the *y*-axis.

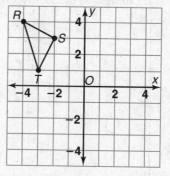

Copy each figure. Does the figure have reflectional symmetry? If it does, draw all the lines of symmetry.

3.

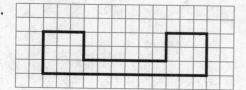

4.

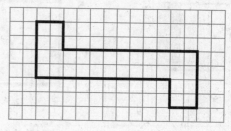

Review 234

A *rotation* is a turn of a figure about a center point, the *center of rotation*.

A figure can be rotated up to 360° counterclockwise.

A figure has *rotational symmetry* if an image matches the original figure after a rotation of 180° or less.

The angle measure the figure rotates is the *angle of rotation*.

The shaded triangle is rotated about its lower vertex.

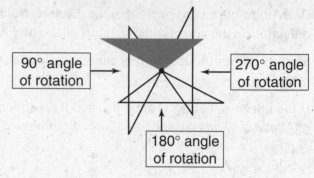

90° angle of rotation

270° angle of rotation

180° angle of rotation

The triangle does not have rotational symmetry.

The shaded figure is rotated 90°, 180°, or 270° about point *X*. The unshaded figure is its image. What is the angle of rotation?

1.

_____

2.

•*X*

_____

3.

_____

Judging by appearance, determine whether each figure has rotational symmetry. If it does, find the angle of rotation.

4.

_____

5.

_____

6.

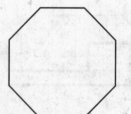

_____

Course 3 Topics

Review 235

A *prime number* is a number with only two factors, 1 and itself.

> The number 17 is prime.
> Its only factors are 1 and 17.

Use a factor tree to find prime factors. The product of prime factors is called the *prime factorization*.

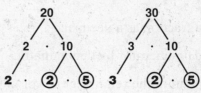

The prime factorization of 40 is $2 \cdot 2 \cdot 2 \cdot 5$ or $2^3 \cdot 5$.

The *greatest common factor (GCF)* of a set of numbers is the greatest factor common to the numbers.

Find the GCF of 20 and 30.

① Use factor trees to find prime factors.

② Circle the common factors. The product of the common factors is the GCF.

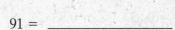

$2 \cdot 5 = 10$
The GCF of 20 and 30 is 10.

Complete these factor trees. Write the prime factorization for each number.

1.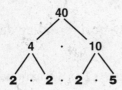

42 = _____

2.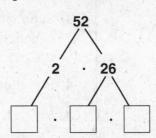

52 = _____

3.

91 = _____

4.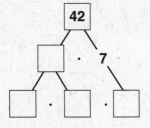

54 = _____

5.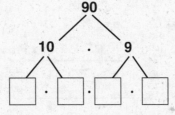

90 = _____

6.

94 = _____

Find the GCF by finding the prime factorization.

7. 10, 12

_____

8. 15, 8

_____

9. 24, 30

_____

10. 12, 18

_____

11. 27, 18

_____

12. 20, 15

_____

Course 3 Topics

Review 236

A fraction is in simplest form when the greatest common factor (GCF) of the numerator and denominator is 1.

Example 1: Write $\frac{24}{36}$ in simplest form.

Use prime factorization and circle the common factors.

$$24 = 2 \cdot 2 \cdot 2 \cdot 3$$
$$36 = 2 \cdot 2 \cdot 3 \cdot 3$$

So, $\frac{24}{36} = \frac{2}{3}$.

To write a fraction as a decimal:

① Divide numerator by denominator.

② Divide until the remainder is 0 or until the remainder repeats.

③ Use a bar to show digits repeating.

Example 2: Write $\frac{5}{6}$ as a decimal.

```
    0.833
 6)5.000
   −48
     20
    −18
      20
     −18
       2  ← Remainder repeats.
```

So, $\frac{5}{6} = 0.833...$, or $0.8\overline{33}$.

Use algebra to write a repeating decimal as a fraction.

Example 3: Write $0.\overline{7}$ as a fraction.

① Let n be the decimal. $n = 0.\overline{7}$

② Multiply each side by 10 because *one* digit repeats. $10n = 7.\overline{7}$

③ Subtract the equations.
$$10n = 7.777...$$
$$-\quad n = 0.777...$$
$$9n = 7$$

④ Solve for n.
$$9n = 7$$
$$\frac{9n}{9} = \frac{7}{9}$$
$$n = \frac{7}{9}$$

So, $0.\overline{7} = \frac{7}{9}$.

Write each fraction in simplest form.

1. $\frac{16}{64}$ _____

2. $\frac{-30}{48}$ _____

3. $\frac{42}{63}$ _____

4. $\frac{-32}{40}$ _____

5. $\frac{12}{-28}$ _____

6. $\frac{18}{27}$ _____

Write each fraction or mixed number as a decimal rounded to three decimal places.

7. $\frac{7}{9}$ _____

8. $-3\frac{2}{7}$ _____

9. $\frac{5}{9}$ _____

10. $5\frac{3}{7}$ _____

11. $\frac{4}{3}$ _____

12. $\frac{1}{11}$ _____

Write each decimal as a mixed number or fraction in simplest form.

13. $0.\overline{1}$ _____

14. $0.1\overline{6}$ _____

15. $0.\overline{3}$ _____

16. $0.\overline{8}$ _____

17. $0.\overline{6}$ _____

18. $0.\overline{36}$ _____

Review 237

The *least common multiple* (LCM) of two or more numbers is the least multiple common to all of the numbers. The LCM of the denominators is called the *least common denominator* (LCD).

| To compare fractions that have the *same* denominator, compare their numerators.

Compare $\frac{3}{4}$ and $\frac{1}{4}$.

$\quad 3 > 1$
$\quad$ So, $\frac{3}{4} > \frac{1}{4}$. | To compare fractions with *different* denominators, rewrite the fractions using the LCD.

Compare $\frac{2}{3}$ and $\frac{7}{9}$.

Rewrite: $\frac{6}{9} \qquad \frac{7}{9}$
$\qquad \frac{6}{9} < \frac{7}{9}$
$\quad$ So, $\frac{2}{3} < \frac{7}{9}$. | Another way to compare numbers involving fractions is to *write them as decimals.*

Compare -1.7 and $-1\frac{3}{4}$.

Rewrite: -1.7 and -1.75
$\qquad -1.7 < -1.75$
$\quad$ So, $-1.7 < -1\frac{3}{4}$. |

Determine which rational number is greater by rewriting each pair of fractions with the *same* common denominator.

1. $\frac{6}{7}, \frac{4}{5}$

2. $\frac{5}{11}, \frac{8}{12}$

3. $\frac{2}{5}, \frac{2}{4}$

_____

_____

_____

4. $\frac{4}{8}, \frac{10}{12}$

5. $\frac{3}{4}, \frac{8}{10}$

6. $\frac{4}{6}, \frac{1}{3}$

_____

_____

_____

7. $\frac{2}{3}, \frac{3}{6}$

8. $\frac{2}{4}, \frac{4}{5}$

9. $\frac{1}{7}, \frac{1}{3}$

_____

_____

_____

10. $\frac{2}{8}, \frac{1}{5}$

11. $\frac{5}{7}, \frac{9}{10}$

12. $\frac{7}{8}, \frac{3}{4}$

_____

_____

_____

Compare. Write >, <, or =.

13. $\frac{8}{9}$ ☐ -2

14. -10.2 ☐ $\frac{-51}{5}$

15. $-\frac{12}{24}$ ☐ $-\frac{9}{24}$

16. 1.2 ☐ $1\frac{1}{2}$

17. $\frac{1}{9}$ ☐ $\frac{1}{3}$

18. $\frac{1}{5}$ ☐ 0.15

19. 0.375 ☐ $\frac{3}{8}$

20. $\frac{-5}{9}$ ☐ $\frac{-7}{12}$

21. $\frac{-1}{2}$ ☐ $\frac{-3}{4}$

22. $-\frac{3}{5}$ ☐ $-\frac{3}{7}$

23. $\frac{3}{10}$ ☐ $\frac{1}{5}$

24. $\frac{5}{6}$ ☐ 0.72

Course 3 Topics

Review 238

To add or subtract fractions and mixed numbers with unlike denominators, first rewrite the fractions using the least common denominator (LCD).

Subtract: $2\frac{3}{4} - 5\frac{1}{3}$

$2\frac{3}{4} - 5\frac{1}{3} = \frac{11}{4} - \frac{16}{3}$

$\phantom{2\frac{3}{4} - 5\frac{1}{3}} = \frac{33}{12} - \frac{64}{12}$ ← The LCD is 12.

$\phantom{2\frac{3}{4} - 5\frac{1}{3}} = \frac{-31}{12}$ ← Subtract numerators.

$\phantom{2\frac{3}{4} - 5\frac{1}{3}} = -2\frac{7}{12}$ ← Simplify.

$2\frac{3}{4} - 5\frac{1}{3} = -2\frac{7}{12}$

You can use addition or subtraction to solve equations with rational numbers.

Solve: $h - \frac{3}{8} = \frac{1}{6}$

$h - \frac{3}{8} + \frac{3}{8} = \frac{1}{6} + \frac{3}{8}$ ← Add $\frac{3}{8}$.

$\phantom{h - \frac{3}{8} + \frac{3}{8}} h = \frac{4}{24} + \frac{9}{24}$ ← The LCD is 24.

$\phantom{h - \frac{3}{8} + \frac{3}{8}} h = \frac{13}{24}$

Find each sum or difference as a fraction or mixed number in simplest form.

1. $6\frac{1}{4} - 2\frac{3}{8}$

2. $\frac{5}{6} + \left(-\frac{1}{2}\right)$

3. $-4\frac{1}{3} - \left(-\frac{3}{5}\right)$

4. $\frac{1}{8} - \left(-\frac{1}{6}\right)$

5. $-1\frac{3}{8} - 4\frac{1}{12}$

6. $\frac{7}{10} + \left(-1\frac{2}{5}\right)$

7. $1\frac{5}{8} - \left(-2\frac{1}{2}\right)$

8. $-2\frac{1}{3} - \left(-1\frac{5}{12}\right)$

9. $-10 - \left(3\frac{11}{12}\right)$

10. $1\frac{1}{3} - 4\frac{3}{4}$

11. $9 + \left(-6\frac{5}{9}\right)$

12. $-2\frac{5}{6} - 5\frac{5}{12}$

Solve each equation. Write each answer as a mixed number or as a fraction in simplest form.

13. $y + \frac{7}{8} = -\frac{1}{4}$

14. $c + -\frac{3}{5} = \frac{1}{2}$

15. $m - 3\frac{2}{3} = 1\frac{1}{6}$

16. $x - 2\frac{1}{4} = -3$

17. $n + \frac{1}{2} = -2\frac{5}{6}$

18. $\frac{1}{2} + d = -3\frac{1}{5}$

19. $7.3 + g = 1\frac{4}{5}$

20. $y - 4.1 = 2\frac{3}{4}$

21. $z + 2.6 = 0.37$

Course 3 Topics

Name _____ Class _____ Date _____

Review 239

To multiply rational numbers in fraction form, multiply numerators, then multiply denominators.

Multiply: $\frac{7}{12} \cdot 1\frac{4}{5}$

$\frac{7}{12} \cdot \frac{9}{5}$ ← fraction form

$\frac{7 \cdot 9}{12 \cdot 5}$ ← Multiply numerators.
        ← Multiply denominators.

$\frac{63}{60} = 1\frac{3}{60} = 1\frac{1}{20}$ ← Simplify.

To divide, multiply by the reciprocal of the divisor.

Divide: $-3\frac{1}{8} \div \frac{2}{3}$

$\frac{-25}{8} \div \frac{2}{3}$ ← fraction form

$\frac{-25}{8} \cdot \frac{3}{2}$ ← reciprocal of divisor

$\frac{-25 \cdot 3}{8 \cdot 2} = \frac{-75}{16}$ ← Multiply.

$= -4\frac{11}{16}$ ← Simplify.

Find each product. Write each answer as a fraction or mixed number in simplest form.

1. $\frac{8}{9} \cdot \left(-\frac{3}{4}\right)$

2. $-\frac{1}{2} \cdot \frac{4}{5}$

3. $-\frac{2}{3} \cdot \left(-\frac{1}{8}\right)$

4. $\frac{5}{6} \cdot \frac{3}{7}$

5. $\frac{3}{4} \cdot \left(-\frac{2}{3}\right)$

6. $3 \cdot 2\frac{1}{4}$

7. $-5\frac{1}{2} \cdot 1\frac{3}{4}$

8. $-2\frac{1}{8} \cdot (-3)$

9. $4\frac{1}{5} \cdot 2\frac{1}{2}$

10. $\frac{13}{15} \cdot \frac{5}{6}$

11. $-3\frac{2}{5} \cdot 2\frac{1}{2}$

12. $-5 \cdot \left(-2\frac{1}{4}\right)$

13. $-\frac{5}{8} \cdot 4\frac{2}{3}$

14. $-5 \cdot 3\frac{3}{10}$

15. $-2\frac{3}{5} \cdot \left(-3\frac{1}{3}\right)$

Find each quotient.

16. $\frac{5}{6} \div \frac{3}{5}$

17. $-\frac{3}{8} \div \left(-\frac{1}{2}\right)$

18. $-6 \div \frac{3}{4}$

19. $4 \div \left(-\frac{2}{3}\right)$

20. $5\frac{1}{4} \div 1\frac{1}{2}$

21. $1\frac{1}{4} \div \left(-\frac{2}{5}\right)$

22. $-\frac{3}{4} \div \left(-1\frac{1}{2}\right)$

23. $-1\frac{3}{5} \div \frac{1}{4}$

24. $2\frac{1}{2} \div \frac{3}{10}$

25. $-\frac{5}{9} \div \left(-\frac{2}{3}\right)$

26. $-6 \div 3\frac{5}{8}$

27. $\frac{3}{4} \div (-9)$

Review 240

You can use a *formula* to find the area of
a figure.

Example: Find the area of a square with side length
1.2 m.

$$A = s \cdot s \qquad \leftarrow \text{Write the formula.}$$
$$A = (1.2)(1.2) \quad \leftarrow \text{Substitute known values.}$$
$$A = 1.44 \qquad \leftarrow \text{Simplify.}$$

The area of the square is 1.44 m^2.

Area Formulas
Rectangle: $A = \text{length} \cdot \text{width}$ $\qquad\qquad A = \ell w$
Square: $\quad A = \text{side length} \cdot \text{side length}$ $\qquad\qquad A = s \cdot s$
Trapezoid: $A = \frac{1}{2}$ height (sum of bases) $\qquad\qquad A = \frac{1}{2} h(b_1 + b_2)$

Knowing how to *transform a formula* by solving
for one of its variables can be useful.

Write a formula to find the width of a rectangle.

Use $A = \ell w$. Solve for w.

$$\frac{A}{\ell} = \frac{\ell w}{\ell}$$
$$\frac{A}{\ell} = w; \text{ or } w = \frac{A}{\ell}$$

Find the area of each figure.

1. Square: side 3.4 ft

2. Rectangle: 6 m $\times$ 2.3 m

3. Trapezoid: $b_1 = 6$ m,
   $b_2 = 12$ m, $h = 4.2$ m

_____

_____

_____

Solve each formula for the variable indicated.

4. Solve for r.
   $d = rt$

5. Solve for ℓ.
   $A = \ell w$

6. Solve for b.
   $y = rx + b$

_____

_____

_____

7. Solve for t.
   $I = prt$

8. Solve for h.
   $A = bh$

9. Solve for h.
   $V = \ell wh$

_____

_____

_____

Use the formula $d = rt$ to find each of the following.

10. time for $d = 500$ miles and $r = 50$ mi/h _____

11. rate for $d = 52.5$ miles and $t = 1.5$ hour _____

12. time for $d = 75$ km and $r = 25$ km/h _____

Course 3 Topics

Review 241

You have $25 left from your paycheck. You spent $200 on rent,
$50 on gas, $150 on food, and $40 on clothing. How much was
your paycheck?

Read and Understand   What do you know? *You have $25 left from your paycheck and
spent $200, $50, $150, and $40.*

Plan and Solve   Use the *Work Backward* strategy to solve.
Add the expenses and the remaining amount.

$$
\begin{array}{rl}
\$\ 25 & \text{remaining} \\
200 & \text{rent} \\
50 & \text{gas} \\
150 & \text{food} \\
+\ \ 40 & \text{clothing} \\
\hline
\$\ 465 & \text{paycheck}
\end{array}
$$

Look Back and Check   How can you check your answer? *Subtract the total expenses from
$465 and see if you get the $25 you have left from your paycheck.*

Solve each problem by either testing and revising or working backward.

1. The next month you get a roommate who pays half the rent. You split a $50 phone bill. How much did you pay for clothing if gas and food expenses and your paycheck remained the same and you were left with $55?

   _____

2. You and your roommate go grocery shopping. At the bakery, you spend $6.50. At the fish market, you spend $4.75. Then you return home with $5.00. How much did you start with?

   _____

3. Your car breaks down. The new battery costs $125 and other necessary parts cost $217. The total cost to fix the car is $650. What is the cost for labor?

   _____

4. In February you deposited $75 in savings. In March you deposited $50, in April you deposited $120, and in May you deposited $20. By June you had $300 in savings. How much money did you start with in January?

   _____

5. If you multiply your roommate's age by 4, add 7, divide by 3, and subtract 9, the result is 20. How old is your roommate?

   _____

6. You spend $20 on gas. You spend half of your remaining cash for lunch. Then you buy a newspaper for $1.75. You have $6.25 left. How much cash did you start with?

   _____

Course 3 Topics

Name _____ Class _____ Date _____

Review 242

The square of 5 is 25.
$5 \cdot 5 = 5^2 = 25$
The *square root* of 25 is 5
because $5^2 = 25$.

$$1^2 = 1$$
$$2^2 = 4$$
$$3^2 = 9 \quad \} \; perfect \; squares$$
$$4^2 = 16$$
$$5^2 = 25$$

$\sqrt{25} = 5$

You can use a calculator to find square roots.
Example: Find $\sqrt{36}$ and $\sqrt{21}$ to the nearest tenth.

$36 \;\boxed{\sqrt{}} = 6 \qquad 21 \;\boxed{\sqrt{}} \approx 4.5825757 \approx 4.6$

You can estimate square roots like $\sqrt{52}$ and $\sqrt{61}$.

Perfect squares

49	$\sqrt{49} = 7$		$\sqrt{49} = 7$
52	Estimate	$\sqrt{52} \approx 7$	Estimate	$\sqrt{61} \approx 8$
64	$\sqrt{64} = 8$		$\sqrt{64} = 8$

Find each square root. Round to the nearest integer if necessary.
Use ≈ to show that a value is rounded.

1. $\sqrt{16}$ 2. $\sqrt{85}$ 3. $\sqrt{26}$ 4. $\sqrt{36}$

_____ _____ _____ _____

5. $\sqrt{98}$ 6. $\sqrt{40}$ 7. $\sqrt{100}$ 8. $\sqrt{18}$

_____ _____ _____ _____

9. $\sqrt{5}$ 10. $\sqrt{121}$ 11. $\sqrt{68}$ 12. $\sqrt{144}$

_____ _____ _____ _____

13. $\sqrt{29}$ 14. $\sqrt{64}$ 15. $\sqrt{37}$ 16. $\sqrt{75}$

_____ _____ _____ _____

17. $\sqrt{225}$ 18. $\sqrt{54}$ 19. $\sqrt{169}$ 20. $\sqrt{103}$

_____ _____ _____ _____

21. $\sqrt{61}$ 22. $\sqrt{400}$ 23. $\sqrt{119}$ 24. $\sqrt{84}$

_____ _____ _____ _____

25. If a whole number is not a perfect square, its square root is an
irrational number. List the numbers from Exercises 1–24
that are irrational.

_____

_____

Course 3 Topics

Name _____ Class _____ Date _____

Review 243

The Pythagorean Theorem The sum of the squares of the lengths of the *legs* of a right triangle is equal to the square of the length of the *hypotenuse*. Also, if $a^2 + b^2 = c^2$, then the triangle is a right triangle.	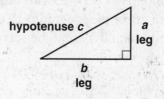 $a^2 + b^2 = c^2$

Example 1: Find the length of a leg of a right triangle if the length of the other leg is 12 cm and the length of the hypotenuse is 13 cm.

$$a^2 + b^2 = c^2$$
$$12^2 + b^2 = 13^2$$
$$144 + b^2 = 169$$
$$144 - 144 + b^2 = 169 - 144$$
$$b^2 = 25$$
$$b = \sqrt{25}$$
$$b = 5$$

The length of the leg is 5 cm.

Example 2: Is a triangle with sides 6 m, 7 m, and 10 m a right triangle?

$$a^2 + b^2 = c^2$$
$$6^2 + 7^2 \stackrel{?}{=} 10^2 \quad \leftarrow \text{Substitute.}$$
$$36 + 49 \stackrel{?}{=} 100 \quad \leftarrow \text{Simplify.}$$
$$85 \neq 100$$

The triangle is *not* a right triangle.

The lengths of two sides of a right triangle are given. Find the length of the third side.

1. legs: 6 ft and 8 ft
hypotenuse:

_____

2. leg: 15 m
hypotenuse: 17 m
leg:

_____

3. leg: 12 in.
hypotenuse: 15 in.
leg:

_____

4. leg: 1.5 km
hypotenuse: 2.5 km
leg:

_____

5. legs: 15 in. and 20 in.
hypotenuse:

_____

6. leg: 16 m
hypotenuse: 34 m
leg:

_____

Is a triangle with the given side lengths a right triangle?

7. 10 cm, 24 cm, 26 cm

_____

8. 5 ft, 7 ft, 9 ft

_____

9. 6 m, 12 m, 15 m

_____

10. 5 in., 12 in., 13 in.

_____

11. 30 mm, 40 mm, 50 mm

_____

12. 2 yd, 5 yd, 8 yd

_____

Course 3 Topics

Review 244

A *ratio* is a comparison between two quantities. Suppose that an apple pie is cut into 12 pieces. 8 are to be served hot and 4 are to be served cold. Two possible ratios are:

$$\frac{hot}{cold} = \frac{8}{4} \; \frac{(part)}{(part)} \quad \frac{hot}{total} = \frac{8}{12} \; \frac{(part)}{(whole)}$$

Example 1: Write the ratios in simplest form.

$$\frac{8}{4} = \frac{8 \div 4}{4 \div 4} = \frac{2}{1} \quad \frac{8}{12} = \frac{8 \div 4}{12 \div 4} = \frac{2}{3}$$

A *rate* compares two different types of quantities. To find a unit rate, divide both the numerator and the denominator by the denominator.

Example 2: Find the unit rate for 150 miles in 6 hours.

① Compare. $\frac{miles}{hours} = \frac{150}{6}$

② Divide. $= \frac{150 \div 6}{6 \div 6}$

③ Simplify. $= \frac{25}{1}$

The unit rate is 25 miles per hour, or 25 mi/h.

Write each ratio in simplest form.

1. 8 in. to 10 in.

2. $\frac{16 \text{ cm}}{12 \text{ cm}}$

3. 15 m : 18 m

_____

_____

_____

4. $\frac{16 \text{ yd}}{24 \text{ yd}}$

5. 30 ft : 10 ft

6. $\frac{9 \text{ mi}}{15 \text{ mi}}$

_____

_____

_____

7. $\frac{12 \text{ ft}}{28 \text{ ft}}$

8. 12 cm to 9 cm

9. 6 m : 16 m

_____

_____

_____

10. 18 km to 10 km

11. $\frac{8 \text{ cm}}{15 \text{ cm}}$

12. 30 in. : 35 in.

_____

_____

_____

Use a calculator, paper and pencil, or mental math to find each unit rate.

13. $3.75 for 3 pounds of bird seed

14. 270 miles for 12 gallons of gas

_____

_____

15. 45 minutes for 15 songs

16. $10.50 for 3 pairs of socks

_____

_____

17. 72 plants in 9 planters

18. 192 jars in 8 cases

_____

_____

19. 3 pounds of cheese for 4 pizzas

20. 270 miles in 6 hours

_____

_____

Review 245

Sometimes you must select the appropriate unit for a measurement.

What customary unit would you use for the weight of a car? *ton, because a ton is a very large unit of weight*

What metric unit would you use for the capacity of a glass of milk? *milliliter, because a milliliter is a small unit of capacity*

Equivalent Units of Measurement	
Customary	**Metric**
1 ft = 12 in.	1 m = 100 cm
1 yd = 3 ft	1 km = 1,000 m
1 mi = 5,280 ft	
1 c = 8 fl oz	1 L = 1,000 mL
1 pt = 2 c	
1 qt = 2 pt	
1 gal = 4 qt	
1 lb = 16 oz	1 kg = 1,000 g
1 t = 2,000 lb	

To convert units of measure, multiply by a conversion factor, or a ratio equal to 1. This process is called *dimensional analysis*.

Example: Convert 4.5 c to fluid ounces.

From the table you know that 1 c = 8 fl oz.

To convert cups to ounces, multiply by $\frac{8 \text{ fl oz}}{1 \text{ c}}$

$$4.5 \text{ c} = \frac{4.5 \text{ c}}{1} \cdot \frac{8 \text{ fl oz}}{1 \text{ c}} = \frac{(4.5)(8) \text{ fl oz}}{1} = 36 \text{ fl oz}$$

So, 4.5 cups equals 36 fluid ounces.

Choose an appropriate customary unit.

1. weight of a peach

    _____

2. capacity of a pitcher of lemonade

    _____

3. length of a crayon

    _____

Choose an appropriate metric unit.

4. distance to Mexico City

    _____

5. mass of a hummingbird

    _____

6. capacity of a jug of milk

    _____

Use dimensional analysis to convert each measure.

7. 48 in. = _?_ ft

    _____

8. 8,400 cm = _?_ m

    _____

9. 6 km = _?_ m

    _____

Use compatible numbers to find a reasonable estimate.

10. 15 qt is about _?_ c.

    _____

11. 32,688 g is about _?_ kg.

    _____

12. 88 oz is about _?_ lb.

    _____

Course 3 Topics

Review 246

You can write an equation as a strategy when solving some problems that have ratios or rates.

A home decorating store offers to mix any paint for free. You need a certain shade of orange that the store person tells you needs 5 parts of red and 3 parts of yellow. If you need 5 gallons of paint, how many ounces of red and orange paint do you need?

Read and Understand   There are 640 oz in 5 gallons. The ratio of paint colors in 5 to 3. Find how many ounces of each color are needed.

Plan and Solve   Setting up an equation will help you solve the problem. Using the ratio given, you know the amount of red paint is a multiple of 5 and the amount of yellow paint is a multiple of 3.

The ratio of red to yellow is 5 : 3. So $5p$ represents the amount of red paint and $3p$ represents the amount of yellow paint.

Words	amount of red	+	amount of yellow	=	total amount of paint
Equation	$5p$	+	$3p$	=	640

$5p + 3p = 640$
   $8p = 640$ ← Combine like terms.
   $\frac{8p}{8} = \frac{640}{8}$ ← Divide each side by 8.
   $p = 80$ ← Simplify.

Substitute 80 for p in the expression for each color
red: $5(80) = 400$ oz
yellow: $3(80) = 240$ oz

Look Back and Check   Since $400 + 240 = 640$, the answer is correct.

Solve each problem by writing an equation.

1. A cleaning solution contains a mixture of ammonia and water in a ratio of 5 : 2. If you need 7 gallons of cleaning solution, how many ounces of ammonia and water do you need?

   _____

2. Concrete is made of cement and sand in a ratio of 1 : 2. How many pounds of cement and sand are needed to make 27 pounds of concrete?

   _____

3. Juice concentrate is mixed with water in a ratio of 1 : 3. How many quarts of concentrate and water do you need to make 12 quarts of juice?

   _____

Review 247

A *proportion* states that two ratios are equal. To solve a proportion that contains a variable, find a value of the variable that makes the statement true. Use *cross products*.

Example 1: Solve the proportion $\frac{3}{4} = \frac{n}{20}$.

  ① Write the proportion. $\frac{3}{4} = \frac{n}{20}$

  ② Use cross products. $3 \cdot 20 = 4 \cdot n$

  ③ Solve. $60 = 4n$
                 $15 = n$

When you write a proportion, remember that matching terms in the ratios should represent the same thing.

Example 2: Minh makes bouquets having 4 roses out of 7 flowers. How many roses are there out of 14 flowers?

  ① Write the proportion. $\frac{4}{7} = \frac{n}{14} \frac{(roses)}{(flowers)}$

  ② Use cross products. $4 \cdot 14 = 7n$

  ③ Solve. $56 = 7n$
                $8 = n$

There are 8 roses out of 14 flowers.

Solve each proportion.

1. $\frac{5}{3} = \frac{n}{6}$

    $30 =$ _____

    $n =$ _____

2. $\frac{s}{4} = \frac{7}{2}$

    $2s =$ _____

    $s =$ _____

3. $\frac{15}{12} = \frac{5}{y}$

    $15y =$ _____

    $y =$ _____

4. $\frac{5}{7} = \frac{w}{21}$

    $105 =$ _____

    $w =$ _____

5. $\frac{b}{10} = \frac{6}{15}$

    $15b =$ _____

    $b =$ _____

6. $\frac{9}{12} = \frac{3}{n}$

    $9n =$ _____

    $n =$ _____

Write a proportion for each situation. Then solve.

7. Eight out of 10 fish are trout. How many trout are there out of 40 fish?

_____

    $w =$ _____

8. There is 1 robin for every 5 birds. How many robins are there for 15 birds?

_____

    $b =$ _____

9. Two flowers cost $.66. How much does 1 flower cost?

_____

    $n =$ _____

Course 3 Topics

Review 248

Similar Figures and Proportions

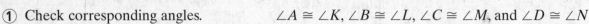

Similar polygons have congruent corresponding angles and corresponding sides that are in proportion.
The symbol ~ means *is similar to*.

Example: Is parallelogram
ABCD ~ parallelogram *KLMN*?

① Check corresponding angles. $\angle A \cong \angle K$, $\angle B \cong \angle L$, $\angle C \cong \angle M$, and $\angle D \cong \angle N$

② Compare corresponding sides.
$\dfrac{AB}{KL} = \dfrac{8}{4} = \dfrac{2}{1}$ $\dfrac{BC}{LM} = \dfrac{12}{6} = \dfrac{2}{1}$
$\dfrac{CD}{MN} = \dfrac{8}{4} = \dfrac{2}{1}$ $\dfrac{DA}{NK} = \dfrac{12}{6} = \dfrac{2}{1}$

Corresponding angles are congruent. Corresponding sides are in proportion. The parallelograms are similar.

You can use proportions to find unknown lengths in similar figures.

① To find *EF*, use a proportion. $\dfrac{AB}{DE} = \dfrac{BC}{EF}$ $\triangle ABC \sim \triangle DEF$

② Substitute. $\dfrac{12}{6} = \dfrac{10}{n}$

③ Use cross products. $12n = 60$

④ Solve. $n = 5$

$EF = 5$

Tell whether each pair of polygons is similar. Explain why or why not.

1.

2.

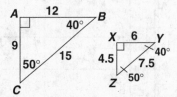

3.

_____   _____   _____

Exercises 4–6 show pairs of similar polygons. Find the unknown length.

4.

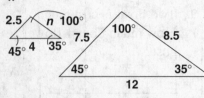

5.

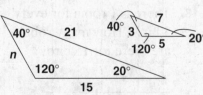

6.

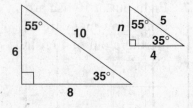

_____   _____   _____

Name _____ Class _____ Date _____

Review 249

Similarity Transformations

Draw the image of quadrilateral $ABCD$
for the *dilation* with *scale factor* 2.
Then graph the image.

Example:

① Write the coordinates of
   each point.

② Multiply the x- and y-
   coordinates of each point
   by the scale factor, 2.

③ Graph the image
   $A'B'C'D'$.

$$A(-2, -1) \longrightarrow A'(-4, -2)$$
$$B(-2, 1) \longrightarrow B'(-4, 2)$$
$$C(2, 1) \longrightarrow C'(4, 2)$$
$$D(1, -1) \longrightarrow D'(2, -2)$$

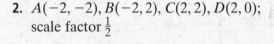

Image $A'B'C'D'$ is an *enlargement* of $ABCD$ because the scale
factor is greater than 1. If the scale factor had been less than 1,
then the dilation of $ABCD$ would be a *reduction*.

**Graph quadrilateral $ABCD$ and its image $A'B'C'D'$ after a
dilation with the given scale factor. Classify each dilation as
an enlargement or a reduction.**

1. $A(-1, 1), B(1, 1), C(0, -1), D(-1, -1)$;
   scale factor 2

2. $A(-2, -2), B(-2, 2), C(2, 2), D(2, 0)$;
   scale factor $\frac{1}{2}$

_____

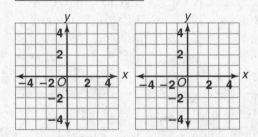

_____

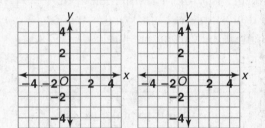

3. $A(-2, -2), B(-2, 2), C(2, 2), D(2, -2)$;
   scale factor $\frac{1}{2}$

4. $A(-2, 2), B(2, 0), C(2, -2), D(-2, -2)$;
   scale factor 2

_____

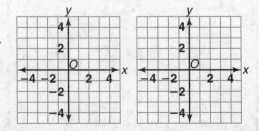

_____

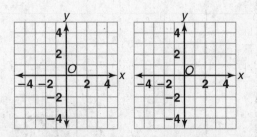

Course 3 Topics

Review 250

A carpenter is making some furniture based on tiny furniture from an old dollhouse. The *scale* of the models is $\frac{5}{2}$ in. : 1 ft. The height of a footstool in the dollhouse is 3 in. What is the height of the carpenter's footstool?

① Write a proportion. Let h = height of the carpenter's footstool. Be sure the terms of the ratios match.

② Use cross products.

③ Solve.

$$\frac{\frac{5}{2}}{1} = \frac{3}{h} \quad \frac{\text{model height (in.)}}{\text{actual height (ft)}}$$

$$\frac{5}{2}h = 3$$

$$h = \frac{6}{5}$$

$$h = 1\frac{1}{5}$$

The height of the carpenter's footstool is $1\frac{1}{5}$ ft.

Write a proportion. Then solve.

1. The carpenter wants to make a dresser based on the dollhouse furniture. The scale is $\frac{5}{2}$ in. : 1 ft. The height of the dresser in the doll-house is 10 in. What is the height of the carpenter's dresser?

   _____

2. The carpenter uses colonial doll furniture with a scale of $\frac{9}{2}$ in. : 1 ft as a model. The length of a doll's bed is 27 in. What is the length of the carpenter's bed?

   _____

3. The scale of some Victorian doll furniture is $\frac{15}{4}$ in. : 1 ft. The height of the doll's table is 12 in. What is the height of the carpenter's table?

   _____

4. The scale of some modern doll furniture is $\frac{7}{2}$ in. : 1 ft. The length of a doll's sofa is 28 in. What is the length of the carpenter's sofa?

   _____

5. The carpenter wants to make a desk like a doll's desk that is $10\frac{1}{2}$ in. high. The scale is $\frac{7}{2}$ in. : 1 ft. What is the height of the carpenter's desk?

   _____

6. Ruth makes a scale drawing of her room. She uses the scale $\frac{3}{2}$ in. : 1 ft. In the drawing, the dimensions of her room are 18 in. by 24 in. What are the actual dimensions of her room?

   _____

Course 3 Topics

Review 251

You can use similar triangles to solve problems.

Example: Sam is 5 ft tall and casts a shadow 8 ft long. The nearby
flagpole casts a shadow 24 feet long. How tall is the flagpole?

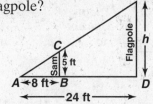

① Draw a diagram. Show similar
   triangles formed by the flagpole, Sam,
   and the shadows. Let h = height of the
   flagpole.

② Write a proportion.
   Use the similar triangles.

$$\frac{\text{flagpole's height}}{\text{Sam's height}} = \frac{\text{length of flagpole's shadow}}{\text{length of Sam's shadow}}$$

③ Substitute.

$$\frac{h}{5} = \frac{24}{8}$$

④ Use cross products.

$$8h = 5 \cdot 24$$

⑤ Solve.

$$h = \frac{120}{8} = 15$$

The height of the flagpole is 15 ft.

In each figure, find h.

1.

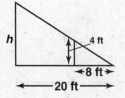

_____

2.

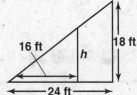

_____

Use similar triangles to answer each question.

3. A child 4 ft tall casts a shadow 12 ft
   long. She stands next to a sculpture
   that has a 36 ft long shadow. How
   tall is the sculpture?

   _____

4. A building 35 ft tall casts a shadow
   105 ft long. Patty casts a shadow
   16.5 ft long. How tall is Patty?

   _____

5. A man 6 ft tall casts a shadow 3 ft
   long. He stands next to a tree that
   has a 47.5 ft shadow. How tall is the
   tree?

   _____

6. A fence post 3 ft tall casts a shadow
   16 ft long. At the same time the barn
   casts a shadow 96 ft long. How tall is
   the barn?

   _____

Course 3 Topics

Review 252

The Sine and Cosine Ratios

Find the sine and cosine ratios for $\angle A$.

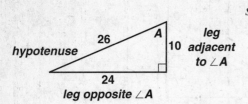

$sine$ of $\angle A = \sin A$ $cosine$ of $\angle A = \cos A$

$= \dfrac{\text{opposite}}{\text{hypotenuse}}$ $= \dfrac{\text{adjacent}}{\text{hypotenuse}}$

$= \dfrac{24}{26}$ $= \dfrac{10}{26}$

$= \dfrac{12}{13}$ $= \dfrac{5}{13}$

You can use a calculator to find the sine and cosine of any acute angle.

Example 1: Find $\sin 47°$.

① Enter the angle measure.

② Press the SIN key.

47 SIN 0.7313537

So, $\sin 47° \approx 0.7314$.

Example 2: Find $\cos 47°$.

① Enter the angle measure.

② Press the COS key.

47 COS 0.6819984

So, $\cos 47° \approx 0.6820$.

You can use the sine and cosine ratios to find measures indirectly.

Example 3: Find the length x to the nearest tenth.

① Use the cosine ratio. $\cos 54° = \frac{x}{35}$

② Solve for x. $x = 35(\cos 54°)$

③ Use a calculator.   35 ✕ 54 COS = 20.5725

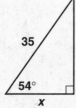

The length x is about 20.6 ft.

Find each trigonometric ratio as a fraction in simplest form.

1. $\sin D$

2. $\cos D$

3. $\sin E$

_____   _____   _____

4. $\cos E$

5. $\sin D$

6. $\sin E$

_____   _____   _____

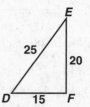

Find each sine or cosine ratio to the nearest ten-thousandth.

7. $\sin 32°$

8. $\cos 56°$

9. $\cos 18°$

10. $\sin 65°$

_____   _____   _____   _____

11. Find n to the nearest tenth. $n =$ _____

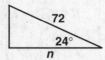

Course 3 Topics

Review 253

A *percent* is a ratio that compares a number to 100.

- To *write a fraction as a percent*, find the equivalent fraction with denominator 100. Write the numerator to show the percent.

$$\frac{3}{10} = \frac{3 \cdot 10}{10 \cdot 10} = \frac{30}{100}$$

- To *write a decimal as a percent*, move the decimal point two places to the right and write the % sign.

$$0.78 = 78\%$$
$$0.054 = 5.4\%$$
$$3.9 = 390\%$$

- To *write a percent as a fraction*, compare the number to 100, then simplify.

$$40\% = \frac{40}{100} = \frac{2}{5}$$

- To *write a percent as a decimal*, remove the % sign and move the decimal point two places to the left.

$$34\% = 0.34$$
$$0.9\% = 0.009$$
$$460\% = 4.6$$

Another way to change between a fraction and a percent is to use a decimal as an intermediate step.

Fraction	→	Decimal	→	Percent
$\frac{3}{8} = 3 \div 8$	=	0.375	=	37.5%

Percent	→	Decimal	→	Fraction
250%	=	2.50	=	$2\frac{50}{100} = 2\frac{1}{2}$

Write each decimal as a percent.

1. 0.39 _____

2. 0.08 _____

3. 4.2 _____

4. 0.5 _____

5. 9 _____

6. 0.056 _____

Write each fraction as a percent.

7. $\frac{3}{4}$ _____

8. $\frac{1}{5}$ _____

9. $\frac{7}{10}$ _____

10. $\frac{5}{8}$ _____

11. $\frac{1}{4}$ _____

12. $\frac{3}{5}$ _____

Write each percent as a decimal.

13. 45% _____

14. 90% _____

15. 0.2% _____

16. 150% _____

17. 4% _____

18. 32% _____

Write each percent as a fraction in simplest form.

19. 25% _____

20. 10% _____

21. 68% _____

22. 450% _____

23. 12% _____

24. 375% _____

Course 3 Topics

Review 254

You can use common percents and their multiples to estimate a percent of a number. Some common percents are listed below.

$25\% = \frac{1}{4}$	$20\% = \frac{1}{5}$	$12\frac{1}{2}\% = \frac{1}{8}$	$10\% = \frac{1}{10}$
$50\% = \frac{1}{2}$	$40\% = \frac{2}{5}$	$37\frac{1}{2}\% = \frac{3}{8}$	$30\% = \frac{3}{10}$
$75\% = \frac{3}{4}$	$60\% = \frac{3}{5}$	$62\frac{1}{2}\% = \frac{5}{8}$	$70\% = \frac{7}{10}$
	$80\% = \frac{4}{5}$	$87\frac{1}{2}\% = \frac{7}{8}$	$90\% = \frac{9}{10}$

Here are two ways to estimate percent.

Use fractions.

Example 1: Estimate 74% of $79.

① Use a fraction that is close to 74%.

$$75\% \approx \frac{3}{4}$$

$$79 \approx 80$$

② Multiply.

$$\frac{3}{4} \times 80 = 60$$

74% of $79 is about $60.

Use decimals.

Example 2: Estimate 18% of 165.

① Use a decimal that is close to 18%.

$$18\% \approx 0.2$$

$$165 \approx 170$$

② Multiply.

$$0.2 \cdot 170 = 34$$

34 is about 18% of 165.

Estimate the percent of each number. Use fractions or decimals.

1. 20% of 36 _____

2. 75% of 41 _____

3. 60% of 49 _____

4. 30% of 42 _____

5. $12\frac{1}{2}\%$ of 66 _____

6. 25% of 17 _____

7. 9.7% of 68 _____

8. 40% of 19.9 _____

9. 5% of 60 _____

10. 69% of 150 _____

11. 0.8% of 153 _____

12. 55% of 400 _____

Estimate a 15% tip for each restaurant bill.

13. $9.25

14. $39.50

15. $28.85

_____

_____

_____

16. $48.45

17. $21.20

18. $12.34

_____

_____

_____

Course 3 Topics

Review 255

You can use proportions to solve percent problems.

Find the part.

Example 1: Find 10% of 92.

① Think of the percent
    as a ratio. $10\% = \frac{10}{100}$

② Write a proportion. $\frac{10}{100} = \frac{n}{92}$

③ Solve. $100n = 920$

$$\frac{100n}{100} = \frac{920}{100}$$

$$n = 9.2$$

10% of 92 is 9.2.

Find the whole.

Example 3: 50 is 20% of what number?

① Write a proportion. $\frac{50}{n} = \frac{20}{100}$

② Solve. $20n = 5,000$

$$\frac{20n}{20} = \frac{5,000}{20}$$

$$n = 250$$ 50 is 20% of 250.

Find the percent.

Example 2: What percent of 80 is 20?

① Write a proportion. $\frac{20}{80} = \frac{n}{100}$

② Solve. $80n = 2,000$

$$\frac{80n}{80} = \frac{2,000}{80}$$

$$n = 25$$

20 is 25% of 80.

Complete the proportion. Then solve each problem.

1. 6 is *n*% of 30.

$\frac{n}{100} =$

n = _____

2. 2 is 25% of *n*.

$\frac{2}{n} =$

n = _____

3. 75% of 80 is *n*.

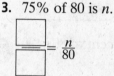 $= \frac{n}{80}$

n = _____

4. *n*% of 50 is 20.

$\frac{n}{100} =$

n = _____

5. 49 is *n*% of 140.

$\frac{n}{100} =$

n = _____

6. 45 is 15% of *n*.

$\frac{45}{n} =$

n = _____

Use a proportion to solve each problem.

7. Find 50% of 90.

_____

8. Find 75% of 980.

_____

9. 60 is 30% of what number?

_____

Course 3 Topics

Review 256

You can use an equation to solve percent problems.

Find the whole.

Example 1: 25% of what number is 20?

① Think of the percent
as a decimal.   25% = 0.25

② Write an equation. $0.25n = 20$

③ Solve. $n = \frac{20}{0.25}$
                                              $= 80$

25% of 80 is 20.

Find the part.

Example 2: Find 12% of 48.

① Think of the percent
as a decimal.   12% = 0.12

② Write an equation. $0.12 \times 48 = n$

③ Solve. $5.76 = n$

12% of 48 is 5.76.

Find the percent.

Example 3: What percent of 48 is 30?

① Write an equation. $n \times 48 = 30$

② Solve. $n = \frac{30}{48}$
                                              $= 0.625$
                                              $= 62.5\%$ 30 is 62.5% of 48.

Use an equation to solve each problem.

1. 30% of what number is 6?

   _____

2. 32 is 25% of what number?

   _____

3. What percent of 80 is 20?

   _____

4. What is 10% of 35?

   _____

5. Find 40% of 90.

   _____

6. What percent of 60 is 27?

   _____

7. What is 11% of 99?

   _____

8. 22 is 55% of what number?

   _____

9. What is 13% of 56?

   _____

10. What percent of 96 is 84?

   _____

Course 3 Topics

Review 257

Percent of Increase

Example 1: Alex collects rare books. In 1997, he bought a book for $10. In 1998, it was worth $12. What is the percent of increase from 1997 to 1998?

$$\text{Percent increase} = \frac{\text{amount of change}}{\text{original amount}}$$

$$= \frac{12 - 10}{10}$$

$$= \frac{2}{10} = 0.2 = 20\%$$

The value of Alex's book increased by 20%.

Percent of Decrease

Example 2: Alex sold one of his books in 1998 for $8. The book cost $12 in 1996. What is the percent of decrease from 1996?

$$\text{Percent increase} = \frac{\text{amount of change}}{\text{original amount}}$$

$$= \frac{12 - 8}{12}$$

$$= \frac{4}{12} = \frac{1}{3} \approx 33.3\%$$

The value of Alex's book decreased by $33\frac{1}{3}\%$.

Find each percent of decrease. Round your answer to the nearest tenth of a percent.

1. $40 to $30

2. $80 to $40

3. 25 to 20

_____

_____

_____

4. 11.5 h to 8 h

5. 99 lb to 87 lb

6. 55 to 30.8

_____

_____

_____

7. 15 ft to 13 ft

8. 75 s to 46 s

9. 25 to 16.4

_____

_____

_____

Find each percent of increase. Round your answer to the nearest tenth of a percent.

10. $50 to $60

11. $90 to $120.50

12. 120 min to 180 min

_____

_____

_____

13. 60 to 77

14. 20 m to 35.7 m

15. 60 to 80

_____

_____

_____

Course 3 Topics

Review 258

Example 1: Carissa's Nursery buys plants for $10. She marks them up 20%. What is the selling price?

① Find the *markup*.

$$\text{cost} \times \text{markup rate} = \text{markup}$$
$$\$10 \times \quad 0.20 \quad = \quad \$2$$

② Find the *selling price*.

$$\text{cost} + \text{markup} = \text{selling price}$$
$$\$10 + \quad \$2 \quad = \quad \$12$$

The selling price is $12.

Example 2: Carissa's Nursery is having a 25% off sale on trees. The regular price for a maple tree is $200. What is the sale price?

① Find the amount of *discount*.

$$\text{price} \times \text{discount rate} = \text{discount}$$
$$\$200 \times \quad 0.25 \quad = \quad \$50$$

② Find the *sale price*.

$$\text{price} - \text{discount} = \text{sale price}$$
$$\$200 - \quad \$50 \quad = \quad \$150$$

The sale price is $150.

Example 3: Carissa's Nursery sells a shrub for $30. This is 20% off the regular price. Find the regular price.

Let c = nursery's cost.

$$c - (0.20 \cdot c) = 30$$
$$0.80c \quad = 30$$
$$\frac{0.80c}{0.80} = \frac{30}{0.8}$$
$$c = 37.50$$

The regular price is $37.50.

Find each selling price. Round to the nearest cent.

1. cost: $20
   markup rate: 20%

   _____

2. cost: $99.99
   markup rate: 10%

   _____

3. cost: $95
   markup rate: 50%

   _____

Find each sale price. Round to the nearest cent.

4. regular price: $500
   discount: 20%

   _____

5. regular price: $23.99
   discount: 15%

   _____

6. regular price: $82.75
   discount: 10%

   _____

Find each regular price. Round to the nearest cent.

7. sale price: $48
   10% off

   _____

8. sale price: $50
   20% off

   _____

9. sale price: $79.99
   30% off

   _____

Course 3 Topics

Review 259

You can write equations to solve many types of problems.

Read and Understand   Katrina is looking for a new sports club. She plans to spend between 10% and 15% of her weekly income on a membership. If Katrina earns $450 per week, find the minimum and maximum amounts that she can spend on a membership.

What are you asked to do?   *Find the minimum and maximum she can spend on a membership.*

Plan and Solve

Minimum	Maximum
$m = 0.10 \cdot 450$	$x = 0.15 \cdot 450$
$= 45$	$= 67.50$

Katrina can spend between $45 and $67.50 per week.

Look Back   Mentally find 10% of $450, which is $45. Take half of $45 to get $22.50. Add $45 and $22.50 to get $67.50. So, the answers are reasonable.

Solve each problem by writing an equation. Check that your answer is reasonable.

1. Madeline has sold $500 worth of merchandise this week. She would like to increase her sales 25% to 30% for next week. Find the minimum and maximum amounts she can increase her sales.

   _____

2. Last year, Miquel ran a total of 1,820 miles. This year he plans to run 15% to 20% more miles than last year. Between how many miles must Miquel run this year to reach his goal?

   _____

3. A manufacturing company sold $150,000 specially produced grommets last year. This year they plan to decrease sales 20% to 30% less than last year. Between what two dollar amounts should the company try to keep their sales?

   _____

4. Juanita currently has a score of 75 points in Mrs. Johnson's science class. She would like to increase her points by 20% to 25%. Between what two point values does Juanita need to raise her points?

   _____

Course 3 Topics

Review 260

Simple Interest

Alicia put $200 in a savings account to earn interest. The interest rate is 5% per year. How much interest will the account earn in $2\frac{1}{2}$ years?

Use this formula to solve:

Interest = *principal* · rate · time in years

$$I = p \cdot r \cdot t$$
$$= 200 \cdot 0.05 \cdot 2.5$$
$$= 25$$

In $2\frac{1}{2}$ years, the account will earn $25 in interest.

Compound Interest

Alex put $500 in an account that earns 6% interest, compounded annually. What will be the account balance after $2\frac{1}{2}$ years?

Use this formula to solve:
Balance = *principal* · (1 + rate)^time in years
$$B = p(1 + r)^t$$

Use a calculator to evaluate:
$$B = 500(1 + 0.06)^{2.5}$$

500 ☒ 1.06 y^x 2.5 ▤ **578.41**

The balance will be $578.41.

Find the interest earned in each account.

1. $300 at 5% simple interest for 1 year

   _____

2. $300 at 5% simple interest for 2 years

   _____

3. $500 at 8% simple interest for 2 years

   _____

4. $1,000 at 6% simple interest for 3 years

   _____

5. $1,200 at 4.5% simple interest for 3 years

   _____

6. $950 at $5\frac{1}{2}$% simple interest for 6 years

   _____

Find the final balance in each account.

7. $800 at 4% compounded annually for 3 years

   _____

8. $1,200 at 5% compounded annually for 4 years

   _____

9. $2,000 at $3\frac{1}{2}$% compounded annually for 2 years

   _____

10. $4,500 at 8% compounded annually for 3 years

    _____

Solve.

11. Ms. Ito is lending her nephew Dan $3,000 for college. She is charging him 2% simple interest each year. He will pay his aunt back in four years. How much interest will he pay?

    _____

Course 3 Topics

Review 261

• •

Angel has eight baseball hats in his collection. There are 2 blue
baseball hats, 1 red, 2 green, and 3 black. What is the probability of
Angel picking a red baseball hat?

If Angel chose a hat at random, there are 8 possible results, or *outcomes*.
A collection of possible outcomes in an experiment is an *event*.

When each outcome has an equal chance of occurring, you can use
the following formula:

Probability of an event = $\frac{\text{number of outcomes in the event}}{\text{total number of possible outcomes}}$

You can list all the possible outcomes. This is called the
sample space. Then you can find the probability.

Sample Space				Probability of red hat
green	green	black	black	$P(\text{red hat}) = \frac{1}{8}$ ← favorable outcomes
black	red	blue	blue	← all possible outcomes

There are 8 possible outcomes.

**A spinner has 12 spaces with the numbers
1, 2, 3, 4, 5, 5, 5, 6, 6, 7, 8, 8. Find each probability.**

1. $P(1)$ _____

2. $P(5)$ _____

3. $P(8)$ _____

4. $P(\text{odd number})$ _____

5. $P(\text{even number})$ _____

6. $P(\text{number less than 5})$ _____

7. $P(\text{number greater than 4})$ _____

8. $P(\text{odd or even number})$ _____

**A box has 10 red, 15 yellow, 20 pink, 25 black, and 30 orange jelly
beans. You pick a jelly bean without looking. Find each probability.**

9. $P(\text{red})$

10. $P(\text{yellow})$

_____

_____

11. $P(\text{pink})$

12. $P(\text{black})$

_____

_____

• •

Review 262

To write a number such as 67,000 in *scientific notation,* move the decimal point to form a number between 1 and 10. The number of places moved shows which power of 10 to use.

- Write 67,000 in scientific notation.

  6.7 is between 1 and 10. So, move the decimal point in 67,000 to the left 4 places and multiply by 10^4.

  $67,000 = 6.7 \times 10^4$

To write scientific notation in *standard form,* look at the exponent. The exponent shows the number of places and the direction to move the decimal point.

- Write 8.5×10^5 in standard form.

  The exponent is positive 5, so move the decimal point 5 places to the right.

  $8.5 \times 10^5 = 850,000$

Write each number in scientific notation.

1. 6,500

2. 65,000

3. 6,520

_____

_____

_____

4. 345

5. 29,100

6. 93,000,000

_____

_____

_____

7. 200

8. 2,300

9. 23,000

_____

_____

_____

10. 450

11. 90,000

12. 96,000

_____

_____

_____

Write each number in standard form.

13. 4×10^4 _____

14. 4×10^5 _____

15. 3.6×10^3 _____

16. 4.85×10^4 _____

17. 4.05×10^2 _____

18. 7.1×10^5 _____

19. 4×10^2 _____

20. 1.3×10^2 _____

21. 7×10^1 _____

22. 2.5×10^3 _____

23. 1.81×10^3 _____

24. 1.6×10^4 _____

25. Jupiter is on the average 7.783×10^8 kilometers from the sun. _____

Which number is greater?

26. 5×10^2 or 2×10^5 _____

27. 2.1×10^3 or 2.1×10^6 _____

28. 6×10^{10} or 3×10^9 _____

29. 3.6×10^1 or 3.6×10^3 _____

Course 3 Topics

Review 263

- To multiply numbers or variables with the same base, add the exponents.

Simplify $3^2 \cdot 3^4$.
$3^2 \cdot 3^4 = 3^{(2+4)}$
$ = 3^6$

Simplify $n^3 \cdot n^4$.
$n^3 \cdot n^4 = n^{(3+4)}$
$ = n^7$

Simplify $-4^3 \cdot -4^5$.
$-4^3 \cdot -4^5 = -4^{(3+5)}$
$ = -4^8$

- To multiply numbers in scientific notation.

Find the product $(5 \times 10^4)(7 \times 10^5)$. Write the result in scientific notation.

$(5 \times 10^4)(7 \times 10^5)$

$(5 \cdot 7)(10^4 \cdot 10^5)$ ← Use the Associative and Commutative properties.

$35 \times (10^4 \cdot 10^5)$ ← Multiply 5 and 7.

$35 \times 10^{4+5}$ ← Add the exponents for the powers of 10.

35×10^9

$3.5 \times 10^1 \times 10^9$ ← Write 35 in scientific notation.

3.5×10^{10} ← Add the exponents.

Write each expression using a single exponent.

1. $5^3 \cdot 5^4$

2. $a^2 \cdot a^5$

3. $(-8)^4 \cdot (-8)^5$

4. $n^6 \cdot n^2$

5. $m^3 \cdot m^6$

6. $(-7)^4 \cdot (-7)^2$

7. $(-3)^2 \cdot (-3)^2$

8. $2^5 \cdot 2^2$

9. $c^5 \cdot c^3$

10. $7^5 \cdot 7^9$

11. $n^3 \cdot n^{11}$

12. $3^5 \cdot 3^2$

Find each product. Write the answer in scientific notation.

13. $(3 \times 10^4)(5 \times 10^3)$

14. $(2 \times 10^3)(7 \times 10^6)$

15. $(8 \times 10^2)(5 \times 10^2)$

16. $(9 \times 10^4)(7 \times 10^4)$

17. $(4 \times 10^2)(7 \times 10^5)$

18. $(8 \times 10^3)(4 \times 10^5)$

Course 3 Topics

Review 264

To divide powers with the same base, subtract exponents.

$$\frac{8^6}{8^4} = 8^{6-4} \qquad \frac{a^5}{a^3} = a^{5-3}$$

$$= 8^2 \qquad\qquad = a^2$$

$$= 64$$

- For any nonzero number a, $a^0 = 1$.

$$3^0 = 1 \qquad\qquad (-6)^0 = 1 \qquad\qquad 4t^0 = 4(1) = 4$$

- For any nonzero number a and any integer n, $a^{-n} = \frac{1}{a^n}$.

$$2^{-4} = \frac{1}{2^4} \qquad 3c^{-2} = \frac{3}{c^2} \qquad \frac{5^3}{5^6} = 5^{3-6} \qquad \frac{10z^3}{5z} = 2z^{3-1}$$

$$\quad = \frac{1}{16} \qquad\qquad\qquad\qquad\qquad = 5^{-3} \qquad\qquad = 2z^2$$

$$\qquad\qquad\qquad\qquad\qquad\qquad\qquad = \frac{1}{5^3}$$

$$\qquad\qquad\qquad\qquad\qquad\qquad\qquad = \frac{1}{125}$$

Write each expression using a single exponent.

1. $\dfrac{6^5}{6^3} =$ _____

2. $(-4)^5 \div (-4)^3 =$ _____

3. $9^8 \div 9^6 =$ _____

4. $(-3)^{-2} =$ _____

5. $\dfrac{2^5}{2^7} =$ _____

6. $(-8)^0 =$ _____

7. $\dfrac{5^0}{5^2} =$ _____

8. $(-4)^{-3} =$ _____

9. $\dfrac{(-6)^4}{(-6)^6} =$ _____

10. $7^3 \div 7^5 =$ _____

11. $9^8 \div 9^{10} =$ _____

12. $\dfrac{2^7}{2^3} =$ _____

Simplify each expression. Use only positive exponents.

13. $w^8 \div w^3 =$ _____

14. $x^6 \div x^1 =$ _____

15. $\dfrac{d^7}{d^3} =$ _____

16. $y^6 \div y^9 =$ _____

17. $a^{10} \div a^4 =$ _____

18. $3m^6 \div m^2 =$ _____

19. $\dfrac{w^2}{w^6} =$ _____

20. $4c^5 \div c^8 =$ _____

21. $\dfrac{8x^2}{4x^5} =$ _____

22. $8a^4 \div 2a^2 =$ _____

23. $6w^2 \div 2w^5 =$ _____

24. $\dfrac{6x^6}{3x^9} =$ _____

Course 3 Topics

Review 265

The expression x^n is a power. It can also be read as x to the nth power.

Raising a Power to a Power

To raise a power to a power, multiply exponents.

Arithmetic:
$(2^4)^6$
$= 2^{(4 \cdot 6)}$ ← Multiply the exponents.
$= 2^{24}$ ← Simplify the exponent.

Algebra:
$(a^x)^y$
$= a^{(x \cdot y)}$ ← Multiply the exponents.
$= a^{xy}$ ← Simplify the exponent.

$(x^{-3})^{-5}$
$= x^{(-3 \cdot -5)}$ ← Multiply the exponents.
$= x^{15}$ ← Simplify the exponent.

Raising a Product to a Power

To raise a product to a power, raise each factor to the power.

Arithmetic:
$(4 \cdot 7)^2$
$= 4^2 \cdot 7^2$ ← Raise each factor to the power.

Algebra:
$(xy)^a$
$= x^a y^a$ ← Raise each factor to the power.

$(4a^2)^3$
$= 4^3(a^2)^3$ ← Raise each factor to the power.
$= 4^3 a^6$ ← Multiply the exponents.
$= 64a^6$ ← Simplify.

Write each expression using one base and one exponent.

1. $(6^2)^{-4}$

2. $(y^6)^{-5}$

3. $(7^{-4})^{-5}$

4. $(x^b)^c$

5. $(5^9)^3$

6. $(a^{-3})^{-8}$

Simplify each expression.

7. $(ht)^n$

8. $(5v)^2$

9. $(7p^4)^2$

10. $(3d^4f^2)^3$

11. $(k^5j^4)^3$

12. $(2s^7u^6)^4$

Use <, >, or = to complete each statement.

13. $2^5 \ \square \ (2^3)^2$

14. $(5^{-4})^2 \ \square \ 5^{-8}$

15. $(6 \cdot 4)^2 \ \square \ 10^2$

Course 3 Topics

Review 266

You can write equations to help solve problems involving scientific notation.

The Pacific Ocean is about 6.4×10^7 square miles. It is about two times bigger than the size of the Atlantic Ocean. About how big is the Atlantic Ocean?

Read and Understand The Pacific Ocean has an area two times the size of the Atlantic Ocean. Your goal is to find the area of the Atlantic Ocean.

Plan and Solve You know the size of the Pacific Ocean. You can write an equation to solve for the size of the Atlantic Ocean.

Let x = the area of the Atlantic Ocean.

$$2x = 6.4 \times 10^7$$
$$x = \frac{6.4 \times 10^7}{2}$$
$$x = 3.2 \times 10^7$$

The Atlantic Ocean is about 3.2×10^7 square miles.

Look Back and Check Half of 6.4 is 3.2 and the exponent on 10 did not change. So the area of the Atlantic Ocean appears to be correct.

Solve each problem by writing an equation.

1. The Artic Ocean is about 5.4×10^6 square miles. The Indian Ocean is about 5 times the size of the Artic Ocean. About how big is the Indian Ocean?

   _____

2. The greatest depth of the Artic Ocean is about 1.8×10^5 ft. The greatest depth of the Pacific Ocean is about two times this amount. About how deep is the greatest depth of the Pacific Ocean?

   _____

3. Joe is 5 years older than Bijan. If the sum of their ages is 25, how old is each boy?

   Joe _____ Bijan _____

4. A chicken dinner costs $2.50 more than a spaghetti dinner. If the cost of both is $18.40, how much does each meal cost?

   Chicken _____ Spaghetti _____

5. Elaine sold twice as many T-shirts as Kim. How many did each girl sell if the total number of T-shirts sold was 27?

   Elaine _____ Kim _____

6. There are 5 more rows of corn than rows of peas in the garden. How many rows of each are there if there are 19 rows in all?

   Corn _____ Peas _____

Course 3 Topics

Review 267

The *binary*, or base-2 number system, uses the digits 0 and 1 with place values using powers of 2. Computers use binary numbers to store information.

- Finding the decimal value of a binary number

Find the decimal value of the binary number 1101_2.

$1101_2 = (1 \cdot 2^3) + (1 \cdot 2^2) + (0 \cdot 2^1) + (1 \cdot 2^0)$ ← Write the binary number in expanded form.
$\quad = 8 + 4 + 0 + 1$ ← Simplify within the parentheses.
$\quad = 13$ ← Add.

Find the decimal value of the binary number 110101_2.

$110101_2 = (1 \cdot 2^5) + (1 \cdot 2^4) + (0 \cdot 2^3) +$ ← Write the binary number in expanded form.
$\quad\quad\quad (1 \cdot 2^2) + (0 \cdot 2^1) + (1 \cdot 2^0)$
$\quad\quad = 32 + 16 + 0 + 4 + 0 + 1$ ← Simplify within the parentheses.
$\quad\quad = 53$ ← Add.

- Changing a decimal to a binary number

Write the decimal number 18 as a binary number.

Begin by completing a table of powers of 2.

2^7	2^6	2^5	2^4	2^3	2^2	2^1	2^0
128	64	32	16	8	4	2	1

Complete the table by using each power of 2 either once or not at all.
Use a 1 if the power is used and a 0 if the power is not used.

2^7	2^6	2^5	2^4	2^3	2^2	2^1	2^0
128	64	32	16	8	4	2	1
			1	0	0	1	0

$18 = 16 + 2$ (Use the digits 1 and 0 to write the binary number.)

$18 = 10010_2$

Write the decimal value for each binary number.

1. $1111_2 = $ _____   **2.** $11100_2 = $ _____   **3.** $10111_2 = $ _____   **4.** $110101_2 = $ _____

Write each decimal number as a binary number.

5. 14 _____   **6.** 7 _____   **7.** 33 _____   **8.** 22 _____

Review 268

- *Vertical angles* are pairs of opposite angles formed by two intersecting lines. They are congruent.

  Example 1: ∠1 and ∠3, ∠4 and ∠2

- *Adjacent angles* have a common vertex and a common side, but no common interior points.

  Example 2: ∠1 and ∠2, ∠1 and ∠4

- Two *supplementary angles* form a 180° angle.

  Example 3: ∠1 and ∠4 are supplementary angles.
  ∠3 is also a supplement of ∠4.

If you know the measure of one supplementary angle, you can find the measure of the other. → If $m\angle 4$ is 120°, then $m\angle 1$ is 180° − 120°, or 60°.

- Two *complementary angles* form a 90° angle.

  Example 4: ∠5 and ∠6 are complementary angles.
  ∠6 is a complement of ∠5.

If you know the measure of one complementary angle, you can find the measure of the other. → If $m\angle 5$ is 30°, then $m\angle 6$ is 90° − 30°, or 60°.

Use the diagrams at the right for Exercises 1–6.

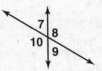

1. Vertical angles ∠7 and _____

2. Adjacent angles ∠10 and _____

3. Supplementary angles ∠8 and _____

4. Complementary angles ∠12 and _____

5. Vertical angles ∠8 and _____

6. Supplementary angles ∠7 and _____

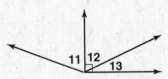

Find the measure of the supplement of each angle.

7. 38°   8. 65°   9. 120°   10. 152°

_____   _____   _____   _____

Find the measure of the complement of each angle.

11. 25°   12. 18°   13. 40°   14. 64°

_____   _____   _____   _____

Review 269

Look at the figure at the right.

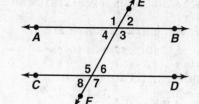

- Line $\overleftrightarrow{AB}$ is parallel to line $\overleftrightarrow{CD}$ ($\overleftrightarrow{AB} \parallel \overleftrightarrow{CD}$)

- Line $\overleftrightarrow{EF}$ is a *transversal*.

Alternate interior angles lie within a pair of lines and on opposite sides of the transversal.

Example 1: $\angle 3$ and $\angle 5$, $\angle 4$ and $\angle 6$

Alternate interior angles are congruent. If $m\angle 4$ is 60°, then $m\angle 6$ is also 60°.

Corresponding angles lie on the same side of the transversal and in corresponding positions.

Example 2: $\angle 1$ and $\angle 5$, $\angle 3$ and $\angle 7$

Corresponding angles are congruent. If $m\angle 1$ is 120°, then $m\angle 5$ is also 120°.

Use the diagram at the right to complete Exercises 1–2.

1. Name the alternate interior angles.

    a. $\angle 11$ and $\angle$ __?__   **b.** $\angle 12$ and $\angle$ __?__

    _____   _____

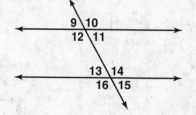

2. Name the corresponding angles.

    a. $\angle 16$ and $\angle$ __?__   **b.** $\angle 14$ and $\angle$ __?__

    _____   _____

    c. $\angle 9$ and $\angle$ __?__   **d.** $\angle 11$ and $\angle$ __?__

    _____   _____

In the diagram at the right, $\ell \parallel m$. Find the measure of each angle.

3. $\angle 1$ 4. $\angle 3$

    _____   _____

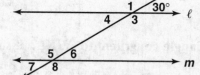

5. $\angle 6$ 6. $\angle 5$

    _____   _____

7. $\angle 8$ 8. $\angle 7$

    _____   _____

Review 270

Congruence statements reveal corresponding parts.

$\triangle ABC \cong \triangle DEF$

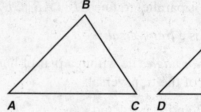

Example 1: $\overline{AB}$ corresponds to $\overline{DE}$

$\angle C$ corresponds to $\angle F$.

Corresponding parts are congruent ($\cong$).

Example 2: $\overline{AB} \cong \overline{DE}$

$\angle C \cong \angle F$

Triangles are congruent if you can show just three parts are congruent.

side-side-side (SSS)
(The marks show which
parts are congruent.)

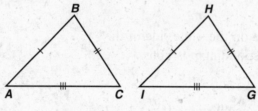

side-angle-side (SAS)
(The arcs show which
angles are congruent.)

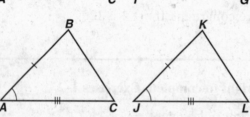

angle-side-angle (ASA)

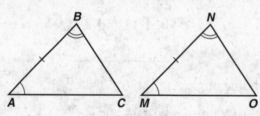

In the diagram at the right, $ABCD \cong JKLM$. **Complete the following.**

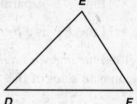

1. $\angle A \cong$ _____

2. $\overline{KL} \cong$ _____

3. $\angle M \cong$ _____

4. $\overline{DC} \cong$ _____

5. $\overline{JM} \cong$ _____

6. $\angle B \cong$ _____

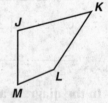

Is the triangle congruent to $\triangle JKL$? **If so, tell why. Use SSS, SAS, or ASA.**

7.

_____

8.

_____

9.

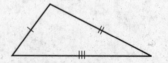

_____

Name _____ Class _____ Date _____

Review 271

Problem Solving: Solve a Simpler Problem and Look for a Pattern

Juan Delgado is creating this mosaic with black and white tiles. If he adds another row, how many tiles in all will be black?

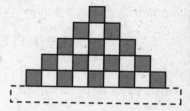

Read and Understand

What do you know? *There is 1 black tile in the top row, 2 in row 2, 3 in row 3, 4 in row 4, and 5 in row 5.*

Plan and Solve

Look for a pattern. You can make a table that shows the total number of black tiles.

Rows	1	2	3	4	5	⑥
Black Tiles	1	3	6	10	⑮	?

      ↑   ↑   ↑   ↑   ↑

      1   1 + 2 3 + 3 6 + 4 10 + 5

How is the total number of black tiles related to the row numbers? *The number of black tiles is equal to the sum of the row numbers.*

Through row 5, there are 15 black tiles.
With row 6, there will be 15 + 6 or 21, black tiles.

Look Back and Check

How could you check your solution? *Draw the sixth row and count the black tiles.*

Solve each problem by solving a simpler problem. Then look for a pattern.

1.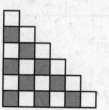

   If another row is added at the bottom, how many tiles in all will be white?

   _____

2.

   If another row is added at the bottom, how many tiles in all will be black?

   _____

3. Find the next number in the pattern: 1, 2, 4, 8, 16, 32, 64, _____

4. Find the next three numbers in the pattern: 1, 1.25, 1.5, 1.75, … _____

5. Draw the fifth figure in the pattern.

Review 272

Classifying Triangles and Quadrilaterals

A *quadrilateral* is a 4-sided polygon. A *triangle* is a 3-sided polygon.

QUADRILATERALS		TRIANGLES	
A *parallelogram* is a quadrilateral with 2 pairs of parallel sides.		An *acute triangle* has 3 angles smaller than 90°.	
A *trapezoid* is a quadrilateral with only 1 pair of parallel sides.		A *right triangle* has 1 angle of 90°.	
A *rhombus* is a parallelogram with 4 congruent sides.		An *obtuse triangle* has 1 angle larger than 90°.	
A *rectangle* is a parallelogram with 4 right angles.		An *equilateral triangle* has 3 congruent sides.	
A *square* is a rectangle with 4 congruent sides or a rhombus with 4 right angles.		An *isosceles triangle* has at least 2 congruent sides.	
		A *scalene triangle* has no congruent sides.	

Name all the figures shown that fit each description. If none are shown, write *none*.

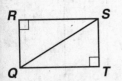 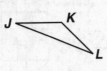

1. obtuse triangle

   _____

2. parallelogram

   _____

3. right triangle

   _____

4. rhombus

   _____

5. trapezoid

   _____

6. isosceles triangle

   _____

7. acute triangle

   _____

8. rectangle

   _____

Course 3 Topics

Review 273

The sum of the angle measures of a polygon with n sides is $(n - 2) \times 180°$.

Example 1: A triangle is a *3*-sided polygon. The sum of the angle measures is:

$$(3 - 2) \times 180° = 1 \times 180°$$
$$= 180°$$

$$m\angle 1 + m\angle 2 + m\angle 3 = 180°$$

Example 2: A quadrilateral is a *4*-sided polygon. The sum of the angle measures is:

$$(4 - 2) \times 180° = 2 \times 180°$$
$$= 360°$$

$$m\angle 1 + m\angle 2 + m\angle 3 + m\angle 4 = 360°$$

In a *regular polygon,* all of the sides are congruent and all of the angles are congruent. The measure of each *interior angle* of a regular polygon is:

    sum of the angle measures ÷ the number of angles

Example 3: Find the measure of each interior angle of a square.

$$360° ÷ 4 = 90°$$

Each angle of a square has a measure of 90°.

Find the sum of the measures of the interior angles of each polygon.

1. pentagon

_____

2. hexagon

_____

3. octagon

_____

4. nonagon

_____

5. decagon

_____

6. heptagon

_____

Find the measure of each angle of the regular polygon. Round to the nearest tenth if necessary.

7.

pentagon

8.

hexagon

9.

heptagon

_____   _____   _____

Review 274

Example 1: Find the area of the parallelogram. Use the formula below.

Area = base × height

$A = bh$

$\quad = 5 \times 2$

$\quad = 10 \text{ cm}^2$

The area of a trapezoid is half the product of the height and the sum of the lengths of the bases.

$A = \frac{1}{2}h(b_1 + b_2)$

Example 2: Find the area of the triangle. You can cut a parallelogram into two congruent triangles. So, the area of a triangle is half the area of a parallelogram.

To find the area of a triangle, use this formula.

Area = $\frac{1}{2}$base × height

$A = \frac{1}{2}bh$

$\quad = \frac{1}{2} \times 5 \times 2$

$\quad = 5 \text{ cm}^2$

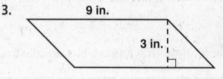

Find the area of each parallelogram.

1.

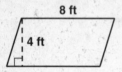

$A = $ _____

2.

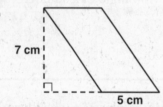

$A = $ _____

3.

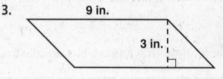

$A = $ _____

Find the area of each triangle.

4.

$A = $ _____

5.

$A = $ _____

6.

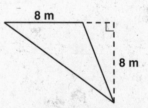

$A = $ _____

Find the area of each trapezoid.

7.

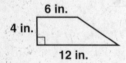

$A = $ _____

8.

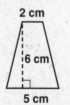

$A = $ _____

9.

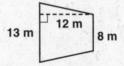

$A = $ _____

Course 3 Topics

Review 275

The distance around a circle is called the *circumference*.

- You can use a formula to find the circumference (C) of a circle. *Pi* (π) is approximately equal to ($\approx$) 3.14.

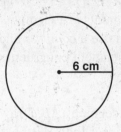

6 cm

$$\text{Circumference} = 2 \times \pi \times \text{radius}$$
$$C = 2\pi r$$

$$\text{Circumference} = 2 \times \pi \times r$$
$$C = 2 \times \pi \times 6$$
$$\approx 37.7 \text{ cm}$$

- If you know the diameter, use this formula:
$$\text{Circumference} = \pi \times \text{diameter}$$
$$C = \pi d$$

To find the *area of a circle*, use this formula:

$$\text{Area} = \pi \times \text{radius}^2$$
$$A = \pi r^2$$

$$\text{Area} = \pi \times r^2$$
$$A = \pi \times 6^2$$
$$\approx 113.1 \text{ cm}^2$$

The circumference of the circle is about 37.7 cm. The area of the circle is about 113.1 cm^2.

Find the circumference and area of each circle. Round to the nearest tenth.

1.

7 m

$C \approx$ _____ $A \approx$ _____

2.

10 km

$C \approx$ _____ $A \approx$ _____

3.

8 cm

$C \approx$ _____ $A \approx$ _____

4.

18 cm

$C \approx$ _____ $A \approx$ _____

5.

6 cm

$C \approx$ _____ $A \approx$ _____

6.

16 cm

$C \approx$ _____ $A \approx$ _____

Course 3 Topics

Review 276

Congruent segments are segments that have the same
length. You can use a *compass* and a straightedge to
construct one segment congruent to another segment.

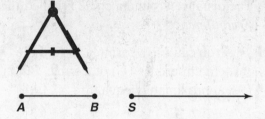

① Start with segment $\overline{AB}$. Draw a ray with endpoint
S that is longer than $\overline{AB}$.

② Place the compass tip on *A*. Draw an arc through *B*.

③ Use the *same* compass setting. Place the compass tip
on *S*. Draw an arc intersecting the ray. Label this
intersection *T*. You have constructed $\overline{ST}$, which should
be congruent to $\overline{AB}$.

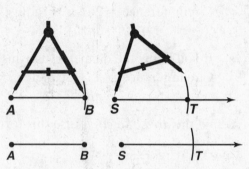

④ To check, measure $\overline{AB}$ and $\overline{ST}$ with a ruler. The
segments should be the same length.

Segment $\overline{AB}$ is congruent to segment $\overline{ST}$.

$$\overline{AB} \cong \overline{ST}$$

Perpendicular bisectors and angle bisectors can be constructed in similar ways. Use the compass and
the endpoints of a segment to draw two arcs that intersect above and below the segment. Connect
the points of intersection to create the perpendicular bisector. To create an angle bisector, use the
compass to draw two intersecting arcs from points on the legs of the angle that are equidistant from
the vertex. Connect the intersection with the vertex of the angle.

Use a compass and a straightedge for each construction.

1. Draw segment $\overline{EF}$ that is 3 inches long.
   Then construct segment $\overline{GH}$ congruent
   to $\overline{EF}$.

2. Draw acute angle *B*. Construct the angle
   bisector of $\angle B$.

Construct a perpendicular bisector to the given segment.

3.

4.

Review 277

These three-dimensional figures are space figures, or *solids*.

cylinder

cone

prism

pyramid

A *cylinder* has two congruent circular bases. $\overline{AB}$ is a radius.

A *cone* has one circular base. $\overline{CD}$ is a diameter.

A *prism* has two bases that are congruent and parallel. The lateral faces are parallelograms. A *pyramid* has one base. The lateral faces are triangles. The shape of a base is used to name the solid. A triangular prism and a square pyramid are shown above.

For each figure, describe the base(s) and name the figure.

1.

_____

2.

_____

3.

_____

4.

_____
_____

5.

_____
_____

6.

_____
_____

For the figure, name a pair parallel lines and a pair of intersecting lines.

7. _____

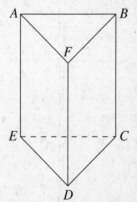

Review 278

A *base plan* for the stack of cubes shows the shape of the base and the number of cubes in each stack. To make a base plan:

① Draw a square for each stack as seen from above.

② Write the number of cubes in each stack inside each square.

③ Label the "Front" and "Right" sides.

An *isometric view* shows a corner view of a solid. From this, three other views can be drawn. The *top view* is suggested by the base plan. The *front view* is what is seen from the front, and the *right view* is what is seen from the right side.

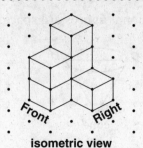

isometric view

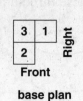

base plan

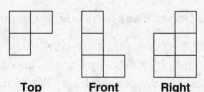

Top   Front   Right

Draw a base plan for each set of stacked cubes.

1.
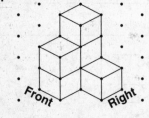

2.
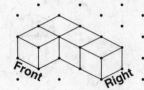

3.
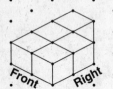

4.
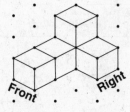

Draw the top, front, and right views of each figure.

5.
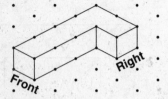

6.
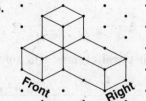

Course 3 Topics

Review 279

You can make *nets*, or flat patterns, of solids.
You can also identify a solid from its net.

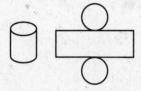

Example 1: The net of a cylinder shows a
rectangle and 2 circles. You can fold the
net to make the cylinder.

Example 2: The net of a cone shows a circle
and a part of a circle.

Example 3: The net of a triangular
pyramid shows 4 triangular surfaces. To
make the pyramid, fold up the outer triangles.

Example 4: The net of a triangular prism
shows 3 rectangles for the lateral faces of
the prism and 2 triangles for the bases.

**List the shapes that make up the net for each figure, and write the
number of times each shape is used.**

1. rectangular prism

   _____

   _____

2. cylinder

   _____

   _____

3. hexagonal prism

   _____

   _____

4. rectangular pyramid

   _____

5. cube

   _____

6. cone

   _____

Identify the solid that each net forms.

7.

8.

9.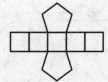

_____ _____ _____

Course 3 Topics

Review 280

The *surface area* of a solid is the sum of the areas of its surfaces. S.A. stands for *surface area* and L.A. stand for *lateral area*.

Example 1: Find the surface area of the prism.

Using a Net to Find Surface Area of a Prism
Draw a net of the prism and find the area of each rectangle in the net.

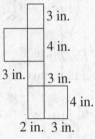

S.A. =
$(2 \cdot 3) + (2 \cdot 3) + (3 \cdot 4) + (3 \cdot 4) + (2 \cdot 4) + (2 \cdot 4)$
$= 6 + 6 + 12 + 12 + 8 + 8$
$= 52 \text{ in.}^2$

Using the Prism Surface Area Formula
The lateral area of a prism is the product of the perimeter of the base and the height of the prism.

L.A. $= ph$
S.A. $= \text{L.A.} + 2B$
$= ph + 2B$
$= (2 + 2 + 3 + 3)4 + 2(2 \cdot 3)$
$= 10(4) + 2(6)$
$= 40 + 12 = 52 \text{ in.}^2$

Example 2: Find the surface area of the cylinder.

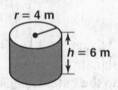

Using a Net to Find Surface Area of a Cylinder
Draw a net of the cylinder and find the area of each shape in the net.

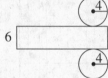

S.A. $= 16\pi + 16\pi + 48\pi$
$= 80\pi$
≈ 251.33

Using the Cylinder Surface Area Formula
S.A. $= 2\pi rh + 2\pi r^2$
$= 2\pi(4)(6) + 2\pi(4^2)$
$= 48\pi + 32\pi$
$= 80\pi$
≈ 251.33

Find the lateral and surface area of each figure to the nearest whole unit.

1.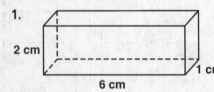

2.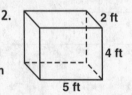

3.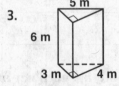

4.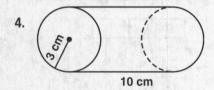

5.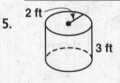

6.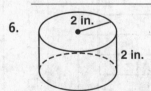

Course 3 Topics

Review 281

Example 1: Find the surface area of the prism.

The lateral area of a square pyramid is four times the area of one of the lateral faces.

$$\text{L.A.} = 4 \cdot \left(\tfrac{1}{2}b\ell\right) = 2b\ell$$

The surface area of a square pyramid is the sum of the lateral area and the area of the base.

$$
\begin{aligned}
\text{S.A.} &= \text{L.A.} + B \\
&= 2b\ell + b^2 \\
&= 2(8)(5) + 8^2 \\
&= 80 + 64 \\
&= 144 \text{ cm}^2
\end{aligned}
$$

Example 2: Find the surface area of the cone.

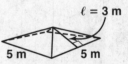

The lateral area of a cone is one half the product of the circumference of the base and the slant height.

$$\text{L.A.} = \tfrac{1}{2}(2\pi r)\ell = \pi r\ell$$

$$
\begin{aligned}
\text{S.A.} &= \text{L.A.} + B \\
&= \pi r\ell + \pi r^2 \\
&= \pi(3)(5) + \pi(3^2) \\
&= 15\pi + 9\pi \\
&= 24\pi \approx 75.4 \text{ m}^2
\end{aligned}
$$

Find the lateral and surface area of each square pyramid.

1.
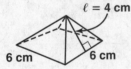

_____

2.
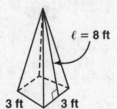

_____

3.
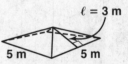

_____

Find the surface area of each cone to the nearest whole unit.

4.
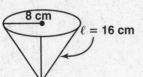

_____

5.
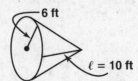

_____

6.
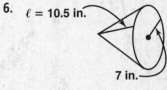

_____

Course 3 Topics

Review 282

To find the volume of a prism or a cylinder, multiply the base area B and the height h.

	① Find the base area B.	② Multiply base area B and height h. $V = Bh$
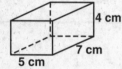 $h = 5$ yd, $w = 4$ yd, $\ell = 6$ yd	$\begin{aligned} B &= \ell w \\ &= 6 \cdot 4 \\ &= 24 \text{ yd}^2 \end{aligned}$	$\begin{aligned} V &= Bh \\ &= 24 \cdot 5 \\ &= 120 \text{ yd}^3 \end{aligned}$ The volume is 120 yd³.
$h = 10$ yd, $r = 3$ yd	$\begin{aligned} B &= \pi r^2 \\ &= \pi \cdot 3^2 \\ &\approx 28.27 \text{ yd}^2 \end{aligned}$	$\begin{aligned} V &= Bh \\ &\approx 28.27 \cdot 10 \\ &\approx 282.7 \text{ yd}^3 \end{aligned}$ The volume is about 283 yd³.

Find the base area and volume of each prism.

1.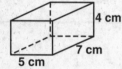
4 cm
5 cm   7 cm

$B =$ _____

$V =$ _____

2.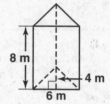
6 ft
6 ft
6 ft

$B =$ _____

$V =$ _____

3.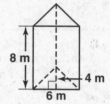
8 m
4 m
6 m

$B =$ _____

$V =$ _____

Find the base area of each cylinder to the nearest hundredth. Then find the volume of each cylinder to the nearest whole unit.

4.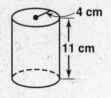
4 cm
11 cm

$B \approx$ _____

$V \approx$ _____

5.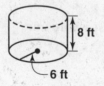
8 ft
6 ft

$B \approx$ _____

$V \approx$ _____

6.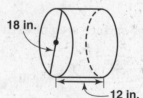
18 in.
12 in.

$B \approx$ _____

$V \approx$ _____

Course 3 Topics

Review 283

To find the volume of a pyramid or cone, multiply $\frac{1}{3}$, the base area
B, and the height h.

	① Find the base area B.	② Multiply $\frac{1}{3}$, the base area B, and the height h. $V = \frac{1}{3}Bh$
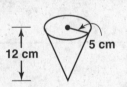 9 cm · 4 cm · 6 cm	$B = \ell w$ $\quad = 6 \cdot 4$ $\quad = 24 \text{ cm}^2$	$V = \frac{1}{3}Bh$ $\quad = \frac{1}{3}(24)(9)$ $\quad = 72 \text{ cm}^3$ The volume is 72 cm³.
12 cm · 3 cm	$B = \pi r^2$ $\quad = \pi \cdot 3^2$ $\quad \approx 28.27 \text{ cm}^2$	$V = \frac{1}{3}Bh$ $\quad \approx \frac{1}{3}(28.27)(12)$ $\quad \approx 113.08 \text{ cm}^3$ The volume is about 113.08 cm³.

Find the volume of each figure to the nearest whole unit.

1.

12 cm · 5 cm

_____

2.
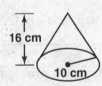
16 cm · 10 cm

_____

3.
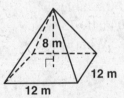
8 m · 12 m · 12 m

_____

4.
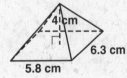
4 cm · 6.3 cm · 5.8 cm

_____

5. Find the height of a cone with an approximate volume of 134 cm³
   and a radius of 4 cm.

_____

Review 284

A farmer has 100 ft of fencing. He wants to enclose the greatest possible area for his garden. He wants the fenced area to be rectangular. What dimensions should he use?

Read and Understand   The goal is to find the dimension of the fence that will give the largest area. The area has to be rectangular.

Plan and Solve   Draw a diagram to help you solve the problem and make a table to show possible dimensions of the fence and area.

> 100 ft of fence

Length (ft)	Width (ft)	Area (ft²)
10	40	400
15	35	525
20	30	600

Length(ft)	Width (ft)	Area (ft²)
25	25	625
30	20	600
35	15	525

Look Back and Check   Can you find a greater area using 2-ft increments?

Length (ft)	Width (ft)	Area (ft²)
10	40	400
12	38	456
14	36	504
16	34	544

Length(ft)	Width (ft)	Area (ft²)
18	32	576
20	30	600
22	28	616
24	26	624

Making the fence 25 ft by 25 ft will result in the largest area.

Make a drawing to help you solve each problem.

1. Fred wants to protect his rectangular workbench by covering it with paper. The workbench is 24 in. by 36 in. He wants the paper to hang over the edges by 4 in. How big should the paper be? What would be its area?

2. The convention center uses cloths cover display tables. The cloths must hang over the edges of the tables by 24 in. The tables are 30 in. by 72 in. How big are the cloths? What is the area of one cloth?

3. Meera is covering a bulletin board with fabric. The bulletin board is 36 in. by 48 in. She needs 6 in. overhang on each side to staple the fabric to the back of the board. How big should the piece of fabric be? What is the area of the fabric?

4. Ethan wants to put a plastic liner in the bed of his truck. The truck bed measures 42 in. by 64 in. He wants 8 in. extra on each side to go against the truck bed walls. How big should the liner be? What would be its area?

Review 285

Two solids are *similar solids* if they have the same shape and all of their corresponding lengths are proportional. A special relationship exists among the measures of similar solids:

- The ratios of the corresponding dimensions of similar solids is $\frac{a}{b}$.

- The ratio of their surface areas is $\frac{a^2}{b^2}$.

- The ratio of their volumes is $\frac{a^3}{b^3}$.

Example: Two similar cylindrical watering cans have diameters of 14 in. and 18 in. Find the volume of the larger watering can if the volume of the smaller watering can is 882 in.^{3}.

① Write the ratio of corresponding dimensions.

   $\frac{14}{18} = \frac{7}{9}$, so the ratio of the volumes is $\frac{a^3}{b^3} = \frac{7^3}{9^3}$, or $\frac{343}{729}$.

② Write a proportion: $\dfrac{\text{volume of small watering can}}{\text{volume of large watering can}} = \dfrac{343}{729}$

$\dfrac{882}{x} = \dfrac{343}{729}$ ← Substitute the known volume.

$343x = (882)(729)$ ← Cross multiply.

$343x = 642{,}978$ ← Divide both sides by 343.

$\quad\ \ x = 1{,}874.57$ ← Simplify.

The volume of the larger watering can is about 1,875 in.^{3}.

For each pair of similar solids find the value of the variable.

1.

2.

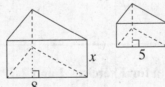

3. A triangular prism has a height of 18 cm, surface area of 463 cm^2, and volume of 279 cm^3. Find the surface area and volume of a similar prism with a height of 12 cm. Round your answers to the nearest whole number.

4. A rectangular prism has a height of 24 inches, a surface area of 1,088 in.^{2} and a volume of 2,112 in.^{3}. Find the surface area and volume of a similar prism with a height of 36 in.

Course 3 Topics

Review 286

The *frequency* of a data item is the number of times it appears. A *frequency table* provides intervals, then tallies each data item in its interval.

The last four digits of 24 phone numbers were chosen from a phone book.

Make a frequency table for the data.

① Choose an appropriate interval. All intervals must be the same size.

② Mark tallies and write totals for the data.

Telephone Numbers (Last Four Digits)

9782	8609	7880	9012	5620	1190	2324	2568
9877	4085	6856	7367	3642	6784	8015	7761
9001	4227	7452	9811	4326	6433	4228	8111

Telephone Numbers

Last Four Digits	Tally	Frequency
1000–1999	I	1
2000–2999	I I	2
3000–3999	I	1
4000–4999	I I I I	4
5000–5999	I	1
6000–6999	I I I	3
7000–7999	I I I I	4
8000–8999	I I I	3
9000–9999	ⅡⅡ	5

You can use a frequency table to make a *histogram*.

In a histogram, there is no space between the bars.

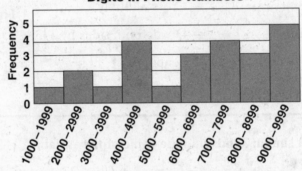

Digits in Phone Numbers

Last Digits of Phone Numbers

Use the following data for Exercises 1 and 2.

Raisins in a small box: 33 32 30 40 29 35 36 33 42 28 41 39 30 29 35 40 33 34 31 28

1. Make a frequency table for the data.

2. Use your frequency table to make a histogram.

Review 287

Two important factors in determining whether a graph gives a correct impression of data are:

- how the scale is chosen and
- whether the entire scale is shown.

The data at the right can be shown in a bar graph.

Countries with Most Universities (2000)	
India	7,513
United States	3,559

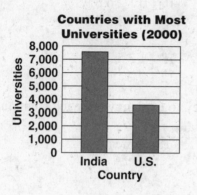

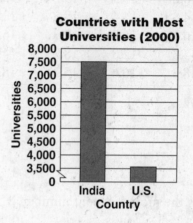

In the first graph, the scale is in multiples of 1,000. The entire scale from 0 through 8,000 is shown. The graph accurately compares the numbers of universities in the two countries.

In the second graph, the scale is in multiples of 500. There is a break in the vertical scale. The graph gives a misleading comparison between the two countries.

Use the bar graphs above for Exercises 1–4.

1. From which graph is it easier to tell that India has about twice the number of universities as the United States?

_____

2. In the second graph, about how many times the number of U.S. universities does India *appear* to have?

_____

3. Which graph makes it easier to estimate the number of universities in each country? Why?

_____

_____

_____

4. Why does the second graph give a misleading impression of the data?

_____

_____

_____

Review 288

A *stem-and-leaf plot* is an easy way to show data arranged in order.

8th Grade 100-M Dash
(Times to Nearest 0.1 s)

13.1	16.2	15.5	15.2	13.5
15.3	14.8	14.4	17.5	12.2
14.1	16.1	16.9	15.3	16.8
16.0	15.3	12.0	18.2	14.6
13.2	18.3	16.6	15.3	18.8

① Choose *stems*. The times range from 12.0 to 18.8. Choose 12 to 18 as stems.

② List the tenths digits as *leaves*.

```
18 | 2 3 8
17 | 5
16 | 0 1 2 6 8 9
15 | 2 3 3 3 3 5
14 | 1 4 6 8
13 | 1 2 5
12 | 0 2
```

③ Make a key to explain what each stem and leaf represents.

18 | 2 means 18.2

The *mode* is the most frequent number.
The mode is 15.3 seconds.

The *median* is the middle number or average of the middle two numbers. The median is 15.3 seconds.

---

1. Complete the stem-and-leaf plot for the data.

8th Grade 200-M Dash
(Times to Nearest 0.1 s)

32.5	32.1	38.5	31.7	34.7
29.3	35.2	34.4	30.2	35.3
34.7	31.9	36.0	32.2	36.7
32.2	31.4	34.7	29.5	36.9
36.4	33.4	38.6	34.7	37.3

Times for the 200-M Dash

```
38 | _____
37 | _____
36 | _____
35 | _____
34 | _____
33 | _____
32 | _____
31 | _____
30 | _____
29 | _____
```

Use your stem-and-leaf plot for Exercises 2–5.

2. The mode is _____.

3. The median is _____.

4. How many 8th grade students finished the race in less than 35 s?

   _____

5. How many 8th grade students finished the race in less than 33 s?

   _____

Course 3 Topics

Review 289

A *box-and-whisker plot* is a graph that summarizes a data set along a number line. Make a box-and-whisker plot for the data in the table at the right.

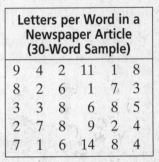

Letters per Word in a Newspaper Article (30-Word Sample)					
9	4	2	11	1	8
8	2	6	1	7	3
3	3	8	6	8	5
2	7	8	9	2	4
7	1	6	14	8	4

① Order the data

1 1 1 2 2 2 2 3 3 3 4 4 4 5 6 6 6 7 7 7 8 8 8 8 8 8 9 9 11 14

② Find the median. The median is 6.

③ Find the medians of the lower and upper halves of the data.

(lower) 1 1 1 2 2 2 2 **3** 3 3 4 4 4 5 6
(upper) 6 6 7 7 7 8 8 **8** 8 8 8 9 9 11 14

④ Mark the least and greatest values below a number line. Mark the three medians.

⑤ Draw a box connecting the lower and upper medians. This box shows where at least half the data lies. Draw a line through the box at the median of all the data.

⑥ Draw whiskers from the box to the least and greatest values.

Complete the steps to make a box-and-whisker plot for the data.

1. Order the data.

   _____

   _____

2. Find the median.

   _____

3. Find the median of the lower and upper halves.

   _____

4. Draw the box-and-whisker plot.

Letters per Word in a Magazine Article (30-Word Sample)				
3	7	8	3	7
4	6	4	3	7
3	1	13	3	2
8	8	2	11	5
5	3	9	9	2
3	2	10	3	2

Course 3 Topics

Review 290

Example Make a scatter plot and find a trend for the data below

① Choose a scale along each axis to represent the two sets of data.

② Locate the ordered pairs on the graph for the data.

③ Is there a trend? Do both sets of values increase? Does one decrease as the other increases? If neither occurs, there is no trend.

④ If there is a trend, draw a trend line that closely fits the data.

Age and Height Survey

Age (y)	Height (in.)	Age (y)	Height (in.)	Age (y)	Height (in.)
11	55	4	39	12	55
10	55	13	62	10	54
8	49	11	52	7	47
6	45	5	41	13	63
10	52	14	62	9	60
11	59	12	56	9	52
7	45	8	52	12	58
12	60	6	44	13	60
6	48	7	48	8	50
5	45	4	39	11	56

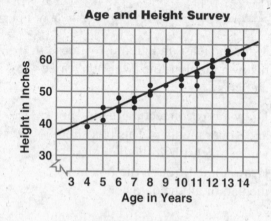

Age and Height Survey

Use the data below for Exercises 1–5.

Weight (lb)	78	63	67	52	81	92	60	34	83	47	73	98	45	31	95	71	76	41
Height (in.)	56	52	55	47	58	60	50	39	58	45	54	61	45	36	60	54	56	41

1. Draw the scatter plot and a trend line.

2. Use your graph to estimate the height of a person who weighs about 90 lb.

   _____

3. Use your graph to estimate the weight of a student 51 in. tall.

   _____

4. Is there a relationship between height and weight?

   _____

5. Write a sentence to explain your answer to Exercise 4.

   _____

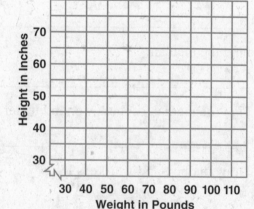

Weight and Height Survey

Course 3 Topics

Review 291

The class look a survey of their favorite breakfast foods.
The results are shown in the table and the circle graph.

1. Find the total number of votes.

2. Find each part of the total as a fraction or percent.

3. Find the measure of each central angle
   in the circle graph by solving for x.

   $\frac{6}{36} = \frac{x}{360°}$; $x = 60°$

4. Draw, label, and title the graph.

Favorite Breakfast Food

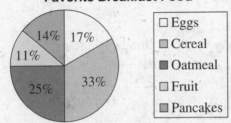

☐ Eggs
☐ Cereal
■ Oatmeal
☐ Fruit
■ Pancakes

Breakfast	Votes	Fraction	%	Degrees
Eggs	6	$\frac{6}{36} = \frac{1}{6}$	17%	60°
Cereal	12	$\frac{1}{3}$	33%	120°
Oatmeal	9	$\frac{1}{4}$	25%	90°
Fruit	4	$\frac{1}{9}$	11%	40°
Pancakes	5	$\frac{5}{36}$	14%	50°
Total	36		100%	360°

**Find the measure of the central angle that could represent each
percent in a circle graph. Round your answer to the nearest degree.**

1. 37% _____   2. 61% _____   3. 26.5% _____   4. 7% _____

5. 19% _____   6. 85% _____   7. 46% _____   8. 54% _____

Make a circle graph for each set of data.

9. a monthly family budget

Monthly Budget	
Item	**Amount**
Rent	$ 425
Food	$ 150
Clothes	$ 50
Gas	$ 75
Phone	$ 25
Water	$ 35
Other	$ 100

10. favorite sport to watch

Favorite Sport to Watch	
Sport	**Votes**
Baseball	255
Football	535
Basketball	593
Soccer	163
Hockey	176
Wrestling	261
Other	368

Review 292

Bar graphs are useful for comparing sets of data.

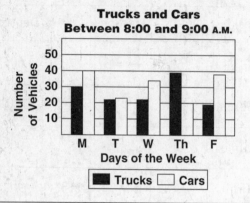

Trucks and Cars Between 8:00 and 9:00 A.M.

Line graphs and multiple line graphs show how data change over time. Line graphs help you see a trend.

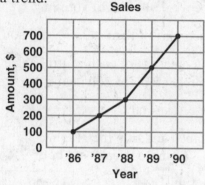

Sales

Circle graphs help you see how a total is divided into parts. The parts may represent actual amounts or percents. If the parts represent percents, the entire circle is 100%.

Sales Per State

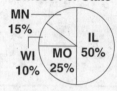

Offices Per State

Decide which type of graph would be the most appropriate for the data: *circle graph*, *line graph*, *multiple line graph*, or *double bar graph*. Explain your choice.

1. two classes' test scores over a school year

_____

2. how a club spends its money

_____

3. the numbers of boys and the numbers of girls who use the playground each day for one week

_____

4. the percents of chemical elements in seawater

_____

5. a company's profit

_____

Name _____ Class _____ Date _____

Review 293

Example 1: Carlos has classes in English, algebra, chemistry, track, and history. Otis has classes in business, English, history, tennis, and computer science. Which classes do both students attend?

Read and Understand   What do you know? *You know which classes each attends.*

Plan and Solve   You can use logical reasoning and a *Venn diagram.* Draw a rectangle. Draw circle *C* showing Carlos's classes. Draw circle *O* showing Otis's classes. The overlap shows the classes both boys attend.

Look Back and Check   Which classes do both attend? *Carlos and Otis both attend English and history classes.*

Example 2: Carlos asks 25 math/science students whether they are taking math or science. Twenty-two students take science classes. Fifteen take math classes. How many students take both math and science if each student takes at least 1 class?

Read and Understand   What do you know? *You know 25 students were surveyed; 22 take science and 15 take math.*

Plan and Solve   You can use logical reasoning and a Venn diagram. What number goes in the overlap? *12*

Look Back and Check   How can you check your answer? *There are 10 + 12 = 22 taking science, 12 + 3 = 15 taking math, and 10 + 12 + 3 = 25 students in all.*

Course 3 Topics

Solve each problem using logical reasoning.

1. Phil's favorite sports are track, basketball, boxing, golf, and soccer. Jerry's favorite sports are boxing, baseball, football, bowling, and soccer. Which sports are favorites of both Phil and Jerry?

2. Barbara asks 18 friends who love to read whether they read fiction or non fiction. Twelve of her friends read fiction. Eleven of her friends read nonfiction. How many read both fiction and nonfiction?

3. Alice likes potatoes, sandwiches, fish, crackers, and steak. Rosie likes vegetables, rice, steak, chicken, and crackers. Which foods are liked by both Alice and Rosie?

4. Nine students like art only. Five students like music only. Twenty students were asked. How many liked both? Draw a Venn Diagram to solve.

Review 294

Andy has 3 pairs of pants: 1 gray, 1 blue, and 1 black. He has 2 shirts: 1 white and 1 red. If Andy picks 1 pair of pants and 1 shirt, how many different outfits does he have?

Andy can choose 1 of 3 pairs of pants and 1 of 2 shirts. A tree diagram can help you count his choices.

pants   shirts

gray — white, red

blue — white, red

black — white, red

3 × 2 = **6 different outfits**

The total number of choices is the product of the number of choices for pants and the number of choices for shirts.

You can also use the *counting principle.*

$$n \quad \times \quad m \quad \text{gives} \quad n \times m$$

first choices   second choices   total choices

Andy has 6 different outfits.

Find the total number of choices.

1. Rich is trying to get from San Francisco to San Jose. He needs to stop in San Bruno on the way. There are 3 major roads or freeways from San Francisco to San Bruno and 3 major roads or freeways from San Bruno to San Jose. How many routes can Rich take?

_____

2. Ralph wants to have soup and salad for lunch There are 5 kinds of soup and 3 kinds of salad on the menu. He picks one of each. From how many possible combinations can he choose?

_____

3. Carla has 4 hats and 4 scarves for winter weather. She picks one of each to wear. How many hat and scarf combinations are there?

_____

4. Lorenzo is looking at 5 color markers and 4 types of paper. He picks one of each. How many choices of color and paper does he have?

_____

5. Eric has 3 baseballs and 4 bats. From how many possible ball and bat combinations can he choose?

_____

6. Ms. Wong is redecorating her office. She has a choice of 3 colors of paint, 4 kinds of curtains, and 4 colors of carpet. How many different ways are there to redecorate?

_____

Course 3 Topics

Review 295

The expression 5! is read "5 *factorial*." It means the product of all whole numbers from 5 to 1.

$5! = 5 \cdot 4 \cdot 3 \cdot 2 \cdot 1 = 120$

Example 1: Evaluate $\frac{5!}{3!}$.

Write the products, then simplify.

$\frac{5!}{3!} = \frac{5 \cdot 4 \cdot 3 \cdot 2 \cdot 1}{3 \cdot 2 \cdot 1} = 5 \cdot 4 = 20$

Example 2: How many 3-letter codes can be made from A, B, C, D, E, F, G, H with no repeating letters?

This is a *permutation* problem. Order is important. ABC is different from ACB.

- There are 8 choices for the first letter.
- There are 7 choices for the second letter.
- There are 6 choices for the third letter.

The number of codes possible = $8 \cdot 7 \cdot 6 = 336$.

You can write this as $_8P_3$, meaning the number of permutations of 8 objects chosen 3 at a time.

Simplify each expression.

1. $4!$ _____

2. $3!$ _____

3. $\frac{4!}{3!}$ _____

4. $\frac{10!}{8!}$ _____

5. $\frac{9!}{9!}$ _____

6. $5! \times 2!$ _____

Simplify each expression.

7. $_6P_3$ _____

8. $_5P_2$ _____

9. $_{12}P_3$ _____

10. $_4P_4$ _____

11. $_{15}P_2$ _____

12. $_6P_4$ _____

Use the counting principle to find the number of permutations.

13. In how many ways can you pick a football center and quarterback from 6 players who try out?

_____

14. For a meeting agenda, in how many ways can you schedule 3 speakers out of 10 people who would like to speak?

_____

Review 296

Mr. Wisniewski wants to pick 2 students from Minh, Joan, Jim, Esperanza, and Tina to demonstrate an experiment. How many different pairs of students can he choose?

In this *combination* problem, the order of the choice of students does not matter. These are the possibilities:

Minh-Esperanza
Minh-Jim   Esperanza-Jim
Minh-Joan   Esperanza-Joan   Jim-Joan
Minh-Tina   Esperanza-Tina   Jim-Tina   Joan-Tina

There are 10 possible combinations.

The number of combinations of 5 students taken 2 at a time is $_5C_2$ where:

$$_5C_2 = \tfrac{1}{2!} \, _5P_2 = \tfrac{1}{2!} \cdot 5 \cdot 4 = 10$$

In general, the number of combinations of n objects taken r at a time is $_nC_r$ where:

$$_nC_r = \tfrac{1}{r!} \cdot \, _nP_r$$

Simplify each expression.

1. $_6C_3$ _____

2. $_5C_2$ _____

3. $_7C_5$ _____

4. $_4C_3$ _____

5. $_8C_2$ _____

6. $_6C_4$ _____

7. $_9C_4$ _____

8. $_5C_3$ _____

9. $_6C_5$ _____

10. $_7C_3$ _____

11. $_8C_3$ _____

12. $_9C_3$ _____

Find the number of combinations.

13. In how many ways can Susie choose 3 of 10 books to take with her on a trip?

_____

14. In how many ways can Rosa select 2 movies to rent out of 6 that she likes?

_____

15. In how many ways can Bill pick 2 of his 7 trophies to show his grandfather?

_____

16. In how many ways can Mr. Wu choose 5 tulip bulbs out of 15 to plant in a flower bed?

_____

17. In how many ways can a town name 5 citizens out of 10 to serve on a committee?

_____

18. In how many ways can Mrs. Harris pick 3 flowers from 8 for a bouquet?

_____

You can collect data through observations or experiments and use the data to state the *experimental probability*.

Alan has a coin. He tosses the coin 100 times and gets 60 heads and 40 tails. The experimental probability of getting heads is:

$$P(\text{heads}) = \frac{\text{number of heads}}{\text{number of trials}} = \frac{60}{100} = 0.6$$

Then Sarita calculated the *theoretical probability* of getting heads on one toss of the coin.

$$P(\text{heads}) = \frac{\text{favorable outcomes}}{\text{number of possible outcomes}} = \frac{1}{2} = 0.5$$

Alan thinks that his coin is unfair since the experimental probability is different from the theoretical probability.

Sarita suggests that they run the experiment again. This time they toss 53 heads and 47 tails. This suggests that the coin is more fair than Alan thinks. To form a more convincing conclusion, they should run the test several more times.

Suppose you have a bag with 75 marbles: 15 red, 5 white, 25 green, 20 black, and 10 blue. You draw a marble, note its color, and then put it back. You do this 75 times with these results: 12 red, 9 white, 27 green, 17 black, and 10 blue. Find each probability as a fraction in simplest form.

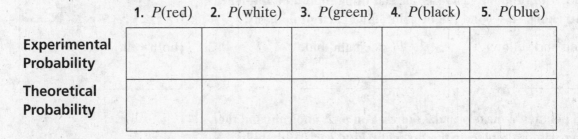

	1. P(red)	**2.** P(white)	**3.** P(green)	**4.** P(black)	**5.** P(blue)
Experimental Probability					
Theoretical Probability					

Suppose you surveyed the students in your class on their favorite juice flavors. Their choices were 6 apple, 10 orange, 1 grapefruit, and 3 mango. Find each probability as a fraction in simplest form.

6. P(apple)   **7.** P(orange)   **8.** P(grapefruit)   **9.** P(not mango)

_____   _____   _____   _____

Review 298

There are 3 chips in a bag. You draw 2 chips from the bag.

Experiment 1: Draw one chip, put it back. Draw a chip again.

Draw 2 *is not* affected by draw 1.

Two events are *independent* when the outcome of the second *is not* affected by the outcome of the first.

If A and B are independent events,
$P(A \text{ and } B) = P(A) \times P(B)$

Suppose 2 chips in the bag are red and 1 chip is blue. You draw 1 chip and then put it back before drawing a second chip. Find the probability that the chip color in both draws is red.

$$P(\text{red and red}) = P(\text{red}) \times P(\text{red})$$
$$= \frac{2}{3} \times \frac{2}{3}$$
$$= \frac{4}{9}$$

Experiment 2: Draw one chip. Then, draw another without replacing the first.

Draw 2 *is* affected by draw 1.

Two events are *dependent* when the outcome of the second *is* affected by the outcome of the first.

If A and B are independent events,
$P(A, \text{ and } B) = P(A) \times P(B \text{ after } A)$.

Suppose 2 chips in the bag are red and 1 chip is blue. You draw 1 chip and then another without putting the first chip back. Find the probability that both chips are red.

$$P(\text{red, then red})$$
$$= P(\text{red}) \times P(\text{red after red})$$
$$= \frac{2}{3} \times \frac{1}{2} = \frac{2}{6} = \frac{1}{3}$$

A store has 3 cans of green paint, 3 cans of blue paint, and 2 cans of yellow paint. You randomly choose one can of paint and then replace it. Then you choose a second can of paint. Find each probability.

1. $P(\text{green and yellow})$ **2.** $P(\text{green and blue})$ **3.** $P(\text{both yellow})$

_____   _____   _____

A jar has 3 pennies, 4 nickels, and 2 dimes. You pick one coin and then pick another without replacing the first coin. Find each probability.

4. $P(\text{nickel, then dime})$ **5.** $P(\text{penny, then nickel})$ **6.** $P(\text{dime, then penny})$

_____   _____   _____

State whether the events are dependent or independent.

7. Flipping a coin twice

_____

8. Choosing a hammer and a paint color in a hardware store

_____

9. Selecting a can of corn and a container of juice in a supermarket

_____

10. Picking a board from a pile, nailing it on a fence, then picking another board from the pile

_____

Course 3 Topics

Review 299

Problem Solving: Make an Organized List and Simulate a Problem

You can use simulation to estimate solutions to probability problems.

A juice company puts one of the five letters, L, E, M, O, and N, inside the bottle cap. The letters are equally distributed among the caps. If you collect all five letters, you get a bottle of juice at half price. Estimate how many bottles you need to buy to collect all five letters.

Read and Understand

What do you want to find? *You want to find how many bottles of juice you need to buy to collect all five letters.*

Plan and Solve

Instead of actually buying bottles of juice, develop a simulation. You can use a five-part spinner. Spin until you get all five letters. Keep track of your results.

Show the results of the simulation in a list. You spun the spinner 7 times before you got all five letters. So you estimate that you would have to buy 7 bottles of juice to collect all five letters.

Spins

M L M O E L N

Look Back and Check

Would you get the same result if you repeat the simulation?

Solve each problem by making an organized list or by simulating the problem. Describe your method.

1. There is one of ten team cards inside a box of cereal. The teams are equally distributed among the boxes. Estimate how many boxes of cereal you need to purchase to collect all ten teams.

   _____

   _____

   _____

2. There is one of five shapes on the inner wrapper of each granola bar. The symbols are equally distributed among the wrappers. Estimate how many bars you need to buy to collect all five shapes and win a free bar.

   _____

   _____

   _____

3. A gas station gives away one of eight drinking glasses each time you buy a tank of gas. There is an equal chance of getting any one of the glasses. Estimate how many tanks you will have to buy to get all eight glasses.

   _____

   _____

4. A store prints one of 12 different symbols on each receipt. Collect all 12 and you get a 10% discount on your next purchase. Symbols are equally placed among the receipts. Estimate how many receipts you would have to get to collect all 12 symbols.

   _____

   _____

Course 3 Topics

Review 300

In a survey, the entire group is called the *population*.
A *sample* is a small part of the population.

For a sample to be fair, it should be *random*. In a random sample,
each member of the population has an equal chance of being
selected.

- Samples can be either systematic or stratified.

  In a *systematic sample*, members are selected using randomness.

  In a *stratified sample*, members are grouped by similar characteristics.

- Survey questions should be fair, not *biased*. They should not make one answer appear better than another.

  Biased question: Did you hate that movie as much as I did?

  Fair question: What did you think of that movie?

**Suppose you want to find out how students feel about new school colors.
Tell whether each survey plan describes a good sample. Justify your answer.**

1. You interview students while they are in art class.

   _____

   _____

   _____

2. You randomly select students from each homeroom in the school.

   _____

   _____

   _____

Describe each sample as systematic or stratified.

3. You ask 25 people coming out of 3 different types of movies if they enjoy the movie.

   _____

4. You pick 5 names from a hat and ask those people their favorite food.

   _____

Explain why each question is biased.

5. Don't you agree that Mrs. Meredith expects too much of her students?

   _____

   _____

6. Were you able to follow that boring movie?

   _____

   _____

Course 3 Topics

Review 301

A *sequence* is a set of numbers that follows a pattern.

In an *arithmetic sequence,* each term is found by *adding* a fixed number to the previous term. The number that you add is called the *common difference.*

Example 1: Find the next three terms in the arithmetic sequence: $8, 5, 2, -1, -4, \ldots$

- The common difference is $5 - 8 = -3$.
- Add -3 for the next three terms.

$$-4 + (-3) = -7$$
$$-7 + (-3) = -10$$
$$-10 + (-3) = -13$$

The next three terms are $-7, -10,$ and -13.

In a *geometric sequence,* each term is found by *multiplying* the previous term by a fixed number. The number that you multiply by is called the *common ratio.*

Example 2: Find the next three terms in the geometric sequence: $2, 6, 18, 54, \ldots$

- The common ratio is $\frac{18}{6} = 3$.
- Multiply by 3 for the next three terms.

$$54 \times 3 = 162$$
$$162 \times 3 = 486$$
$$486 \times 3 = 1{,}458$$

The next three terms are $162, 468,$ and $1{,}458$.

The sequence: $1, 4, 9, 16, \ldots$ is neither arithmetic nor geometric.

Its pattern is $1^2, 2^2, 3^2, 4^2, \ldots$

Its next three terms are $5^2, 6^2, 7^2,$ or $25, 36, 49$.

Find the common difference or ratio in each sequence.

1. $2, 6, 10, 14, \ldots$

_____

2. $30, 20, 10, 0, \ldots$

_____

3. $-12, -4, 4, 12, \ldots$

_____

4. $6, 12, 24, 48, \ldots$

_____

5. $1, \frac{1}{3}, \frac{1}{9}, \frac{1}{27}$

_____

6. $250, 25, 2.5, 0.25, \ldots$

_____

Identify each sequence as *arithmetic, geometric,* or *neither.* Find the next three terms of the sequence.

7. $4, 2, 1, \frac{1}{2} \ldots$

_____

8. $0.2, 0.4, 0.6, 0.8, \ldots$

_____

9. $1, \frac{1}{4}, \frac{1}{9}, \frac{1}{16}$

_____

10. $70, 50, 30, 10, \ldots$

_____

11. $1, 2, 1, 2, 1, 2, \ldots$

_____

12. $4, 8, 16, 32, \ldots$

_____

Review 302

A *function* describes the relationship between two variables called the *input* and the *output*. In a function, each input value has only one output value.

Function:

$$y = 2x + 4$$

↑ ↑

output variable y   *input variable x*

You can list input/output pairs in a table.

$y = 2x + 4$

Input x	Output y
−10	−16
−5	−6
0	4
1	6

To find output *y*, substitute values for input *x* into the function equation.

For $x = -10$: $y = 2(-10) + 4$
$$y = -16$$

You can also show input/output pairs using *function notation*.

Function rule:

$$f(x) = 2x + 4$$
$$f(-10) = 2(-10) + 4 = -16$$

↑   ↑

input   *output*

Find $f(0)$.

$$f(0) = 2(0) + 4$$
$$f(0) = 4$$

Complete the table of input/output pairs for each function.

1. $y = 3x$

Input x	Output y
5	
7	
9	
11	

2. $d = 20r$

Input r	Output d
1	
2	
3	
	160

3. $y = 25 - 2x$

Input x	Output y
0	
1	
	21
	19

Use the function rule $f(x) = 3x + 1$. Find each output.

4. $f(0)$

  $= 3(\_\_\_\_) + 1$

  $= _____$

5. $f(1)$

  $= 3(\_\_\_\_) + 1$

  $= _____$

6. $f(2)$

  $= 3(\_\_\_\_) + 1$

  $= _____$

7. $f(-2)$

  $= 3(\_\_\_\_) + 1$

  $= _____$

8. $f(5)$

_____

9. $f(-6)$

_____

10. $f(10)$

_____

11. $f(5.5)$

_____

Course 3 Topics

Review 303

You can graph a function in the coordinate plane. To plot points for the graph, use *input* as *x*-values (*x*-axis) and *output* as *y*-values (*y*-axis).

output as y-values   *input as x-values*

↓   ↓

$y = 2x + 4$

This function has the form of a linear equation and is called a *linear function.* To draw its graph, use

slope and *y*-intercept: $y = 2x + 4$

slope = 2

y-intercept = 4

or

a table of input/output pairs.

x	y
0	4
1	6
2	8

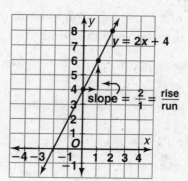

Graph each linear function.

1. $y = 3x$

2. $y = 2x - 2$

3. $y = \frac{1}{2}x + 1$

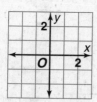

4. $y = 2 - x$

Review 304

Sometimes you can write a function rule to describe a situation.

Cookies at a bazaar sell for $2 each. The booth costs $25 to rent for the day. The profit depends on how many cookies are sold.

Words: Profit = 2 × (number of cookies sold) − $25

Function rule: $y = 2x - 25$

The output y is the profit.

The input x is the number of cookies sold.

You can use the graph of a linear function to write its function rule. First, you need to find the slope and the y-intercept.

① From the graph, the slope (m) is $-\frac{1}{2}$.

② The point $(0, 3)$ is on the graph so the y-intercept (b) is 3.

③ Substitute in the slope-intercept form.

$$y = mx + b$$

$$y = -\frac{1}{2}x + 3$$

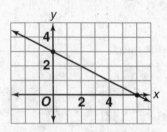

The function rule is $y = -\frac{1}{2}x + 3$.

Write a function rule for each situation. Identify the input and output variables.

1. A person burns 350 calories for every hour of bicycling. The number of calories burned is a function of the number of hours spent bicycling.

   _____

   _____

2. Janice earns $150 a week plus a commission of $3 for every magazine she sells. Her total pay depends on how many magazines she sells.

   _____

   _____

Identify the slope and y-intercept of each graph. Then write a linear function rule.

3.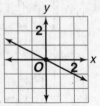

   _____

   _____

4.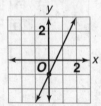

   _____

   _____

5.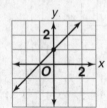

   _____

   _____

Course 3 Topics

Review 305

The graph at the right shows the outside temperature during 16 hours of one day.

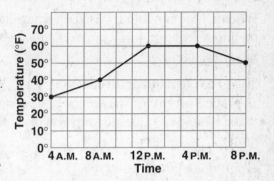

- You can see how the temperature changed throughout the day. *The temperature rose 10°F from 4 A.M. to 8 A.M. The temperature remained at 60°F for 4 hours, from 12 P.M. to 4 P.M.*

- You can also compare the temperatures throughout the day. *The temperature at 8 P.M. was 20° higher than it was at 4 A.M.*

The graph at the right shows a train moving between stations. *The train moves slowly while leaving the station. Then it picks up speed until it reaches a cruising speed. It slows down as it approaches the next station and gradually comes to a stop.*

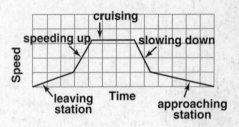

- Since the graph is *sketched* to show relationships, the axes do not need number scales. But the axes and the parts of the graph should have labels to show what they represent.

The graph at the right shows the altitude of an airplane during a flight. Use the graph for Exercises 1–3.

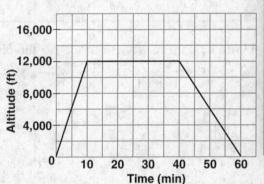

1. What was the airplane's altitude for most of the flight?

   _____

2. How long did it take the airplane to reach an altitude of 12,000 ft?

   _____

3. The third segment in the graph is not as steep as the first segment. What does this mean?

   _____

   _____

Sketch and label a graph of the relationship.

4. You enter the freeway in your car, constantly accelerating until you are on the freeway. Then you turn the cruise control on and drive at a constant speed. When you reach your exit you slow down as you exit the freeway until you stop at the stop light.

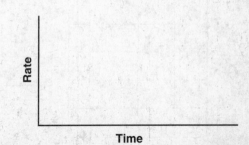

Course 3 Topics

Review 306

When a function rule is based on squaring the input variable, it is a *quadratic function*. Study the table.

The graph of a quadratic function is a ∪-shaped curve called a *parabola*. You can make a table of values to help you draw the graph.

Example 1: Graph $y = 2x^2 - 3$

x	$2x^2 - 3 = y$
-2	$2(-2)^2 - 3 = 5$
-1	$2(-1)^2 - 3 = -1$
0	$2(0)^2 - 3 = -3$
1	$2(1)^2 - 3 = -1$
2	$2(2)^2 - 3 = 5$

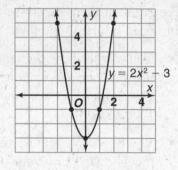

A nonlinear function has a graph that is not straight.

To graph a nonlinear function

① Make a table of values.

② Plot the points from the table.

③ Draw the graph to contain the points following the pattern suggested by the points.

Example 2: Graph $y = \frac{16}{x} + 1$ for positive values of x.

x	$\frac{16}{x} + 1 = y$
1	$\frac{16}{1} + 1 = 16 + 1 = 17$
2	$\frac{16}{2} + 1 = 8 + 1 = 9$
4	$\frac{16}{4} + 1 = 4 + 1 = 5$
8	$\frac{16}{8} + 1 = 2 + 1 = 3$
16	$\frac{16}{16} + 1 = 1 + 1 = 2$

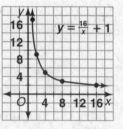

Write a quadratic function rule for the data in each table.

1.

x	0	1	2	3	4
y	4	5	8	13	20

_____

2.

x	0	1	2	3	4
y	-1	0	3	8	15

_____

Complete the table for each function. Then graph the function.

3. $y = 2x^2 - 1$

x	$2x^2 - 1 = y$
-2	
-1	
0	
1	
2	

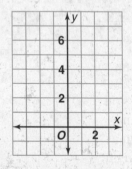

4. $y = 3^x - 5$

x	$3^x - 5 = y$
1	
2	
3	

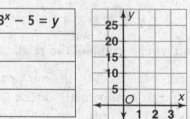

Review 307

You can write equations to solve many types of problems.

Read and Understand   A bacteria culture starts with 5 cells. The number of cells doubles every day. Write a function rule that relates the number of bacteria cells in the culture to the amount of time that has passed. Use the rule to find the number of cells there are in the culture after 12 days.

What are you asked to do?   *Write a function rule that relates bacteria cells to the amount of time that has passed.*

Plan and Solve   Start by making a table that shows the first few days and the number of cells per day.

Day	Cells
1	5
2	10
3	20
4	40

Notice that each output is equal to 5 times 2 raised to the power of the input. So, the number of cells is 5 times 2 raised to the number of days. Let d = the number of days that have passed. Let y = the number of bacteria cells.

Function: $y = 5 \cdot 2^d$

Evaluate the function rule to find how many cells there are after 12 days.

$$y = 5 \cdot 2^{12}$$
$$= 5 \cdot 4{,}096$$
$$= 20{,}480$$

Look Back and Check   How could you check your answer? *You can solve a simpler problem to check the function rule. Extend the table for 5 and 6 days and then evaluate the rule for these times.*

Solve each problem by writing a function rule.

1. Suppose you save $30 this year. You plan to double the amount you save each year. Write a function rule that relates the amount you save in a given year to the number of years that have passed. Use the rule to find out how much you will save after the sixth year and after the eighth year.

    _____

2. A population of 10 rabbits is released into a wildlife refuge. The population triples each year. Write a function rule that relates the population of the rabbits to the number of years that have passed. Use the rule to find out how many rabbits will be in the refuge after 5 years.

    _____

Course 3 Topics

Review 308

Algebra tiles:

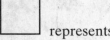 represents x^2, represents x, ☐ represents 1,

 represents $-x^2$, ▮ represents $-x$, ▪ represents -1.

You can use the algebra tiles to model variable expressions.

 is a model for $2x^2 - 3x + 5$.

The expression $2x^2 - 3x + 5$ is a *polynomial*.
To simplify a polynomial, combine like terms.

Example: Simplify $2x^2 - 3x + 5 + 2x$.

$$2x^2 - 3x + 5 + 2x$$
$$= 2x^2 - 3x + 2x + 5$$
↑
Use the Commutative Property

Group tiles of the same size together.
Remove zero pairs.

Write a variable expression for each model.

1.

_____

2.

_____

3.

_____

4.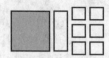

_____

Simplify each polynomial.

5. $x^2 - 2x^2 - 5x - 1 + 4$

6. $3x^2 + 2x^2 + 4x - 5x - 1$

7. $x^2 + x^2 - x - 1 + 5$

_____ _____ _____

8. $3x^2 - x - x^2 + 6x + 2$

9. $4x^2 - 2x + 6x - 2$

10. $x^2 - 3x + 2x^2 - x$

_____ _____ _____

Course 3 Topics

Review 309

To add polynomials, combine like terms. Add the *coefficients* in the like terms.

Example 1: Add $(3x^2 - 5x - 1)$ and $(x^2 - 6x + 3)$.

$3x^2 - 5x - 1 + x^2 - 6x + 3$ ← Write the sum.

$\quad = (3x^2 + x^2) + (-5x - 6x) + (-1 + 3)$ ← Group like terms.

$\quad = (3 + 1)x^2 + (-5 - 6)x + (-1 + 3)$ ← Use the Distributive Property.

$\quad = 4x^2 - 11x + 2$ ← Add and subtract.

To subtract a polynomial, rewrite the second polynomial to be the opposite and add to the first polynomial.

Example 2: Subtract $(2x^2 + x - 3)$ from $(x^2 - 3x + 1)$.

$(x^2 - 3x + 1) - (2x^2 + x - 3)$

$\quad = (x^2 - 3x + 1) + (-2x^2 - x + 3)$ ← Add the opposite of each term in the second polynomial.

$\quad = (x^2 - 2x^2) + (-3x - x) + (1 + 3)$ ← Group like terms.

$\quad = (1 - 2)x^2 + (-3 - 1)x + (1 + 3)$ ← Use the Distributive Property.

$\quad = -x^2 - 4x + 4$ ← Add and subtract.

Add.

1. $(x^2 + 4x) + (2x^2 - 6x)$

    _____

2. $(3x^2 - x - 1) + (2x^2 + 2x - 1)$

    _____

3. $(y^2 - y - 1) + (y^2 + y + 3)$

    _____

4. $(2y^2 - y) + (y^2 + 3)$

    _____

5. $(2k^2 + 1) + (k^2 - 2k + 5)$

    _____

6. $(4n^2 + n - 2) + (n^2 - 3n)$

    _____

Subtract.

7. $(2x^2 + 3x) - (x^2 + x)$

    _____

8. $(3l^2 - 2l + 1) - (2l^2 + l - 3)$

    _____

9. $(x^2 + 1) - (2x^2 + x - 1)$

    _____

10. $(m^2 - 2m + 6) - (4m^2 - 3)$

    _____

11. $(z^2 - 4z) - (3z^2 + 2z + 1)$

    _____

12. $(p^2 + 6p + 5) - (3p^2 - 2p)$

    _____

Course 3 Topics

Review 310

The tile model suggests how to find the area of a rectangle with length $3x + 1$ and width $2x$.

The area of the rectangle is $6x^2 + 2x$.

$\ell \cdot w = (3x + 1) \cdot 2x = 6x^2 + 2x$

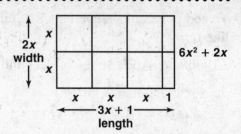

A polynomial with one term is called a *monomial*. To multiply monomials, multiply the coefficients and use the properties of exponents.

Example 1: Multiply $(-5x^2)(2x)$.

$(-5x^2)(2x)$

$= -10 \cdot x^2 \cdot x \leftarrow$ Multiply coefficients.

$= -10x^3 \quad \leftarrow$ Add exponents.

A polynomial with two terms is called a *binomial*. Use the distributive property to find the product of a monomial and a binomial.

Example 2: Multiply $4x$ by $(2x + 3)$.

$4x(2x + 3)$

$= 4x(2x) + 4x(3) \leftarrow$ Use the Distributive Property.

$= 8x^2 + 12x \quad \leftarrow$ Multiply monomials.

Find the area of each rectangle.

1.
$2x + 1$ ⬚
$\quad 3x$

_____

2.
$2x$ ⬚
$\quad 2x + 4$

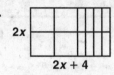

_____

Simplify each expression.

3. $y^2 \cdot 2y$

4. $3x^2 \cdot 5x$

5. $(-2n^3)(2n)$

_____   _____   _____

6. $(2x^2)(6x^2)$

7. $(8j^2)(-4j^3)$

8. $(-x^3)(-3x)$

_____   _____   _____

Use the Distributive Property to simplify each expression.

9. $z(z + 2)$

10. $x(3x - 1)$

11. $2b(b + 5)$

_____   _____   _____

12. $-5x(x - 4)$

13. $-2k(k^2 + 4)$

14. $3x^2(2x - 2)$

_____   _____   _____

Course 3 Topics

Answers

Grade 6 Topics *(Course 1)*

Review 1

1. 6,104   **2.** 15,021,000   **3.** 60,112
4. 2,009,006,001   **5.** 0.017   **6.** 0.29
7. 8,290   **8.** 1,000,030,050   **9.** <   **10.** >
11. >   **12.** >   **13.** <   **14.** >   **15.** >
16. <   **17.** >   **18.** <   **19.** <   **20.** >
21. 782, 783, 785, 790   **22.** 1,240; 1,346; 1,364; 1,420
23. 6,124; 6,214; 6,241; 6,421
24. 92,385; 92,835; 93,258; 93,582
25. 45,923; 45,932; 54,923; 54,932
26. 1,011; 1,101; 1,110; 1,111

Review 2

1. $3 + 0.6$ **2.** $4 + 0.7 + 0.02$
3. $1 + 0.2 + 0.08 + 0.003$ **4.** $20 + 1 + 0.5$
5. $7 + 0.03$ **6.** $10 + 5 + 0.3 + 0.008$
7. $30 + 2 + 0.2 + 0.07$ **8.** $6 + 0.4 + 0.07 + 0.005$
9. two tenths   **10.** fifteen hundredths
11. twenty-nine hundredths   **12.** eleven hundredths
13. sixty hundredths   **14.** nine tenths
15. fifty hundredths   **16.** four tenths
17. thirty-seven hundredths   **18.** 0.7   **19.** 0.1   **20.** 0.04
21. 0.07 **22.** 0.22 **23.** 0.46 **24.** 0.80 **25.** 0.30 **26.** 0.03

Review 3

1. <   **2.** >   **3.** >   **4.** <   **5.** >   **6.** <
7. =   **8.** <   **9.** <   **10.** >   **11.** >   **12.** =
13. >   **14.** <   **15.** <   **16.** 3.46, 3.59, 3.64
17. 21.79, 22.86, 22.97   **18.** 43, 43.022, 43.22
19. 1.02, 10.02, 10.2   **20.** 1.09, 1.1, 1.9
21. 7.4, 7.54, 75.4   **22.**

23.

24.

Review 4

1. 1.68 **2.** 4.98 **3.** 12.60 **4.** 32.97 **5.** 0.16 **6.** 2.01
7. 6.5 **8.** 15.1 **9.** 0.1 **10.** 1.0 **11.** 25.7 **12.** 6.4
13–16. Estimates may vary.
13. $10   **14.** $8   **15.** $3   **16.** $53
17–22. Accept reasonable estimates.
17. about 2 **18.** about 6 **19.** about 600 **20.** about 450
21. about 600 **22.** about 300

Review 5

1. $1 + 7 = 8; 7.6$ **2.** $3 + 9 = 12; 12.5$
3. $5 + 8 = 13; 13.07$
4. 23.8   **5.** 7   **6.** 22.104
7. $9 - 4 = 5; 4.3$ **8.** $7 - 3 = 4; 4.15$
9. $5 - 3 = 2; 2.27$ **10.** 3; 3.361   **11.** 4; 4.434
12. 8; 8.449   **13.** 11; 10.64   **14.** 5; 5.22   **15.** 1; 0.911

Review 6

1. 6 packs of AA, 2 packs of D
2. three $5 packs and one $4 pack
3. 4 new CDs and 2 used CDs
4. 1 ES brand and 2 CW brand

Review 7

1. $0.5 \times 1.2 = 0.60$ **2.** $0.3 \times 1.5 = 0.45$ **3.** 2.52
4. 238.7   **5.** 49.76   **6.** 39.788   **7.** 5.92
8. 479.08   **9.** 75.03   **10.** 7.08   **11.** 121.68
12. 201.6   **13.** 114.08   **14.** 912   **15.** 7.245

Review 8

1. 27   **2.** 25   **3.** 210   **4.** 77   **5.** 2
6. 100   **7.** 284   **8.** 7,500   **9.** 20   **10.** 0.04
11. 0.023 **12.** 0.07 **13.** 5.23 **14.** 0.003 **15.** 0.41
16. >   **17.** <   **18.** <   **19.** =   **20.** <
21. =   **22.** <   **23.** =

Review 9

1. 0.45   **2.** 0.67   **3.** 14   **4.** 3.375   **5.** 2.592
6. 2.5   **7.** 0.04   **8.** 7   **9.** 0.25; 5 **10.** 25
11. 56   **12.** 5   **13.** 3.7   **14.** 0.8   **15.** 1.37
16. 1.5   **17.** 1.87   **18.** 10.5

Review 10

1a. 5   **1b.** 5; 10   **1c.** 10; 13   **2a.** 8   **2b.** 8; 3
2c. 3; 1   **3.** 8   **4.** 6   **5.** 11   **6.** 14
7. =   **8.** >   **9.** =   **10.** <   **11.** >
12. <   **13.** =   **14.** <

Review 11

1. 14, 17, 20; Start with 2 and add 3 repeatedly.
2. 48, 96, 192; Start with 3 and multiply by 2 repeatedly.
3. 45, 54, 63; Start with 9 and add 9 repeatedly.
4. 32, 24, 16; Start with 64 and subtract 8 repeatedly.
5. 256, 1,024, 4,096; Start with 1 and multiply by 4 repeatedly.
6. 55, 50, 45; Start with 75 and subtract 5 repeatedly.
7. 54, 45, 36; Start with 90 and subtract 9 repeatedly.
8. 64, 128, 256; Start with 4 and multiply by 2 repeatedly.

Review 12

1. $p + 2$ **2.** $2p$ **3.** $3p + 6$ **4.** 8; 20
5. 6; 42   **6.** 20; 10   **7.** 21   **8.** 7
9. 20   **10.** 28   **11.** 24   **12.** 3
13. 1   **14.** 36   **15.** 7

Review 13

1. $n + 8$ **2.** $3n$ **3.** $n - 2$ **4.** $6 + y$
5. $8 \div e$ **6.** $h - 3$ **7.** $4w$ **8.** $s - 8$
9. $r \div 2$ **10.** $n + 5$ **11.** $6m$

Answers (continued)

Review 14
1. 7 games   2. 45 games   3. $1,400
4. Every other team has lost at least 1 game.

Review 15
1. $q = 3$ 2. $w = 5$ 3. $h = 9$ 4. $h = 6$
5. $h = 36$ 6. $m = 20$ 7. $y = 20$ 8. $w = 13$
9. false   10. true   11. true   12. false
13. false   14. true   15. false   16. false

Review 16
1. 15; 15; 16   2. 20; 20; 25   3. 32   4. 23
5. 30   6. 100   7. 21   8. 412
9. 20   10. 200
11. $2,000 + p = $3,200; p = $1,200

Review 17
1. yes   2. no   3. no   4. yes
5. yes   6. no   7. 4; 4; 3   8. 9; 9; 36
9. 5   10. 81   11. 4   12. 15
13. 476   14. 5   15. 576   16. 4
17. 88   18. 22   19. 42   20. 3

Review 18
1. 3; 6   2. 6; 2   3. 8; 4   4. 9^3; 9; 3
5. 6^4; 6; 4   6. 1^5; 1; 5   7. 36   8. 243
9. 10,000   10. 41   11. 4   12. 52
13. 28   14. 22   15. 14   16. 4
17. 50   18. 14

Review 19
1. 3; 8   2. 5; 6   3. 9; 4; 3   4. 6; 5   5. 4; 5
6. 6; 12; 6   7. $2 \times (7 + 5)$; 24
8. $(8 \times 60) - (8 \times 5)$; 440   9. $7 \times (8 - 6)$; 14
10. $12 \times (3 + 4)$; 84   11. 81   12. 215
13. 472   14. 427   15. 420   16. 318
17. 384   18. 364   19. 342

Review 20
1. 8; 26; 42; 218   2. 10; 25; 975; 1,005; 2,340
3. 100; 60; 250   4. 51; 75; 12; 93; 153
5. 27; 36; 108; 126; 387   6. yes   7. yes   8. yes
9. yes   10. yes   11. no   12. no   13. yes
14. yes   15. yes   16. no   17. no   18. yes
19. no   20. yes   21. no   22. no   23. no
24. 2, 5, 10   25. 5   26. 2, 5, 10

Review 21
1. composite   2. prime   3. prime
4. composite   5. composite   6. prime
7. prime   8. composite   9. prime
10. composite   11. prime   12. composite
13.   14.

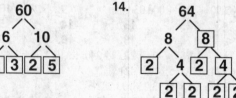

15.

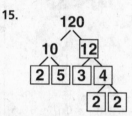

16. 3×7 17. $2 \times 2 \times 2 \times 3$
18. $3 \times 3 \times 3 \times 3$ 19. $2 \times 2 \times 2 \times 2 \times 7$
20. $3 \times 3 \times 7$ 21. $2 \times 2 \times 5 \times 5$
22. 1×103 23. 5×31

Review 22
1. 1, 2, 5, 10; 1, 3, 5, 15; 5   2. 1, 2, 7, 14; 1, 3, 7, 21; 7
3. 1, 3, 9; 1, 3, 7, 21; 3   4. 1, 2, 3, 4, 6, 12; 1, 13; 1
5. 1, 3, 5, 15; 1, 5, 25; 5   6. 1, 3, 5, 15; 1, 2, 3, 6, 9, 18; 3
7. 1, 2, 3, 4, 6, 9, 12, 18, 36; 1, 2, 3, 4, 6, 8, 12, 16, 24, 48; 12
8. 1, 2, 3, 4, 6, 8, 12, 24; 1, 2, 3, 5, 6, 10, 15, 30; 6
9. 3   10. 15   11. 8   12. 6   13. 10
14. 21   15. 4   16. 24   17. 30

Review 23
1. $\frac{10}{12}, \frac{15}{18}$ 2. $\frac{6}{14}, \frac{9}{21}$ 3. $\frac{14}{16}, \frac{21}{24}$ 4. $\frac{6}{22}, \frac{9}{33}$
5. $\frac{6}{12}, \frac{1}{2}$ 6. $\frac{2}{10}, \frac{3}{15}$ 7. no; $\frac{4}{5}$ 8. yes
9. no; $\frac{3}{7}$ 10. yes   11. no; $\frac{7}{15}$ 12. no; $\frac{5}{14}$
13. $\frac{1}{2}$ 14. $\frac{1}{20}$ 15. $\frac{7}{8}$ 16. $\frac{1}{3}$
17. $\frac{13}{17}$ 18. $\frac{3}{4}$ 19. $\frac{1}{7}$ 20. $\frac{2}{3}$
21. $\frac{2}{15}$ 22. $\frac{7}{33}$

Review 24
1. $\frac{16}{7}$ 2. $\frac{23}{4}$ 3. $\frac{13}{2}$ 4. $\frac{53}{8}$ 5. $\frac{34}{10}$
6. $\frac{23}{5}$ 7. $\frac{28}{3}$ 8. $\frac{24}{5}$ 9. $\frac{15}{8}$ 10. $\frac{27}{8}$
11. $\frac{17}{7}$ 12. $\frac{49}{6}$ 13–18. Check students' work.
19. $1\frac{1}{8}$ 20. $3\frac{1}{2}$ 21. $2\frac{2}{5}$ 22. $2\frac{2}{3}$ 23. $1\frac{3}{4}$
24. $1\frac{1}{5}$ 25. $6\frac{2}{3}$ 26. $3\frac{2}{5}$ 27. $4\frac{1}{2}$ 28. $1\frac{4}{5}$
29. $3\frac{5}{8}$ 30. $2\frac{2}{3}$

Answers

Answers (continued)

Review 25

1. 4, 8, 12, 16, 20; 5, 10, 15, 20; 20
2. 6, 12, 18, 24, 30, 36, 42; 7, 14, 21, 28, 35, 42; 42
3. 9, 18, 27, 36, 45; 15, 30, 45; 45
4. 10, 20, 30, 40, 50; 25, 50; 50
5. 8, 16, 24; 24; 24   6. 8, 16, 24; 12, 24; 24
7. 4, 8, 12, 16, 20, 24, 28; 7, 14, 21, 28; 28
8. 15, 30, 45, 60, 75; 25, 50, 75; 75
9. 15, 30, 45, 60; 20, 40, 60; 60
10. 4, 8, 12, 16, 20, 24, 28, 32, 36; 9, 18, 27, 36; 36
11. 63 12. 24 13. 72 14. 200 15. 294 16. 12

Review 26

1. < 2. < 3. > 4. > 5. =
6. > 7. < 8. = 9. > 10. >
11. < 12. < 13. $\frac{1}{2}, \frac{5}{8}, \frac{3}{4}$ 14. $\frac{5}{8}, \frac{2}{3}, \frac{5}{6}$
15. $\frac{5}{12}, \frac{1}{2}, \frac{2}{3}$ 16. $\frac{7}{12}, \frac{3}{5}, \frac{2}{3}$ 17. $\frac{3}{8}, \frac{1}{2}, \frac{3}{5}$ 18. $\frac{3}{4}, \frac{13}{16}, \frac{7}{8}$
19. Eugene; $1\frac{1}{9} = 1\frac{4}{36}; 1\frac{5}{12} = 1\frac{15}{36}; 1\frac{15}{36} > 1\frac{4}{36}$

Review 27

1. $\frac{4}{5}$ 2. $\frac{11}{20}$ 3. $1\frac{1}{4}$ 4. $1\frac{3}{4}$ 5. $3\frac{3}{8}$
6. $\frac{1}{8}$ 7. $1\frac{8}{25}$ 8. $\frac{17}{50}$ 9. $\frac{21}{250}$ 10. $\frac{3}{500}$
11. $\frac{13}{20}$ 12. $4\frac{19}{20}$ 13. 0.65 14. $0.1\overline{6}$ 15. 0.35
16. $2.\overline{6}$ 17. 0.76 18. $0.\overline{4}$ 19. $0.6\overline{36}$ 20. 1.625
21. $1.\overline{2}$ 22. 2.25 23. 0.04 24. $0.41\overline{6}$
25–30. Check students' work
25. less than 26. equal to 27. less than
28. greater than 29. greater than 30. less than

Review 28

1. 6 packs of AA, 2 packs of D
2. three $5 packs and one $4 pack
3. 4 new CDs and 2 used CDs
4. 1 ES brand and 2 CW brand

Review 29

1. 1 2. 2 3. 1 4. 0 5. 1
6. $\frac{1}{2}$ 7. $\frac{1}{2}$ 8. 2 9. $\frac{1}{2}$ 10. $\frac{1}{2}$
11. 0 12. 0 13. $1\frac{1}{2}$ 14. 0 15. $\frac{1}{2}$
16. 9 17. 0 18. 9 19. 7 20. 9
21. 6 22. 12 23. 9 24. $16\frac{1}{2}$ 25. 18
26. 6 27. 6 28. yes 29. 6 mi

Review 30

1. $\frac{4}{5}$ 2. $\frac{5}{6}$ 3. $\frac{1}{2}$ 4. $1\frac{1}{10}$ 5. $\frac{1}{2}$
6. $\frac{3}{4}$ 7. $\frac{3}{4}$ 8. $1\frac{1}{2}$ 9. $1\frac{1}{8}$ 10. $\frac{3}{8}$
11. $\frac{3}{5}$ 12. $\frac{1}{2}$ 13. $\frac{1}{2}$ 14. $\frac{1}{5}$ 15. $\frac{1}{3}$
16. $\frac{2}{5}$ 17. $\frac{1}{12}$ 18. $\frac{1}{2}$ 19. $\frac{3}{7}$ 20. $1\frac{1}{5}$
21. 1 22. $\frac{4}{11}$ 23. $\frac{1}{2}$ 24. $\frac{47}{80}$ 25. $\frac{1}{5}$

Review 31

1. $1\frac{1}{4}$ 2. $\frac{3}{8}$ 3. $\frac{1}{2}$ 4. $\frac{3}{8}$ 5. $1\frac{2}{5}$
6. $1\frac{2}{9}$ 7. $1\frac{1}{5}$ 8. $\frac{1}{3}$ 9. $\frac{7}{8}$ 10. $\frac{11}{16}$
11. $\frac{1}{4}$ 12. $1\frac{1}{6}$ 13. $\frac{5}{8}$ 14. $\frac{23}{30}$ 15. $\frac{11}{60}$
16. $\frac{23}{40}$ 17. $1\frac{1}{12}$ 18. $\frac{1}{24}$ 19. $1\frac{7}{24}$ 20. $\frac{1}{10}$
21. $\frac{13}{40}$ 22. $\frac{1}{10}$ 23. $\frac{2}{5}$ 24. $\frac{9}{10}$

Review 32

1. $5\frac{5}{7}$ 2. $4\frac{2}{3}$ 3. $6\frac{1}{2}$ 4. $12\frac{1}{2}$ 5. $9\frac{7}{8}$
6. $5\frac{9}{10}$ 7. $8\frac{2}{3}$ 8. $10\frac{5}{14}$ 9. $11\frac{7}{8}$ 10. $6\frac{5}{8}$
11. $16\frac{1}{2}$ 12. $11\frac{1}{15}$ 13. $15\frac{11}{20}$ 14. $9\frac{1}{2}$ 15. $11\frac{1}{10}$
16. $9\frac{2}{5}$ 17. $10\frac{1}{2}$ 18. $12\frac{11}{16}$

Review 33

1. $5\frac{2}{5}$ 2. $2\frac{1}{4}$ 3. $4\frac{1}{2}$ 4. $2\frac{1}{8}$ 5. $5\frac{1}{4}$
6. $6\frac{1}{12}$ 7. $2\frac{2}{3}$ 8. $3\frac{7}{8}$ 9. $2\frac{11}{14}$ 10. $2\frac{5}{6}$
11. $3\frac{15}{16}$ 12. $4\frac{11}{15}$ 13. $3\frac{1}{16}$ 14. $3\frac{2}{3}$ 15. $6\frac{5}{8}$
16. $5\frac{3}{20}$ 17. $7\frac{1}{12}$ 18. $1\frac{3}{10}$

Review 34

1. $\frac{3}{5}; \frac{3}{5}, \frac{3}{5} + \frac{1}{5} = \frac{4}{5}, \frac{4}{5} = \frac{4}{5}$
2. $9; x - \frac{3}{9} = \frac{2}{9}, \frac{5}{9}, \frac{5}{9}, \frac{5}{9} - \frac{3}{9} = \frac{2}{9}, \frac{2}{9} = \frac{2}{9}$
3. $\frac{2}{4} = \frac{1}{2}$ 4. $\frac{6}{8} = \frac{3}{4}$ 5. $\frac{3}{10}$ 6. $\frac{23}{12} = 1\frac{11}{12}$
7. $\frac{2}{12} = \frac{1}{6}$ 8. $\frac{4}{6} = \frac{2}{3}$ 9. $\frac{3}{12} = \frac{1}{4}$ 10. $\frac{3}{12} = \frac{1}{4}$
11. $\frac{3}{8}$ 12. $\frac{37}{40}$

Review 35

1. 205 min 2. 137 min 3. 168 min
4. 318 min 5. 373 min 6. 339 min
7. 2 h 35 min 8. 2 h 14 min 9. 5 h 45 min
10. 7 h 29 min 11. 13 h 54 min 12. 18 h 28 min
13. 1 h 20 min 14. 2 h 45 min

Review 36

1. 176 ft 2. 70 ft less; 176 ft − 106 ft
3. 24 ft 4. 16 ft

Review 37

1. $\frac{3}{4} \times \frac{1}{2} = \frac{3}{8}$ 2. $\frac{1}{2} \times \frac{2}{3} = \frac{2}{6} = \frac{1}{3}$ 3. $\frac{2}{27}$ 4. $\frac{1}{7}$
5. $3\frac{3}{4}$ 6. $\frac{3}{7}$ 7. $\frac{7}{30}$ 8. $\frac{5}{8}$ 9. $\frac{21}{80}$
10. $\frac{1}{12}$ 11. $1\frac{7}{9}$ 12. $\frac{2}{3}$ 13. $2\frac{2}{9}$ 14. $\frac{3}{10}$
15. $1\frac{1}{4}$ c

Answers

Answers (continued)

Review 38

1. $3\frac{1}{3}$ 2. $10\frac{4}{5}$ 3. $8\frac{4}{5}$ 4. $\frac{5}{9}$ 5. 30

6. $5\frac{2}{3}$ 7. 10 8. $1\frac{4}{5}$ 9. 10 10. $4\frac{2}{7}$

11. $4\frac{1}{8}$ 12. 12 13. $\frac{2}{5}$ 14. $\frac{1}{4}$ 15. $\frac{1}{2}$

16. 11 17. $5\frac{5}{6}$ 18. $6\frac{1}{15}$ 19. $\frac{8}{35}$ 20. $5\frac{1}{10}$

21. $8\frac{1}{2}$ 22. $12\frac{1}{3}$ 23. $3\frac{5}{7}$ 24. $\frac{3}{14}$ 25. 4

26. 66 in.^{2} 27. 8.75 in.

Review 39

1. 4 2. $\frac{3}{5}$ 3. 20 4. $\frac{9}{8}$ 5. $\frac{1}{14}$

6. $\frac{1}{18}$ 7. $\frac{9}{5}$ 8. $\frac{11}{3}$ 9. $\frac{7}{9}$ 10. $\frac{12}{11}$

11. $\frac{7}{2}$ 12. $\frac{15}{3}$ 13. 3 14. 8 15. 12

16. 15 17. $7\frac{1}{2}$ 18. $16\frac{4}{5}$ 19. $1\frac{2}{5}$ 20. $1\frac{1}{8}$

21. $\frac{2}{7}$ 22. $1\frac{5}{16}$ 23. $\frac{1}{8}$ 24. $\frac{8}{15}$ 25. $\frac{3}{10}$

26. $\frac{3}{25}$ 27. $\frac{1}{16}$ 28. $\frac{6}{7}$ 29. $2\frac{1}{2}$ 30. $1\frac{2}{9}$

Review 40

1. 3 2. 5 3. 17 4. 2 5. 3

6. 3 7. 2 8. 5 9. 3 10. 3

11. 3 12. 2 13. 10 14. $16\frac{1}{50}$ 15. $2\frac{4}{9}$

16. $2\frac{9}{20}$ 17. $13\frac{8}{11}$ 18. $\frac{7}{16}$ 19. $2\frac{6}{13}$ 20. $12\frac{4}{27}$

21. $\frac{3}{5}$

Review 41

1. $\frac{4}{5}$ 2. $\frac{3}{5}$ 3. 12 4. $\frac{6}{2} = 3$ 5. $\frac{2}{5}$

6. $\frac{1}{5}$ 7. $\frac{2}{9}$ 8. $\frac{7}{12}$ 9. $\frac{3}{5}$ 10. $\frac{2}{9}$

11. $110\frac{1}{4}$ lb 12. $40\frac{1}{2}$

Review 42

1. $168,070 2. $164,640 3. 15 games 4. $1,051.20

Review 43

1. Gardens can be quite long, so use feet or yards.
2. Hummingbirds are quite small, so use inches.
3. A letter is not heavy, so use ounces.
4. Steel girders are heavy, so use tons.
5. A pitcher can be large or small, so use quarts or ounces.
6. There is a lot of water in an aquarium, so use gallons.
7. > 8. ≈

Review 44

1. 4 2. 8 3. 7,920 4. $7\frac{1}{2}$ 5. $\frac{1}{4}$

6. 5,000 7. 74 8. $2\frac{1}{2}$ 9. 99 10. 8 pt

11. 2 yd 2 ft 12. 15 lb 13. < 14. =

15. < 16. = 17. > 18. < 19. $4\frac{1}{4}$ t

Review 45

1–8. Sample answers are given.

1. $\frac{4}{10},\frac{6}{15},\frac{8}{20}$ 2. $\frac{2}{6},\frac{3}{9},\frac{4}{12}$ 3. $\frac{6}{8},\frac{9}{12},\frac{15}{20}$ 4. $\frac{10}{16},\frac{15}{24},\frac{20}{32}$

5. $\frac{4}{14},\frac{6}{21},\frac{8}{28}$ 6. $\frac{2}{10},\frac{3}{15},\frac{4}{20}$ 7. $\frac{24}{40},\frac{36}{60},\frac{48}{80}$ 8. $\frac{12}{32},\frac{18}{48},\frac{24}{64}$

9. $\frac{2}{1}$ 10. $\frac{7}{12}$ 11. $\frac{18}{25}$ 12. $\frac{12}{5}$ 13. $\frac{5}{8}$

14. $\frac{1}{3}$ 15. $\frac{5}{8}$ 16. $\frac{4}{1}$ 17. 12 18. 50

19. 108 20. 70 21. $\frac{1}{3}$ 22. 360 23. 500

24. 35 25. 72

Review 46

1. $17/shirt 2. $50/game 3. $4/toy 4. $20/shirt

5. $9/box 6. $44/book 7. $20/racket 8. $8/h

9. $.33/can 10. $21.25 11. 84 cheerleaders

12. $101 13. 12.7 cm 14. $25.50

15. 24 points in 2 games 16. 4 in. in 2 mo

17. 4 mi in 32 min 18. 10 c in 12 min

Review 47

1. yes 2. no 3. no 4. yes 5. yes

6. no 7. no 8. no 9. yes 10. 5

11. 8 12. 3 13. 10 14. 5 15. 7

16. 18 17. 5 18. 81 19. 4 times 20. 4 mi

Review 48

1. yes 2. yes 3. no 4. yes 5. no

6. yes 7. no 8. yes 9. no 10. no

11. yes 12. yes 13. $n = 1$ 14. $n = 1$

15. $a = 45$ 16. $x = 14$ 17. $t = 9$ 18. $r = 24$

19. $m = 48$ 20. $e = 20$ 21. $h = 30$ 22. $w = 30$

23. $y = 42$ 24. $x = 18$ 25. $t = 3$ 26. $a = 15$

27. $b = 8$ 28. $n = 3$

Review 49

1. 72 yd 2. 360 yd 3. 18 yd 4. 54 yd

5. about 90 yd 6. about 36 yd 7. 1 in. to 5 ft

8. 1 in. to 3 in. 9. 1 cm to 7 cm 10. 1 in. to 6 ft

Review 50

1. $0.30, \frac{3}{10}$ 2. $0.14, \frac{7}{50}$ 3. $0.16, \frac{4}{25}$ 4. $0.05, \frac{1}{20}$

5. $0.92, \frac{23}{25}$ 6. $0.80, \frac{4}{5}$ 7. $0.21, \frac{21}{100}$ 8. $0.38, \frac{19}{50}$

9. 68% 10. 85% 11. 16% 12. 12.5% 13. 3.5%

14. 10% 15. 64% 16. 0.8% 17. 45% 18. 40%

19. 32% 20. 7% 21. 13% 22. 90% 23. 1%

24. 60%

Review 51

1. 27 2. 96 3. 33 4. 72 5. 21

6. 245 7. 24 8. 255 9. 24 10. 110

11. 148 12. 170 13. 25 14. 49 15. 7

16. 30 17. 40 18. 7.2 19. 19.2 20. 40.5

21. 43.2 22. 66 23. 171 24. 12.8

Answers

Answers (continued)

Review 52

1. 20 **2.** 20 **3.** 7 **4.** 24 **5.** 1
6. 15 **7.** 350 **8.** 25 **9.** 38 **10.** 72
11. 18 **12.** 60 **13.** 9 **14.** 36 **15.** 15
16. 50 **17.** 40 **18.** 6 **19.** 27 **20.** 280
21. 56 **22.** $24

Review 53

1. $173.32 **2.** 284 subscriptions **3.** 4 packages
4. $60 **5.** 120 grams

Review 54

1. 8 **2.** 14 **3.** 9 **4.** 111 **5.** 69
6. 70 **7.** 7 **8.** 15 **9.** 16 **10.** 46
11. 55 **12.** 7 **13.** 5 **14.** 1 **15.** 3
16. 33 **17.** 98 **18.** 110, 121

Review 55

1.

First Letter	Tally	Frequency
A		2
B		1
D		1
F		2
H		1
J		4

2.

Month	Tally	Frequency
March		2
April		1
May		5
June		2
July		2

3. 3;

Students' Ages

```
        X
   X    X
   X    X
   X    X    X
   X    X    X
X  X    X    X
11 12  13   14
```

4. 4;

Questions Answered Correctly

```
             X
      X  X   X
   X  X  X   X
X  X  X  X   X
X  X  X  X   X
6  7  8  9  10
```

Review 56

1. day 10 **2.** 6 ways
3. 16 different combinations **4.** 34 days overdue

Review 57

1. 20 books **2.** January **3.** 10 books
4. October and November
5. Bar graph; data shows amounts, but not changes over time.
6. Line graph; data shows change over time.

Review 58

1. English and Spanish **2.** 12 people
3. 12 people **4.** Polish

5.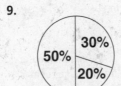

6.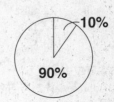

7.

8.

9.

10.

11–13. Answers may vary.

11.

12.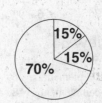

13.

Review 59

1. A2–A5 **2.** C2–C5 **3.** E2 **4.** F5
5. 1 hour **6.** 9 hours **7.** 3 hours **8.** 0 hours
9. 5 hours **10.** =B4 + C4 + D4
11. =B5 + C5 + D5 **12.** =B2 + C2 + D2
13. =E5/3 or = (B5 + C5 + D5)/3

Answers

Answers (continued)

Review 60

1. 18 years old
2. 2 entries
3. 9 people
4. 28 people
5.

stem	leaf
47	9
48	0 9
49	3
50	4 8
51	4 9
52	3 7

Review 61

1. graph A
2. graph B
3. graph D
4. graph C
5. All of the scores but one are well above the mean. The score of 12 is an outlier and greatly decreases the mean.

Review 62

1. false
2. false
3. true
4. true
5. false
6. false
7. false
8. false
9. true
10. false
11. b
12. c
13. d
14. a

Review 63

1. obtuse
2. right
3. acute
4. right

5–8. Sample answers are given.

5. 75°
6. 90°
7. 120°
8. 60°

Review 64

1. 55°
2. 115°
3. 90°
4. complementary
5. supplementary
6. supplementary and congruent
7. complementary
8. supplementary
9. supplementary and congruent

Review 65

1. right
2. obtuse
3. acute
4. acute
5. right
6. acute
7. obtuse
8. acute
9. scalene
10. isosceles
11. equilateral
12. isosceles

Review 66

1. parallelogram, rectangle, rhombus, square
2. parallelogram, rhombus
3. parallelogram, rectangle
4. trapezoid
5. quadrilateral
6. hexagon
7. octagon
8. quadrilateral
9. pentagon
10. triangle
11. hexagon
12. decagon

Review 67

1. Patrick in the blue house, Tony in the white house, and Neil in the green house
2. tulips, hyacinths, daisies, daffodils, snapdragons
3. Kendra, Carlos, John, Amber
4. parents, grandparents, brother, sister

Review 68

1. yes
2. no
3. no
4. b, c
5. congruent and similar
6. similar
7. similar

Review 69

1. yes
2. no
3. yes
4. no
5. yes
6. yes
7. no
8. yes; H̶A̶H̶
9. no
10. yes; ~~COB~~

Review 70

1–4. See sample drawings.

1.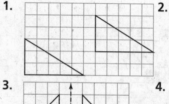
2.
3.
4.

5. b; 90°

Review 71

1. millimeters
2. centimeters
3. kilometers
4. meters
5. liters
6. kiloliters
7. milligrams
8. grams

Review 72

1. 2,500 m
2. 3.71 m
3. 0.49 m
4. 0.48 m
5. 4,000 m
6. 1.5 m
7. 600 L
8. 7.99 L
9. 0.0009 L
10. 0.0356 L
11. 6 L
12. 0.018 L
13. 4,000 g
14. 6.61 g
15. 1.5 g
16. 0.02 g
17. 1,950 g
18. 0.0023 g
19. 0.019
20. 5,500
21. 0.049
22. 0.73
23. 60
24. 254

Review 73

1. $A \approx 12\frac{1}{2}$ in.^{2}
2. $A \approx 6$ in.^{2}
3. $A \approx 14$ in.^{2}
4. 28 cm; 24 cm^2
5. 33 ft; 67.5 ft^2
6. 10 m; 6.25 m^2
7. 22 in.; 30.25 in.^{2}
8. 19.2 in.; 21.08 in.^{2}
9. 10.5 ft; 3.375 ft^2
10. 32 cm; 64 cm^2
11. 31.4 m; 54.6 m^2
12. 62 in.; 198 in.^{2}
13. 225 m^2

Answers (continued)

Review 74

1. 48 ft^2 **2.** 108 in.^{2} **3.** 72 yd^2 **4.** 9.52 in.^{2}
5. 589 yd^2 **6.** 20.25 m^2 **7.** 105 cm^2 **8.** 97.11 ft^2
9. 93.6 m^2 **10.** 56 cm^2 **11.** 63 in.^{2} **12.** 25.3 m^2
13. 11.2 ft^2 **14.** 2,860 in.^{2} **15.** 12.39 cm^2 **16.** 2.805 m^2
17. 16.82 yd^2 **18.** 3.44 in.^{2}

Review 75

1. $\overline{TY}$ **2.** $\overline{TZ}$, $\overline{ZY}$, or $\overline{TY}$
3. $\overline{QT}$, $\overline{QX}$, $\overline{QY}$ **4.** 16 cm **5.** 55 in.
6. 24 ft **7.** 72 in. **8.** 45 yd **9.** 21 m
10. 39 ft **11.** 126 yd **12.** 114 cm

Review 76

1. 28.3 m^2 **2.** 12.6 m^2 **3.** 113.1 m^2 **4.** 201.1 cm^2
5. 530.9 in.^{2} **6.** 616 m^2 **7.** 452.4 ft^2 **8.** 38.5 m^2
9. 132.7 cm^2 **10.** 5.1 ft^2 **11.** 660.5 in.^{2} **12.** 415.3 ft^2
13. 19.6 yd^2 **14.** 1,808.6 in.^{2} **15.** 1,133.5 cm^2

Review 77

1. triangular prism **2.** pentagonal pyramid
3. hexagonal pyramid **4.** square pyramid
5. 7 faces; 15 edges; 10 vertices

Review 78

1. 96 m^2 **2.** 56 cm^2 **3.** 368 cm^2 **4.** 188.4 cm^2
5. 75.4 cm^2

Review 79

1. 64 cm^3 **2.** 180 m^3 **3.** 180 cm^3 **4.** 162 in.^{3}
5. 36.75 cm^3 **6.** 720 mm^3 **7.** 120.9 m^3
8. 1,809.6 m^3 **9.** 904.8 m^3

Review 80

1. 168 ears **2.** 70 lb **3.** 88 potatoes **4.** 68 lb

Review 81

1. -7 **2.** 212 **3.** -49 **4.** $-1,991$ **5.** 78
6. -16 **7.** > **8.** < **9.** < **10.** >
11. < **12.** < **13.** < **14.** < **15.** >
16. < **17.** > **18.** < **19.** > **20.** >
21. < **22.** < **23.** 2 **24.** 100 **25.** 16
26. 8 **27.** 25 **28.** 250 **29.** 16 **30.** 12
31. 75

Review 82

1. 5 **2.** 10 **3.** -5 **4.** -12 **5.** 3
6. 2 **7.** -4 **8.** 3 **9.** 8 **10.** -8
11. -2 **12.** 2 **13.** -10 **14.** 5 **15.** -7
16. 7 **17.** -12 **18.** 16 **19.** -19 **20.** -7
21. 0 **22.** 0 **23.** -4 **24.** 6 **25.** 0
26. -12 **27.** 1 **28.** 1 **29.** -1 **30.** -8

Review 83

1. 9 **2.** 6 **3.** -3 **4.** 2 **5.** -5
6. 8 **7.** -10 **8.** 10 **9.** -6 **10.** -11
11. -12 **12.** 0 **13.** -11 **14.** 12 **15.** -5
16. 19 **17.** -15 **18.** 28 **19.** 15 **20.** -12
21. -26 **22.** 10 **23.** 28 **24.** 6 **25.** -2
26. -12 **27.** 3 **28.** -18 **29.** 24 **30.** -12
31. $s = -22$ **32.** $x = 5$ **33.** $b = -6$
34. $x = 19$ **35.** $s = -75$ **36.** $y = 4$
37. $c = -5$ **38.** $x = -25$ **39.** $b = -5$

Review 84

1. -28 **2.** 45 **3.** -22 **4.** -72 **5.** -45
6. 42 **7.** -72 **8.** -65 **9.** 20
10. -6 pounds **11.** -108 **12.** 245
13. -45 **14.** -112 **15.** -125 **16.** 243
17. -48 **18.** -363 **19.** 100

Review 85

1. -3 **2.** 5 **3.** -5 **4.** -7 **5.** -5
6. 3 **7.** -3 **8.** -3 **9.** 2
10. $y = -6$ **11.** $p = -60$ **12.** $y = 10$
13. $x = -4$ **14.** $x = -6$ **15.** $s = 28$
16. $x = -96$ **17.** $x = -6$ **18.** $x = 10$
19. -9 ft/s

Review 86

1–14.

15. $(4, -1)$ **16.** $(-3, 5)$ **17.** $(0, 1)$ **18.** $(-3, -2)$
19. U **20.** R

Review 87

1. 8 **2.** -32 **3.** 60 **4.** 15 **5.** 0
6. -403 **7.** 273 **8.** 329 **9.** -983 **10.** 3,766
11. 2,079 **12.** $-2,841$ **13.** $2,147 **14.** $49

Answers

Answers (continued)

Review 88

1. 7; 8   **2.** 8; 10   **3.** 25; 30

4.

Quarts	Cups
1	4
2	8
3	12
4	16

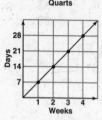

5.

Weeks	Days
1	7
2	14
3	21
4	28

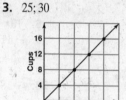

Review 89

1. $4.25;

Federal Minimum Wage

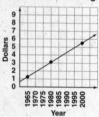

2. 900,000 civilians;

Civilian Staff in the Military

Review 90

1. $\frac{2}{5}$ **2.** $\frac{2}{7}$ **3.** $\frac{1}{4}$ **4.** $\frac{2}{6}$ or $\frac{1}{3}$ **5.** $\frac{1}{2}$

6. $\frac{3}{5}$ **7.** 0   **8.** $\frac{1}{2}$ **9.** likely

10. certain   **11.** unlikely   **12.** unlikely

13. impossible   **14.** impossible

Review 91

1. $\frac{1}{6}$ **2.** $\frac{4}{6}$ or $\frac{2}{3}$

3. No; the probabilities are not close to being the same.

4. $\frac{5}{20}$ or $\frac{1}{4}$ **5.** $\frac{9}{20}$ **6.** $\frac{11}{20}$ **7.** $\frac{12}{20}$ or $\frac{3}{5}$ **8.** $\frac{7}{20}$

Review 92

1. 10; 60   **2.** 190; 350   **3.** 600; 32,700

4. 300; 1,200   **5.** 100; 160   **6.** 150; 480

Review 93

1. about $\frac{1}{4}$ **2.** about $\frac{1}{10}$ **3.** about $\frac{1}{9}$ **4.** about $\frac{1}{12}$

Review 94

1–2. Check students' diagrams.   **1.** $\frac{1}{9}$ **2.** $\frac{1}{4}$

3. 16 ways   **4.** 40 ways   **5.** 30 ways   **6.** 200 ways

Review 95

1. COW, OWC, WOC, CWO, OCW, WCO

2. 238, 328, 823, 283, 382, 832   **3.** IF, FI   **4.** 79, 97

5. 120 ways   **6.** 40,320 ways   **7.** 6 ways

8. 362,880 games

Review 96

1. no   **2.** yes   **3.** yes   **4.** no

5. $\frac{1}{64}$ **6.** $\frac{9}{49}$ **7.** $\frac{1}{12}$ **8.** $\frac{1}{4}$

9. 0   **10.** $\frac{1}{4}$ **11.** $\frac{1}{8}$

Review 97

1a. Add 5.   **1b.** Divide by 7.   **1c.** $x = 3$

2a. Subtract 8.   **2b.** Multiply by 5.   **2c.** $t = 20$

3. $y = 2$ **4.** $x = 29$ **5.** $c = 40$

6. $f = 5$ **7.** $k = 1$ **8.** $e = 100$

Review 98

1a. x is less than or equal to -4.

1b. closed

1c.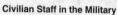

2a. x is greater than or equal to -1.

2b. closed

2c.

3a. x is less than 4.

3b. open

3c.

Review 99

1. $x < 7$ **2.** $y > 6$ **3.** $a \geq 4$ **4.** $x \leq -1$

5. $y \geq 9$ **6.** $d \geq 20$ **7.** $c \leq 20$ **8.** $b \geq 16$

9. $w \geq 14$ **10.** $x < -24$

Review 100

1. 63 mugs   **2.** 112.5 miles

3. 16 ft × 12 ft   **4.** 2 m

Review 101

1. no   **2.** yes   **3.** yes   **4.** yes   **5.** 3

6. 5   **7.** 2   **8.** 10   **9.** 20   **10.** 50

11. yes   **12.** no   **13.** yes   **14.** yes   **15.** yes

16. no   **17.** 6 and 7; 6.5   **18.** 9 and 10; 9.4

19. 7 and 8; 7.9   **20.** 8 and 9; 8.7   **21.** 5 and 6; 5.5

22. 9 and 10; 9.8

Review 102

1. 20 in.   **2.** 13 cm   **3.** 10 in.   **4.** 25   **5.** 65

6. 150   **7.** 117   **8.** 28   **9.** 5

10. about 7.4 ft

Answers

Answers (continued)

Grade 7 Topics (*Course 2*)

Review 103

Sample answers are given.

1. 9
    +7
    16

2. 13
    −8
    5

3. $16
    −5
    $11

4. 2.4
    +0.8
    3.2

5. 2
    ×5
    10

6. 7
    ×1
    7

7. $12
    −11
    $1

8. 6.1
    +0.7
    6.8

9. 70
    −20
    50

10. 30
    ×3
    90

11. $9 \div 3; 3$

12. $110 \div 11; 10$

Review 104

1. 12.11   2. 12.385   3. 1.86   4. 91.26
5. 9.937   6. 6.01   7. 11.802   8. 3.8
9. 31.49   10. 0.132   11. 7.14   12. 11.909
13. 6.497   14. 101.1   15. 0.0035   16. 0.1898
17. 11.06   18. 4.526

Review 105

1. 10.224   2. 9.02   3. 1.533   4. 21.344
5. 0.140   6. 1.015   7. 10.143   8. 5.208
9. 0.0225   10. 3,465.6   11. $51\overline{)3,519}$ 12. $18\overline{)149}$
13. $32\overline{)3,968}$ 14. $6\overline{)94.8}$ 15. $8\overline{)21.12}$ 16. $49\overline{)945.7}$
17. 7.9   18. 5.5   19. 11   20. 4.5
21. 201   22. 8

Review 106

1. larger to smaller unit; multiply; 1,000; 16,000
2. smaller to larger unit; divide; 1,000; 1.6
3. 600   4. 162,000   5. 4
6. 25   7. 1 mm   8. 50 m

Review 107

1. about 8 students   2. 80.25 m

Review 108

1. >   2. <   3. >   4. >   5. <
6. >   7. <   8. <   9. >   10. >
11. <   12. >   13. 6   14. 3   15. 8
16. 9   17. 5   18. 0   19. 6   20. 10
21. 20   22. −4, −2, 0, 1 5
23. −6, −5, −3, 4, 6   24. −7, −5, −4, 0, 3, 4
25. −7, −6, −2, 1, 3, 5

Review 109

1. 6   2. −5   3. 1   4. 10
5. 25   6. −4   7. 9   8. −8
9. −3   10. −2   11. 11   12. 1
13. (−4); −7   14. (−2); 3   15. 10; 4   16. 2; 10
17. −1   18. −9   19. −1   20. 25
21. −22   22. −22   23. 1   24. 1
25. 16   26. −3   27. −2   28. 10

Review 110

1. positive   2. negative   3. positive
4. positive   5. positive   6. negative
7. positive   8. negative   9. positive
10. negative   11. negative   12. positive
13. positive   14. negative   15. negative
16. negative   17. positive   18. positive

Review 111

1. 8; 11   2. 20 + 6; 26   3. 20 + 3 − 2; 21
4. 14; 19   5. 48 + 16; 64   6. 12 + 6; 18
7. 40   8. 18   9. 25
10. 4   11. 38   12. 5
13. 8; 8; 56   14. 4; 0.4; 22.4   15. 5; 52
16. 4; 4; 52   17. 3; 6; 81   18. 14; 70

Review 112

1. 9   2. 12.3 points
3. 9, 10, 10, 10, 11, 12, 15, 16, 18; 11 points
4. 10 points   5. 28; 30; 23
6. 8; 8; 9

Review 113

1. 3, 12, 21   2. 8, 32, 25   3. 8, 8, 40, 8, 48
4. 8, 3, 8, 6, 14   5. 18   6. 30
7. 30   8. 192   9. 36
10. 24   11. 70   12. 28
13. 9 plus a number   14. 6 times a number
15. 8 less than a number   16. a number divided by 5
17. $x + 10$ 18. $x − 4$ 19. $x + 3$ 20. $6x$

Review 114

1. $t = 6$ 2. $w = 15$ 3. $p = 8$ 4. $a = 9$
5. $h = 21$ 6. $g = 28$ 7. $y = 22$ 8. $d = 20$
9. $d = 14$ 10. $c = 25$ 11. $a = 41$ 12. $q = 440$
13. $b = −9$ 14. $r = 9$ 15. $n = 8$ 16. $s = 21$

Review 115

1. 6, 2   2. 3, 23   3. (−3), (−3), −4
4. 5, 5, −7   5. (−4), (−4), −6   6. 16, 16, −7
7. 16   8. 1   9. −4   10. 53
11. 32   12. 47   13. −22   14. −23
15. $m − 2\frac{1}{2} = 7; m = 9\frac{1}{2}$ min

Answers (continued)

Review 116

1. $-5, -5, -6$ **2.** $2, 2, -32$ **3.** $-2, -2, 2$
4. $8, 8, -4$ **5.** $6, 6, 30$ **6.** $-3, -3, 15$ **7.** -4
8. -25 **9.** -80 **10.** 8 **11.** 4
12. 16 **13.** -9 **14.** -7 **15.** -48
16. -7 **17.** 24 **18.** 35 **19.** 19
20. -1 **21.** -18 **22.** 5

Review 117

1. $4h + 3$ **2.** $6t - 4$ **3.** $\frac{1}{2}m + 8$ **4.** $2c + 30$
5. $4h + 5; \$13$ **6.** $10 + 15h; \$70$
7. $s = 3$ **8.** $f = 30$ **9.** $r = 4$
10. $x = 10$ **11.** $n = 10$ **12.** $s = 6$

Review 118

1. $2x, 3, 9, 3$ **2.** $3x, 4, 7, 1$ **3.** $7, 7, 5, 5, -1$
4. $1, 1, 2, 2, 5$ **5.** 2 **6.** 6 **7.** -3
8. 5 **9.** 1 **10.** -7

Review 119

1–4. Check students' answers.
1. $2s + 28 = 152; \$62$
2. $q = \frac{(22.75 - 10.50)}{0.25}$; 49 quarters
3. $25 + 4.50m = 56.50; m = 7$
4. $7 + (4 \times 20) = c; c = 87$

Review 120

1a. x is less than or equal to -3.
1b. closed; -3 satisfies inequality
1c.

2a. x is greater than or equal to -1.
2b. closed; -1 satisfies inequality
2c.

3a. x is less than 3. **3b.** open
3c.

Review 121

1. $a > 4$
2. $w \le 4$
3. $a \ge 5$
4. $w \le 3$
5. $y < 2$
6. $g \ge 6$
7. $x > 5$
8. $r < 6$

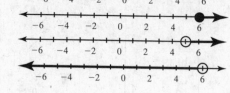

Review 122

1. $a > 5$
2. $w > -4$
3. $r \ge -4$
4. $2 \le a$
5. $a < 3$
6. $g < 1$
7. $x \le 2$
8. $m < 0$

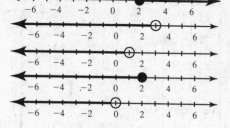

Review 123

1. 6^5 **2.** 0.2^3 **3.** 9^4 **4.** 12^5
5. $12 \times 12; 144$ **6.** $8 \times 8 \times 8; 512$
7. $0.4 \times 0.4 \times 0.4; 0.064$
8. $5 \times 5 \times 5 \times 5 \times 5; 3,125$
9. $3 \times 3 \times 3 \times 3 \times 3 \times 3; 729$
10. $1.4 \times 1.4; 1.96$
11. 76 **12.** 24 **13.** 5 **14.** 4
15. 40 **16.** 225 **17.** 113 **18.** 48

Review 124

1. 3, left; $3.5, 10^3$ **2.** 6, left; $1.4, 10^6$
3. 9.3×10^7 **4.** 1.2×10^6
5. 1.7×10^4 **6.** 7.5×10^5
7. 2.4×10^3 **8.** 6.532×10^6
9. 5.6×10^{11} **10.** 3.48×10^7
11. $2,580$ **12.** $8,000,000$
13. $481,600$ **14.** 811
15. $18,500,000$ **16.** $3,750.9$
17. 80.03 **18.** $5,660,000,000$
19. 423 **20.** $99,920,000,000$

Answers

Answers (continued)

Review 125

1. Yes, because 336 is divisible by 8.
2. Yes, because the number ends in a zero.
3. No, because the number does not end in 0 or 5.
4. Yes, because the sum of the digits is divisible by 3.
5. No, because the sum of the digits is not divisible by 9.
6. No, because 21 is not divisible by 4.
7. 2   8. 5   9. 2, 3, 4, 8
10. 3, 9   11. 2, 5, 10   12. 2, 4

Review 126

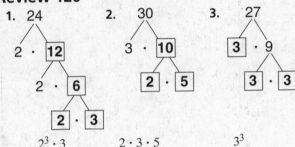

1. 24
2. 30
3. 27

$2^3 \cdot 3$ $2 \cdot 3 \cdot 5$ 3^3

4. $2^2 \cdot 5$ 5. $2 \cdot 3^3$ 6. $2^3 \cdot 5$
7. $2^4 \cdot 3$ 8. $2^3 \cdot 7$ 9. $2 \cdot 3 \cdot 5^2$

Review 127

1. $\dfrac{10}{20} = \dfrac{10 \div \boxed{2}}{20 \div 2} = \dfrac{5 \div \boxed{5}}{10 \div \boxed{5}} = \dfrac{1}{2}$

2. $\dfrac{24}{60} = \dfrac{24 \div \boxed{6}}{60 \div \boxed{6}} = \dfrac{4 \div \boxed{2}}{10 \div \boxed{2}} = \dfrac{2}{5}$

3. $\dfrac{6}{7}, 2$ 4. $\dfrac{3}{5}, 3$ 5. $\dfrac{5}{6}, 7$ 6. $\dfrac{4}{5}, 10$
7. $\dfrac{7}{10}$ 8. $\dfrac{5}{9}$ 9. $\dfrac{9}{10}$ 10. $\dfrac{1}{3}$
11. $\dfrac{3}{4}$ 12. $\dfrac{2}{9}$ 13. $\dfrac{3}{5}$ 14. $\dfrac{9}{16}$
15. $\dfrac{1}{3}$ 16. $\dfrac{13}{15}$ 17. $\dfrac{2}{3}$ 18. $\dfrac{10}{19}$

Review 128

1a. 10, 9   1b. >   2a. 4, 5   2b. <
3a. 9, 9   3b. =   4. <   5. <
6. =   7. <   8. >   9. =
10. >   11. <   12. $\dfrac{1}{4}, \dfrac{1}{2}, \dfrac{4}{5}$ 13. $\dfrac{3}{8}, \dfrac{1}{2}, \dfrac{2}{3}$
14. $\dfrac{1}{4}, \dfrac{5}{6}, \dfrac{7}{8}$ 15. $\dfrac{1}{2}, \dfrac{5}{8}, \dfrac{5}{6}$ 16. $\dfrac{1}{5}, \dfrac{2}{3}, \dfrac{7}{10}$ 17. $\dfrac{1}{4}, \dfrac{2}{3}, \dfrac{11}{12}$

Review 129

1.
Add one box on the left each time.
2. 54 diagonals
3a. −1   3b. 1   3c. −1   3d. 1   3e. 1
4. −1 to any even power is 1.   5. $88.50

Review 130

1. $\dfrac{13}{4}$ 2. $\dfrac{8}{3}$ 3. $\dfrac{11}{8}$ 4. $\dfrac{37}{7}$ 5. $\dfrac{27}{4}$
6. $\dfrac{10}{9}$ 7. $\dfrac{9}{2}$ 8. $\dfrac{19}{5}$ 9. $\dfrac{31}{6}$ 10. $\dfrac{10}{3}$
11. $\dfrac{47}{8}$ 12. $\dfrac{33}{8}$ 13. $3\dfrac{1}{2}$ 14. 6   15. $4\dfrac{2}{5}$
16. $5\dfrac{1}{3}$ 17. $5\dfrac{7}{8}$ 18. 8   19. $4\dfrac{1}{4}$ 20. $3\dfrac{1}{2}$
21. $2\dfrac{3}{5}$ 22. $5\dfrac{3}{4}$ 23. $1\dfrac{4}{9}$ 24. 7

Review 131

1. 0.8   2. 0.75   3. $0.1\overline{6}$ 4. 0.25   5. $0.\overline{6}$
6. 0.7   7. $0.\overline{5}$ 8. 0.2   9. 0.375   10. $\dfrac{2}{5}$
11. $\dfrac{3}{4}$ 12. $1\dfrac{1}{2}$ 13. $\dfrac{7}{20}$ 14. $2\dfrac{7}{10}$ 15. $1\dfrac{4}{5}$
16. $\dfrac{5}{8}$ 17. $\dfrac{39}{50}$ 18. $\dfrac{22}{25}$ 19. $\dfrac{13}{6}, 2.\overline{6}, 2\dfrac{5}{6}$
20. $2\dfrac{1}{200}, 2.0202, 2.\overline{02}$ 21. $\dfrac{5}{4}, 1.\overline{4}, 1\dfrac{4}{5}$

Review 132

1. >   2. <   3. <   4. >
5. <   6. =   7. $-0.35, -\dfrac{1}{3}, -\dfrac{3}{10}, 0.3$
8. $-0.25, \dfrac{1}{5}, 0.21, \dfrac{3}{10}$ 9. $-6.25, \dfrac{-5}{12}, 2.1, 2\dfrac{8}{9}$
10. $\dfrac{-9}{11}, \dfrac{-3}{4}, -0.5\overline{5}, \dfrac{-12}{25}$
11. Your brother's investment is worth more.

Review 133

1. 1   2. 0   3. 1
4. 1   5. $1\dfrac{1}{2}$ 6. 2
7. 1   8. 0   9. 4
10. 12   11. 9   12. 7
13. $5 \cdot 2$ 14. $12 \div 4$ 15. $7 \cdot 9$
16. $20 \div 4$ 17. $5 \cdot 7$ 18. $40 \div 5$
19. 24   20. 3   21. 8
22. 50   23. 4   24. 33

Review 134

1. $\dfrac{3}{10} + \dfrac{4}{10} = \dfrac{7}{10}$ 2. $\dfrac{3}{12} + \dfrac{6}{12} = \dfrac{9}{12} = \dfrac{3}{4}$
3. $\dfrac{5}{8} + \dfrac{2}{8} = \dfrac{7}{8}$ 4. $\dfrac{3}{4} - \dfrac{2}{4} = \dfrac{1}{4}$
5. $\dfrac{5}{9} - \dfrac{3}{9} = \dfrac{2}{9}$ 6. $\dfrac{9}{15} - \dfrac{5}{15} = \dfrac{4}{15}$
7. $1\dfrac{3}{5}$ 8. $\dfrac{1}{4}$ 9. $\dfrac{1}{6}$ 10. $\dfrac{1}{6}$
11. $1\dfrac{1}{8}$ 12. $\dfrac{5}{8}$ 13. $\dfrac{1}{2}$ 14. $\dfrac{1}{4}$
15. $1\dfrac{1}{15}$ 16. $1\dfrac{2}{5}$ 17. $\dfrac{7}{12}$ 18. $\dfrac{2}{5}$
19. $1\dfrac{1}{8}$ 20. $\dfrac{1}{10}$ 21. $\dfrac{1}{4}$

Answers

Answers (continued)

Review 135

1. $4\frac{6}{8} - 2\frac{3}{8} = 2\frac{3}{8}$

2. $4\frac{7}{12} + 2\frac{10}{12} = 6\frac{17}{12} = 7\frac{5}{12}$

3. $4\frac{5}{15} - 1\frac{9}{15} = 3\frac{20}{15} - 1\frac{9}{15} = 2\frac{11}{15}$

4. $3\frac{7}{10}$ 5. $6\frac{5}{18}$ 6. $1\frac{3}{10}$ 7. $\frac{5}{6}$

8. $3\frac{1}{12}$ 9. $7\frac{5}{6}$ 10. $4\frac{9}{10}$ 11. $13\frac{7}{12}$

12. $11\frac{3}{10}$ 13. $5\frac{9}{16}$ 14. $1\frac{7}{10}$ 15. $3\frac{7}{8}$

16. $8\frac{1}{10}$ 17. $3\frac{13}{20}$ 18. $2\frac{3}{8}$ 19. $11\frac{3}{10}$

20. $\frac{1}{6}$ 21. $9\frac{1}{5}$ 22. $19\frac{1}{8}$ in.

Review 136

1. $\frac{1}{5} \cdot \frac{2}{3} = \frac{2}{15}; \frac{2}{15}$ 2. $\frac{1}{4} \cdot \frac{33}{8} = \frac{33}{32}; 1\frac{1}{32}$

3. $\frac{11}{4} \cdot \frac{5}{3} = \frac{55}{12}; 4\frac{7}{12}$ 4. $\frac{1}{4}$ 5. 6

6. $\frac{1}{8}$ 7. $1\frac{7}{20}$ 8. $2\frac{7}{12}$ 9. $\frac{19}{30}$

10. $8\frac{1}{3}$ 11. $5\frac{1}{2}$ 12. $\frac{13}{20}$ 13. $2\frac{11}{40}$

14. 3   15. $1\frac{1}{16}$ 16. $8\frac{5}{8}$ 17. $3\frac{13}{21}$

18. $16\frac{3}{7}$ 19. $14\frac{2}{3}$ 20. 3   21. $15\frac{1}{2}$

Review 137

1. $\frac{8}{7}$ 2. $\frac{6}{1}$ 3. $\frac{3}{8}$ 4. $\frac{10}{9}$

5. $\frac{3}{2}; \frac{2}{3}$ 6. $\frac{7}{3}; \frac{3}{7}$ 7. $\frac{9}{5}; \frac{5}{9}$ 8. $\frac{11}{4}, \frac{4}{11}$

9. $\frac{2}{3} \cdot \frac{8}{3} = \frac{16}{9}; 1\frac{7}{9}$

10. $\frac{10}{1} \div \frac{7}{8} = \frac{10}{1} \cdot \frac{8}{7} = \frac{80}{7}; 11\frac{3}{7}$

11. $\frac{18}{5} \div \frac{6}{5} = \frac{18}{5} \cdot \frac{5}{6} = \frac{90}{30}; 3$

12. $\frac{2}{5}$ 13. $\frac{9}{16}$ 14. 10   15. 8

16. $\frac{15}{32}$ 17. $1\frac{1}{5}$

Review 138

1. $\frac{1}{5}; \frac{1}{5}; \frac{2}{5}$ 2. $\frac{1}{4}; \frac{1}{4}; 1\frac{2}{4} = 1\frac{1}{2}$

3. $\frac{3}{8}; \frac{3}{8}; \frac{10}{8} = 1\frac{1}{4}$ 4. $2\frac{1}{3}; 2\frac{1}{3}; 3$

5. $3\frac{2}{5}$ 6. 3   7. $1\frac{2}{9}$ 8. $1\frac{1}{2}$

9. $1\frac{1}{3}$ 10. $\frac{3}{4}$ 11. $6\frac{5}{6}$ 12. $1\frac{5}{6}$

13. $\frac{4}{15}$ 14. $1\frac{3}{7}$ 15. $7\frac{7}{8}$ 16. $1\frac{8}{9}$

17. $1\frac{7}{18}$ 18. $3\frac{1}{10}$ 19. $1\frac{1}{12}$ 20. $\frac{4}{21}$

Review 139

1. $11.00   2. 100   3. 19 years old

4. $13\frac{1}{2}$ ft

Review 140

1. 42 in.; 1 ft = 12 in.   2. 12 oz; 1 c = 8 fl oz

3. 80 oz; 1 lb = 16 oz   4. 11 pt; 1 qt = 2 pt

5. 13 qt; 1 gal = 4 qt   6. 8 c; 1 pt = 2 c

7. 10,560 ft; 1 mi = 5,280 ft   8. 12 pt; 1 qt = 2 pt

9. 3,000 lb; 1 t = 2,000 lb   10. 3 c; 1 c = 8 fl oz

11. 2 lb; 1 lb = 16 oz   12. $2\frac{1}{2}$ gal; 1 gal = 4 qt

13. $1\frac{1}{2}$ pt; 1 pt = 2 c   14. 2 t; 1 t = 2,000 lb

15. $1\frac{1}{16}$ lb; 1 lb = 16 oz   16. $3\frac{1}{2}$ qt; 1 qt = 2 pt

17. 9 yd; 1 yd = 3 ft   18. $2\frac{1}{2}$ ft; 1 ft = 12 in.

19. 2,540 miles

Review 141

1. 8,448 ft   2. 8.87 km   3. 13 in.   4. 5.64 cm

5. 4.3 yd.   6. 17.33 mm   7. 56.5 ft

8. 3.25 km   9. 1,700 cm   10. 3,500 in.^{2}

11. 8.6 in.   12. 86 cm^2 13. 31 cm^2

14. 15.4 ft   15. 8 mm   16. 14 yd

Review 142

1. 2 to 6; 2 : 6; $\frac{2}{6}$ 2. 3 to 5; 3 : 5; $\frac{3}{5}$

3. 6 to 5; 6 : 5; $\frac{6}{5}$ 4. 2 to 3; 2 : 3; $\frac{2}{3}$

5. 6 to 16; 6 : 16; $\frac{6}{16}$ 6. 5 to 16; 5 : 16; $\frac{5}{16}$

7. 8 to 8; 8 : 8; $\frac{8}{8}$ 8. 3 to 8; 3 : 8; $\frac{3}{8}$

9. 2 to 16; 2 : 16; $\frac{2}{16}$ 10. 2 to 5; 2 : 5; $\frac{2}{5}$

11. Sample answers: $\frac{1}{2}; \frac{10}{20}$

12. Sample answers: 4 : 10; 6 : 15

13. Sample answers: 3 to 5; 36 to 60

14. $\frac{1}{2}$ 15. 4 to 1   16. 2 : 3

17. $\frac{2}{1}$ 18. $\frac{3}{50}$ 19. 4 : 9

Review 143

1. 25; 25; $.10/copy   2. 100; 100; $.06 /copy

3. 50; 50; $.09/copy   4. 60 mi/h

5. 26 mi/gal   6. $333\frac{1}{3}$ m/min

7. $1.50/ticket   8. 38 mi/gal

9. 4.5 c/cake   10. $.07/oz; $.0875/oz; 18 oz

11. $1.58/yd; $1.30/yd; 6 yd

12. $1.75/pair; $1.50/pair; 6 pairs

13. $.30/oz; $.50/oz; 1 lb

Review 144

1. 606 digits   2. 24 posts   3. 60 miles

4. 90 plants   5. 4 miles

Answers (continued)

Review 145

1. 60; 60; yes
2. 48; 2; 48; yes
3. 8; 64; 16; 80; no
4. yes
5. no
6. yes
7. no
8. yes
9. yes
10. yes
11. yes
12. yes
13. yes
14. yes
15. yes
16. no
17. no
18. yes

Review 146

1. $10.85
2. 336
3. 6; n; 1
4. 30; 30n; 1
5. 162; 9n; 18
6. $n = 5$
7. $n = 3$
8. $n = 6$
9. $n = 6$
10. $n = 2$
11. $n = 12$
12. $n = 66$
13. $n = 10$
14. $n = 5$

Review 147

1. $\overline{QR}$; $\overline{RS}$; $\overline{SQ}$
2. $\overline{BC}$; $\frac{12}{n}$; 30
3. 80
4. 7.5

Review 148

1. 2; 4; 200 m
2. 2; 2; 100 m
3. 2; n; 4.5 cm
4. 2; n; 3 cm
5. $\frac{2}{100} = \frac{n}{175}$; 3.5 cm

Review 149

1. 30%
2. 40%
3. 55%
4. 40%
5. 65%
6. 45%
7. 60%
8. 17%
9. 72%
10. 65%
11. 80%
12. 25%
13. 34%
14. 44%
15. 35%
16. 84%
17. 30%
18. 64%
19. 40%
20. 99%
21. 55%
22. 52%
23. 10%
24. 78%
25. 95%
26. 24%

Review 150

1. 75%
2. 48%
3. 80%
4. 575%
5. $\frac{9}{20}$
6. $\frac{3}{5}$
7. $\frac{4}{25}$
8. $\frac{1}{4}$
9. $\frac{3}{8}$
10. $\frac{99}{100}$
11. $\frac{2}{5}$
12. $\frac{43}{50}$
13. 0.35
14. 0.48
15. 1.16
16. 0.08
17. 0.12
18. 0.055
19. 4
20. 0.006
21. 39%
22. 73.5%
23. 86%
24. 34%
25. 40%
26. 60%
27. 0.4%
28. 600%

Review 151

1. $\frac{1}{10,000}$; 0.0001
2. $\frac{9}{2000}$; 0.0045
3. $\frac{1}{500}$; 0.002
4. $\frac{67}{10,000}$; 0.0067
5. $\frac{3}{2} = 1\frac{1}{2}$; 1.5
6. $\frac{9}{4} = 2\frac{1}{4}$; 2.25
7. $\frac{93}{50} = 1\frac{43}{50}$; 1.86
8. $\frac{201}{100} = 2\frac{1}{100}$; 2.01

Review 152

1. 0.15; 0.15; 12
2. 0.04; 0.04; 2.8
3. 0.7; 0.7; 14
4. 8
5. 16
6. 40
7. 60
8. 6.3
9. 1.32
10. 14
11. 15
12. 5.6
13. 20.68
14. 16.5
15. 18
16. 36
17. 77
18. 320
19. 450
20. 113.1
21. 74.8
22. 574
23. 287.5
24. $63
25. $1,468.50

Review 153

1. n; 12; 16
2. n; n; 82; 410
3. 9; 5n; 100 · 9; 180
4. 60; 60; 1,200
5. 100; 4.8; 100; 80
6. 170; 51; 170n; 100 · 51; 30
7. $n = 75$
8. $n = 55$
9. $n = 150$
10. 92.4
11. 60
12. 80%

Review 154

1. $0.09 \cdot 150 = n$
2. 13.5
3. 120
4. 61.5
5. 8
6. 256
7. p% of 75 is 12
8. 16%
9. 30%
10. 70%

Review 155

1. $10.40
2. $9.21
3. $65.27
4. $340.80
5. $6.80
6. $28.76
7. $180
8. $6,000
9. $96
10. $132

Review 156

1. 20; 20; 20; 50; increase of 50%
2. 6; 6; 6; 40; decrease of 40%
3. 0.5; 0.5; 100; 0.5 · 100; 125; increase of 125%
4. 150%
5. 200%
6. 100%
7. 10%
8. 100%
9. 25%
10. 40%
11. 10%
12. 25%
13. 43%
14. 50%
15. 50%
16. 10%
17. 4%
18. 1%
19. 15%

Review 157

1. $K + 8 = 26$; 18 years old
2. $36 + 2l = 100$; 32 in.
3. $(s \cdot 2) + 28 = 152$; $62
4. $(22.75 - 10.50) \div 0.25 = q$; 49
5. $(x + 6) + x = 20$; 13
6. $(s + 11) + s = 61$; 25

Answers

Answers (continued)

Review 158

1. parallel
2. perpendicular
3–6. Sample answers are given.
3. $\overline{XZ}, \overline{WZ}, \overline{WX}, \overline{XY}, \overline{YZ}, \overline{ZM},$ or $\overline{MX}$
4. M
5. $\overleftrightarrow{WX}$ and $\overleftrightarrow{XY}$
6. $\overleftrightarrow{WZ}$ and $\overleftrightarrow{XY}$
7.
7a. parallel
7b. perpendicular
8.
9.
10.

Review 159

1. 120°; obtuse
2. 50°; acute
3. 60°; acute
4. 110°; obtuse
5. acute
6. obtuse
7. acute
8. obtuse
9. acute
10. obtuse
11. acute
12. obtuse

Review 160

1.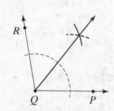
2.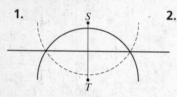
3.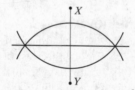
4.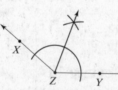
5.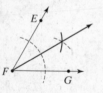
6.

Review 161

1. scalene; obtuse
2. equilateral; acute
3. isosceles; right
4. scalene; obtuse
5. scalene; acute
6. isosceles; acute
7. 105°
8. 34°
9. 90°

Review 162

1. rectangle
2. rhombus
3. trapezoid
4. parallelogram
5–8. Samples drawings are shown.
5.
6.
7.
8.

Review 163

1. 48°
2. 48°, 84°
3. 32 posts
4. 7 cuts
5. 45 mi
6. 50 km east

Review 164

1. $\overline{QR}; \angle R$
2. $\overline{YW}; \angle X$
3a. $\angle D$
3b. $\angle E$
3c. $\angle F$
3d. $\overline{DF}$
3e. $\overline{EF}$
3f. $\overline{DE}$
4. No, because corresponding angles and sides are not congruent.
5. Yes, because all corresponding sides and angles are congruent.

Review 165

1. $\overline{PR}, \overline{SP}, \overline{PT}$
2. $\overline{SQ}, \overline{ST}$
3. Sample answers: $\overline{SQ}, \overline{RT}, \overline{SQT}$
4. $\overline{LK}, \overline{HG}$
5. $\angle HML, \angle HMK, \angle KMG$
6. $\overline{LK}, \overline{HG}$
7. $\widehat{KHL}, \widehat{KGL}$
8. $\overline{ML}, \overline{MK}$

Review 166

Tuesday's Music CD Sales

Type of Music	Number of CDs Sold	Central Angle Measure
Country	10	75°
Rock	8	60°
Jazz	16	120°
Rap	14	105°
Total	**48**	**360°**

Tuesday's Music CD Sales

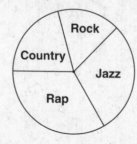

Answers

Answers (continued)

Review 167
1. 3 in.　　2. 1 in.　　3. 5 cm　　4. 3 cm
5. 6 ft; a refrigerator is about the height of a person.
6. 8 ft; a stop sign is a little taller than a person.
7. 220 mi^2　8. 140 mi^2

Review 168
1. 30 cm^2　2. 32 ft^2　3. 35 m^2　4. 30 cm^2
5. 8 m^2　6. 35.1 cm^2　7. 28 in.^2　8. 13.5 m^2
9. 2.5 cm^2

Review 169
1. 33 ft^2　2. 748 ft^2　3. $33\frac{1}{4} \text{ in.}^2$
4. 98 m^2　5. 838 km^2　6. $2,586 \text{ yd}^2$

Review 170
1. $44 \text{ cm}; 154 \text{ cm}^2$　2. $13 \text{ in.}; 13 \text{ in.}^2$　3. $31 \text{ m}; 79 \text{ m}^2$
4. $6 \text{ cm}; 3 \text{ cm}^2$　5. $19 \text{ ft}; 28 \text{ ft}^2$　6. $50 \text{ yd}; 201 \text{ yd}^2$

Review 171
1. 12　2. 6　3. 10　4. 50　5. 18
6. 20　7. 7 cm　8. 9 in.　9. 12 cm　10. 25 in.
11. 26 ft　12. 60 yd　13. rational　14. irrational
15. rational　16. rational

Review 172
1. $a = 18 \text{ ft}$　2. $c = 26 \text{ in.}$　3. $b = 15 \text{ cm}$
4. $x = 9.4 \text{ m}$　5. $x = 4.2 \text{ cm}$　6. $x = 12.7 \text{ in.}$
7. 6.7 ft　8. 24.1 cm

Review 173
1. rectangular prism　2. cylinder
3. square pyramid　4. cone
5. triangular prism　6. hexagonal prism
7. cylinder　8. rectangular prism
9. sphere

Review 174
1. 10 ft^2　2. 103 cm^2　3. $1,570.8 \text{ yd}^2$　4. 124 m^2

Review 175
1. $6; 2; 3; 36 \text{ in.}^3$　2. $8; 8; 4; 803.8 \text{ cm}^3$
3. 79 cm^3　4. 24 m^3　5. 75 cm^3

Review 176
1. 45, 50　2. 36 ft　3. 88, 89　4. 9 cm
5. 10 m　6. $14.50

Review 177
1.
2.

Review 178
1. Start with 4 and add 3 repeatedly. 16, 19, 22
2. Start with 2 and add 2 repeatedly. 10, 12, 14
3. Start with 20 and add 15 repeatedly. 65, 80, 95
4. Start with 5 and multiply by 5 repeatedly. 3,125; 15,625; 78,125
5. Start with 7 and multiply by 7 repeatedly. 16,807; 117,649; 823,543
6. Start with 0.3 and multiply by 3 repeatedly. 24.3, 72.9, 218.7

Review 179
1. 4　　2. $4n$
3. Multiply each term number by 4.
4. 24, 28　5. $2n + 3$
6. Multiply each term number by 2, then add 3
7. 15, 17　8. $3n - 1$　9. n^2　10. $5n$

Review 180
1. output = 2 · input　2. output = input + 2
3. output = 45 · input

4.
x	y
0	0
1	10
2	20
3	30

5.
x	y
0	−4
1	−3
2	−2
3	−1

6.
x	y
0	4
1	6
2	8
3	10

7.
x	y
0	−1
1	2
2	5
3	8

8a. $y = 9x$　8b. 135 pages　8c. 675 minutes

Answers

Answers (continued)

Review 181

1. $4\,(-2, 4);\ 0\,(0, 0);\ -2\,(1, -2);\ -6\,(3, -6);\ -8\,(4, -8)$

2.
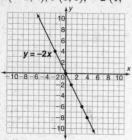

Review 182

1. C **2.** B **3.** A

4.
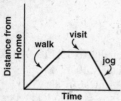

5.
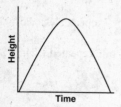

Review 183

1. 800; 0.04; 5; $160
2. 1,200; 0.055; 25; $1,650
3. $96
4. $1,710
5. $10,500
6. 600; 0.06; $714.61
7. 9,000; 0.05; 4; $10,939.56

Review 184

1. $168 = 14w$; 12 ft; The width is 12 ft.
2. $48 = 15 + b$; the blouse costs $33.
3. $m - 1 = 12$; Mary baked 13 muffins.

Review 185

1a. $r = \dfrac{d}{t}$
1b. 6 mi/hr
2. $A = 770\ \text{m}^2$
3. $l = 8$ in.
4. $t = 12$ hr
5. $C = 62.8$ cm
6. $l = 4$ ft
7. $I = \$10$

Review 186

1. A **2.** E **3.** C **4.** F **5.** H
6. B **7.** R **8.** T **9.** $(2, -4)$
10. $(0, 6)$ **11.** $(-4, -7)$ **12.** $(0, -3)$
13. $(-8, 2)$ **14.** $(5, 3)$ **15.** $(8, 8)$
16. $(-7, 5)$ **17.** III **18.** I
19. IV **20.** II **21.** II
22. III **23.** II **24.** IV
25. vertical **26.** horizontal **27.** vertical

Review 187

1.

x	x − 4	y	(x, y)
2	2 − 4	−2	(2, −2)
4	4 − 4	0	(4, 0)
6	6 − 4	2	(6, 2)

2.

x	3x	y	(x, y)
−1	3(−1)	−3	(−1, −3)
0	3(0)	0	(0, 0)
3	3(3)	9	(3, 9)

3.

x	−x + 1	y	(x, y)
0	0 + 1	1	(0, 1)
2	−2 + 1	−1	(2, −1)
−3	−(−3) + 1	4	(−3, 4)

4.
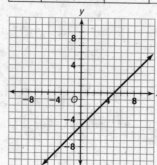

5.
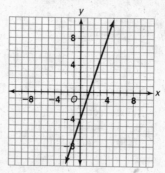

Review 188

1. $\dfrac{3}{4}$ **2.** -1 **3.** 2

4.
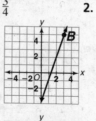

5.
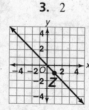

6.

Answers

Name ______________________ Class ______________ Date ____________

Answers (continued)

Review 189

1.

x	y
−2	2
−1	−1
0	−2
1	−1
2	2

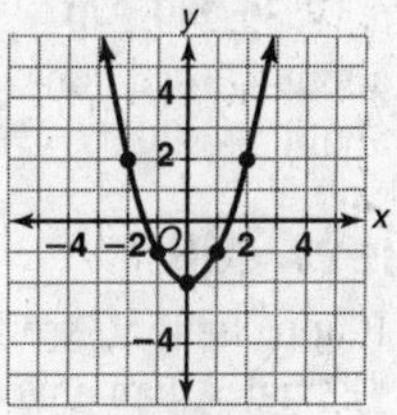

2.

x	y
−2	5
−1	−1
0	−3
1	−1
2	5

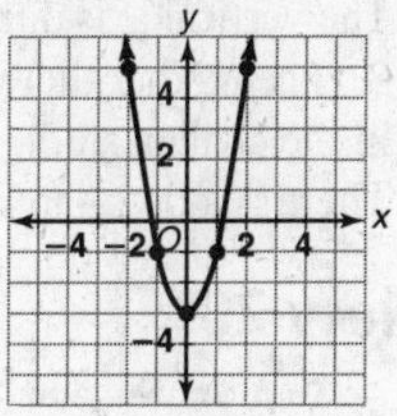

3.

x	y
−4	3
−2	2
0	1
2	2
4	3

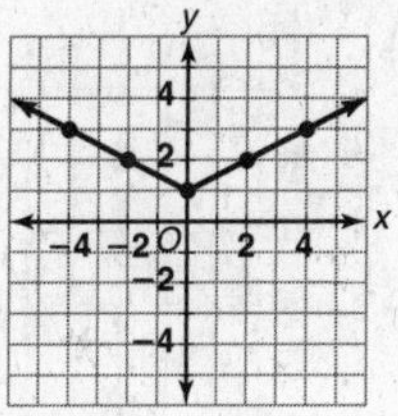

Review 190

1–2. Check students' graphs and tables.

1. 784 ft **2.** \$4.03

Review 191

1. −1; 4 **2.** 3; 6 **3.** 1; 3; 5; 2

4.

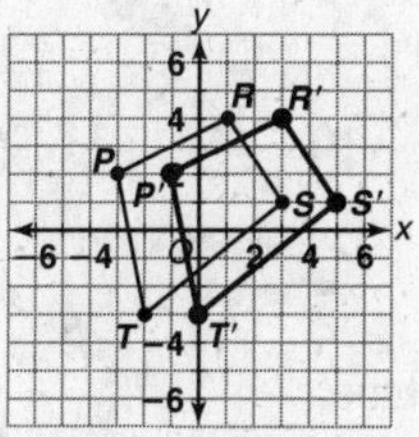

5.

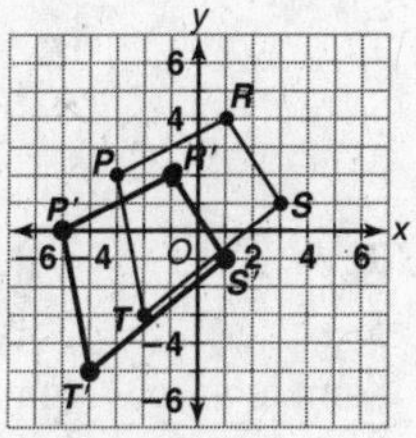

6.

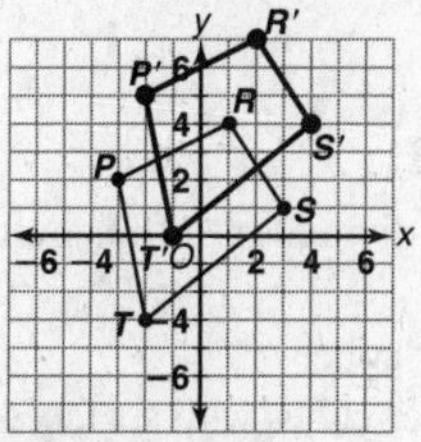

7. $(x + 3, y + 1)$ **8.** $(x - 4, y + 5)$

9. $(x - 1, y - 9)$ **10.** $(x, y) \rightarrow (x - 1, y - 3)$

11. $(x, y) \rightarrow (x + 1, y + 2)$ **12.** $(x, y) \rightarrow (x - 3, y + 2)$

Review 192

1.

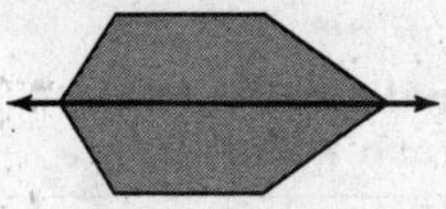

2. none

3.

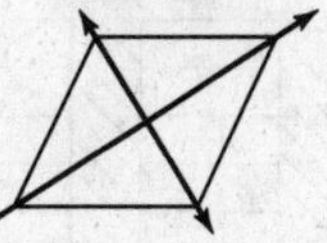

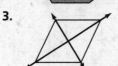

4. (−4, −4); (−2, 0); (0, −2)

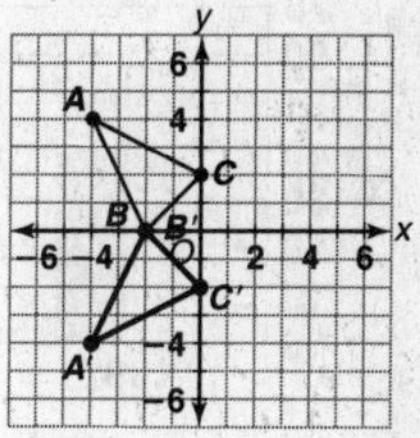

5. (4, 4); (2, 0); (0, 2)

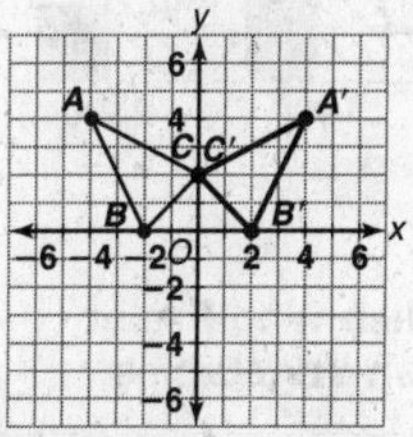

Review 193

1. yes **2.** no **3.** yes

4.

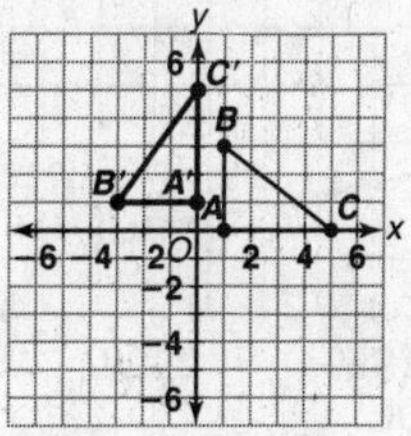

5.

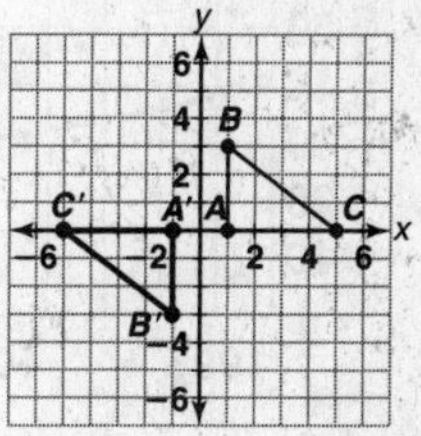

6.

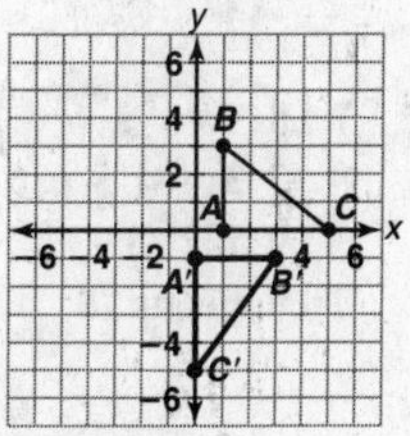

Review 194

1.

Number of Rose Bushes	1	2	3	4	5	6
Tally	I	IIII	III	~~IIII~~ I	I	I
Frequency	1	4	3	6	1	1

2.

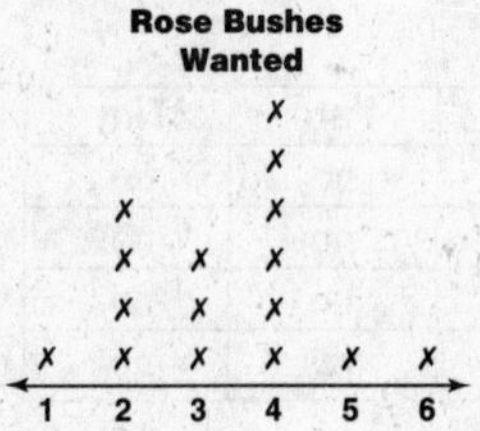

3.

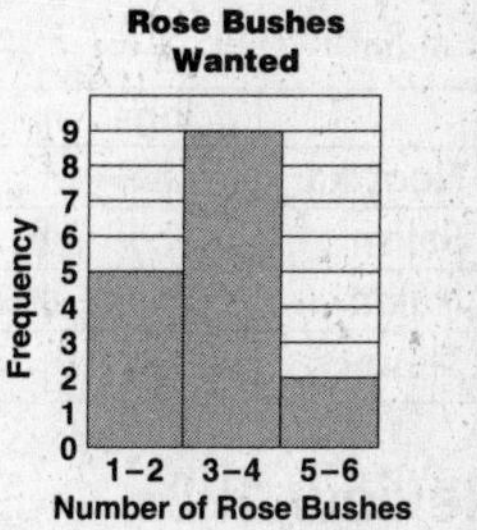

Answers

Answers (continued)

Review 195

1. 78, 39   **2.** A5; A2

3.

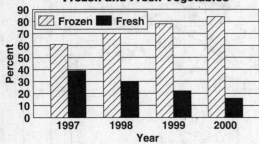

Percents of Families Who Prefer
Frozen and Fresh Vegetables

4.

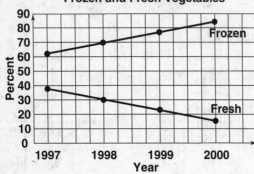

Percents of Families Who Prefer
Frozen and Fresh Vegetables

Review 196

1.
```
1 | 5 6
2 | 4 7
3 | 6 6 9
4 | 2 5
5 | 1 4 9
6 | 1 3 4
1 | 5 means 15
```

2.
```
7 | 8 9
8 | 2 3 4 4 5 6 6 7 9
9 | 0 1 2
7 | 8 means 78
```

3.

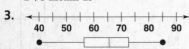

Review 197

Tim; Sara; Iona; Pete

	Iona	Sara	Pete	Tim
Noottka	no	no	no	yes
Salish	no	yes	no	no
Haida	yes	no	no	no
Tlingit	no	no	yes	no

Review 198

1. a shopping mall   **2.** biased   **3.** fair
4. No; you are more likely to interview homeowners.
5. No; you are more likely to interview renters.
6. Yes; you can't tell if people own or rent.

Review 199

1. 5; 15; 80; 240; 240   **2.** 45; 3; 20 · 45; 300; 300
3. about 472 sea lions   **4.** about 9 owls
5. about 54 rabbits   **6.** about 1,600 pigeons

Review 200

1a. It appears that Aretha Franklin had many more
#1 singles than anyone else.
1b. The vertical axis does not start at zero.
2a. It appears that there has been a great amount of change
in the civilian staff.
2b. There is a break in the vertical axis.

Review 201

1.

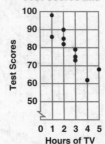

Test Scores and TV

2. Negative; as one value goes up, the other goes down.
3. The more TV students watch, the lower their test scores.

Review 202

1. 1; 0.2; 20%   **2.** 5; 0.4; 40%   **3.** $\frac{1}{2}$, 0.5; 50%
4. $\frac{3}{10}$, 0.3; 30%   **5.** $\frac{9}{10}$, 0.9; 90%   **6.** $\frac{2}{9}$
7. $\frac{2}{3}$ **8.** $\frac{8}{9}$ **9.** $\frac{1}{4}$ **10.** $\frac{3}{22}$ **11.** $\frac{22}{23}$

Review 203

1. 5; $\frac{1}{4}$ **2.** $\frac{7}{20}$; 35%   **3.** $\frac{2}{5}$ **4.** $\frac{4}{15}$ **5.** $\frac{1}{3}$
6. Sample answer: Flip a coin 20 times.
7. Sample answer: Spin a spinner divided into six equal
sections.

Review 204

1. Sample answer: Use a spinner divided into four parts, one
for each symbol.
2. Sample answer: Toss a number cube.
3. Sample answer: Roll two number cubes with six faces each.
4. Sample answer: Use two sets of cards each numbered 1–10.

Review 205

1.

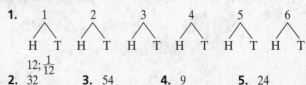

$12; \frac{1}{12}$
2. 32   **3.** 54   **4.** 9   **5.** 24

Answers

Answers (continued)

Review 206

1. $\frac{6}{25}$ **2.** $\frac{9}{25}$ **3.** $\frac{4}{25}$ **4.** $\frac{4}{15}$ **5.** $\frac{1}{3}$

6. $\frac{2}{15}$ **7.** $\frac{1}{28}$ **8.** $\frac{1}{32}$

Review 207

1. 3; 2; 24 **2.** 10; 9; 8; 720 **3.** 24 **4.** 20

5. 720 **6.** 60 **7.** 6 **8.** 12

9. 30 **10.** 42 **11.** 6 **12.** 60

13. 24 **14.** 120

Review 208

1. 3 combinations: EO, EU, OU

2. 10 combinations: CMP, CMT, CMR, MPT, MPR, PTR, PTC, TRC, TRM, CRP

3. 3 combinations **4.** 20 combinations **5.** 15 ways

6. 276 ways **7.** 10 ways **8.** 120 sets

Grade 8 Topics *(Course 3)*

Review 209

1. 36 **2.** 6 **3.** 8 **4.** 52 **5.** 12

6. 36 **7.** 23 **8.** 18 **9.** 6 **10.** 10

11. 16 **12.** 5 **13.** 10 **14.** 23 **15.** 9

16. 14 **17.** 15 **18.** 11

19. $P = 2(2) + 2(4)$; multiply 2 and 2 in. and 2 and 4 in.

Review 210

1. 15 years old; 10 years old **2.** $10.45; $7.95

3. 18 T-shirts; 9 T-shirts **4.** 12 rows of corn; 7 rows of peas

5. 15 **6.** $100

Review 211

1.

$$\underset{-7\ -6\ -5\ -4\ -3\ -2\ -1\ \ 0\ \ 1\ \ 2\ \ 3\ \ 4\ \ 5\ \ 6\ \ 7}{}$$

2.

$$\underset{-65-60-55-50-45-40-35-30-25-20-15-10\ -5\ \ 0\ \ 5\ \ 10\ \ 15}{}$$

3. > **4.** < **5.** < **6.** > **7.** >

8. > **9.** < **10.** > **11.** = **12.** >

13. < **14.** > **15.** 3 **16.** 2 **17.** 10

18. 4 **19.** 4 **20.** 0 **21.** 1 **22.** 18

23. 50

Review 212

1. 4 **2.** 12 **3.** −4 **4.** −6 **5.** 4

6. −5 **7.** 4 **8.** 12 **9.** −4 **10.** −19

11. 20 **12.** −3 **13.** 12 **14.** 4 **15.** −13

16. 0 **17.** −20 **18.** 17 **19.** −15 **20.** 8

21. 26 **22.** 1 **23.** 5 **24.** −7 **25.** −20

26. 57 **27.** −39 **28.** $15 **29.** 15 inches

Review 213

1. − **2.** − **3.** + **4.** − **5.** +

6. + **7.** − **8.** + **9.** − **10.** +

11. + **12.** − **13.** −36 **14.** 81 **15.** −9

16. 32 **17.** 350 **18.** 24 **19.** 50 **20.** −72

21. 28 **22.** −42 **23.** 48 **24.** −125 **25.** 6

26. 9 **27.** −5 **28.** 1 **29.** −6 **30.** 20

31. −4 **32.** 11 **33.** −7 **34.** −11 **35.** −20

36. −25

Review 214

1. mean: 3; median: 3; mode: 4

2. mean: 8.1; median: 8; mode: 5

3. mean: 0.58; median: 0.5; mode: 0

4. mean: $3.25; median: $3.25; mode: $4

5. Median; there is no mode and the median is greater than the mean.

6. Mode; both the median and the mean are less than the mode.

Review 215

1. 7^3 **2.** $(-6)^5$ **3.** 10^4 **4.** 1^6 **5.** $(-8)^5$

6. 2^7 **7.** 72 **8.** 19 **9.** 51 **10.** −30

11. 10 **12.** 32 **13.** −47 **14.** 3 **15.** −36

16. −48

Review 216

1. 6 **2.** −20 **3.** 92 **4.** 30 **5.** 70

6. −240 **7.** 1,800 **8.** 90 **9.** −280 **10.** 3,600

11. −96 **12.** −14 **13.** $8(4 - 0.1) = 31.2$

14. $6(20 + 1) = 126$ **15.** $4(7 + 0.2) = 28.8$

16. $5(40 - 2) = 190$ **17.** $6(10 + 0.1) = 60.6$

18. $7(40 + 2) = 294$

Review 217

1. 5; 5; 6; 6; 11 **2.** 13; 13; 14; 14; 27

3. $y - 18 + 18 = 24 + 18$; $y = 42$; $y - 18 = 24$; $42 - 18 \stackrel{?}{=} 24$; $24 = 24$

4. 3; 3; 6; 18 **5.** −5; −5; 65; 65; −13

6. $\frac{y \cdot 8}{8} = \frac{24}{8}$; $y = 3$; $3 \cdot 8 \stackrel{?}{=} 24$; $24 = 24$ **7.** −6

8. 5 **9.** $-3\frac{1}{2}$ **10.** 2 **11.** 0.64 **12.** 5

Review 218

1. 5; 5; 2; 2; 10; 10; 25 **2.** 2; 2; 2; 2; 8; 8; 2

3. $7y - 17 + 17 = -38 + 17$; $\frac{7y}{7} = \frac{-21}{7}$; $y = -3$; $7y - 17 = -38$; $7 \cdot (-3) - 17 \stackrel{?}{=} -38$; $-38 = -38$

4. 4 **5.** 7 **6.** $\frac{1}{30}$ **7.** −1 **8.** −10

9. −12

Answers

Answers (continued)

Review 219

1. $8x$ 2. $3c$ 3. $-2h$ 4. y 5. $-4m$
6. $7n$ 7. $-4s$ 8. $-3t$ 9. $-6b$ 10. $-7p$
11. $10v$ 12. $-3j$ 13. $8c - 40$ 14. $4d + 24$
15. $6n + 3$ 16. $2x + 3y$ 17. $-2m + 12$
18. $5v - 20$ 19. $-4a + 3$ 20. $5s + 11$
21. $-2u + 12$ 22. $6x + y - 9$ 23. $-2x - 3y$
24. $5v$ 25. $-3s + 2$ 26. $3x - 8$
27. $3j - 2k$ 28. $3a - 5$

Review 220

1. -12 2. 10 3. 3 4. $\frac{1}{3}$ 5. 9
6. 6 7. 22 8. -3 9. -1 10. 4
11. 7 12. 5 13. -1 14. -5 15. 4
16. 3 17. -2 18. -2 19. $\frac{1}{4}$ 20. 14
21. 5

Review 221

1. adult $6.50, child $4.50 2. width 9 ft, length 12 ft
3. 409 mi the first day and 433 mi the second day
4. 5 bags
5. 1st day: 28 pgs; 2nd day: 42 pgs; 3rd day: 56 pgs

Review 222

1.
2.
3.
4.
5. $a > 2$
6. $r < 4$
7. $n < 3$
8. $s \le 4$

Review 223

1. $a > 4$
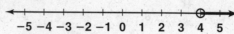

2. $r < -4$
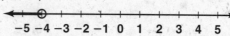

3. $n > 3$
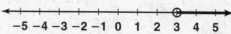

4. $s \le 2$
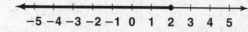

5. $m < 4$
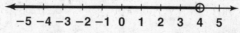

6. $q \ge 1$
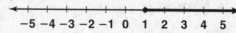

7. $x \ge -2$
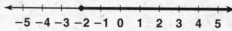

8. 4
9. 8 songs

Review 224

1. $x < 10$ 2. $x < 300$ 3. $x < 5$ 4. $x \le 21$
5. $x \ge 9$ 6. $x \le 88$ 7. $x \ge 20$
8. $x < -108$ 9. $x < 125$ 10. $x < 28$
11. $x \ge 2$ 12. $x \ge 2.3$

Review 225

1.
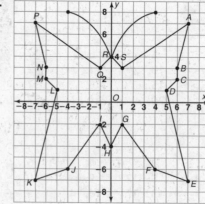

Answers (continued)

Review 226

1.

x	y
−2	2
0	3
2	4
4	5

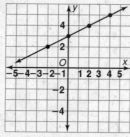

2.

x	y
−1	3
0	1
1	−1
2	−3

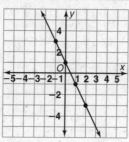

Review 227

1. 1 **2.** $\frac{1}{3}$ **3.** −2 **4.** −1

Review 228

1. 2; 3 **2.** −5; −2 **3.** −3, 2 **4.** 1; −3 **5.** $\frac{1}{2}$; −4
6. 5; 0 **7.** $y = x − 2$ **8.** $y = −2x + 1$

Review 229

1. $t = 200 + 10p$; 130 people

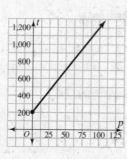

Review 230

1. $168 = 6x + 24y$ **2.** $30 = 2x + 5y$

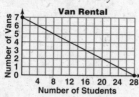 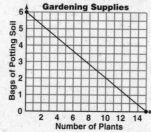

3. $(−2, 0); (0, 6)$ **4.** $(8, 0); (0, 4)$

Review 231

1. Sample answers:

x	0	1	2
y	1	0	−1

2. Sample answers:

x	0	2	4
y	2	1	0

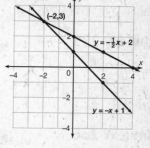

3. $(−2, 3)$
4. $y = −x + 1$ $y = −\frac{1}{2}x + 2$
   $3 = −(−2) + 1$ $3 = −\frac{1}{2}(−2) + 2$
   $3 = 3$ ✔ $3 = 3$ ✔

Review 232

1. $A'(1, 2), B'(4, 2), C'(2, −1), D'(1, −1)$

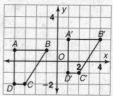

2. $A'(−2, 1), B'(−1, 1), C'(0, −1), D'(−1, −1)$

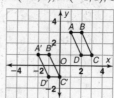

3. $(x, y) \rightarrow (x + 4, y + 1)$
4. $(x, y) \rightarrow (x − 4, y)$

Review 233

1. 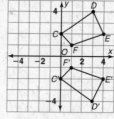 **2.**

3. yes

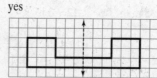

4. no

Answers (continued)

Review 234

1. 90° **2.** 180° **3.** 270°
4. yes; 180° **5.** no **6.** yes; 45°

Review 235

1. 6; 2; 3; 7; 2 · 3 · 7 **2.** 2; 2; 13; 2^2 · 13
3. 13; 13 · 7 **4.** 6; 2; 3; 3; 3; 2 · 3^3
5. 2; 5; 3; 3; 2 · 3^2 · 5 **6.** 2; 47; 2 · 47
7. 2 **8.** 1 **9.** 6 **10.** 6 **11.** 9 **12.** 5

Review 236

1. $\frac{1}{4}$ **2.** $\frac{-5}{8}$ **3.** $\frac{2}{3}$ **4.** $\frac{-4}{5}$ **5.** $\frac{3}{-7}$
6. $\frac{2}{3}$ **7.** 0.778 **8.** -3.286 **9.** 0.556 **10.** 5.429
11. 1.333 **12.** 0.091 **13.** $\frac{1}{9}$ **14.** $\frac{1}{6}$ **15.** $\frac{1}{3}$
16. $\frac{8}{9}$ **17.** $\frac{2}{3}$ **18.** $\frac{4}{11}$

Review 237

1. $\frac{6}{7}$ **2.** $\frac{8}{12}$ **3.** $\frac{2}{4}$ **4.** $\frac{10}{12}$ **5.** $\frac{8}{10}$ **6.** $\frac{4}{6}$
7. $\frac{2}{3}$ **8.** $\frac{4}{5}$ **9.** $\frac{1}{3}$ **10.** $\frac{2}{8}$ **11.** $\frac{9}{10}$ **12.** $\frac{7}{8}$
13. > **14.** = **15.** < **16.** < **17.** < **18.** >
19. = **20.** > **21.** > **22.** < **23.** > **24.** >

Review 238

1. $3\frac{7}{8}$ **2.** $\frac{1}{3}$ **3.** $-3\frac{11}{15}$ **4.** $\frac{7}{24}$ **5.** $-5\frac{11}{24}$ **6.** $\frac{-7}{10}$
7. $4\frac{1}{8}$ **8.** $\frac{-11}{12}$ **9.** $-13\frac{11}{12}$ **10.** $-3\frac{5}{12}$ **11.** $2\frac{4}{9}$
12. $-8\frac{1}{4}$ **13.** $-1\frac{1}{8}$ **14.** $1\frac{1}{10}$ **15.** $4\frac{5}{6}$ **16.** $\frac{-3}{4}$
17. $-3\frac{1}{3}$ **18.** $-3\frac{7}{10}$ **19.** -5.5 **20.** 6.85 **21.** -2.23

Review 239

1. $\frac{-2}{3}$ **2.** $\frac{-2}{5}$ **3.** $\frac{1}{12}$ **4.** $\frac{5}{14}$ **5.** $\frac{-1}{2}$ **6.** $6\frac{3}{4}$
7. $-9\frac{5}{8}$ **8.** $6\frac{3}{8}$ **9.** $10\frac{1}{2}$ **10.** $\frac{13}{18}$ **11.** $-8\frac{1}{2}$ **12.** $11\frac{1}{4}$
13. $-2\frac{11}{12}$ **14.** $-16\frac{1}{2}$ **15.** $8\frac{2}{3}$ **16.** $1\frac{7}{18}$ **17.** $\frac{3}{4}$ **18.** -8
19. -6 **20.** $3\frac{1}{2}$ **21.** $-3\frac{1}{8}$ **22.** $\frac{1}{2}$ **23.** $-6\frac{2}{5}$ **24.** $8\frac{1}{3}$
25. $\frac{5}{6}$ **26.** $-1\frac{19}{29}$ **27.** $\frac{-1}{12}$

Review 240

1. $A = 11.56 \text{ ft}^2$ **2.** $A = 13.8 \text{ m}^2$ **3.** $A = 37.8 \text{ m}^2$
4. $r = \frac{d}{t}$ **5.** $\ell = \frac{A}{w}$ **6.** $b = y - rx$
7. $t = \frac{I}{pr}$ **8.** $h = \frac{A}{b}$ **9.** $h = \frac{V}{\ell w}$
10. 10 h **11.** 35 mi/h **12.** 3 h

Review 241

1. $85 **2.** $16.25 **3.** $308 **4.** $35
5. 20 years old **6.** $36

Review 242

1. 4 **2.** ≈ 9 **3.** ≈ 5 **4.** 6 **5.** ≈ 10
6. ≈ 6 **7.** 10 **8.** ≈ 4 **9.** ≈ 2 **10.** 11
11. ≈ 8 **12.** 12 **13.** ≈ 5 **14.** 8 **15.** ≈ 6
16. ≈ 9 **17.** 15 **18.** ≈ 7 **19.** 13 **20.** ≈ 10
21. ≈ 8 **22.** 20 **23.** ≈ 11 **24.** ≈ 9
25. $\sqrt{85}, \sqrt{26}, \sqrt{98}, \sqrt{40}, \sqrt{18}, \sqrt{5}, \sqrt{68}, \sqrt{29}, \sqrt{37}, \sqrt{75}, \sqrt{54}, \sqrt{103}, \sqrt{61}, \sqrt{119}, \sqrt{84}$

Review 243

1. 10 ft **2.** 8 m **3.** 9 in. **4.** 2 km **5.** 25 in.
6. 30 m **7.** yes **8.** no **9.** no **10.** yes
11. yes **12.** no

Review 244

1. 4 to 5 **2.** $\frac{4}{3}$ **3.** 5 : 6 **4.** $\frac{2}{3}$ **5.** 3 : 1
6. $\frac{3}{5}$ **7.** $\frac{3}{7}$ **8.** 4 to 3 **9.** 3 : 8 **10.** 9 to 5
11. $\frac{8}{15}$ **12.** 6 : 7 **13.** $1.25/lb
14. 22.5 mi/gal **15.** 3 min/song **16.** $3.50/pair
17. 8 plants/planter **18.** 24 jars/case
19. 0.75 lb/pizza **20.** 45 mi/h

Review 245

1. ounce **2.** quart **3.** inch **4.** kilometer
5. gram **6.** liter **7.** 4 **8.** 84
9. 6,000 **10.** 60 **11.** 33 **12.** 6

Review 246

1. 640 oz bleach and 256 oz water
2. 9 lb of cement and 18 lb of sand
3. 3 qt of concentrate and 9 qt of water.

Review 247

1. $3n$; 10 **2.** 28; 14 **3.** 60; 4 **4.** $7w$; 15
5. 60; 4 **6.** 36; 4 **7.** $\frac{8}{10} = \frac{n}{40}$; 32 trout
8. $\frac{1}{5} = \frac{n}{15}$; 3 robins **9.** $\frac{2}{0.66} = \frac{1}{n}$; $.33

Review 248

1. no **2.** yes $\triangle ABC \sim \triangle XYZ$
3. no **4.** $n = 5.3$ **5.** $n = 9$ **6.** $n = 3$

Answers

Answers (continued)

Review 249

1. enlargement

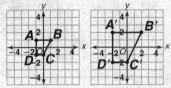

2. reduction

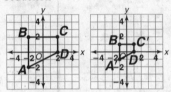

3. reduction

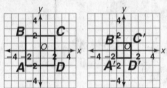

4. enlargement

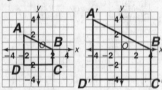

Review 250

1. $\frac{5}{1} = \frac{10}{h}$; 4 ft
2. $\frac{9}{1} = \frac{27}{l}$; 6 ft
3. $\frac{\frac{15}{4}}{1} = \frac{12}{h}$; $3\frac{1}{5}$ ft
4. $\frac{7}{1} = \frac{28}{l}$; 8 ft
5. $\frac{7}{1} = \frac{10\frac{1}{2}}{l}$; 3 ft
6. $\frac{3}{1} = \frac{24}{l}$, $\frac{3}{1} = \frac{18}{w}$; 12 ft by 16 ft

Review 251

1. $h = 10$ ft
2. $h = 12$ ft
3. 12 ft
4. 5.5 ft
5. 95 ft
6. 18 ft

Review 252

1. $\frac{4}{5}$
2. $\frac{3}{5}$
3. $\frac{3}{5}$
4. $\frac{4}{5}$
5. $\frac{4}{5}$
6. $\frac{3}{5}$
7. 0.5299
8. 0.5592
9. 0.9511
10. 0.9063
11. 65.8

Review 253

1. 39%
2. 8%
3. 420%
4. 50%
5. 900%
6. 5.6%
7. 75%
8. 20%
9. 70%
10. 62.5%
11. 25%
12. 60%
13. 0.45
14. 0.9
15. 0.002
16. 1.5
17. 0.04
18. 0.32
19. $\frac{1}{4}$
20. $\frac{1}{10}$
21. $\frac{17}{25}$
22. $4\frac{1}{2}$
23. $\frac{3}{25}$
24. $3\frac{3}{4}$

Review 254

1–12. Sample answers are given.
1. 7
2. 30
3. 30
4. 12
5. 8
6. 4
7. 6.8
8. 8
9. 3
10. 105
11. 1.5
12. 200
13–18. Sample answers are given.
13. $1.50
14. $6.00
15. $5.00
16. $7.50
17. $3.00
18. $1.80

Review 255

1. 6; 30; 20
2. 25; 100; 8
3. 75; 100; 60
4. 20; 50; 40
5. 49; 140; 35
6. 15; 100; 300
7. 45
8. 735
9. 200

Review 256

1. $0.30n = 6$; $n = 20$
2. $0.25n = 32$; $n = 128$
3. $n \times 80 = 20$; $n = 25\%$
4. $0.10 \times 35 = n$; $n = 3.5$
5. $0.40 \times 90 = n$; $n = 36$
6. $n \times 60 = 27$; $n = 45\%$
7. $0.11 \times 99 = n$; $n = 10.89$
8. $0.55n = 22$; $n = 40$
9. $0.13 \times 56 = n$; $n = 7.28$
10. $n \times 96 = 84$; $n = 87.5\%$

Review 257

1. 25%
2. 50%
3. 20%
4. 30.4%
5. 12.1%
6. 44%
7. 13.3%
8. 38.7%
9. 34.4%
10. 20%
11. 33.9%
12. 50%
13. 28.3%
14. 78.5%
15. 33.3%

Review 258

1. $24
2. $109.99
3. $142.50
4. $400
5. $20.39
6. $74.48
7. $53.33
8. $62.50
9. $114.27

Review 259

1. $125 to $150
2. 2,093 to 2,184 mil
3. $105,000 to $120,000
4. 15 to 18.75 points

Review 260

1. $15
2. $30
3. $80
4. $180
5. $162
6. $313.50
7. $899.89
8. $1,458.61
9. $2,142.45
10. $5,668.70
11. $240

Review 261

1. $\frac{1}{12}$
2. $\frac{1}{4}$
3. $\frac{1}{6}$
4. $\frac{1}{2}$
5. $\frac{1}{2}$
6. $\frac{1}{3}$
7. $\frac{2}{3}$
8. 1
9. $\frac{1}{10}$
10. $\frac{3}{20}$
11. $\frac{1}{5}$
12. $\frac{1}{4}$

Answers

Answers (continued)

Review 262

1. 6.5×10^3
2. 6.5×10^4
3. 6.52×10^3
4. 3.45×10^2
5. 2.91×10^4
6. 9.3×10^7
7. 2×10^2
8. 2.3×10^3
9. 2.3×10^4
10. 4.5×10^2
11. 9×10^4
12. 9.6×10^4
13. 40,000
14. 400,000
15. 3,600
16. 48,500
17. 405
18. 710,000
19. 400
20. 130
21. 70
22. 2,500
23. 1,810
24. 16,000
25. 778,300,000 km
26. 2×10^5
27. 2.1×10^6
28. 6×10^{10}
29. 3.6×10^3

Review 263

1. 5^7
2. a^7
3. $(-8)^9$
4. n^8
5. m^9
6. $(-7)^6$
7. $(-3)^4$
8. 2^7
9. c^8
10. 7^{14}
11. n^{14}
12. 3^7
13. 1.5×10^8
14. 1.4×10^{10}
15. 4.0×10^5
16. 6.3×10^9
17. 2.8×10^8
18. 3.2×10^9

Review 264

1. 36
2. 16
3. 81
4. $\frac{1}{9}$
5. $\frac{1}{4}$
6. 1
7. $\frac{1}{25}$
8. $-\frac{1}{64}$
9. $\frac{1}{36}$
10. $\frac{1}{49}$
11. $\frac{1}{81}$
12. 16
13. w^5
14. x^5
15. d^4
16. $\frac{1}{y^3}$
17. a^6
18. $3m^4$
19. $\frac{1}{w^4}$
20. $\frac{4}{c^3}$
21. $\frac{2}{x^3}$
22. $4a^2$
23. $\frac{3}{w^3}$
24. $\frac{2}{x^3}$

Review 265

1. 6^{-8}
2. y^{-30}
3. 7^{20}
4. x^{bc}
5. 5^{27}
6. a^{24}
7. $h^n t^n$
8. $25v^2$
9. $49p^8$
10. $27d^{12}f^6$
11. $k^{15}j^{12}$
12. $16s^{28}u^{24}$
13. $<$
14. $=$
15. $>$

Review 266

1. $2.7 \times 10^7 \text{ mi}^2$
2. $3.6 \times 10^5 \text{ ft}$
3. 15; 10
4. $10.45; $7.95
5. 18; 9
6. 12; 7

Review 267

1. 15
2. 28
3. 23
4. 53
5. 1110_2
6. 111_2
7. 100001_2
8. 10110_2

Review 268

1. $\angle 9$
2. $\angle 7$ or $\angle 9$
3. $\angle 7$ or $\angle 9$
4. $\angle 13$
5. $\angle 10$
6. $\angle 8$ or $\angle 10$
7. $142°$
8. $115°$
9. $60°$
10. $28°$
11. $65°$
12. $72°$
13. $50°$
14. $26°$

Review 269

1a. 13
1b. 14
2a. 12
2b. 10
2c. 13
2d. 15
3. $150°$
4. $150°$
5. $30°$
6. $150°$
7. $150°$
8. $30°$

Review 270

1. $\angle J$
2. $\overline{BC}$
3. $\angle D$
4. $\overline{ML}$
5. $\overline{AD}$
6. $\angle K$
7. yes; SAS
8. no
9. yes; SSS

Review 271

1. 16 tiles
2. 28 tiles
3. 128
4. 2, 2.25, 2.5
5.

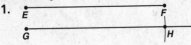

Review 272

1. $\triangle JKL$
2. $QRST, DEFG$
3. $\triangle QRS, \triangle STQ$
4. $DEFG$
5. none
6. $\triangle ABC$
7. $\triangle ABC$
8. $QRST$

Review 273

1. $540°$
2. $720°$
3. $1{,}080°$
4. $1{,}260°$
5. $1{,}440°$
6. $900°$
7. $108°$
8. $120°$
9. $128.6°$

Review 274

1. 32 ft^2
2. 35 cm^2
3. 27 in.^2
4. 24 ft^2
5. 30 in.^2
6. 32 m^2
7. 36 in.^2
8. 21 cm^2
9. 126 m^2

Review 275

1. 44.0 m; 153.9 m^2
2. 62.8 km; 314.0 km^2
3. 25.1 cm; 50.2 cm^2
4. 56.5 cm; 254.3 cm^2
5. 18.8 cm; 28.3 cm^2
6. 50.2 cm; 201.0 cm^2

Review 276

1–4. Sample answers are shown.

1.

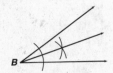

2.

3.

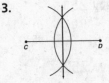

4.

Review 277

1. circle; cone
2. pentagon; pentagonal prism
3. triangle; triangular pyramid
4. circle; cylinder
5. square; square pyramid
6. triangle; triangular prism
7. Sample answer: $\overleftrightarrow{AE}$ and $\overleftrightarrow{BC}$; $\overleftrightarrow{AF}$ and $\overleftrightarrow{FD}$

Answers

Answers (continued)

Review 278

1.
2.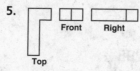
3.

4.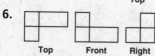
5.

6.

Review 279

1. 6 rectangles
2. 2 circles and 1 rectangle
3. 2 hexagons and 6 rectangles
4. 1 rectangle and 4 triangles
5. 6 squares
6. 1 circle and 1 part of a circle
7. square prism
8. rectangular pyramid
9. pentagonal prism

Review 280

1. 28 cm^2; 40 cm^2
2. 56 ft^2; 76 ft^2
3. 72 m^2; 84 m^2
4. 188 cm^2; 245 cm^2
5. 38 ft^2; 63 ft^2
6. 25 in.^{2}; 50 in.^{2}

Review 281

1. 48 cm^2; 84 cm^2
2. 48 ft^2; 57 ft^2
3. 30m^2; 55 m^2
4. 603 cm^2
5. 302 ft^2
6. 385 in.^{2}

Review 282

1. 35 cm^2; 140 cm^3
2. 36 ft^2; 216 ft^3
3. 12 m^2; 96 m^3
4. 50.27 cm^2; 553 cm^2
5. 113.10ft^2; 905 ft^3
6. 254.47 in.^{2}; 3,054 in.^{3}

Review 283

1. 314 cm^3
2. 1,676 cm^3
3. 384 m^3
4. 49 cm^3
5. 8 cm

Review 284

1. 32 in. by 44 in.; 1,408 in.^{2}
2. 78 in. by 120 in.; 9,360 in.^{2}
3. 48 in. by 60 in.; 2,880 in.^{2}
4. 58 in. by 80 in.; 4,640 in.^{2}

Review 285

1. $x = 6$
2. $x = 3.2$
3. 206 cm^2; 83 cm^3
4. 2,448 in.^{2}; 7,128 in.^{3}

Review 286

1.

Number of Raisins	Tally	Frequency
25–29	IIII	4
30–34	IIII III	8
35–39	IIII	4
40–44	IIII	4

2.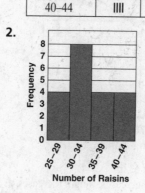

Review 287

1. the first graph
2. about 9 times
3. The second graph; since the scale is smaller, the bars can be read more accurately.
4. By using the break, most of the bar for the United States has been left out.

Review 288

1. Times for the 200-M Dash

38	5 6
37	3
36	0 4 7 9
35	2 3
34	4 7 7 7 7
33	4
32	1 2 2 5
31	4 7 9
30	2
29	3 5

38 | 5 means 38.5

2. 34.7 s
3. 34.7 s
4. 16 students
5. 10 students

Review 289

1. 1 2 2 2 2 3 3 3 3 3 3 3 3 4 4 5 5 6 7 7 7 8 8 8 9 9 10 11 13
2. median = 4
3. lower median = 3; upper median = 8
4.

Answers (continued)

Review 290

1.

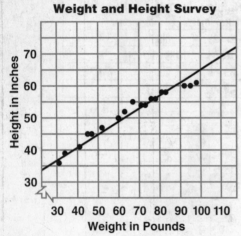

Weight and Height Survey

2. about 61 in. **3.** about 63 lb **4.** yes
5. Sample answer: As height increases, weight increases.

Review 291

1. 133° **2.** 220° **3.** 95° **4.** 25° **5.** 68°
6. 306° **7.** 166° **8.** 194°

9.

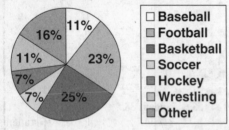

Monthly Budget Amount

Rent 49%, Food 17%, Clothes 6%, Gas 9%, Phone 3%, Water 4%, Other 12%

10.

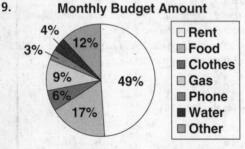

Favorite Sport to Watch Votes

Baseball 11%, Football 23%, Basketball 25%, Soccer 7%, Hockey 7%, Wrestling 11%, Other 16%

Review 292

1. multiple line graph; shows changes in two sets of data over time
2. circle graph; shows how the club's budget is divided into parts
3. double bar graph; compares two sets of data
4. circle graph; shows how 100% is divided into parts
5. line graph; shows change over time

Review 293

1. boxing and soccer **2.** 5 friends
3. crackers and steak **4.** 6 students

Review 294

1. 9 **2.** 15 **3.** 16 **4.** 20
5. 12 **6.** 48

Review 295

1. 24 **2.** 6 **3.** 4 **4.** 90 **5.** 1
6. 240 **7.** 120 **8.** 20 **9.** 1,320 **10.** 24
11. 210 **12.** 360 **13.** $_6P_2 = 30$
14. $_{10}P_3 = 720$

Review 296

1. 20 **2.** 10 **3.** 21 **4.** 4 **5.** 28
6. 15 **7.** 126 **8.** 10 **9.** 6 **10.** 35
11. 56 **12.** 84 **13.** $_{10}C_3 = 120$
14. $_6C_2 = 15$ **15.** $_7C_2 = 21$ **16.** $_{15}C_5 = 3,003$
17. $_{10}C_5 = 252$ **18.** $_8C_3 = 56$

Review 297

1. $\frac{4}{25}; \frac{1}{5}$ **2.** $\frac{3}{25}; \frac{1}{15}$ **3.** $\frac{9}{25}; \frac{1}{3}$ **4.** $\frac{17}{75}; \frac{4}{15}$ **5.** $\frac{2}{15}; \frac{2}{15}$
6. $\frac{3}{10}$ **7.** $\frac{1}{2}$ **8.** $\frac{1}{20}$ **9.** $\frac{17}{20}$

Review 298

1. $\frac{6}{64} = \frac{3}{32}$ **2.** $\frac{9}{64}$ **3.** $\frac{4}{64} = \frac{1}{16}$ **4.** $\frac{1}{9}$
5. $\frac{1}{6}$ **6.** $\frac{1}{12}$ **7.** independent
8. independent **9.** independent **10.** dependent

Review 299

1. Sample answer: Use a set of number cards 1–10 and draw one card at a time from a bag. Then replace the card.
2. Sample answer: Roll a number cube letting each of the numbers represent a different shape.
3. Sample answer: Use a spinner with 8 equal parts.
4. Sample answer: Roll a 12-sided number cube, letting each of the numbers represent a different symbol.

Review 300

1. No; the sample includes only students interested in art, not the whole population.
2. Yes; every student has an equal chance of being selected.
3. stratified **4.** systematic
5. Questioner is giving away his or her own feelings.
6. Question assumes that the movie was boring.

Review 301

1. 4 **2.** −10 **3.** 8 **4.** 2 **5.** $\frac{1}{3}$
6. 0.1 **7.** geometric; $\frac{1}{4}, \frac{1}{8}, \frac{1}{16}$
8. arithmetic; 1, 1.2, 1.4 **9.** neither; $\frac{1}{25}, \frac{1}{36}, \frac{1}{49}$
10. arithmetic; −10, −30, −50
11. neither; 1, 2, 1 **12.** geometric; 64, 128, 256

Answers

Answers (continued)

Review 302

1.

Input x	Output y
5	15
7	21
9	27
11	33

2.

Input r	Output d
1	20
2	40
3	60
8	160

3.

Input x	Output y
0	25
1	23
2	21
3	19

4. 0; 1 **5.** 1; 4 **6.** 2; 7 **7.** −2; −5 **8.** 16
9. −17 **10.** 31 **11.** 17.5

Review 303

1. 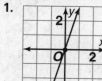 **2.**

3. 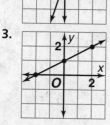 **4.**

Review 304

1. $y = 350x$; x = number of hours; y = number of calories
2. $y = 3x + 150$; x = number of magazines; y = total pay
3. $m = -\frac{1}{2}$; $b = 0$; $y = -\frac{1}{2}x$
4. $m = 2$; $b = -1$; $y = 2x - 1$
5. $m = 1$; $b = 1$; $y = x + 1$

Review 305

1. 12,000 ft **2.** 10 min
3. The airplane ascends faster than it descends.
4.

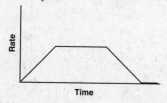

Review 306

1. $y = x^2 + 4$ **2.** $y = x^2 - 1$

3.

x	$2x^2 - 1 = y$
−2	7
−1	1
0	−1
1	1
2	7

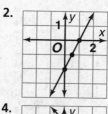

4.

x	$y = 3^x - 5$
1	−2
2	4
3	22

Review 307

1. $y = 30 \cdot 2^x$; \$1,920; \$7,680
2. $y = 10 \cdot 3^x$; 2,430 rabbits

Review 308

1. $x^2 - 3x - 1$ **2.** $-2x^2 - 2x + 4$
3. $2x^2 - x + 3$ **4.** $-x^2 + x + 6$
5. $-x^2 - 5x + 3$ **6.** $5x^2 - x - 1$
7. $2x^2 - x + 4$ **8.** $2x^2 + 5x + 2$
9. $4x^2 + 4x - 2$ **10.** $3x^2 - 4x$

Review 309

1. $3x^2 - 2x$ **2.** $5x^2 + x - 2$
3. $2y^2 + 2$ **4.** $3y^2 - y + 3$
5. $3k^2 - 2k + 6$ **6.** $5n^2 - 2n - 2$
7. $x^2 + 2x$ **8.** $l^2 - 3l + 4$
9. $-x^2 - x + 2$ **10.** $-3m^2 - 2m + 9$
11. $-2z^2 - 6z - 1$ **12.** $-2p^2 + 8p + 5$

Review 310

1. $6x^2 + 3x$ **2.** $4x^2 + 8x$ **3.** $2y^3$
4. $15x^3$ **5.** $-4n^4$ **6.** $12x^4$
7. $-32j^5$ **8.** $3x^4$ **9.** $z^2 + 2z$
10. $3x^2 - x$ **11.** $2b^2 + 10b$ **12.** $-5x^2 + 20x$
13. $-2k^3 - 8k$ **14.** $6x^3 - 6x^2$

Answers